INTERSECTIONALITY

INTERSECTIONALITY
A FOUNDATIONS AND FRONTIERS READER

FIRST EDITION

PATRICK R. GRZANKA

WESTVIEW PRESS

A Member of the Perseus Books Group

Westview Press was founded in 1975 in Boulder, Colorado, by notable publisher and intellectual Fred Praeger. Westview Press continues to publish scholarly titles and high-quality undergraduate- and graduate-level textbooks in core social science disciplines. With books developed, written, and edited with the needs of serious nonfiction readers, professors, and students in mind, Westview Press honors its long history of publishing books that matter.

Westview Press books are available at special discounts for bulk purchases in the United States by corporations, institutions, and other organizations. For more information, please contact the Special Markets Department at the Perseus Books Group, 2300 Chestnut Street, Suite 200, Philadelphia, PA 19103, or call (800) 810-4145, ext. 5000, or e-mail special.markets@perseusbooks.com.

Designed by Jack Lenzo

Library of Congress Cataloging-in-Publication Data

Intersectionality : a foundations and frontiers reader / [compiled and edited by] Patrick R. Grzanka. — First edition.
    pages cm
  Includes bibliographical references and index.
  ISBN 978-0-8133-4908-4 (pbk.)
  1. Sociology—Study and teaching. 2. Critical theory. 3. Marginality, Social. 4. Social justice. 5. Interdisciplinary approach to knowledge. I. Grzanka, Patrick R.
  HM571.I56 2014
  301.07—dc23
                                2013039732

10 9 8 7 6 5 4 3 2 1

CONTENTS

UNIT III: IDENTITIES

UNIT IV: SPACE, PLACE, COMMUNITIES, AND GEOGRAPHIES

UNIT V: CULTURE AND THE POLITICS OF REPRESENTATION

UNIT VI: VIOLENCE, RESISTANCE, AND ACTIVISM

UNIT VII: NATIONS, BORDERS, AND MIGRATIONS

ACKNOWLEDGMENTS

This book has at least two beginnings, depending on how you look at it. One beginning is 2004, when Bonnie Thornton Dill offered me a graduate assistantship at the Consortium on Race, Gender and Ethnicity (CRGE) at the University of Maryland, where I spent the next two years working and studying intersectionality. At CRGE, I found the body of scholarship and network of scholar-activists who would shape so much of my intellectual career and plant the seeds of this book. Another starting point of this project came nearly a decade later when Leanne Silverman called me from Westview and pitched the idea to me. Less than two years later, this book had come to fruition. Without these two inspiring women, I can't imagine how any of this would have happened.

So, the story of this book—which in many ways is about origin stories—has quite a few origins of its own. As I developed this project, I consulted with friends and colleagues who provided invaluable guidance on how to create a good book on intersectionality. I hope to someday return huge favors to (in particular): Christine Muller, Amelia Wong, Justin Maher, Dan Greene, Clare Jen, Mel Michelle Lewis, and, as always, my dear Emily Mann. Sheri Parks and Laura Mamo both continued in their roles as mentors throughout this process, and I remain grateful for their intellectual and emotional generosity. My community of friends at Arizona State University provided kindness, support, and inspiration during the tricky first years of being a junior faculty member; I especially thank Jacquie Scott, John Lynch, Wendy Cheng, Aviva Dove-Viebahn, Chris Callahan, Breanne Fahs, Mary Ingram-Waters, John Parker, Hilary Harp, and my partner in fun and foolishness, Jenny ("Ryan") Brian. There are countless other colleagues in the greater sociological and psychological communities who have influenced my thinking and feelings about this book, such as Jackie Orr, Ruth Zambrana, Kelly Joyce, Jyoti Puri, C. J.

Pascoe, Elizabeth Cole, Helen Neville, Lisa Spanierman, Anthony Hatch, and Ruth Fassinger; there are truly too many to try to name here, and that makes me feel all the more fortunate.

In addition to Leanne Silverman's pitch-perfect blend of flexibility, humor, smarts, and pushiness (e.g., "Get it done, Patrick"), Brooke Smith, Grace Fujimoto, Melissa Veronesi, and Deborah Heimann provided excellent editorial support at Westview. The following manuscript reviewers offered substantive criticism and much-needed encouragement from proposal to completion: Michelle Corbin, Worcester State University; Heather Dillaway, Wayne State University; Laura Gillman, Virginia Tech; Marla H. Kohlman, Kenyon College; Betsy Lucal, Indiana University South Bend; Gary Kinte Perry, Seattle University; Hillary Potter, University of Colorado at Boulder; and Julie A. Raulli, Wilson College. But no one person did more to help me in the preparation of this manuscript than my amazing research assistant, Candice Bain, who devoted a semester and a summer to digging through the library, tracking down permissions, calculating word counts, carving out excerpts, and catching my mistakes. I told you that I needed you to be perfect, and you were. Candice, you are my hero . . . and I still owe you a car.

My friends and family give my work meaning. I am fortunate to have such wonderful people in my life with whom to celebrate accomplishments and who distract me from disappointment, including Cassandra Hunsdon, Peg and Jim Connolly, Erin Dieterich, Ehren Reed, Leah Dieterich, Debbie Van Camp, Matt Goldmark, Kelly Barnes, Angela Gunder, Julie Arseneau, Jill Paquin, Colin Callahan, Trish Raque-Bogdan, Illya Riske, Erin Whiteside, Jackie Zajac, Stephen Brookman, Tara Fischer, Michelle Ruiz, Katie Zeiders, Caitlin Haney, Janet Gibson, Anna Lucas, Tanya Jung, and Mao-Lin Shen. I am most thankful for my partner, who makes me smarter and kinder and happier every day. Thank you for traveling to exciting and boring places with me, Joe Miles. I hope we are together soon.

I am very lucky to have my wonderful mother, Sharon, who inspires me every day with her strength, compassion, and intellect. I am also very unlucky to have lost my father when he and I were both too young and before this book was even in my imagination. I dedicate this book to him. He was braver than me, but he helped me to be courageous and to be myself. Thank for you for loving me, Butchie.

INTRODUCTION

Intersectional Objectivity

Patrick R. Grzanka

As I was completing this book in June 2013, the US Supreme Court held the country in suspense: it was about to deliver decisions on four court cases that struck at the core of civil rights law and the role of social categories, namely race, gender, and sexuality, in the production and distribution of those rights. In one case, *Fisher v. University of Texas,* a young White woman, Abigail Fisher, sued her state's major public university after being denied admission to the prestigious flagship campus at Austin. Her claim is that the university's use of race in admissions—which was legal at the time under affirmative action laws that had been to the Supreme Court in a similar 2003 case against the University of Michigan—was the reason she was not admitted. The conservative activist who helped to build Fisher's case and bring it all the way to the Supreme Court, Edward Blum, summed up the core of Fisher's complaint to the press: "It's our belief that but for the fact that she's [W]hite, she would have been admitted to [the University of Texas]" (quoted in Chuck 2013). Edward Blum and his nonprofit legal organization Project on Fair Representation also facilitated Shelby County, Alabama's case (*Shelby County v. Holder*), in which Shelby County argued against the constitutional legitimacy of the Voting Rights Act of 1965, chiefly section 5. This portion of the law requires certain state and local jurisdictions most notorious for racial discrimination and voter intimidation tactics prior to the passage of the Act to receive "preclearance" from the federal government before making any changes to their voting laws and procedures. The preclearance procedures were positioned before the Supreme Court as an unconstitutional extension of the federal government's powers: a history of blatant racism should not, according to the plaintiffs from Shelby County, mean that a jurisdiction should have to comply with preclearance laws in the future.

Two other cases before the court that have commanded significant public attention in this session are about same-sex marriage: *Hollingsworth v. Perry,* in which the State of California's ability to define marriage as the union of a man and a woman is at stake, and *United States v. Windsor,* in which the constitutionality of the federal Defense of Marriage Act (DOMA) will likely be decided. In these cases, the judicial branch of the federal government has been placed in a position to rule on cases that could create sweeping legal and social changes, reinforce the status quo, or create new legal pathways to the state-by-state acquisition of marriage equality—which has been the primary goal of mainstream lesbian, gay, bisexual, and transgender (LGBT) activist organizations for the past twenty years. Regardless of the decisions in all four cases, these legal contentions have captivated scholars, activists, and even individuals who perceive no personal stake in the cases, because they signify moments of potential social transformation, particularly in terms of race and sexuality.

In legal analysis and media coverage, the four cases above are grouped into two categories, reflecting both the logic of contemporary social politics in the United States and the limits of the law: *Fischer* and *Shelby* are about race, whereas *Hollingsworth* and *Windsor* are about sexuality. Infinitely less common in the media and popular discourse are conversations about how these cases overlap historically and conceptually, and how race, sexuality, gender, and other organizing elements of social life are implicated in all four cases. In *Fischer,* a young woman argued that being White is a disadvantage when applying to colleges that unfairly use affirmative action to discriminate against White people. This is a particularly ironic claim for a White woman to make about affirmative action; no single constituency in the United States has been better served by affirmative action than White women (Cho 2002). And yet Fisher's case frames her racial privilege as a disadvantage, and ignores her gender completely. Shelby County, an overwhelmingly White, solidly middle-class region with a population of 200,000 and a median household incoming of $69,000, finds itself in a legal alliance with ultra-wealthy conservative activists who have fostered a racial coalition across class lines in the interest of dismantling voting protections for African Americans and Latinos who, in Shelby, make up a combined 17 percent of the county's population (United States Census Bureau 2013). In the wake of the passage of Proposition 8 in California, Black voters were an immediate target of White liberal and LGBT activists who believed that homophobia in African American communities, and particularly African American churches, was to blame for Proposition 8's success (Savage 2008; see also Wilds Lawson 2009, and Wadsworth 2011). Meanwhile, the Mormon Church, which up until 1978 did not allow African

American men to be ordained in its priesthood, had contributed $20 million via its members and canvassed throughout California in support of Proposition 8 (Mencimer 2013), and 51 percent of White men voted "yes" on Proposition 8 to define marriage as between a man and a woman. And in the broader context of LGBT activism, the Employment Non-Discrimination Act (ENDA), which would protect individuals from employment discrimination on the basis of sexual orientation and gender identity, has spent two decades in legislative limbo and taken a backseat to marriage equality initiatives in mainstream LGBT politics as determined by the Human Rights Campaign and other leading LGBT activist and lobbying organizations. ENDA's political subordination to marriage equality is particularly interesting given that employment discrimination based on perceived sexual orientation and gender identity affects *all* people, regardless of how they identify sexually or in terms of gender, whereas marriage equality—though certainly valuable in terms of access to institutions, benefits, and privileges—pertains to a much smaller percentage of the LGBT community and ultimately disregards all those who choose to not or cannot marry. Furthermore, rates of unemployment, job discrimination, and workplace harassment are especially high for LGBT people of color, particularly transgender people of color (Stachelberg and Burns 2013).

So while Proposition 8, the Voting Rights Act, same-sex marriage, affirmative action, and employment discrimination are often framed as having to do with race *and not* gender, sexuality *and not* race, or race *and not* class, the reality of our social structures, including the law, media, education, government, and economy, is much more complicated than a zero-sum game. When viewed from the perspective of where these dynamics of inequality intersect, everything is not, as they say, so black and white. This book foregrounds precisely these kinds of concerns, exploring the ways in which race, class, gender, sexuality, and other dimensions of identity and inequality shape the contours of social life and structures in the United States and around the world. "Intersectionality," or the study of how these dimensions of inequality co-construct one another, is a leading paradigm in women's studies, American studies, ethnic studies, and allied fields, and is increasingly becoming an indispensible tool for social scientists and humanists across the disciplines who do research and activism on historical and contemporary social injustices. This book charts the foundational moments of intersectionality as a political and intellectual movement and traces several "origin stories" that lead to the issues facing intersectionality today. Through ten units that focus on key elements of social inquiry—such as geography, culture, and identities—intersectionality's historical foundations and emergent frontiers are showcased as potent tools for research, pedagogy, and activism.

Theory on the Move

The organization of this book and the selection of readings to include were driven by three groups of questions. The first concerns the movement of intersectionality through history and across disciplines: *Where does intersectionality come from? Where has it been? And where is intersectionality going?* As sociologist Roderick Ferguson has reflected, "No one can really say when the theory emerged. Some say the legal scholar Kimberlé Crenshaw created it. Others locate it even further back, with the Combahee River Collective Statement of 1977. Most agree that the category was a way to address the simultaneity of modes of difference" (2012, 91). Rather than settle on one creation story, these units craft overlapping and intertwined narratives about the origins of intersectionality in US Black women's community activism and intellectual labor, but also include contributions from other women of color feminists from within and outside the United States whose work has influenced how we understand the key concepts and concerns of the field. And while each unit is focused on a basic sociological concept, the insights of each author's contribution are hardly limited to the unit in which it is placed.

Kimberlé Crenshaw's work in critical legal studies serves as a launching point, but not the only place from which theorizing intersectionality begins. Importantly, Crenshaw (1989) posits the root metaphor and rhetoric of intersections, crafted from an analysis of Black women's positionality in the US legal system, specifically in antidiscrimination doctrine:

> Consider an analogy to traffic in an intersection, coming and going in all four directions. Discrimination, like traffic through an intersection, may flow in one direction, and it may flow in another. If an accident happens in an intersection, it can be caused by cars traveling from any number of directions and, sometimes, from all of them. Similarly, if a Black woman is harmed because she is in the intersection, her injury could result from sex discrimination or race discrimination. (149)

In developing and proposing the intersection metaphor, Crenshaw (1991) explained:

> My objective there was to illustrate that many of the experiences Black women face are not subsumed within the traditional boundaries of race or gender discrimination as these boundaries are currently understood, and that the intersection of racism and sexism factors into Black women's lives in ways that cannot be captured wholly by looking at the race or gender dimensions of those experiences separately. (1244)

To paraphrase Crenshaw (1989), Black women sometimes experience discrimination in ways that resemble White women's experiences, and sometimes in ways that are similar to Black men; they often experience double-discrimination, which refers to the combined effects of race and gender; and sometimes they experience discrimination as *Black women*—not the sum of racism and sexism (i.e., race + sex), but as Black women whose identity and social location are not simply derivative of White women's or Black men's lives. Crenshaw's insights can appear at once obvious and profound: considering the experiences of a social group on its own terms seems like a sufficiently reasonable enough proposition, and yet Crenshaw's and others' work in critical legal studies has shown that Black women are rarely treated on such terms by the law and other institutions that filter Black women's demands and needs through *single-axis* categorical analysis (e.g., Williams 1992, Unit I, reading 1; Crenshaw 2000, Unit I, reading 3). "Single-axis" is the term used in intersectional research to denote those perspectives, methods, and modes of analysis that privilege one dimension of inequality (e.g., race *or* gender *or* class) and which derive ideas, knowledge, and policy from that single dimension such that all members of a racial, gender, or class group are thought to have essentially the same experiences of race, gender, or class. Single-axis paradigms generally position racism and sexism as *parallel* or *analogous*, as opposed to *intersecting* or *co-constitutive*, phenomena. Conversely, in intersectionality and Black feminist thought, racism and sexism are viewed as intimate allies in the production of inequality.

Though Crenshaw, sociologist Patricia Hill Collins (2000), and others (e.g., Barbara Smith 1980, Unit II, reading 5; Angela Davis 1990, Unit III, reading 10) begin from Black women's unique position to theorize intersectionality, they do not reduce intersectionality to a theory about *identity*. Intersectionality is a structural analysis and critique insomuch as it is primarily concerned with how social inequalities are formed and maintained; accordingly, identities and the politics thereof are the *products* of historically entrenched, institutional systems of domination and violence. While intersectionality helps us to explore social and personal identities in complex and nuanced ways (Sengupta 2006, Unit III, reading 12), intersectional analyses direct their critical attention to categories, structures, and systems that produce and support multiple *dimensions of difference* (Dill, Nettles, and Weber 2001). In intersectionality, "dimensions of difference" is the term used to denote systems of inequality, such as heterosexism and ageism, that are organized around and coproduce social identity categories, such as sexual orientation and age. In other words, though this book offers much to think about with regard to identity, intersectionality is foremost about studying multiple dimensions of inequality and developing ways to resist and challenge these various forms of oppression.

Another "origin story" of intersectionality stretches back historically much earlier than the development of Critical Race Theory in the late 1980s; by looking beyond traditional academic disciplines and institutions, we can uncover a rich history of intersectional thinking that long predates the term. In *Black Feminist Thought* (2000), Patricia Hill Collins insists that redefining what counts as "intellectual" is essential to recovering the silenced and marginalized voices of women of color in the United States and worldwide whose radical, disruptive voices attempted to unsettle hegemonic systems of racism, sexism, and classism. Black women were forcefully prohibited from formal higher education for centuries in the United States, so we must look outside the ivory tower for sites of intellectual expression that take various forms, including oral history, poetry, music, journalism, creative nonfiction, and social activism. For important civil rights figures Sojourner Truth and Ida B. Wells-Barnett, for example, radical social transformation was at the core of their life's work, and their activism happened largely outside of universities, though their work is now studied widely in academia. In the 1970s, the Combahee River Collective formed in Boston to address the needs of Black lesbians working within Black feminist movements. Their hugely influential statement on Black feminism (1977) is thought to be another turning point in the development of intersectionality, and it was firmly grounded in the lived experiences of Black lesbian feminist authors, artists, and activists, such as Barbara Smith (1980, Unit II, reading 5) and Audre Lorde (1984, Unit VI, reading 22), whose perspectives had been marginalized by traditional approaches to antiracism and sexism, which often elided Black lesbian women's existence. Closely aligned with US Black feminist thought but bringing to bear the distinct experiences of non-Western women of color feminists, the writings of Chandra Talpade Mohanty (1984, Unit VII, reading 26; 1993, Unit III, reading 11), Gayatri Chakravorty Spivak (1988), Chela Sandoval (2000), and others foregrounded postcolonial criticism in their articulations of intersectionality. Likewise, Gloria Anzaldúa (1987, Unit IV, reading 14) and Cherríe Moraga (Moraga and Anzaldúa 1984) also spoke to interlocking systems of oppression, but from the position of Chicana lesbian feminists; Anzaldúa and Moraga's work was also strongly influenced by their identities as artists and creative writers. Collectively, these various women of color contributed to a multivoiced dialogue about the experiences of women of color living in oppressive contexts but resisting domination in extraordinary ways that illuminate the realities of oppression *and* activism.[*]

---

[*] This list is necessarily selective and is not meant to represent an exhaustive or comprehensive account of early intersectional scholarship. Each unit, however, does offer a more detailed elaboration on foundations of the field beyond the scholars mentioned here.

As intersectionality was institutionalized during the 1990s and 2000s (e.g., Dill, Nettles, and Weber 2001), new questions were posed and new problems arose for the movement as it became popular and traveled widely. How would intersectionality apply outside of the study of Black women's experiences (Carbado 2013; c.f., Frankenberg 1993)? What might happen to its political investments as it became institutionalized within predominantly White institutions that historically restricted Black women's access and continue to subordinate women of color and similarly oppressed groups in academic ghettoes (e.g., women's studies and African American studies) and outside positions of leadership (Dill 2009; Mohanty 2013)? How would intersectional research be evaluated by colleagues and within disciplines to which multidimensional social analysis was unintelligible and threatening (Dill, Zambrana, and McLaughlin 2009)? Would intersectionality transform disciplines, or be transformed by them (e.g., Cole 2009, Unit X, reading 41)? How would new generations of scholars and activists be trained, and what are the risks of doing intersectional work that may be dismissed as biased, too political or, worst of all, branded as lacking scholarly merit (Gines 2011)? Despite these precarious threats to intersectionality's viability and success in academic institutions, the field has flourished. Even a quick Google search of the term offers a digital snapshot of the pervasiveness of intersectionality and a window into its impact. One finds links to anthologies with titles such as *The Intersectional Approach* (Berger and Guidroz 2009), *Emerging Intersections* (Dill and Zambrana 2009), and *Gender, Race, Class and Health: Intersectional Approaches* (Schulz and Mullings 2005); syllabi for courses at numerous colleges and universities; articles such as Leslie McCall's "The Complexity of Intersectionality," which has been cited over 1,250 times since its publication in 2005; research centers at Tulane University, the University of Maryland, and the University of South Carolina; and conferences, book series, and calls for papers from organizations around the world. Its success prompted even further dilemmas, nonetheless: Would "intersectionality" become a fad, or an empty buzzword (Davis 2008)? Would scholars prematurely "settle" on intersectionality and let social justice research stagnate (Nash 2008; Ferguson 2012)? Though some have been occasionally interested in esoteric conversations about theory that pull intersectionality further away from its political, pragmatic commitments (see Collins 1998, Unit II, reading 7, for an overview), intersectionality's most committed critics (including those represented in this volume, e.g., Puar 2007, Unit X, reading 42) have pushed the field forward and identified new frontiers for social justice interventions, such as the queer of color critique (Ferguson 2004, Unit II, reading 9), social studies of science, technology, and medicine (Bridges 2011, Unit IX, reading 37), and transnational feminisms (Patil 2013; Brah and Phoenix 2004, Unit X, reading 39).

Over and Against Multiculturalism

As we chart these new frontiers of intersectionality, the second set of questions driving this volume is: *What does intersectionality do? How do we do intersectionality?* The application of intersectional ideas across disciplines and in novel contexts leads to inevitable concerns about what intersectionality actually means and how precisely it should be applied methodologically. What these heterogeneous applications of intersectionality should look like has been the subject of much writing and debate, and this concern challenges us to consider whether intersectionality should be conceptualized as a theory alone, a theory with methodological implications, or perhaps something else entirely. Scholars throughout this book take up this question seriously, but methodological concerns are showcased in Unit X with various elaborations of how intersectionality can be executed as/in empirical inquiry.

The term itself always suggests at least two denotations: first, "intersectional" and "intersectionality" signify a kind of theory, method, or mode of analysis that incorporates the tenets of the field, broadly construed (e.g., "an intersectional approach to Latina public health," or "applying intersectionality to studies of political economy"); and second, "intersectionality" refers to actual intersecting oppressions as they manifest in the empirical universe (i.e., "the case of homosexual asylum in the U.S. represents a moment of intersectionality"; e.g., Reddy 2005, Unit I, reading 4). Cho, Crenshaw, and McCall (2013) remind us that much intersectional scholarship goes by other names and may not identify as such: "If intersectionality is an analytic disposition, a way of thinking about and conducting analyses, then what makes an analysis intersectional is not its use of the term 'intersectionality,' nor its being situated in a familiar genealogy, nor its drawing on lists of standard citations" (795). Opening up what counts as intersectional—judging what analyses do rather than what they say they do—enables us to trace new histories of the field and identify new elaborations of intersectionality in unexpected places. In this book, for example, *most* authors will not use the term "intersectionality," but all adopt "an intersectional way of thinking about the problem of sameness and difference and its relation to power" (Cho, Crenshaw, and McCall 2013, 795).

As intersectionality travels and is elaborated across disciplines, unifying themes have emerged beyond the foundational logic of interlocking oppressions. Some of these themes can be articulated as what intersectionality does and does not do. In the latter, we can say with confidence that intersectionality is not about inclusion, per se. As Devon Carbado (2013) has recently stressed, intersectionality is not "an effort to identify, in the abstract, an exhaustive list of intersectional social categories and to add them up to determine—once and for all—the different intersectional configurations those categories can form" (815). Melamed (2006, Unit VIII, reading 31), Duggan (2003, Unit VIII, reading 30), Boyd (2008, Unit IV, reading 16), and Bowleg (2008, Unit X, reading 40) elaborate on how efforts to include multiple social categories into systems that are foundationally oppressive, explicitly about the accumulation of power, or implicitly committed to institutional inertia are not likely to result in radical social transformation. Adding difference into systems that are opposed to difference all but guarantees that human cultural diversity will be incorporated into hegemonies. The incorporation of difference into businesses, higher education, and government—what Duggan pithily terms "Equality, Inc."—is the hallmark of contemporary multiculturalisms that pursue superficial diversity to escape critiques of their actual agendas, which are generally much more regressive and conservative (see also Ahmed 2006, 2012; Grzanka and Maher 2012). Intersectionality has provided a potent critique of "neoliberalism," explored throughout this volume but especially in Unit VIII on politics, because neoliberalism's mantra of inclusion obfuscates the reality of neoliberal politics' cooptation and commodification of difference and diversity. Herman Gray (2005) likewise refers to such politics as "palace discourses," which are centers of power/knowledge that reinforce oppression even as they effectively and insidiously develop ways to incorporate diversity toward their own exclusionary and discriminatory aims.

Similarly, as intersectionality continues to grow in popularity and become institutionalized, different research may take on the label of intersectionality without doing anything that involves systematic critique. Dill and Kohlman (2011) have distinguished between two forms of intersectionality—"weak" and "strong"—in order to better discern between those approaches that *include* differences and those that *critique* systems. The former, weak intersectionality, is characterized by the incorporation of multiple forms of diversity and identity into research questions, participant samples, data analysis, and interpretation, but has the effect of reproducing hegemonic knowledge rather than challenging assumptions about social worlds and systems. We might think of this as putting a different kind of fuel into a gas tank and expecting to wind up with an entirely different car. Strong intersectionality, on the other hand, has the possibility of producing counterhegemonic knowledge about marginalized and subjugated social groups and/or about the operations of power and privilege, because these "strong" approaches analyze systems of inequality in relation to one another. This relational critique, according to Dill and Kohlman, is a hallmark of strong intersectionality and remains one of its most effective analytic tools.

Intersectionality is therefore a critique of multiculturalism as it is produced, practiced, and elaborated within "palace discourse" (Gray 2005). Intersectionality imagines alternative ways of knowing and doing in the interest of forging efficacious tools for social justice. Intersectional scholars therefore practice self-reflexivity and are constantly engaged in critique of their own work and refinement of their ideas and practices. In this book, Lisa Bowleg (2008, Unit X, reading 40) and Patricia Ticineto Clough and Michelle Fine (2007, Unit VI, reading 24) offer exemplars of self-reflexive "scholar-activism." Bowleg details how she went about a psychological study of Black lesbian women only to find—in the midst of data collection—that the study had been configured along an additive model of identity that could not account for the intersectionality of her participants' experiences. As a result, she has become an advocate not only of intersectionality as a theory, but of cultivating critical methods to better capture intersectional dynamics in psychological research. Clough and Fine, alternatively, explain their respective experiences working as academic researchers with incarcerated women of color and people leaving prison after periods of incarceration. They share deeply personal stories of having their positions of privilege highlighted and intensified during the research process, and of questioning the politics and efficacy of participant action research (PAR) and other forms of scholar-activism that often do more for those on the "scholar" side of the equation than for those being studied—the individuals and groups under the social scientific microscope.

Intersectional Objectivity

The activist orientation of intersectionality leads us to the final questions that organized this volume: *What are intersectionality's objectives? What are its transformative potentials?* Many of the field's goals have already been elaborated in terms of research and methods, but the question of intersectionality's objectives is a central part of self-reflexivity that will keep intersectionality on its theoretical, methodological, and political toes, so to speak. For example, Ferguson has written critically about intersectionality's proponents (the dominant affirmation) and its detractors (the dominant objection); he sums it up accordingly:

> In its dominant affirmation, intersectionality is engaged as an assemblage of social relations that can be observed as empirical truths. Hence, the affirmation designates intersectionality as the occasion for a positivism that will grant us authentic and true knowledge. The dominant objection, though, characterizes the category as one that preserves ideologies of discreteness, identity politics and so forth. Despite their antinomy to one another, the dominant affirmation and the dominant objection share an affinity: they both are invested in a belief that intersectionality as a signifier is *destined toward a meaning of discreteness, truth, and legibility.* (2012, 91) [emphasis added]

Ferguson's framing of these debates warrants serious consideration. He asks us to consider if claiming to be for or against intersectionality is ultimately reflective of the same investment: uncovering a legible form of truth. He suggests that such an investment threatens to, on the one hand, "produce a policing consensus that potentially assigns past work to the dustbin of history," and, on the other, to "address minority social formations and modes of difference as fixed and stable entities that are in the service of empiricist and positivist analytics" (91–92). In other words, Ferguson warns against: a) an intersectionality that serves as a normative yardstick on which all forms of scholarship past and future are measured, and also against b) an allegedly "new" paradigm that does the same old work but is dressed up in fancy intersectional clothes.

Antiracist, feminist, and anticolonialist discourse has long been critical of deployments of truth that claim to offer new, definitive knowledge—and with good reason. "Truth"—the ability to produce it, declare it, use it, and have people believe it—is a primary tool through which oppression is consolidated. Science, including social science, has been a "palace discourse" of truth since at least the Enlightenment, and has accordingly been a target of intersectional critiques that seek to destabilize the certainty with which scientific discourses construct and deploy assertions about how the universe works. Siobhan Somerville (1994, Unit IX, reading 34), for example, looked to early forms of sexology (i.e., the science of sexuality) in the nineteenth century to examine how European and American cultural beliefs about Africans' racial inferiority, gender politics, and sexual behavior influenced the biological constitution of two of modernity's most powerful creations: race and sexual orientation. "Is it merely a historical coincidence," she asks, "that the classification of bodies as either 'homosexual' or 'heterosexual' emerged at the same time that the United States was aggressively policing the imaginary boundary between 'black' and 'white' bodies?" (245). Somerville's intersectional reading of early sexology reveals how "structures and methodologies that drove dominant ideologies of race also fueled the pursuit of scientific knowledge about the homosexual body: both sympathetic and hostile accounts of homosexuality were steeped in assumptions that had driven previous scientific studies of race" (247). In this case, the "truth" about sexuality, gender, and race produced by nineteenth- and early-twentieth century biosciences, including anatomy, anthropometry (i.e., the measurement of bodies), biological anthropology, medicine, and psychiatry, was a historically contingent, culturally motivated, and intensely violent choreography of body types and categories of personhood that science "knew" to be inferior. If these discourses remained inside textbooks or the laboratory, that would present one kind of social problem; of course, we know that these knowledges traveled far and continue to circulate in popular culture and public policy, even as the social construction of race, gender, and sexual orientation categories has become widely accepted in the scientific community (Fausto-Sterling 2000; Gould 1996; Duster 2003). In the domain of epidemiology, Janet Shim (2005, Unit IX, reading 35) likewise finds that the "truth" of cardiovascular disease (CVD) is a hotly contested playing field, particularly when it comes to patients' and clinicians' different understandings of the meaning of "risk." Whereas epidemiologists acknowledge the limitations of race as a medical category, Shim finds that scientists "ritualistically" adopt the category in research, conflating "race" with what they perceive to be "cultural differences" that account for behavioral and physiological variations between racial groups that place African Americans at special risk for CVD. The CVD patients that Shim interviews, on the other hand, possess elaborate and sophisticated "lay" critiques of this scientific logic, and instead exercise sociological reasoning derived from their lived experiences of racism, sexism, and classism to produce an alternative explanation of risk. Whereas risky behaviors and choices are at the forefront of epidemiologists' account of CVD risk, actual CVD patients centralize the role that living under the constant stresses of economic hardship, racial discrimination, and gender-based harassment has played in their development of CVD.

As Shim's, Somerville's, and many others' work in this book attests, questioning normative, taken-for-granted knowledge can undermine oppressive versions of "truth" and generate alternative accounts of reality that potentially represent our social worlds more accurately, fairly, and justly. The answer to Ferguson's concerns over intersectionality's investment in "discreetness, truth and legibility," their scholarship suggests, is not to close up shop or disregard Ferguson's concerns. This volume represents interventions and interruptions in hegemonic knowledge production, rather than conclusions and declarations meant to foreclose debate or preempt dialogue. Ferguson compels ongoing, difficult negotiations about what we as students, scholars, and activists are invested in and what kinds of futures we can imagine for our communities by way of intersectionality. I stress "by way of" intersectionality, because *theorizing* oppression was never the end point, and those futures—beyond multiculturalism, against "diversity," and better than Equality, Inc.—demand new theorizing, new methods, and new forms of social action.

When it comes to the objectives of intersectionality, new configurations of *objectivity* may very well be one of them. Philosopher of science Donna Haraway (1988, Unit II, reading 6) helps shed some light on how objectivity can be a tool for injustice *or* justice. As she describes in Unit II on epistemology, Haraway was in the middle of contentious debates in the late 1980s about antiracist feminism's relationship to truth, objectivity, and science; she recounts that two camps were stuck in a holding pattern over the "science question in feminism." The radical postmodernists, on the one hand, thought science was an illusion: to them, science is all language games to misrepresent reality in the interest of power and should therefore be abandoned. Haraway's response:

"So much for those of us who still want to talk about reality" (577). (Patricia Hill Collins [1998] offers her thoughts on a similar debate, as well, in Unit II, reading 7.) On the other side were the feminist scientists, those who thought that science needed some serious tweaking in terms of its ethical practices and political commitments but was overall a sound path to objective truth. To Haraway's dissatisfaction, this group failed to interrogate the core assumptions of science (e.g., its epistemology) and, therefore, what science can actually accomplish when it comes to knowledge production. Haraway's contribution was an attempt to shift the conversation by offering a new way of thinking about objectivity. She explains:

> So, with many other feminists, I want to argue for a doctrine and practice of objectivity that privileges contestation, deconstruction, passionate construction, webbed connections, and hope for transformation of systems of knowledge and ways of seeing. But not just any partial perspective will do; we must be hostile to easy relativisms and holisms built out of summing and subsuming parts. "Passionate detachment" requires more than acknowledged self-critical partiality. We are also bound to seek perspective from those points of view, which can never be known in advance, that promise something quite extraordinary, that is, knowledge potent for constructing worlds *less organized by axes of domination*. (1988, 584–585) [emphasis added]

By advocating for feminist objectivity or "situated knowledges," Haraway suggested a version of truth-seeking that insists upon modest claims about the world that are always embodied and always situated within history, politics, and the material world. No objectivity is total, and all knowledge is partial. Situating knowledge, to Haraway, is the feminist ethic of accountability and means taking responsibility for your claims about how things are and how things should be. Whereas masculinist, racist, colonialist forms of objectivity pretend to have no position—to see everything from nowhere—Haraway's feminist objectivity is about stitching together perspectives and foregrounding "tensions, resonances, transformations, resistances, and complicities" (588). And situated knowledges are not disinterested; they are knowledges made for doing something—truths with a purpose.

I do not think that Haraway offers all of the answers, but I think she provides a starting point to seriously contemplate Ferguson (2012) and others' calls for thinking about intersectionality's objectives, which are perhaps new forms of objectivity. Whereas many traditional approaches to social science may still promise disembodied truth claims that abdicate responsibility for the harm they do to real people (e.g., see the controversy over sociologist

Mark Regnerus's study of the children of same-sex parents: Cohen 2012), intersectionality offers other ways of thinking critically about reality, conducting politically engaged research, and doing real social activism. The scholars in this volume take on the political, intellectual, and emotional burden of speaking out against inequality and claiming to see how oppressions operate more clearly than those who examine social worlds using only a single lens of race, class, or gender. They provide tentative answers to the question of intersectionality's objectives, but they do not finally decide on its transformative potentials. That work is still very much ongoing.

References

Ahmed, S. 2006. "The Nonperformativity of Antiracism." *Meridians: Feminism, Race, Transationalism* 7: 104–126.

Ahmed, S. 2012. *On Being Included: Racism and Diversity in Institutional Life.* Durham, NC: Duke University Press.

Anzaldúa, G. 1987. *Borderlands/La Frontera.* San Francisco: Aunt Lute Books.

Berger, M. T., and K. Guidroz, eds. 2009. *The Intersectional Approach: Transforming the Academy Through Race, Class, and Gender.* Chapel Hill, NC: University of North Carolina Press.

Bowleg, L. 2008. "When Black + Woman + Lesbian ≠ Black Lesbian Woman: The Methodological Challenges of Qualitative and Quantitative Intersectionality Research." *Sex Roles* 59: 312–325.

Boyd, N. A. 2008. "Sex and Tourism: The Economic Implications for the Gay Marriage Movement." *Radical History Review* 100: 223–235.

Brah, A., and A. Phoenix. 2004. "Ain't I a Woman? Revisiting Intersectionality." *Journal of International Women's Studies* 5: 75–86.

Bridges, K. M. 2011. *Reproducing Race: An Ethnography of Pregnancy as a Site of Racialization.* Berkeley: University of California Press.

Carbado, D. W. 2013. "Colorblind Intersectionality." *Signs: The Journal of Women in Culture and Society* 38: 811–845.

Cho, S. 2002. "Understanding White Women's Ambivalence Towards Affirmative Action: Theorizing Political Accountability in Coalitions." *University of Missouri Kansas City Law Review* 71: 399–418.

Cho, S., K. W. Crenshaw, and L. McCall. 2013. "Intersectionality Studies: Theory, Applications, and Praxis." *Signs: The Journal of Women in Culture and Society* 38: 785–810.

Chuck, E. 2013. "Meet the Supreme Court Matchmaker: Edward Blum." *NBCNews.com*. Accessed June 11. http://usnews.nbcnews.com/_news/2013/06/11/18750240-meet-the-supreme-court-matchmaker-edward-blum?lite.

Clough, P. T., and M. Fine. 2007. "Activism and Pedagogies: Feminist Reflections." *Women's Studies Quarterly* 35: 255–275.

Cohen, P. 2012. "Regnerus Study Controversy Guide." *Family Inequality*. Accessed June 11. http://familyinequality.wordpress.com/2012/08/15/regnerus-study-controversy-guide/.

Cole, E. R. 2009. "Intersectionality and Research in Psychology." *American Psychologist* 64: 170–180.

Collins, P. H. (1990) 2000. *Black Feminist Thought: Knowledge, Consciousness, and the Politics of Empowerment.* Second edition. New York: Routledge.

Collins, P. H. 1998. *Fighting Words: Black Women and the Search for Justice.* Minneapolis: University of Minnesota Press.

Combahee River Collective. (1977) 2007. "A Black Feminist Statement." In *The Essential Feminist Reader,* edited by E. B. Freedman, 325–330. New York: Modern Library.

Crenshaw, K. W. 1989. "Demarginalizing the Intersection of Race and Sex: A Black Feminist Critique of Antidiscrimination Doctrine, Feminist Theory and Antiracist Politics." *University of Chicago Legal Forum* 140: 139–167.

Crenshaw, K. W. 1991. "Mapping the Margins: Intersectionality, Identity Politics, and Violence Against Women of Color." *Stanford Law Review* 46: 1241–1299.

Crenshaw, K. W. 2000. Background Paper for the Expert Meeting on the Gender-Related Aspects of Race Discrimination. United Nations.

Davis, A. Y. 1990. *Women, Culture, and Politics.* New York: Vintage.

Davis, K. 2008. "Intersectionality as Buzzword: A Sociology of Science Perspective on What Makes a Feminist Theory Successful." *Feminist Theory* 9: 67–85.

Dill, B. T. 2009. "Intersections, Identities, and Inequalities in Higher Education." In *Emerging Intersections: Race, Class, and Gender in Theory, Policy, and Practice,* edited by B. T. Dill and R. E. Zambrana, 229–252. New Brunswick, NJ: Rutgers University Press.

Dill, B. T., and M. H. Kohlman. 2011. "Intersectionality: A Transformative Paradigm in Feminist Theory and Social Justice." In *The Handbook of Feminist Research: Theory and Praxis,* second edition, edited by S. N. Hesse-Biber, 154–174. Thousand Oaks, CA: SAGE Publications.

Dill, B. T., S. M. Nettles, and L. Weber. 2001. "Defining the Work of the Consortium: What Do We Mean by Intersections?" *Connections.* Consortium on Race, Gender and Ethnicity. http://www.crge.umd.edu/pdf/RC2001_spring.pdf.

Dill, B. T., and R. E. Zambrana, eds. 2009. *Emerging Intersections: Race, Class, and Gender in Theory, Policy, and Practice.* New Brunswick, NJ: Rutgers University Press.

Dill, B. T., R. E. Zambrana, and A. E. McLaughlin. 2009. "Transforming the Campus Climate through Institution, Collaboration, and Mentoring." In *Emerging Intersections: Race, Class, and Gender in Theory, Policy, and Practice,* edited by B. T. Dill and R. E. Zambrana, 253–273. New Brunswick, NJ: Rutgers University Press.

Duggan, L. 2003. *The Twilight of Equality?: Neoliberalism, Cultural Politics, and the Attack on Democracy.* Boston: Beacon Press.

Duster, T. 2003. "Buried Alive: The Concept of Race in Science." In *Genetic Nature/Culture: Anthropology and Science Beyond the Two-Culture Divide,* edited by A. H. Goodman, D. Heath, and M. S. Lindee, 258–277. Berkeley, CA: University of California Press.

Fausto-Sterling, A. 2000. *Sexing the Body: Gender Politics and the Construction of Sexuality.* New York: Basic Books.

Ferguson, R. A. 2004. *Aberrations in Black: Toward a Queer of Color Critique.* Minneapolis: University of Minnesota Press.

Ferguson, R. A. 2012. "Reading Intersectionality." *Trans-Scripts* 2: 91–99.

Frankenberg, R. 1993. *The Social Construction of Whiteness: White Women, Race Matters*. Minneapolis, MN: University of Minnesota Press.

Gines, K. 2011. "Being a Black Woman Philosopher: Reflections on Founding the Collegium of Black Women Philosophers." *Hypatia* 26: 429–437.

Gould, S. J. 1996. *The Mismeasure of Man*. Second edition. New York: W. W. Norton & Company.

Gray, H. S. 2005. *Cultural Moves: African Americans and the Politics of Representation*. Berkeley: University of California Press.

Grzanka, P. R., and J. T. Maher. 2012. "Different, Like Everyone Else: *Stuff White People Like* and the Marketplace of Diversity." *Symbolic Interaction* 35: 368–393.

Haraway, D. 1988. "Situated Knowledges: The Science Question in Feminism and the Privilege of Partial Perspective." *Feminist Studies* 14: 579–599.

Lorde, A. 1984. *Sister Outsider: Essays and Speeches*. Berkeley, CA: The Crossing Press.

McCall, L. 2005. "The Complexity of Intersectionality." *Signs: The Journal of Women in Culture and Society* 30: 1711–1800.

Melamed, J. 2006. "The Spirit of Neoliberalism: From Racial Liberalism to Neoliberal Multiculturalism." *Social Text* 89: 1–24.

Mencimer, S. 2013. "Mormon Church Abandons Its Crusade Against Gay Marriage." *Mother Jones,* April 12. http://www.motherjones.com/politics/2013/04/prop-8-mormons-gay-marriage-shift.

Mohanty, C. T. 1984. "Under Western Eyes: Feminist Scholarship and Colonial Discourses." *boundary 2* 12: 333–358.

Mohanty, C. T. 2013. "Feminist Crossing: On Neoliberalism and Radical Critique." *Signs: The Journal of Women in Culture and Society* 38: 967–991.

Moraga, C., and G. Anzaldúa, eds. 1984. *This Bridge Called My Back: Writings by Radical Women of Color*. Second edition. Cambridge, MA: Kitchen Table: Women of Color Press.

Nash, J. C. 2008. "Re-thinking Intersectionality." *Feminist Review* 89: 1–15.

Patil, V. 2013. "From Patriarchy to Intersectionality: A Transnational Feminist Assessment of How Far We've Really Come." *Signs: The Journal of Women in Culture and Society* 38: 847–867.

Puar, J. K. 2007. *Terrorist Assemblages: Homonationalism in Queer Times*. Durham, NC: Duke University Press.

Reddy, C. 2005. "Asian Diasporas, Neoliberalism, and Family: Reviewing the Case for Homosexual Asylum in the Context of Family Rights." *Social Text* 23: 101–119.

Sandoval, C. 2000. *Methodology of the Oppressed*. Minneapolis: University of Minnesota Press.

Savage, D. 2008. "Black Homophobia." *The Stranger: SLOG News & Arts,* November 5. Accessed June 11, 2013. http://slog.thestranger.com/2008/11/black_homophobia.

Schulz, A. J., and L. Mullings, eds. 2005. *Gender, Race, Class, and Health: Intersectional Approaches*. San Francisco, CA: Jossey-Bass.

Sengupta, S. 2006. "I/Me/Mine: Intersectional Identities as Negotiated Minefields." *Signs: The Journal of Women in Culture and Society* 31: 629–639.

Shim, J. K. 2005. "Constructing 'Race' Across the Science-Lay Divide: Racial Formation in the Epidemiology and Experience of Cardiovascular Disease." *Social Studies of Science* 35: 405–436.

Smith, B. 1980. "Racism and Women's Studies." *Frontiers: A Journal of Women's Studies* 5: 48–49.

Somerville, S. 1994. "Scientific Racism and the Emergence of the Homosexual Body." *Journal of the History of Sexuality* 5: 243–266.

Spivak, G. C. 1988. "Can the Subaltern Speak?" In *Marxism and the Interpretation of Culture,* edited by C. Nelson and L. Grossberg, 271–313. Urbana: University of Illinois Press.

Stachelberg, W., and C. Burns. 2013. "10 Things to Know About the Employment Non-Discrimination Act." Center for American Progress, April 24. Accessed June 11, 2013. http://www.americanprogress.org/issues/lgbt/news/2013/04/24/61294 /10-things-to-know-about-the-employment-non-discrimination-act/.

United States Census Bureau. 2013. "Shelby County, Alabama." *State and County QuickFacts.* Accessed June 11, 2013. http://quickfacts.census.gov/qfd/states/01 /01117.html.

Wadsworth, N. D. 2011. "Intersectionality in California's Same-Sex Marriage Battles: A Complex Proposition." *Political Research Quarterly* 64: 200–216.

Wilds Lawson, T. 2009. *Faith Without Funding, Values Without Justice: The Bush Campaign's Successful Targeting of African American Evangelical Pastors and Churches in the 2004 Presidential Election* (doctoral dissertation). Retrieved from Digital Repository at the University of Maryland (DRUM).

Williams, P. 1992. *The Alchemy of Race and Rights: Diary of a Law Professor.* Cambridge: Harvard University Press.

LAW

Systems of Oppression
Patrick R. Grzanka

There are innumerable ways to begin thinking about the history of intersectionality, but the law is perhaps the most obvious place to start. Critical Race Theory (CRT), the prominent segment of critical legal studies that explores the persistence of race and racism in the law and society, preceded the formal elaboration of intersectionality and in many ways served as the harbinger of intersectionality as an intellectual and activist project. While figures such as Derrick Bell, Richard Delgado, and Jean Stefancic were developing CRT into a potent tool for uncovering how racism and White supremacy are reinforced by the law in the United States, Black feminist law scholars such as Patricia Williams and Kimberlé Williams Crenshaw were skeptical of CRT's focus on race at the expense of other dimensions of identity and difference, namely gender and class. As the story goes, it was in critical legal studies that the term "intersectionality" first originated in print (Crenshaw 1989), and twenty-five years later the law remains a preoccupying site for intersectional critics for reasons that speak to the overarching commitments of the field as recently detailed by Crenshaw, fellow legal studies scholar Sumi Cho, and sociologist Leslie McCall (Cho, Crenshaw, and McCall 2013). First, the law is a discursive and deeply material arena in which social norms are both produced and reflected; identities and subjects are both crafted and transformed; equality is promoted and undermined; and diverse elements of society and the social contract are both reinforced and resisted. In this way, the law is a quintessential example of the kind of structural forces that are the target of intersectional teaching, research, and activism.

Second, the law is a site of thinking, debate, and working through of what it is that "intersectionality" itself actually means. A key part of theory construction—including the testing, revision, elaboration, and re-testing of theory in the interest of validity, reliability, and overall explanatory power—is debate among a given theory's practitioners about what the theory is designed to do (and not do), where it applies (and does not apply), and what its strength are (and are not). Specifically, because intersectionality as a term is basically always metaphorical, a significant part of the development of intersectionality has been scholarly debate about the practical and theoretical utility of the intersection metaphor. As Kathy Davis explains, "Controversies have emerged about whether intersectionality should be conceptualized as a crossroad (Crenshaw 1991), as 'axes' of difference (Yuval-Davis 2006) or as a dynamic process (Staunæs 2003)" (2008, 68). The dynamic nature of the law and the unique ways in which the law affects and is affected by individuals, history, social forces, political economy, and large-scale structural dynamics makes it an especially inviting place to consider the efficacy of the intersection metaphor itself and to propose alternative configurations of theory and praxis that explain, critique, and challenge various forms of oppression.

Finally, the law is a site of activism and resistance in which many of the key social problems facing our global society are advocated. From economic justice to immigration reform, to military interventions and prison abolition, to environmental activism and organized labor, the law is a contested field in which multiple social groups and actors seek power, control, restitution, and social transformation. "These concerns," according to Cho, Crenshaw, and Mc-Call, "reflect the normative and political dimensions of intersectionality and thus embody a motivation to go beyond mere comprehension of intersectional dynamics to transform them" (2013, 786). Therefore, the law contains both forms of intersectionality delineated by Crenshaw (2000, reading 3): *structural* intersectionality, or the material consequences of intersecting oppressions, and *political* intersectionality, which denotes the ways the multiply marginalized and vulnerable social groups resist their oppression.

Though the law is heterogeneous and refers to a broad range of rules and regulations that are created and implemented by diverse institutions (e.g., the state, local jurisdictions, and international agencies such as the International Criminal Court) in widely varying ways, the law can be understood as a *system of oppression*. While many intersectional scholars will use anecdotal evidence, lived experiences, and case studies to define and critique instances of oppression, intersectionality as a field is generally committed to the critique of systemic social forces. This means that while major historical events, such as Hurricane Katrina, and everyday occurrences, such as street harassment, happen in particular spaces in particular moments in time, intersectional analyses work to understand how those specific incidents reflect systemic patterns of discrimination, exploitation, privilege, and disinvestment. When it comes to the law, therefore, studies of intersectionality investigate how unfair sentencing practices (e.g., Farrell, Ward, and Rousseau 2010), gaps in legal doctrine (e.g., antidiscrimination law; Crenshaw 1989), and crises in individual families (Reddy 2005, reading 4) are produced and managed by systemic forces that create and shape landscapes of inequality.

In this unit, Chandan Reddy (2005) refers to the law as an "archive" to signal both the historical dimensions of the law and how institutions and stakeholders, who are always invested in difference, actively construct it. He posits, "Contending with the law as an active archive, or technique of self-making and the making of selves . . . requires that we not simply 'take up' its narrative and framework. Instead, we need to ask how regulation marks its interest in difference." It has long been acknowledged that history is not a passive record of all that has happened; rather, history is a *political* construction of what certain people think has happened. As Donna Haraway (1988, reading 6) reminds us in Unit II, this does not mean that we should give up on history, that all history is a lie, or that history is a useless pursuit. On the contrary, history is field of power, and attending to history means considering what has been omitted, remembered, memorialized, and distorted. The implications of history speak not only to the past but also to the future, as Reddy insists. The active archive of the law necessitates attention to the legal record and sensitivity to how differences (such as those defined by citizenship, race, gender, and sexuality) are *presently* being made and remade by the law. Carbado explains Crenshaw's initial goals:

> Crenshaw also sought to highlight courts' refusal to permit Black women to represent a class of plaintiffs that included white women or Black men: here, courts were essentially saying that Black women were too different to represent either white women or Black men as a group. The problem, then, was not simply that courts were prohibiting Black women from representing themselves; the problem was also that courts were prohibiting Black women from representing gender or race per se. Too similar to be different and too different to be the same, Black women were "impossible subjects" (Ngai, 2004) of antidiscrimination law. (2013, 813).

The late 1980s and 1990s marked a period of paramount importance for Black women's status in the US legal code as major court cases, Supreme Court appointments (e.g., Clarence Thomas), and legislative battles (e.g., Clinton-era welfare reform) predicated the future of gender, racial, and sexual politics. Today, we look back upon these events and decisions to understand the processes of social formation engendered by the law and to see how today's systemic inequalities are rooted in legal dynamics of the far and recent past.

Moreover, as contemporary legal battles over same-sex marriage, immigration reform, right to digital privacy, and corporate involvement in elections persist, the active archive is both a record of injustice and a potential tool for social justice. In Reddy's framework, we must take the literal record of the law to task in order to create alternative possibilities for rights and equality. We do history, then, in the interest of the future.

And while we begin here in the law, legal concerns are not restricted to formal studies of jurisprudence and legislation. The law pervades social life, and legal criticism therefore echoes throughout this book in studies that inevitably implicate the law in domains such as politics, community activism, and identity. There is no line—real or imagined—that demarcates the place where the law begins and ends, even as much as traditional legal practice might seek to carve out the social universe in such a way, as Patricia Williams (1992, reading 1) explains. Though lawyers and judges are professionally mandated to consider where the law does and does not have jurisdiction, intersectionality transcends these concerns, and intersectional studies look to unexpected and unpredictable places where the legal ordering of society influences where power, resources, and life chances flow to and from.

References and Further Reading

Bell, D. 1993. *Faces at the Bottom of the Well: The Permanence of Racism*. New York: BasicBooks.

Carbado, D. W. 2013. "Colorblind Intersectionality." *Signs: The Journal of Women in Culture and Society* 38: 811–845.

Cho, S., K. W. Crenshaw, and L. McCall. 2013. "Intersectionality Studies: Theory, Applications, and Praxis." *Signs: The Journal of Women in Culture and Society* 38: 785–810.

Conaghan, J. 2009. "Intersectionality and the Feminist Legal Project in Law." In *Law, Power and the Politics of Subjectivity: Intersectionality and Beyond*, edited by E. Grabham, D. Cooper, J. Krishnadas, and D. Herman, 21–48. London: Routledge.

Crenshaw, K. W. 1989. "Demarginalizing the Intersection of Race and Sex: A Black Feminist Critique of Antidiscrimination Doctrine, Feminist Theory and Antiracist Politics." *University of Chicago Legal Forum* 140: 139–167.

Crenshaw, K. W. 1991. "Mapping the Margins: Intersectionality, Identity Politics, and Violence Against Women of Color." *Stanford Law Review* 46: 1241–1299.

Crenshaw, K. W. 2000. Background Paper for the Expert Meeting on the Gender-Related Aspects of Race Discrimination. United Nations.

Crenshaw, K. W., N. Gotanda, G. Peller, and K. Thomas, eds. 1996. *Critical Race Theory: The Key Writings That Formed the Movement*. New York: New Press.

Davis, K. 2008. "Intersectionality as Buzzword: A Sociology of Science Perspective on What Makes a Feminist Theory Successful." *Feminist Theory* 9: 67–85.

Delgado, R., and J. Stefancic. 2012. *Critical Race Theory: An Introduction*. Second edition. New York: New York University Press.

Farrell, A., G. Ward, and D. Rousseau. 2010. "Intersections of Gender and Race in Federal Sentencing: Examining Court Contexts and the Effects of Representative Court Authorities." *Journal of Gender, Race and Justice* 14: 85–126.

Haraway, D. 1988. "Situated Knowledges: The Science Question in Feminism and the Privilege of Partial Perspective." *Feminist Studies* 14: 579–599.

Ngai, M. M. 2004. *Impossible Subjects: Illegal Aliens and the Making of Modern America*. Princeton, NJ: Princeton University Press.

Puar, J. K. 2007. *Terrorist Assemblages: Homonationalism in Queer Times*. Durham, NC: Duke University Press.

Reddy, C. 2005. "Asian Diasporas, Neoliberalism, and Family: Reviewing the Case for Homosexual Asylum in the Context of Family Rights." *Social Text* 23: 101–119.

Reddy, C. 2008. "Time for Rights? *Loving*, Gay Marriage, and the Limits of Legal Justice." *Fordham Law Journal* 76: 2849–2872.

Roberts, D. E. 1993a. "Crime, Race, and Reproduction." *Tulane Law Review* 67: 1945–1977.

Roberts, D. E. 1993b. "Racism and Patriarchy in the Meaning of Motherhood." *American University Journal of Gender and Law* 1: 1–38.

Spade, D. 2013. "Intersectional Resistance and Legal Reform." *Signs: The Journal of Women in Culture and Society* 38: 1031–1055.

Staunæs, D. 2003. "Where Have All the Subjects Gone? Bringing Together the Concepts of Intersectionality and Subjectification." *Nora* 11: 101–110.

Williams, P. 1992. *The Alchemy of Race and Rights: Diary of a Law Professor*. Cambridge: Harvard University Press.

Yuval-Davis, N. 2006. "Intersectionality and Feminist Politics." *European Journal of Women's Studies* 13: 193–210.

Patricia Williams

Patricia Williams is currently a James L. Dohr Professor of Law at Columbia University and one of the founding theorists of intersectionality. Though she is professionally situated in legal studies, the traditional "birthplace" of intersectionality, her *Alchemy of Race and Rights: Diary of a Law Professor* (1991) integrates critical literary theory, autobiography, and cultural studies to weave an argument about the intersectionality of race, gender, and class. In doing so, she presents an interdisciplinary methodological framework that has been hugely influential to scholars in the broad genealogy of intersectionality, because she shows how the use of multiple methods and texts (from Oprah Winfrey to the law school classroom) is often the best way to break out of disciplinary rubrics that encourage single-axis (e.g., race *or* gender *or* class) approaches to the study of difference and oppression.

In the book, Williams takes up the ancient concept of alchemy to metaphorically cast the law as a contemporary alchemist of seemingly opposing forces, such as wealth and poverty, the Constitution and big business, sanity and insanity, objectivity and subjectivity. The excerpt below includes one of the most famous passages from the text, in which Williams makes the rhetorically simple but philosophically profound statement: "life is complicated." The complexity of our lives traditionally sits in opposition to the law, explains Williams, because the law—not entirely unlike science—seeks to reduce and simplify the universe into generalizable principles that can be applied across the population without concern to the particularities of context, life history, emotions, and subjectivity. Though many essays throughout this volume will take up unfair and unjust manifestations of legal practice, Williams is concerned with challenging the hegemony of the law itself, particularly its status as a bastion of "high objectivity." If we are to begin to take life's complexity seriously, then we must reconsider the architecture of the social contract and the mechanisms by which society is organized. The law, of course, in all of its messiness, is at the center of such a project.

1. Life is Complicated, and Other Observations[*]

It is my deep belief that theoretical legal understanding and social transformation need not be oxymoronic. I want this book to occupy the gaps between those ends that the sensation of oxymoron marks. What I hope will be filled in is connection; connection between my psyche and the readers', between lived experience and social perception, and between an encompassing historicity and a jurisprudence of generosity.

"Theoretical legal understanding" is characterized, in Anglo-American jurisprudence, by at least three features of thought and rhetoric:

1. The hypostatization of exclusive categories and definitional polarities, the drawing of bright lines and clear taxonomies that purport to make life simpler in the face of life's complication: rights/needs, moral/immoral, public/private, white/black.
2. The existence of transcendent, acontextual, universal legal truths or pure procedures. For example, some conservative theorists might insist that the tort of fraud has always existed and that it is part of a universal system of right and wrong. A friend of mine demanded of a professor who made just such an assertion: "Do you mean to say that when the first white settlers landed on Fiji, they found tortfeasors waiting to be

---

[*] Excerpted from P. J. Williams, *The Alchemy of Race and Rights: Diary of a Law Professor* (Cambridge: Harvard University Press, 1991), 8–14. Copyright © 1991 by the President and Fellows of Harvard College.

discovered?" Yes, in a manner of speaking, was the professor's response. This habit of universalizing legal taxonomies is very much like a cartoon I once saw, in which a group of prehistoric fish swam glumly underwater, carrying baseball bats tucked beneath their fins, waiting to evolve, looking longingly toward dry land, where a baseball was lying in wait on the shore. The more serious side of this essentialized world view is a worrisome tendency to disparage anything that is nontranscendent (temporal, historical), or contextual (socially constructed), or nonuniversal (specific) as "emotional," "literary," "personal," or just Not True.

3. The existence of objective, "unmediated" voices by which those transcendent, universal truths find their expression. Judges, lawyers, logicians, and practitioners of empirical methodologies are obvious examples, but the supposed existence of such voices is also given power in romanticized notions of "real people" having "real" experiences—not because real people have experienced what they really experienced, but because their experiences are somehow *made* legitimate—either because they are viewed as empirically legitimate (directly corroborated by consensus, by a community of outsiders) or, more frequently, because those experiences are corroborated by hidden or unspoken models of legitimacy. The Noble Savage as well as the Great White Father, the Good-Hearted Masses, the Real American, the Rational Consumer, and the Arm's-Length Transactor are all versions of this Idealized Other whose gaze provides us either with internalized censure or externalized approval; internalized paralysis or externalized legitimacy; internalized false consciousness or externalized claims of exaggerated authenticity.

The degree to which these three features of legal thought are a force in laws ranging from contracts to crimes, from property to civil liberties, will be a theme throughout the rest of this book. For the moment, however, a smaller example might serve to illustrate the interpretive dynamic of which I am speaking.

A man with whom I used to work once told me that I made too much of my race. "After all," he said, "I don't even think of you as black." Yet sometime later, when another black woman became engaged in an ultimately unsuccessful tenure battle, he confided to me that he wished the school could find more blacks like me. I felt myself slip in and out of shadow, as I became nonblack for purposes of inclusion and black for purposes of exclusion; I felt the boundaries of my very body manipulated, casually inscribed by definitional demarcations that did not refer to me.

The paradox of my being black yet notblack visited me again when, back to back, the same (white) man and then a (black) woman wondered aloud if I "really identified as black." When the white man said this, I was acutely aware that the choice of identifying as black (as opposed to white?) was hardly mine; that as long as I am identified as black by the majority of others, my own identifying as black will almost surely follow as a simple fact of human interdependency. When the black woman told me the very same thing, I took it to heart as a signpost of self-denial; as possible evidence within myself of that brand of social distress and alienation to which blacks and oppressed people are so peculiarly subject; and as a call for unity in a society that too often helps us turn against ourselves.

I heard the same words from each, and it made no difference to me. I heard the same words from each, but differently: one characterized me as more of something I am not, white; the other called for me to be more conscious of something I am, black. I heard the same-different words addressed to me, a perceived white-male-socialized black woman, as a challenge to mutually exclusive categorization, as an overlapping of black and female and right and male and private and wrong and white and public, and so on and so forth.

That life is complicated is a fact of great analytic importance. Law too often seeks to avoid this truth by making up its own breed of narrower, simpler, but hypnotically powerful rhetorical truths. Acknowledging, challenging, playing with these *as* rhetorical gestures is, it seems to me, necessary for any conception of justice. Such acknowledgment complicates the supposed purity of gender, race, voice, boundary; it allows us to acknowledge the utility of such categorizations for certain purposes and the necessity of their breakdown on other occasions. It complicates definitions in its shift, in its expansion and contraction according to circumstance, in its room for the possibility of creatively mated taxonomies and their wildly unpredictable offspring.

I think, though, that one of the most important results of reconceptualizing from "objective truth" to rhetorical event will be a more nuanced sense of legal and social responsibility. This will be so because much of what is spoken in so-called objective, unmediated voices is in fact mired in hidden subjectivities and unexamined claims that make property of others beyond the self, all the while denying such connections. I remember A., a colleague, once stating that he didn't like a book he had just read because he had another friend who was a literary critic and he *imagined* that this critical friend would say a host of negative things about the book. A. disclaimed his own subjectivity, displacing it onto a larger-than-life literary critic; he created an authority who was imaginary but whose rhetorical objectivity was as smooth and convincing as the slice of a knife. In psychobabble, this is known as "not taking responsibility." In racial contexts, it is related to the familiar offensiveness of people who will say, "Our maid is black and *she* says that blacks want . . . "; such statements both universalize the lone black voice and disguise, enhance, and "objectify" the authority of the individual white speaker. As a legal tool, however, it is an extremely common device by which not just subject positioning is obscured, but by which agency and responsibility are hopelessly befuddled.

The propagated mask of the imagined literary critic, the language club of hyperauthenticity, the myth of a purely objective perspective, the godlike image of generalized, legitimating others—these are too often reified in law as "impersonal" rules and "neutral" principles, presumed to be inanimate, unemotional, unbiased, unmanipulated, and higher than ourselves. Laws like masks, frozen against the vicissitudes of life; rights as solid as rocks; principles like baseballs waiting on dry land for us to crawl up out of the mud and claim them.

This semester I have been teaching a course entitled Women and Notions of Property. I have been focusing on the semantic power and property of individualistic gendered perspectives, gender in this instance having less to do with the biology of male and female than with the semiotics of power relations, of dominance and submission, of assertion and deference, of big and little; as well as on gender issues specifically based in biology, such as reproductive rights and the complicated ability of women in particular to live freely in the territory of their own bodies. An example of the stories we discuss is the following, used to illustrate the rhetoric of power relations whose examination, I tell my students, is at the heart of the course.

Walking down Fifth Avenue in New York not long ago, I came up behind a couple and their young son. The child, about four or five years old, had evidently been complaining about big dogs. The mother was saying, "But why are you afraid of big dogs?" "Because they're big," he responded with eminent good sense. "But what's the difference between a big dog and a little dog?" the father persisted. "They're *big*," said the child. "But there's really no difference," said the mother, pointing to a large slathering wolfhound with narrow eyes and the calculated amble of a gangster, and then to a beribboned Pekinese the size of a roller skate, who was flouncing along just ahead of us all, in that little fox-trotty step that keep Pekinese from ever being taken seriously. "See?" said the father. "If you look really closely you'll see there's no difference at all. They're all just dogs."

And I thought: Talk about your iron-clad canon. Talk about a static, unyielding, totally uncompromising point of reference. These people must be lawyers. Where else do people learn so well the idiocies of High Objectivity? How else do people learn to capitulate so uncritically to a norm that refuses to allow for difference? How else do grown-ups sink so deeply into the authoritarianism of their own world view that they can universalize their relative bigness so completely that they obliterate the subject positioning of their child's relative smallness? (To say nothing of the position of the slathering wolfhound, from whose own narrow perspective I dare say the little boy must have looked exactly like a lamb chop.)

I used this story in my class because I think it illustrates a paradigm of thought by which children are taught not to see what they see; by which blacks are reassured that there is no real inequality in the world, just their own bad dreams; and by which women are taught not to experience what they experience, in deference to men's ways of knowing. The story also illustrates the possibility of a collective perspective or social positioning that would give rise to a claim for the legal interests of groups. In a historical moment when individual rights have become the basis for any remedy, too often group interests are defeated by, for example, finding the one four-year-old who has wrestled whole packs of wolfhounds fearlessly to the ground; using that individual experience to attack the validity of there ever being any generalizable four-year-old fear of wolfhounds; and then recasting the general group experience as a fragmented series of specific, isolated events rather than a pervasive social phenomenon ("You have every right to think that that wolfhound has the ability to bite off your head, but that's just your point of view").

My students, most of whom signed up expecting to experience that crisp, refreshing, clear-headed sensation that "thinking like a lawyer" purportedly endows, are confused by this and all the stories I tell them in my class on Women and Notions of Property. They are confused enough by the idea of property alone, overwhelmed by the thought of dogs and women as academic subjects, and paralyzed by the idea that property might have a gender and that gender might be a matter of words.

But I haven't been able to straighten things out for them because I'm confused too. I have arrived at a point where everything I have ever learned is running around and around in my head; and little bits of law and pieces of everyday life fly out of my mouth in weird combinations. Who can blame the students for being confused? On the other hand, everyday life is a confusing bit of business. And so my students plot my disintegration, in the shadowy shelter of ivy-covered archways and in the margins of their notebooks. . . .

Lisa Lowe

Lisa Lowe is a professor of English and American studies at Tufts University, and also holds the title of professor emeritus at the University of California, San Diego, where she was chair of the Department of Comparative Literature. She studied European intellectual history and critical theory at the University of California, Santa Cruz, and her scholarship has long reflected a concern for the persistence of colonialism in contemporary cultural politics. She has published multiple books, including *Critical Terrains: French and British*

Orientalisms (1991), *The Politics of Culture in the Shadow of Capital* (1997, co-edited with D. Lloyd), and *Immigrant Acts: On Asian American Cultural Politics* (1996), which is excerpted here.

The term "immigrant acts" is a kind of double entendre that refers to, as Lowe explains, how a) Asian peoples were both subjected to racist immigration laws (e.g., the Chinese Exclusion Act of 1882) throughout their historical relationship with the US nation-state and b) the heterogeneous ways in which Asian American cultural politics have always involved opposition to these exclusions, exploitations, and subordinations: "the *acts* of labor, resistance, memory, and survival, as well as the politicized cultural work that emerges from dislocation and disidentification." The law, to Lowe, is a discursive arena in which subjects (i.e., categories of personhood) are not merely managed but produced. This production of the Asian American subject in US legal doctrine has been marked by contradictions that are signified by the phrase "immigrant acts." Lowe seeks to highlight the murkiness and inconsistencies of the alien/citizen, legal/illegal, US-born/permanent resident dualisms through which the liberal state "discriminates, surveys, and produces immigrant identities." To access these complexities and to deconstruct the binary logic of the law, Lowe directs her critique toward the connections between the law and extralegal sociohistorical dynamics that simultaneously and differentially racialized, gendered, and Othered Asian American subjects in contrast to the White supremacist, capitalist, and heteromasculine US nation-state. Lowe argues that gender, race, and citizenship are therefore coproduced by and through the law, economy, and culture.

2. Immigrant Acts*

"Immigrant acts," then, attempts to name the *contradictions* of Asian immigration, which at different moments in the last century and a half of Asian entry into the United States have placed Asians "within" the U.S. nation-state, its workplaces, and its markets, yet linguistically, culturally, and racially marked Asians as "foreign" and "outside" the national polity. Under such contradictions, late-nineteenth-century Chinese immigrants labored in mining, agriculture, and railroad construction but were excluded from citizenship and political participation in the state. The contradiction of immigration and citizenship took a different but consistently resonant form during World War II, when U.S.-born Japanese Americans were nominally recognized as citizens

---

* Excerpted from L. Lowe, "Immigration, Citizenship, Racialization: Asian American Critique," in *Immigrant Acts* (Durham, NC: Duke University Press, 1996), 1–36. Copyright, 1996, Duke University Press. All rights reserved. Republished by permission of the copyright holder, www.dukeupress.edu.

and hence recruited into the U.S. military, yet were dispossessed of freedoms and properties explicitly granted to citizens, officially condemned as "racial enemies," and interned in camps throughout the Western United States. Philippine immigration after the period of U.S. colonization animates yet another kind of contradiction. For Filipino immigrants, modes of capitalist incorporation and acculturation into American life begin not at the moment of immigration but rather in the "homeland" already deeply affected by U.S. influences and modes of social organization. The situations of Filipino Americans, or U.S. Filipinos, foreground the ways in which Asian Americans emigrating from previously colonized sites are not exclusively formed as racialized minorities within the United States but are simultaneously determined by colonialism and capital investment in Asia. These different contradictions express distinct yet continuous formations in the genealogy of the racialization of Asian Americans: the Chinese as alien noncitizen, the American citizen of Japanese descent as racial enemy, and the American citizen of Filipino descent as simultaneously immigrant and colonized national.

By insisting on "immigrant acts" as contradictions and therefore as dialectical and critical, I also mean to emphasize that while immigration has been the *locus* of legal and political restriction of Asians as the "other" in America, immigration has simultaneously been the site for the emergence of critical negations of the nation-state for which those legislations are the expression. If the law is the apparatus that binds and seals the universality of the political body of the nation, then the "immigrant," produced by the law as margin and threat to that symbolic whole, is precisely a generative site for the critique of that universality. The national institutionalization of unity becomes the measure of the nation's condition of heterogeneity. If the nation proposes American culture as the key site for the resolution of inequalities and stratifications that cannot be resolved on the political terrain of representative democracy, then that culture performs that reconciliation by naturalizing a universality that exempts the "non-American" from its history of development or admits the "non-American" only through a "multiculturalism" that aestheticizes ethnic differences as if they could be separated from history. In contrast, the cultural productions emerging out of the contradictions of immigrant marginality displace the fiction of reconciliation, disrupt the myth of national identity by revealing its gaps and fissures, and intervene in the narrative of national development that would illegitimately locate the "immigrant" before history or exempt the "immigrant" from history. The universals proposed by the political and cultural forms of the nation precisely generate the critical *acts* that negate those universals. "Immigrant acts" names the *agency* of Asian immigrants and Asian Americans: the *acts* of labor, resistance, memory, and survival, as well as the politicized cultural work that emerges from dislocation and disidentification. Asian immigrants and Asian Americans have not only been "subject to" immigration exclusion and restriction but have also been "subjects of" the immigration process and are agents of political change, cultural expression, and social transformation.

The period from 1850 to World War II was marked by legal exclusions, political disenfranchisement, labor exploitation, and internment for Asian-origin groups in the United States. While some of the legal and political exclusions have been lifted in the period following the McCarran-Walter Act of 1952 and the Immigration and Nationality Act of 1965, the problems of legal definition have continued for Asian origin communities. Indeed, the McCarran-Walter Act, an expression of the cold war era, legislated strict quotas, created an area called the "Asia-Pacific triangle" based on a strategically territorial mapping, and contained language delineating the exclusion of and right to deport "any alien who has engaged or has had purpose to engage in activities 'prejudicial to the public interest' or 'subversive to national security.'" The 1965 act has initiated not fewer but indeed more specifications and regulations for immigrants of Asian origins. Immigration, thus, can be understood as the most important historical and discursive site of Asian American formation through which the national and global economic, the cultural, and the legal spheres are modulated. Whether that determination is expressed through immigration "exclusion" or "inclusion," the U.S. nation-state attempts to "produce" and regulate the Asian as a means of "resolving" economic exigencies, primarily through the *loci* of citizenship and political representation but also in ways that extend to the question of culture. As the state legally transforms the Asian *alien* into the Asian American *citizen,* it institutionalizes the disavowal of the history of racialized labor exploitation and disenfranchisement through the promise of freedom in the political sphere. Yet the historical and continued racialization of the Asian American, as citizen, exacerbates the contradictions of the national project that promises the resolution of material inequalities through the political domain of equal representation.

In the following discussion, I place the legal regulations of the Asian as *alien* noncitizen and the Asian American as *citizen* in terms of the material contradictions that have emerged as the nation has intersected with the global economy during the last century and a half. The economic contradictions of capital and labor on the national level, and the contradictions of the political nation within the global economy, have given rise to the need, over and over again, for the nation to resolve *legally* capitalist contradiction around the definition of the Asian immigrant subject. The history of the legislation of the Asian as *alien* and the administration of the Asian American as *citizen* is at once the genealogy of this attempt at resolution and the genealogy of a distinct "racial formation" for Asian Americans, defined not primarily in terms of biological racialism but in terms of institutionalized, legal definitions of race and national origin. Michael Omi and Howard Winant observe that for most of its history, the U.S. state's racial policy has been one of repression and exclusion, and they read the role of the state in racial formation through a consideration of these state policies and laws. While noting the deep involvement of the state in the organization and interpretation of race, Omi and Winant also note the inadequacy of state institutions to carry out these functions. Therefore, they observe that race is "an unstable and 'decentered' complex of social meanings constantly being transformed by political struggle."

Racialization along the legal axis of definitions of citizenship has also ascribed "gender" to the Asian American subject. Up until 1870, American citizenship was granted exclusively to white male persons; in 1870, men of African descent could become naturalized, but the bar to citizenship remained for Asian men until the repeal acts of 1943–1952. Whereas the "masculinity" of the citizen was first inseparable from his "whiteness," as the state extended citizenship to nonwhite male persons, it formally designated these subjects as "male," as well. Though the history of citizenship and gender in relation to the enfranchisement of white women is distinct from the history of citizenship and race in relation to enfranchisement of nonwhite males, it is not entirely separate, for the legally defined racial formation of Chinese Americans and, later, other Asian Americans has likewise been a gendered formation. The 1943 enfranchisement of the Chinese American into citizenship, for example, constituted the Chinese immigrant subject as male; in the 1946 modification of the Magnuson Act, the Chinese wives of U.S. citizens were exempted from the permitted annual quota; as the law changed to reclassify "Chinese immigrants" as eligible for naturalization and citizenship, female immigrants were not included in this reclassification but were in effect specified only in relation to the changed status of "the Chinese immigrant," who was legally presumed to be male. Thus, the administration of citizenship was simultaneously a "technology" of racialization and gendering. From 1850 until the 1940s, Chinese immigrant masculinity had been socially and institutionally marked as different from that of Anglo- and Euro-American "white" citizens owing to the forms of work and community that had been historically available to Chinese men as the result of the immigration laws restricting female immigration. The Page Law of 1875 and a later ban on Chinese laborers' spouses had effectively halted the immigration of Chinese women, preventing the formation of families and generations among Chinese immigrants; in addition, female U.S. citizens who married an "alien ineligible to citizenship" lost their own citizenship. In conjunction with the relative absence of Chinese wives and family among immigrant "bachelor" communities and because of the concentration of Chinese men in "feminized" forms of work—such as laundry, restaurants, and other service-sector jobs—Chinese male immigrants could be said to occupy, before 1940, a "feminized" position in relation to white male citizens and, after 1940, a "masculinity" whose *racialization* is the material trace of the history of this "gendering."

Immigration regulations and the restrictions on naturalization and citizenship have thus racialized and gendered Asian Americans, and this history has situated Asian Americans, even as citizens, in a differential relationship to the political and cultural institutions of the nation-state. The racialization of Asian Americans in relation to the state locates Asian American culture as a site for the emergence of another kind of political subject, one who has a historically "alien-ated" relation to the category of citizenship. That historical alienation situates the Asian American political subject in critical apposition to the category of the citizen, as well as to the political sphere of representative democracy that the concept of the citizen subtends. The differentiation of Asian immigrants from the national citizenry is marked not only politically but culturally as well: refracted through images, memories, and narratives— submerged, fragmented, and sedimented in a historical "unconscious"—it is rearticulated in Asian American culture through the emergence of alternative identities and practices.

The emergence of successful capitalist states in Asia has necessitated global restructuring for U.S. capital, reinvigorating American anxiety about Asia, but such anxiety about the Asian is clearly not new. Throughout the twentieth century, the figure of the Asian immigrant has served as a "screen," a phantasmatic site, on which the nation projects a series of condensed, complicated anxieties regarding external and internal threats to the mutable coherence of the national body: the invading multitude, the lascivious seductress, the servile yet treacherous domestic, the automaton whose inhuman efficiency will supersede American ingenuity. Indeed, it is precisely the unfixed liminality of the Asian immigrant—geographically, linguistically, and racially at odds with the context of the "national"—that has given rise to the necessity of endlessly fixing and repeating such stereotypes. Stereotypes that construct Asians as the threatening "yellow peril," or alternatively, that pose Asians as the domesticated "model minority," are each equally indices of these national anxieties. (Yet the discursive fixing of the Asian is not exclusively a matter of stereotypical representation in the cultural sphere; as I have been arguing, it has historically been instantiated through the state's classification of racialized Asian immigrant identities. The state announces its need to fix and stabilize the identity of the immigrant through legal exclusions and inclusions, as well as through juridical classifications. "Legal" and "illegal," "citizen" and "noncitizen," and "U.S.-born" and "permanent resident" are contemporary modes through which the liberal state discriminates, surveys, and produces immigrant identities. The presence of Asia and Asian peoples that currently impinges on the national consciousness sustains the figuration of the Asian immigrant as a transgressive and corrupting "foreignness" and continues to make "Asians" an object of the law, the political sphere, as well as national culture.

Kimberlé Williams Crenshaw

Kimberlé Crenshaw is professor of law at the University of California, Los Angeles, and the Columbia University School of Law. In addition to coining the term "intersectionality," Crenshaw is also a founder of the closely related Critical Race Theory movement and an internationally renowned expert on race, gender, and the law. She is a widely cited scholar and a public intellectual; Crenshaw is a regular commentator on NPR and MSNBC, and she has written for *Ms. Magazine, The Nation,* and other print media. Her work has made her a high-profile consultant for major social justice projects. For example, her research was influential in the drafting of the South African Constitution, and she authored the background paper on race and gender discrimination for the United Nations' World Conference on Racism, excerpted here.

This document, released in 2000, represents a key moment in the development of intersectionality for at least two primary reasons. First, it stands as elaboration of intersectionality theory in that Crenshaw posits a "provisional framework" that distinguishes between two forms or levels of intersectionality: 1) *structural* intersectionality, which denotes "a full range of circumstances in which policies intersect with background structures of inequality to create a compounded burden for particularly vulnerable victims," such as gendered discrimination toward women who are already marginalized due to race and/ or class, and 2) *political* intersectionality, which refers to how "women who are members of communities that are racially, culturally, or economically marginalized have actively organized in large and small ways to challenge the conditions of their lives." In this framework, structural intersectionality charts the material consequences of intersectional oppression, whereas political intersectionality describes the strategies of resistance employed by individuals, social groups, and organizations in the face of intersectional oppression.

The second reason this document is so important to the history of intersectionality is that it marks the inclusion of intersectional theory, research, and politics at the highest levels of international diplomacy. Though it may be an overstatement to call this "mainstreaming," because the uptake of Crenshaw's recommendations have been mixed, the consideration of intersectionality at the level of the United Nations (UN) and in more than rhetoric signifies an undeniable degree of political legitimacy and recognition for the movement. Furthermore, Crenshaw's work for the UN (among other human rights and social justice organizations) embodies key tenets of Black feminists' original configuration of intersectionality as an *activist* project for social transformation. After decades as a guiding figure in the movement, Crenshaw continues to be emulated by scholar-activists seeking to realize the ambitions of the Combahee River Collective and other women of color feminists for whom intersectional theories were the stepping stones to racial social change and justice for US Black women and similarly oppressed groups worldwide.

3. The Structural and Political Dimensions of Intersectional Oppression*

The conjoining of multiple systems of subordination has been variously described as compound discrimination, multiple burdens, or double or triple discrimination. Intersectionality is a conceptualization of the problem that attempts to capture both the structural and dynamic consequences of the interaction between two or more axes of subordination. It specifically addresses the manner in which racism, patriarchy, class oppression and other discriminatory systems create background inequalities that structure the relative positions of women, races, ethnicities, classes—and the like. Moreover, it addresses the way that specific acts and policies create burdens that flow along these axes constituting the dynamic or active aspects of disempowerment.

To use a metaphor of an intersection, we first analogize the various axes of power—i.e., race, ethnicity, gender, or class—as constituting the thoroughfares which structure the social, economic or political terrain. It is through these avenues that disempowering dynamics travel. These thoroughfares are sometimes framed as distinctive and mutually exclusive axes of power, for example racism is distinct from patriarchy which is in turn distinct from class oppression. In fact, the systems often overlap and cross each other, creating complex intersections at which two, three or four of these axes meet. Racialized women are often positioned in the space where racism or xenophobia, class and gender meet. They are consequently subject to injury by the heavy flow of traffic traveling along all these roads. Racialized women and other multiply burdened groups who are located at these intersections by virtue of their specific identities must negotiate the "traffic" that flows through these intersections. This is a particularly dangerous task when the traffic flows simultaneously from many

---

* Excerpted from K. W. Crenshaw, Background Paper for the Expert Meeting on the Gender-Related Aspects of Race Discrimination (United Nations, 2000).

directions. Injuries are sometimes created when the impact from one direction throws victims into the path of oncoming traffic while in other occasions, injuries occur from fully simultaneous collisions. These are the contexts in which intersectional injuries occur—disadvantages or conditions interact with preexisting vulnerabilities to create a distinct dimension of disempowerment.

Categorizing the Intersectional Experience: A Provisional Framework

While it is now widely accepted that women do not always experience sexism in the same way, and that men and women do not experience racism in the same way, the project of framing the actual circumstances in which experiences of racism and sexism converge is only gradually developing on a global level. Provided below is only a provisional framework intended to assist in cataloging and organizing existing knowledge about the multiple ways that intersectionality might play out in shaping the lives of women around the globe. The objective of these initial topologies is to introduce a language for people to attach to their own experience. It also serves to illustrate the imperative of expanding conceptual parameters of existing treaty discourses. As the topologies show, the intersectional problem is not simply that one discreet form of discrimination is not fully addressed, but that an entire range of human rights violations are obscured by the failure to address fully the intersectional vulnerabilities of marginalized women and occasionally marginalized men, as well.

1. The tragic incidents of racially motivated rape are sometimes preceded by another manifestation of intersectional oppression, the propagation of explicitly raced and gendered propaganda directed against ethnic women in efforts to rationalize sexual aggression against them. This was explicitly deployed in Bosnia and Rwanda, as reported by Human Rights Watch reports from both regions.

2. Women are not the only victims of this intersectional subordination. Racialized gender stereotypes have also been deployed against men to rationalize a sex-inflected form of violence against them. In the US, for example, racist propaganda often preceded and subsequently rationalized the lynching of African American men.

3. Even where sexualized propaganda does not culminate in mass scale sexual violence, there is reason to believe that such targeted propaganda against women is damaging in a host of other ways, and thus forms yet another example of intersectional oppression. Propaganda against poor and racialized women may not only render them likely targets of sexualized violence, it may also contribute to the tendency of many people to doubt their truthfulness when they attempt to seek the protection

of authorities. According to Human Rights Watch, Dalit women who attempt to press charges against accused rapists are highly unlikely to have their cases prosecuted, particularly in cases involving higher caste perpetrators. In the US, Black and Latino women are least likely to see the men accused of raping them prosecuted and incarcerated. Studies suggest that the racial identity of the victim plays a significant role in determining such outcomes, and there is evidence that jurors may be influenced by sexualized propaganda to believe that racialized women were more likely to consent to sex in circumstances that they would find doubtful if the victim were not a racial minority.

4. Sexualized propaganda targeted at racialized women may also contribute to their political subordination, particularly in contexts relating to reproductive policies and social welfare. Justifications for policies that compromise the reproductive rights of poor and minority women such as sterilization, forced birth control, and the imposition of economic penalties and other disincentives for childbearing are sometimes premised on pre-existing images of poor and ethnic women as sexually undisciplined. This might usefully be framed as intersectional discrimination in that the subordinating aspects of these images simultaneously draw upon pre-existing gender stereotypes that draw distinctions between women based on perceived sexual conduct, and also racial or ethnic stereotypes that characterize some race, ethnic or class groups as sexually undisciplined. The consequence for women at the intersection of these stereotypes is that they are particularly vulnerable to punitive measures based largely on who they are.

5. Targeted acts of intentional discrimination are not limited to sexual violence. In employment, education and in other arenas, racialized women are sometimes subject to discriminations and burdens specifically because they are not men and because they are not members of racially or ethnically dominant groups in society. This is in effect compound discrimination: they are excluded on the basis of race from jobs designated for women, and they are excluded from jobs reserved for men on the basis of gender. In effect, they are specifically excluded as minority or ethnic women because there is no role for applicants with their particular ethno-racial and gendered profile.

6. For example, in some workforces, particularly those that are gender and race segregated, racialized women may encounter compound discrimination where as a rule, women are hired for office jobs or positions that involve interaction with the public, while racial or ethnic minorities are hired for industrial work or some other form of gender segregated work. In such instances racialized women experience discrimination because

the women's work is not appropriate for racialized women and the work designated for racialized men is deemed inappropriate for women.

7. There are also instances where the overlap between race and gender exclusion also limits the employment or educational opportunities for men. Where industrial jobs or other male specific modes of employment are limited, and the work that remains is oriented toward women's work, men too might experience compound discrimination: the work that is available to women is not deemed to be appropriate for men, and the work available to more privileged men is not available to racially subordinate men.

8. In education, as well, women of a particular ethno-racial identity may be specifically excluded from educational opportunity, or perhaps undereducated relative to men in their ethno-racial group or more elite women. Recent reports suggest that Albanian girls in Bosnia are specifically excluded from education . . . while in India, Dalit girls are significantly less likely to be educated and sustain extremely high school drop-out rates.

9. A slightly distinct manifestation of intersectional subordination might be framed as structural intersectional subordination. This phenomenon represents a full range of circumstances in which policies intersect with background structures of inequality to create a compounded burden for particularly vulnerable victims. In some instances, a gendered discrimination occurs within a context in which some women are already vulnerable due to race and/or class. In other instances, a policy, practice or individual act on the basis of race, ethnicity or some other factor occurs in a context of a gendered structure that effects women (or sometimes men) in a unique way. The vulnerability of refugee women to sexual violence constitutes an example of an intersectional problem that should be only partially analyzed as ethnic discrimination. As reported by Human Rights Watch, Burundian refugee women in Tanzania report a very high incidence of rape. Their vulnerability to sexual violence is partially structured by gender in that they are often most vulnerable to abuse when they undertake the gender based responsibilities of collecting firewood and other essentials for home. Under prevailing conditions of refugee life, honoring this responsibility requires them to travel alone or in small groups several miles from the refugee camps. Over the course of pursuing these responsibilities, they are often assaulted, sometimes because of their identity as powerless refugee women. Here their condition is the product of ethnoracial disempowerment and patriarchy twice over: because they are women, part of the structure of gender relations requires them to risk their safety to fulfill their responsibilities. As Hutus, they are dislocated aliens in a foreign land; more broadly,

the conditions that prevail in their camp, particularly the lack of bare essentials for survival, are also products of broader patterns of racial power, in particular, the differential resources available to African refugees as opposed to those who are victims of European conflict. Finally, the dynamic nature of their sexual violence is both raced and gendered: the specific abuse to which they are subject is obviously based on their gender while their specific identity as Hutu women renders them particularly vulnerable to racial stereotypes prevalent among Tanzanian men.

10. Another example of structural intersectionality can be captured by the overlapping effects of background structures that interact with a policy or some other decision that create burdens that are disproportionately visited upon marginalized women. What distinguishes this intersectional problem from the examples above is that the policy in question is not in any way targeted toward women or toward any other marginalized people; it simply intersects with other structures to create a subordinating effect. Examples of this kind of subordination might be illustrated in the burdens placed on women by structural adjustment policies within developing economies. The gendered consequences of structural adjustment policies, for example, have already been articulated by a range of critics who note the heavy burden placed on women. It is often women who must pick up the additional burdens created by the retraction of services that were once performed by the state. As the state withdraws resources for the care for the young, infirm and elderly, for example, the consequences of these unmet needs subsequently fall largely on those to whom such responsibilities have been traditionally distributed—women. Yet additional class structures determine which women will physically perform this work, and which women will have this work performed by paying other economically disadvantaged women to do it. Thus poor women must pick up the burden of caring for the families of others as well as their own.

The consequences of structural adjustment—particularly where devaluation of their currencies has reduced their wages—place them in a position in which they are economically forced to take on even more work, often the gendered work that more elite women can turn to the market to secure. The buck stops not at the top but at the bottom, a bottom which is often gendered, classed, and frequently racialized.

Political Intersectionality

The examples set forth above primarily track the material consequences of intersectionality. There is, however, another aspect of the overlap between race and gender subordination that bears noting. Women who are members of communities that are racially, culturally, or economically marginalized have actively organized in large and small ways to challenge the conditions of their lives. They do so against some of the same obstacles that more elite women face, as well as obstacles that are unique to them. One such obstacle is often framed in terms of their obligation to their social or national group, an obligation that is at times deployed to suppress any critique of such practices or problems that might in some way draw negative attention to the group. Women who insist on pursuing their rights against certain abuses that occur within their communities risk ostracism or other forms of disapproval for allegedly betraying or embarrassing their communities. For example, Anita Hill garnered the world's attention when she accused Clarence Thomas of sexual harassment. Although Hill effectively broke the silence about this widespread problem and raised the level of awareness about sexual harassment in an important way, she was widely regarded by many in the African American community as having betrayed the group's interests. This particular burden is not one that women in racially dominant groups ordinarily face.

Women who challenge discriminatory practices which are defended by others as cultural often find themselves in a particularly precarious position. On one hand, it is sometimes the case that outsiders are all too willing to unleash harsh criticism toward the practices of ethnically or racially different groups even in the face of similarly questionable abuses within their own cultures. On the other hand, when women allow their challenges to patriarchal cultural traditions within their own communities to be silenced, they lose the opportunity to transform practices that are damaging to women.

Chandan Reddy

Chandan Reddy is an associate professor of English at the University of Washington. In addition to his often-cited work on the literary, cultural, and legal study of race, migration, and political economy, Reddy is a leading figure in the research on non-Western and immigrant sexualities. Accordingly, his scholarship is profoundly intersectional, as illustrated by his most recent book, *Freedom with Violence: Race, Sexuality, and the U.S. State* (2011), in which he argues that the modern, liberal nation-state's ability to promise freedom *from* violence is dependent upon its systematic deployment *of* violence against those labeled nonnormative, particularly in terms of race and sexuality. In this excerpt from his 2005 *Social Text* essay on homosexual asylum and US immigration law, Reddy links transformations in the economy of the welfare state, immigration reform legislation, and the "deployment of sexuality" to the figure of the gay immigrant seeking asylum in the United States. Reddy begins with postcolonial critic Gayatri Spivak and travels from macrolevel geopolitics to the micropolitics of organizations working to resist state power, charting along the way a history of "neoliberalism," which he explains as the massive redistribution of income, the privatization of all sectors of civil society, and the denial of security and social rights for the racialized poor and the "noncitizen class." Note that Reddy uses philosopher Michel Foucault's concept of "governmentality" to denote the disciplining of the population in the image of the state—in this case, the constitution of noncitizens and sexual citizenship that adhere to US neocolonial and neoliberal interests.

Reddy's work represents a leading edge of intersectional analyses, especially that of the relationship between racialized sexualities and citizenship. In comparison to Crenshaw's work in this unit (reading 3), which privileges gender and race as the key axes on which structural oppression operates, Reddy insists that critical attention to sexuality transforms our understanding of gendered and racial dynamics, not to mention what constitutes citizenship. Accordingly, we will see echoes of his work in later units as we learn more about the emergent "queer of color critique" and transnational studies. He concludes with a reformulation of the law itself as an "archive," which is meant to catalyze a rethinking of the law as a site of confrontation and regulated social formation, rather than a passive, indifferent, universal record of how legal rights have been distributed.

4. Diaspora, Asylum, and Family*

As Spivak argues, the particular structural economic constraints on global Southern countries (the postcolonial and decolonizing countries) continue to effect a dismantling of the state and the national economy as agencies and sites for social redistribution. Under such constraints, the national citizen as a figure of recent decolonization is by necessity disinterred from the state. This citizen then operates as the persistent reminder of the state's inability and failure to achieve security for its citizenry against the ravages that daily accompany neoliberal capitalism. Importantly, the seizure of citizenship discourse by the "new social movements" in the global South remains a compelling catachresis in the globalized fight for just life, in part because it necessarily foregrounds the splitting of nation and state from their modernist configuration as the "nation-state" because of the pressures of neoliberal capitalism.

---

* Excerpted from C. Reddy, "Asian Diasporas, Neoliberalism, and Family: Reviewing the Case for Homosexual Asylum in the Context of Family Rights," *Social Text* 23 (2005): 101–119. Copyright, 2005, Duke University Press. All rights reserved. Republished by permission of the copyright holder, Duke University Press. www.dukeupress.edu.

Yet, as Spivak reminds us, immigrant advocacy and social justice proj-ects in the global North that make their appeals to the state are implicated in the very structure of global inequity that continues to separate nation from state in the global South. For in the global North, Spivak reveals, the citizen remains consonant with the state, not despite but precisely because of neo-liberalism. We must therefore ask after how the promulgation of a politics of citizenship—most often expressed as the desire to partake in civil society and the social safety net designed by the welfare state—might only further the ends of neoliberalism rather than thwart it.

Indeed, this observation suggests that we respecify what has colloquially been understood as the contemporary "dismantling of the welfare state" in the United States. For, in actuality, neoliberalism has not precipitated entirely the state's dismemberment or the erosion of its social safety net. Rather, it has en-tailed the reorganization of the state through, first, the consolidation of a wel-fare state for lower-middle through upper-class U.S. citizens and citizen clones (professional green-card holders). This consolidation promises not "social redis-tribution" but rather the *distribution of entitlements* and the security to wield and exercise those entitlements in a now "internationalized" civil society. In this process, the redistributive functions traditionally associated with the wel-fare state are indistinguishable from the social reproduction and growth of capital. Put otherwise, we can say that while the welfare state is organized to reproduce labor power and simultaneously regulate/capture labor, the current "postwelfare state" governmentality is organized to produce wealth through the extension and production of new domains and modes of valorization. The privatization and public investment of retirement funds and the growth of the 401 (k) capital investment sector are a case in point.

Second, we have witnessed the state's revocation of this welfare structure and of social rights for the racialized poor and the noncitizen class, also in the name of citizen security. Since the mid-1990s, this has become a particularly salient phenomenon. The 1996 passage of three linked federal laws—the Wel-fare Reform Act, the Illegal Immigration Reform Act, and the Counterterrorism Act—together worked to politically and economically disenfranchise the nonci-tizen and simultaneously to redirect capital's surpluses back into the economy. In each instance, such acts were facilitated discursively through practices of security. Moreover, these acts specifically denied immigrants the basic rights of all workers at a time when the immigrant is a category primarily composed of Latino, Asian, and Caribbean people. Or take, for example, that the ending of affirmative ac-tion in major revenue states such as California and Texas coincided with the buildup of the "prison-industrial complex" in these very same states.

The current conditions suggest that it is imperative that we refuse the figure of the citizen as the subject of knowledge and as the trope of unity.

Moreover, in the context of U.S. asylum cases, as Spivak argues, a narrative that promotes the racially and sexually excluded's desire to enter into U.S. civil society that also fails to situate that desire within the context of other "desires" (of the gendered subaltern, for example) that are structurally foreclosed, violently refused, or made impossible by the "fulfillment" of the former trajectory in neoliberal times risks producing current struggles as alibis for exploitation. It also risks foreclosing and "forgetting" the critical disruptions and radical possibilities these very struggles open up.

That is, I want to explore how "family" as a regulative formation in the current governmentality organizes the conditions for "gay asylum." Hence we can resituate that supplementary figure as the site for a critique of the regulative function of family.

In our contemporary moment in the United States we are witnessing a certain recrossing of what Foucault has named the "deployment of alliances" with the "deployment of sexuality." These different historical currents have once again found their point of convergence and intersection in the space of "family." And, moreover, this domain of family, whose centrality to the current governmentality is as indisputable as it is unstable, is also the effect of new articulations of race and sexuality, articulations whose investigation poses specific challenges and critical opportunities for those of us working in the domain of queer studies.

It would appear that the current moment would require us to think also about how the deployment of sexuality subtends and is anchored by the contemporary capitalist mode of production. In the United States, that mode of production continues to rely on nonnational differences (of gender, race, and sexuality) to expand the proletarian class. Diaspora and migration have increasingly come to define and restructure these differences, subtending new formations of nonnormative sexualities. How might we enter the "focus on family," as the U.S. Christian Right names it, in order to pursue an inquiry into the functions of capital, the U.S. state, and contemporary strategies of accumulation? In particular, what might be the different functionings of family in the current elaboration of racial and neoliberal capitalism?

For the last three years the Audre Lorde Project (ALP), a queer people of color organizing center in New York City, has been involved in developing a report on queer immigrants of color and the politics of immigration. The report reveals that since the 1980s the state has actively worked to produce a racialized and gendered labor migration through the rubric of family reunification. Designed to assess how current immigration policy creates the conditions for a certain "homophobia" within immigrant communities and yet remains unaddressed by both gay and lesbian and immigrant rights groups, the report and the broader organizing initiative sought to reveal how the depoliticization of certain social forms, such as the "family" deployed by the state at the current moment, became the very means by which the state racially stratified immigrant communities in relation to the broader citizenry and actively organized a social structure for global capital in the city while appearing to be pursuing facially "neutral," and even just, social policy—one that corrected historical exclusions.

Since 1986 a large quotient of low-wage immigrant workers came to New York City through the Family Reunification program. For example, though many scholars have suggested that the major pull factor for immigration in the 1990s was a shortage within the United States of workers, especially for those located within the domestic, low-end services, and "unskilled" labor markets, the Immigration Act of 1990 capped the number of immigrant visas for so-called unskilled workers at a paltry ten thousand while it increased family-based immigrant visas to 480,000 annually beginning in 1995. While family immigration obviously includes minors and seniors who are either legally or functionally unable to enter the labor market, family-based immigration offers by far the largest pool of immigrant visas for so-called unskilled workers.

In other words, while immigrants are recruited by the persistence of entry-level jobs in the services, industrial, and informal sectors of New York, the federal government continues to recruit such workers through the language and networks of family reunification. The effect of creating economic pull factors that recruit immigrants to the United States while using bureaucratic categories like "family reunification" to code that migration as essentially produced by the petitioning activity of resident immigrants living in the United States is to enable the appeasement of capital's need for immigrant workers while projecting the state as either a benevolent actor reuniting broken families or an overburdened and effete agent unable to prevent immigrants' manipulations of its (mandatory) democratic and fair laws. In either case, the recruitment of low-wage workers—who compose the majorities of the immigrant of color populations in New York City—is displaced from the state's responsibility and relocated back onto immigrants themselves. In this manner, the state is absolved politically from having created and expanded the conditions of noncitizen life within the territorial parameters of the United States and, at the same time, distinguishes itself as the apotheosis of Western Democracy by achieving the status of depoliticized neutrality.

Indeed, since its original passage of the Family Reunification Act in 1986, the federal government has increasingly elected to attach the wardship of the welfare of all incoming immigrants to the petitioning families themselves. In a rather stunning move that has effectively destroyed the state's redistributive function within a managed economy, the government's mandate that petitioning families must now absorb the state's welfare functions for immigrants, in the context of the government's continuing bid to dismantle the welfare economy, has meant that it is now the role of the poor to absorb the social costs of poverty and a "healthy" unemployment rate! The state has effectively managed to both increase the numbers of immigrants arriving into the United States, as the economy continues to demand low-wage noncitizen labor, and at the same time to use immigration as the vehicle to dismantle its welfare responsibilities.

In addition to the benefits the state accrues through the recruitment of labor under family reunification, these governmental practices also engender conditions within which the family unit is now a site and apparatus (willy-nilly) of state regulatory and capitalist power. For immigrants recruited through family reunification, patriarchal and heterosexual mandates have often become prerequisites to gaining family or welfare support. With the effective dismantling of welfare benefits of noncitizen racialized workers, workers brought in through family reunification have increasingly been forced to depend on family ties for access to room and board, employment, and other services, such as (what amounts to) workplace injury insurance, health care, child care, etc. In other words, federal immigration policies such as Family Reunification extend and institute heteronormative community structures as a requirement for accessing welfare provisions for new immigrants by attaching those provisions to the family unit.

In sum, the new federal structure has increased immigrants' exposure and structural dependence on heteropatriarchal relations and regulatory structures. Many queer immigrant interviewees spoke about the impossibility of "being gay" in a context in which one's dependence on "family"—broadly defined—is definitional to living as an immigrant in the City. While this is something spoken about commonly enough in progressive circles, the tendency is to immediately assume the supposedly more essential homophobic nature of immigrant cultures over "American" culture or to blame the extraordinary willingness of queer immigrants to accept homophobic silencing and closeting. However, such "culturalist" arguments only further mask the state's role (as I have described it) in exactly engendering and enforcing the very immigrant homophobias that many claim are brought over by immigrants from their home countries. Both the intensity and specificity of homophobia in queer immigrants of color's lives are founded on local conditions (and not because of the "culture" that they bring from abroad, as so many scholars are quick to suggest) and are produced at the intersection of state immigration policies and their fixation on the heteropatriarchal family unit. Rather, the category of "gay" presumes a particular liberal order of "family," "civil society," and the "state" discursively and ideologically impossible for queer immigrants, deferring the queer of color into the status of the nonnational, produced at the limit of civil society. More pointedly, the liberal isomorphism of family, society, and state requires as its condition of possibility the "queer of color" immigrant as a nonindividuated, nonrights-bearing "subject," whose conditions of existence confounds that isomorphism.

In addition to the state's official immigration policy, federal and state governments since the Clinton years also have been empowered to shift the delivery of services away from public and private nonprofit secular providers and toward religious organizations and groups. In New York City, rising numbers of church organizations petition for government money and an increasing number of immigrants access church services as their primary service provider. Again, it is the dislocating of the state's function as a welfare agent that has exposed queer immigrants of color in particular to remarkable heteropatriarchal coercion and that produces the disproportionate enforcement of heteropatriarchal relations within immigrant of color communities.

Some scholars have pointed to what they believe is a potential silver lining in the end of the traditional welfare state: the diminishing importance of the state in the private and social lives of citizens and residents. However, as I have argued, the erosion of the welfare state has not only been manifested by the withdrawal of economic and social resources to working and poor people. In fact, and in addition, the continued deterioration of the welfare system will not result in the withdrawal of state power from the lives of immigrants of color, or queer immigrants of color in particular, but will instead foster the expansion of social regulation through a growing reliance on state-circumscribed or sponsored social forms, such as family and religion.

By naming the law an "archive" I mean to observe how the law seeks to be the record of the confrontation of social groups with the universality of "community" and the "state" posited by liberal political theory and epistemologies. Not just the law of record, the law's textuality is also the expression of the law *as* record. And, as an archive or mode of record keeping, the law seeks to produce an account of social differences that preserves the conditions for universality. Put otherwise, historical and social differences (of gender, race, sexuality, etc.) are subjugated by the law, as a precondition of their entrance into the national record, forced to preserve the liberal narrative of universality on which the legal sphere bases its notion of justice and the nation is said to be founded. As an archive, the law organizes social and historical differences in ways that promise both knowledge (of difference) and membership. In this way the law as an archive is not a dispassionate or disinterested space of records. Rather, it is the privileged ledger by which knowledge, idealized as dispassionate and disinterested, is, paradoxically, made coincident with community, idealized as nonalienated experience, producing that peculiar epistemo-affect associated with the "citizen."

Like all archives, the law, and the broader textual legal sphere, as an archive is not simply an institutional site for the recording of the past and of historical and social difference. Rather, it is a framework that, ironically, promises its reader agency only through the perpetual subjugation of differences, a subjugation, then, that targets not only the past but also the future. Indeed the law as an archive addressed to the citizen or potential subject of "civility" seeks, above all, to be an archive of the future.

Hence the archive is not a passive domain in which differences, such as the gay Pakistani immigrant, can be found, extracted, and restored to their fullness, if necessary. It is the active technique by which sexual, racial, gendered, and national differences, both historical and futural, are suppressed, frozen, and redirected as the occasion for a universal knowledge. It is the technique by which the modern U.S. state promotes the citizen as a universal agent through that knowledge production—to women, queers, people of color, etc.—demanding that we take up its framework for difference (both historical and social) as a prerequisite for a validated agency.

Contending with the law as an active archive, or technique of selfmaking and the making of selves, as I do here, requires that we not simply "take up" its narrative and framework. Instead, we need to ask how regulation marks its interest in difference. Asking after this regulation requires reading these figures against the grain of the archive, situating that archive within and against the social formation—the forces and relations that constitute it—which bourgeois law cites but which it, haplessly, cannot comprehend. In other words, we need to read the figure as the limit of the archive, the point at which the archive's own conditions for existence might be retraced.

EPISTEMOLOGY

Power/Knowledge/Position
Patrick R. Grzanka

To challenge the order of things—literally, the way knowledge is organized—one must inevitably attend to issues of epistemology (Foucault 1970). "Epistemology" can be defined as the "theory of knowledge," but in critical domains of the social sciences and humanities, epistemology more generally refers to "ways of knowing." By recognizing multiple epistemolog*ies* across time, space, and cultures, we are better able to illuminate how knowledge is socially constructed and historically contingent. In other words, how we come to know what we know, what we believe to be true, and which forms of knowledge are legitimated is a socially, historically, and culturally mediated practice. Critical studies of epistemology can be profound precisely because they help to destabilize taken-for-granted knowledges, such as beliefs in fundamental differences between races, genders, and people of different sexual orientations. Beliefs in natural or "essential" differences between socially constructed groups of people are often reinforced by "legitimate," respected, and therefore *powerful* scientific discourses (Habermas 1975; Kuhn 1962). Accordingly, to intervene in such dominant, "normative" discourses, intersectional scholars have not only cultivated new knowledge, but directed their energies toward critiquing the racist, classist, masculinist, and colonialist epistemologies that have produced oppressive knowledges and, consequently, oppressive social structures, institutions, and inequalities.

This unit represents a constellation of thinking about epistemology from Black feminist social science, lesbian women of color activism, feminist philosophy of science, Black queer sociology, and literary criticism. These categories are not mutually exclusive, and these essays collectively overlap and transect in both predictable and unexpected ways across a thirty-year time span. What links them, most importantly for our conversation here, is an unapologetic insistence that knowledge is *always* political. From Barbara Smith's 1980 "Racism and Women's Studies" (reading 5), which comes from what is largely considered a watershed moment for intersectionality in women's studies, to Roderick Ferguson's (2004) more recent call for a "queer of color critique" in sociology (reading 9), each of these authors demonstrates how intersectional analysis provides a robust critique of dominant epistemologies and avenues for producing new, counterhegemonic knowledges. What's at stake is nothing less than what counts as knowledge, and who gets to be called an "intellectual." Patricia Hill Collins (2000) argues in *Black Feminist Thought* that the concept of "intellectual" itself has been used by those in power to restrict Black women's access to education, politics, labor, and other institutions of power. "Black women's exclusion from positions of power within mainstream institutions," she explains, "has led to the elevation of elite White male ideas and interests and the corresponding suppression of Black women's ideas and interests in traditional scholarship" (5). The effects of such suppression and marginalization extend outside the walls of the academy: "Moreover, this historical exclusion means that stereotypical images of Black women permeate popular culture and public policy" (5). If one cannot attend university, be elected to political office, or lead a corporation, how can one be called an "intellectual"? The answer, to Collins, is a reformulation of what constitutes intellectualism, and a reclaiming of Black women's knowledge from the periphery of social thought and from forms, such as oral history, creative arts, and music, that have been marginalized by "traditional" centers of knowledge and power, namely universities:

> The concept of *intellectual* must itself be deconstructed. Not all Black women intellectuals are educated. Not all Black women intellectuals work in academia. Furthermore, not all highly educated Black women, especially those who are employed in US Colleges or universities, are automatically intellectuals. . . . One is neither born an intellectual nor does one become one by earning a degree. Rather, doing intellectual work of the sort envisioned within Black feminism requires a process of self-conscious struggle on behalf of Black women, regardless of the actual social location where that work occurs. (2000, 15)

Opening up what constitutes intellectuals and intellectualism allows, on the one hand, for recognition of meaningful knowledge production in unexpected spaces and places; on the other hand, it facilitates a critique of assumptions, "facts," and theories for how they represent the interests and investments of those legitimated to do the work of creating and disseminating knowledge.

Collins and others call this combination of identity, politics, and location a "standpoint."

Standpoint feminisms, such as those theorized by Collins (2000), Bonnie Thornton Dill (1979; Baca Zinn and Dill 1996), Gloria Anzaldúa (1987), and Donna Haraway (1988), do the work of situating knowledge production within the fields of power and social forces that shape human experiences. Claiming knowledge from a particular standpoint bonds personal life experiences and social location to the notion of "truth." Not all standpoint feminisms make exactly the same point, nor do they use the same language or tactics to articulate standpoints. Nonetheless, some general themes link these ideas under the broad category of standpoint feminisms. For intersectional theorists, the concept of standpoint has been a critical tool with which to understand how multiple axes of identity and difference order, rank, and hierarchize knowledge in terms of race, gender, class, and other systems of social inequality. The standpoint, in this sense, functions as a critique: first, of intersecting systems of oppression, and second, of the knowledge produced and legitimated within those systems. The standpoint also has the productive and pragmatic purpose of cultivating knowledge that is self-reflexive, self-conscious, and self-critical. Haraway (1988, reading 6), for example, posits a feminist refashioning a "vision" as an analytic tool and metaphor with which to understand feminist knowledge production in the interest of making claims to truth that are both responsible (i.e., accountable) and embodied (i.e., coming from someone, somewhere):

> I would like to suggest how our insisting metaphorically on the particularity and embodiment of all vision (although not necessarily organic embodiment and including technological mediation), and not giving in to the tempting myths of vision as a route to disembodiment and second-birthing allows us to construct a usable, but not an innocent, doctrine of objectivity. . . . So, not so perversely, objectivity turns out to be about particular and specific embodiment and definitely not about the false vision promising transcendence of all limits and responsibilities. (1988, 582–583)

Haraway is committed to developing a feminist version of objectivity in the sciences, which she terms "situated knowledges." To Haraway, situated knowledges allow feminists to critique scientific knowledge production and to do the infinitely important work of actually *practicing* science.

Postmodern and radical social constructionist theories that deny any and all accounts of reality or truth fail, from Haraway's perspective, to provide a path to alternative forms of knowledge production or avenues through which to promote social justice. To the radical postmodernist, she says we must not abandon the goal of crafting more accurate and fair claims about reality, even if reality itself is a contested concept. Collins (1998, reading 6) echoes a similar critique of postmodernism, of which certain strands seem to deconstruct, decenter, and destabilize identity and power to the point of nothingness. Such nihilism may inadvertently undermine the ability for oppressed groups to make any claims about social injustice and, therefore, disempower movements that seek to promote social justice. In these radical postmodern frameworks, even "social justice" itself is subject to deconstruction, and Collins suspects that such analytic moves benefit only those for whom the stakes of social justice projects are not so high, for example, White, middle-class men in faculty positions in universities where vanguard, esoteric theories written in inaccessible language are highly valued and rewarded. Collins, Haraway, and other standpoint feminist theorists, on the other hand, insist upon potent, pragmatic, hybrid, alternative forms of knowledge or "knowledges." According to Haraway, by pluralizing the notion of knowledge, situating all knowledges and rejecting singular truth claims that pretend to see "everything from nowhere" (1988, 581), we can foster a "no-nonsense commitment to faithful accounts of a 'real' world, one that can be partially shared and that is friendly to earthwide projects of finite freedom, adequate material abundance, modest meaning in suffering, and limited happiness" (579).

Intersectional theorists have also found analytic utility and explanatory power in "dialectics," which describe the interaction of two opposing concepts (i.e., thesis and antithesis) that produces a synthesis. For Collins (2000), the dialectical relationship of Black feminist thought links "oppression" and "activism," or domination and resistance, which highlights how Black feminist epistemology cannot be understood through an all-encompassing, one-dimensional theory of hegemony or a utopian model of liberation. Furthermore, many Black women's experiences are defined by an "outsider-within" standpoint, which Collins uses to explain how Black women find themselves simultaneously included and excluded by various discourses and social structures, such as antiracist movements dominated by Black men or the White households in which so many women of color have served and continue to labor as primary caregivers to White children. In some of her earliest writing on Black feminism and intersectionality, sociologist Bonnie Thornton Dill (1979) likewise argued that Black women's lives are characterized by the complex interplay of multiple, seemingly oppositional forces and outcomes. "Too often," Dill writes, "social science researchers have sought to describe Black women and their families as if they were a monolithic whole, without regard for differences in social class. At the other extreme is the contention that social class differences obliterate distinctions of race" (551). In the interest of developing a more honest and valid sociological account of Black women's lives,

Dill advocates a dialectical epistemology that is sensitized to complexity, as opposed to statistical and other empirical strategies that seek to "control" multiple variables of experience or that minimize the impact of history and culture on life experiences and sociological consequences, such as birth rates, education attainment, migration, and income.

Like so much of intersectionality theory, these insights about standpoints, the "outsider-within," and epistemology more broadly locate their origins in Black feminist thought. But Black feminists such as Collins, Dill, and Audre Lorde are insistent that intersectionality's foundation in Black feminism does not foreclose on the capacity of intersectionality to explain multiply marginalized and privileged social groups' experiences in United States and worldwide. Collins (2000) notably distinguishes intersectionality as a critical social theory because of its "commitment to justice, both for U.S. Black women as a collectivity and for that of other similarly oppressed groups" around the world (9). Gloria Anzaldúa's (1988, Unit III, reading 14) "borderlands" theory, which represents intellectual work done outside the traditional structures of academic research and writing, is derived from creative, auto-ethnographic (i.e., writing about the self) exploration of Anzaldúa's own life as a Chicana, lesbian feminist. Anzaldúa's work—along with Philip Brian Harper's work on intuition included in this unit (reading 8)—reminds us that binaries and dualisms, such as Black/White, gay/straight, native/immigrant, are wholly insufficient to capture life at the borderlands, where national boundaries, cultures, identities, and histories overlap, collide, and grind against one another to create new forms of consciousness. Poet and essayist Audre Lorde's (1984) timeless call for new tools with which to dismantle "the master's house" deconstructs the "second-wave" of American feminism for its uncritical relationship to class, race, and sexuality in the name of promoting an all-inclusive sisterhood. Here, "tools" denote not only the methods of feminist activism, but also the very knowledge structures and theoretical assumptions that feminism takes as its starting points. And at the forefront of intersectional epistemological criticism in the social sciences and humanities today sits the queer of color critique, represented in this unit by the work of Roderick Ferguson (see reading 9). Ferguson's (2004) *Aberrations in Black* targets canonical sociology, African American studies, and dominant strands of queer theory for their respective failures to adequately study and theorize the intersections of sexuality and race. The queer of color critique exemplifies an emergent frontier of scholarship on intersectionality that reverberates throughout multiple readings in this volume. This argument, variations on which will be articulated by Harper, Jasbir Puar (Unit X, reading 42), Kara Keeling (Unit V, reading 20), and others, illuminates existing queer theories' elision of race, ethnicity, and nation, as well as "mainstream" Black studies' limitations as a lens through which to understand

and critique how sexual practices, identities, and desires cocreate how we understand race, ethnicity, and racism.

For reasons that should become increasingly obvious to readers, "epistemology" is the second unit in this text because of the heterogeneous ways in which knowledge/power relations prefigure our understanding of intersectional oppressions, activisms, and sites of resistance. These themes will certainly recur and reemerge in multiple units, but the readings within Unit II lay the groundwork for a serious reconsideration of how we comprehend social worlds and identities. Knowledge *itself* is a launching pad from which to explore what it means to make claims about oppression, which always precede claims for justice. And as philosopher Michel Foucault's (1972) work notably bound the concepts of knowledge and power together—knowledge is always about power, and power is created by way of the production of (what counts as) knowledge—an intersectional approach qualifies this framework by foregrounding the politics of positionality in the study of epistemology. Knowledge is power, and knowledge/power relations always happen somewhere, in some bodies, in particular historical contexts. Cultivating emancipatory knowledges starts with understanding these relations of power/knowledge/position.

References and Further Reading

Anzaldúa, G. (1987) 1999. *Borderlands/La Frontera: The New Mestiza.* Second edition. San Francisco: Aunt Lute Books.

Baca Zinn, M., and B. T. Dill. 1996. "Theorizing Difference from Multiracial Feminism." *Feminist Studies* 22: 321–331.

Collins, P. H. 1986. "Learning from the Outsider Within: The Sociological Significance of Black Feminist Thought." *Social Problems* 33(6): S14–S32.

Collins, P. H. (1990) 2000. *Black Feminist Thought: Knowledge, Consciousness, and the Politics of Empowerment.* Second edition. New York: Routledge.

Collins, P. H. 1998. *Fighting Words: Black Women and the Search for Justice.* Minneapolis: University of Minnesota Press.

Combahee River Collective. (1977) 2007. "A Black Feminist Statement." In *The Essential Feminist Reader,* edited by E. B. Freedman, 325–330. New York: Modern Library.

Davidson, M. D. G., K. T. Gines, and D-D. L. Marcano, eds. 2010. *Convergences: Black Feminism and Continental Philosophy.* Albany, NY: State University of New York Press.

Davis, K. 2008. "Intersectionality as Buzzword: A Sociology of Science Perspective on What Makes a Feminist Theory Successful." *Feminist Theory* 9: 67–85.

Dill, B. T. 1979. "The Dialectics of Black Womanhood." *Signs: The Journal of Women in Culture and Society* 4: 543–555.

Ferguson, R. A. 2004. *Aberrations in Black: Toward a Queer of Color Critique.* Minneapolis: University of Minnesota Press.

Foucault, M. (1970) 1994. *The Order of Things: An Archaeology of the Human Sciences.* New York: Random House.

Foucault, M. 1972. *The Archaeology of Knowledge and the Discourse on Language.* Translated by A. M. Sheridan Smith. New York: Pantheon Books.

Habermas, J. 1975. *Legitimation Crisis.* Boston: Beacon Press.

Haraway, D. 1988. "Situated Knowledges: The Science Question in Feminism and the Privilege of Partial Perspective." *Feminist Studies* 14: 579–599.

Harding, S. 1993. "Rethinking Standpoint Epistemology: "What Is Strong Objectivity?" In *Feminist Epistemologies,* edited by L. Alcoff and E. Potter, 49–82. New York: Routledge.

Kuhn, T. 1962. *The Structure of Scientific Revolutions.* Chicago: University of Chicago Press.

Lorde, A. 1984. *Sister Outsider: Essays and Speeches.* Berkeley, CA: The Crossing Press.

Sandoval, C. 2000. *Methodology of the Oppressed.* Minneapolis: University of Minnesota Press.

Smith, B. 1980. "Racism and Women's Studies." *Frontiers: A Journal of Women's Studies* 5: 48–49.

Stoetzler, M., and N. Yuval-Davis. 2002. "Standpoint Theory, Situated Knowledge and the Situated Imagination." *Feminist Theory* 3: 315–334.

Yuval-Davis, N. 2012. "Dialogical Epistemology—An Intersectional Resistance to the 'Oppression Olympics.'" *Gender & Society* 26: 46–54.

Barbara Smith

Barbara Smith has been a leading Black feminist writer and activist since the 1960s. Among her most notable accomplishments in the development of intersectional perspectives on social life and inequality was the cofounding of Kitchen Table: Women of Color Press, the first US publisher specifically for women of color, and the cofounding of the Combahee River Collective, a Black lesbian feminist organization based in Boston whose "Combahee River Collective Statement" (1977) is considered a key document in the development of contemporary Black feminism. Her writing has appeared in leading publications, including *Ms. Magazine,* the *New York Times Book Review,* and *The Nation*, and she has published several books, including the classic *All the Women Are White, All the Blacks Are Men, But Some of Us Are Brave* (coedited with Gloria T. Hull and Patricia Bell Scott, 1982), and *Home Girls: A Black Feminist Anthology* (1983). In this piece, Smith targets the center of women's studies as an academic discipline and addresses the salience of and silence around race and racism in White academic feminism. This essay was delivered as an address at the National Women's Studies Association Conference in 1979, which then remained dominated by White heterosexual women and, as Smith explicates, the NWSA was organized around their ideological and political interests. Though the title of this piece is "Racism and Women's Studies," readers should pay careful attention to how Smith integrates sexuality, gender, race, nation, and class concerns here; in many ways, the title oversimplifies the complexities of Smith's critique and the issues that face women's studies as an ongoing academic *and* activist movement. She begins our conversation on epistemology, because Smith views women's studies itself as a site of knowledge production that is capable of both subverting *and* reinforcing racism, classism, and heterosexism—interlocking systems of oppression that serve as the exigency for US Black feminist activism in the late 1970s. Unless women's studies becomes a self-reflexive, activist movement that divests from its "white patriarchal legacy," Smith suggests that women's studies will continue to reinforce rather than undermine intersectional oppressions.

5. Racism and Women's Studies*

Although my proposed topic is black women's studies, I have decided to focus my remarks in a different way. Given that this is a gathering of predominantly white women and given what has occurred during this conference, it makes much more sense to discuss the issue of racism: racism in women's studies and racism in the women's movement generally.

"Oh no," I can hear some of you groaning inwardly. "Not that again. That's all we've talked about since we got here." This of course is not true. If it had been all *we* had all talked about since we got here, we might be at a point of radical transformation on the last day of this Conference that we clearly are not. For those of you who are tired of hearing about racism, imagine how much more tired we are of constantly experiencing it, second by literal second, how much more exhausted we are to see it constantly in your eyes. The degree to which it is hard or uncomfortable for you to have the issue raised is the degree to which you know inside of yourselves that you aren't dealing with the issue, the degree to which you are hiding from the oppression that undermines Third World women's lives. I want to say right here that this is not a "guilt trip." It's a fact trip. The assessment of what's actually going on.

Why is racism being viewed and taken up as a pressing feminist issue at this time and why is it being talked about in the context of women's studies? As usual the impetus comes from the grassroots, activist women's movement. In my six years of being an avowed black feminist I have seen much change in how white women take responsibility for their racism, particularly within the last year. The formation of C.R. groups to deal solely with this issue, study

* Reprinted from B. Smith, "Racism and Women's Studies," *Frontiers: A Journal of Women Studies* 5 (1980): 48–49. Reproduced with permission from the University of Nebraska Press. Copyright 1980 by Frontiers Editorial Collective, Inc.

groups, community meetings and workshops, articles in our publications, letters in newspapers, and the beginning of real and equal coalitions between Third World and white women are all phenomena that have begun to really happen and I feel confident that there will be no turning back.

The reason racism is a feminist issue is easily explained by the inherent definition of feminism. Feminism is the political theory and practice that struggles to free *all* women: women of color, working-class women, poor women, disabled women, lesbians, old women, as well as white, economically privileged heterosexual women. Anything less than this vision of total freedom is not feminism, but merely female self-aggrandizement.

Let me make it quite clear at this point before going any further something you must understand: white women don't work on racism to do a favor for someone else, to solely benefit Third World women. You have got to comprehend how racism distorts and lessens your own lives as white women, that racism affects your chances for survival too and that it is very definitely your issue. Until you understand this no fundamental change will come about.

Racism is being talked about in the context of women's studies because of it being raised in the women's movement generally, but also because women's studies is a context in which white and Third World women actually come together, a context that should be about studying and learning about all of our lives. I feel at this point it's not only about getting Third World women's materials into the curriculum, although this must be done. This has been happening and it's clear that racism still thrives, just as the inclusion of women's materials in a college curriculum does not prevent sexism from thriving. The stage we're at now is having to decide to change fundamental attitudes and behavior, the way people treat each other. In other words, we're at a stage of having to take some frightening risks.

I'm sure that many women here are telling themselves they aren't racist because they are capable of being civil to black women, having been raised by their parents to be anything but. It's not about merely being polite: "I'm not racist because I do not snarl and snap at black people." It's much more subtle than that. It is not white women's fault that they have been raised for the most part not knowing how to talk to black women, not knowing how to look us in the eye and laugh *with* us. Racism and racist behavior is our white patriarchal legacy. What is your fault is making no serious effort to change old patterns of contempt. To look at how you still believe yourselves to be superior to Third World women and how you communicate these attitudes in blatant and subtle ways.

A major roadblock for women involved in women's studies to changing their individual racism and challenging it institutionally is the pernicious ideology of professionalism. That word "professionalism" covers such a multitude of sins. I always cringe when I hear *anyone* describe themselves as "professional," because what usually follows is an excuse for inaction, an excuse for ethical irresponsibility. It's a word and concept we don't need because it is ultimately a way of dividing ourselves from others and escaping from reality. I think the way to be "successful" is to do work with integrity and work that is good. Not to play cutthroat tricks and insist on being called "Doctor." When I got involved in women's studies six years ago and particularly during my three and a half years as the first Third World woman on the Modern Language Association Commission on the Status of Women, I quickly began to recognize what I call women's studies or academic feminists. Women who teach, research, and publish about women, but who are not involved in any way in making radical social and political change, women who are not involved in making the lives of living breathing women more viable. The grassroots/community women's movement has given women's studies its life. How do we relate to it? How do we bring our gifts and our educational privilege back to it? Do we realize also how very much there is to learn in doing this essential work? Ask yourself what the women's movement is working on in your town or city. Are you a part of it? Ask yourself what women are living in the worst conditions in your town and how does your work positively affect and directly touch their lives? If it doesn't, why not?

The question has been raised here whether this should be an activist association or an academic one. In many ways this is an immoral question, an immoral and false dichotomy. The answer lies in which emphasis and what kinds of work will lift oppression off of not only women, but all oppressed people: poor and working class people, people of color in this country and in the colonized Third World. If lifting this oppression is not a priority to you then it's problematic whether you are a part of the actual feminist movement.

There are two other roadblocks to our making feminism real which I'll mention briefly. First, there is Third World women's anti-feminism which I sometimes sense often gets mixed up with opposition to white women's racism and is fueled by a history of justified distrust. To me racist white women cannot be said to be actually feminist, at least not in the way I think and feel about the word. Feminism in and of itself would be fine. The problems arise with the mortals who practice it. As Third World women we must define a responsible and radical feminism for ourselves and not assume that bourgeois female self-aggrandizement is all that feminism is and therefore attack feminism wholesale.

The other roadblock is homophobia, that is antilesbianism, an issue that both white and Third World women still have to deal with. Need I explicate in 1979 how enforced heterosexuality is the extreme manifestation of male domination and patriarchal rule and that women must not collude in the oppression of women who have chosen each other, that is, lesbians. I also wish I had time here to speak about the connections between the lesbian-feminist movement, being woman identified and the effective anti-racist work that is being done by many, though not all lesbians.

In conclusion, I'll say that I don't consider my talk today to be in anyway conclusive or exhaustive. It has merely scratched the surface. I don't know exactly what's going on in your schools or in your lives. I can only talk about those qualities and skills that will help you to bring about change: integrity, awareness, courage, and redefining your own success.

I also feel that the women's movement will deal with racism in a way that it has not been dealt with before in any other movement—fundamentally, organically, and nonrhetorically. White women have a materially different relationship to the system of racism than white men. They get less out of it and often function as its pawns whether they recognize this or not. It is something that living under white male rule has imposed on us and overthrowing racism is the inherent work of feminism and by extension feminist studies.

Donna Haraway

Donna Haraway is a notoriously perplexing writer, but the importance of her ideas and their impact across the humanities and social sciences warrants the challenge of reading her work. Haraway is currently Distinguished Professor Emerita at the University of California, Santa Cruz's History of Consciousness Department, which has produced such important thinkers in intersectionality as Ruth Frankenberg, Chela Sandoval, Michael Omi, and Howard Winant, among numerous others. She is a feminist philosopher of science trained in biology, and Haraway is best known for her "A Cyborg Manifesto" (1991), in which she famously challenged the boundaries between organic and nonorganic life and contemplated what feminist theory and politics might look like in the age of advanced technoscience. Though Haraway's feminist theory is explicitly antiracist and deeply invested in confronting how science reproduces racism, Haraway's writing in the late 1980s is often overlooked for its contributions to intersectionality theory in traditional genealogies of the field, perhaps because Patricia Hill Collins's *Black Feminist Thought* and Kimberelé Williams Crenshaw's "Mapping the Margins" were published concurrently and more directly spoke to the agenda of the emerging Black feminist project of intersectionality. In "Situated Knowledges" (1988), however, originally published in the leading journal *Feminist Studies,* Haraway offers a potent framework for thinking about how antiracist, Marxist, anticolonial feminists might retain an investment in critical social constructionism *and* the always tricky concept of "objectivity." Haraway's version of standpoint theory here comes in the form of a protracted metaphor about vision or "partial perspectives." The part of the essay not included here begins with Haraway outlining an ongoing debate between radical social constructionists—whom she says render all science a conspiratorial power play and all of reality a series of rhetorical moves—and the "feminist critical empiricists," who advocate feminist ethics and politics in science but do little to challenge the epistemological (i.e., positivist) assumptions that undergird contemporary science. Haraway has grown tired of this debate, which does not seem to be advancing answers to the question of how feminists might produce *better* (more equitable, truthful, fair, modest) science. So, she says, it's time to switch metaphors . . . and that is where we begin here. Haraway's writing is at once playful and experimental while conveying the seriousness of her project: feminism must offer productive, powerful ways of conceptualizing truth, defying masculinist science, and adapting to the context of advanced technologies and industrialized science projects that are literally rearranging the knowledge and logics of race, gender, sexuality, and species in the early twenty-first century. Of special concern to Haraway here is the need to resist an all-too-common impulse in Western feminism to appropriate and/or "fetishize" the vision of the "Third World Woman" and the subjugated knowledges of "the Other."

6. Situated Knowledges and the Persistence of Vision*

So, I think my problem, and "our" problem, is how to have *simultaneously* an account of radical historical contingency for all knowledge claims and knowing subjects, a critical practice for recognizing our own "semiotic technologies" for making meanings, *and* a no-nonsense commitment to faithful accounts of a "real" world, one that can be partially shared and that is friendly to earthwide projects of finite freedom, adequate material abundance, modest meaning in suffering, and limited happiness. [Sandra] Harding calls this necessary multiple desire a need for a successor science project and a postmodern insistence on irreducible difference and radical multiplicity of local knowledges. *All* components of the desire are paradoxical and dangerous, and their combination is both contradictory and necessary. Feminists don't need a doctrine of objectivity that promises transcendence, a story that loses track of its mediations just where

---

* Excerpted from D. Haraway, "Situated Knowledges: The Science Question in Feminism and the Privilege of Partial Perspective," *Feminist Studies* 14(3) (Fall 1988): 575–599. Reproduced by permission of the publisher, Feminist Studies Inc.

someone might be held responsible for something, and unlimited instrumental power. We don't want a theory of innocent powers to represent the world, where language and bodies both fall into the bliss of organic symbiosis. We also don't want to theorize the world, much less act within it, in terms of Global Systems, but we do need an earth-wide network of connections, including the ability partially to translate knowledges among very different—and power-differentiated—communities. We need the power of modern critical theories of how meanings and bodies get made, not in order to deny meanings and bodies, but in order to build meanings and bodies that have a chance for life.

Natural, social, and human sciences have always been implicated in hopes like these. Science has been about a search for translation, convertibility, mobility of meanings, and universality—which I call reductionism only when one language (guess whose?) must be enforced as the standard for all the translations and conversions. What money does in the exchange orders of capitalism, reductionism does in the powerful mental orders of global sciences. There is, finally, only one equation. That is the deadly fantasy that feminists and others have identified in some versions of objectivity, those in the service of hierarchical and positivist orderings of what can count as knowledge. That is one of the reasons the debates about objectivity matter, metaphorically and otherwise. Immortality and omnipotence are not our goals. But we could use some enforceable, reliable accounts of things not reducible to power moves and agonistic, high-status games of rhetoric or to scientistic, positivist arrogance. This point applies whether we are talking about genes, social classes, elementary particles, genders, races, or texts; the point applies to the exact, natural, social, and human sciences, despite the slippery ambiguities of the words "objectivity" and "science" as we slide around the discursive terrain. In our efforts to climb the greased pole leading to a usable doctrine of objectivity, I and most other feminists in the objectivity debates have alternatively, or even simultaneously, held on to both ends of the dichotomy, a dichotomy which Harding describes in terms of successor science projects versus postmodernist accounts of difference and which I have sketched in this essay as radical constructivism versus feminist critical empiricism. It is, of course, hard to climb when you are holding on to both ends of a pole, simultaneously or alternatively. It is, therefore, time to switch metaphors.

I would like to proceed by placing metaphorical reliance on a much maligned sensory system in feminist discourse: vision. Vision can be good for avoiding binary oppositions. I would like to insist on the embodied nature of all vision and so reclaim the sensory system that has been used to signify a leap out of the marked body and into a conquering gaze from nowhere. This is the gaze that mythically inscribes all the marked bodies, that makes the unmarked category claim the power to see and not be seen, to represent while escaping representation. This gaze signifies the unmarked positions of Man and White, one of the many nasty tones of the word "objectivity" to feminist ears in scientific and technological, late-industrial, militarized, racist, and male-dominant societies, that is, here, in the belly of the monster, in the United States in the late 1980s. I would like a doctrine of embodied objectivity that accommodates paradoxical and critical feminist science projects: Feminist objectivity means quite simply *situated knowledges*.

The eyes have been used to signify a perverse capacity—honed to perfection in the history of science tied to militarism, capitalism, colonialism, and male supremacy—to distance the knowing subject from everybody and everything in the interests of unfettered power. The instruments of visualization in multinationalist, postmodernist culture have compounded these meanings of disembodiment. The visualizing technologies are without apparent limit. The eye of any ordinary primate like us can be endlessly enhanced by sonography systems, magnetic reasonance imaging, artificial intelligence-linked graphic manipulation systems, scanning electron microscopes, computed tomography scanners, color-enhancement techniques, satellite surveillance systems, home and office video display terminals, cameras for every purpose from filming the mucous membrane lining the gut cavity of a marine worm living in the vent gases on a fault between continental plates to mapping a planetary hemisphere elsewhere in the solar system. Vision in this technological feast becomes unregulated gluttony; all seems not just mythically about the god trick of seeing everything from nowhere, but to have put the myth into ordinary practice. And like the god trick, this eye fucks the world to make techno-monsters. Zoe Sofotilis calls this the cannibaleye of masculinist extra-terrestrial projects for excremental second birthing.

But, of course, that view of infinite vision is an illusion, a god trick. I would like to suggest how our insisting metaphorically on the particularity and embodiment of all vision (although not necessarily organic embodiment and including technological mediation), and not giving in to the tempting myths of vision as a route to disembodiment and second-birthing allows us to construct a usable, but not an innocent, doctrine of objectivity. I want a feminist writing of the body that metaphorically emphasizes vision again, because we need to reclaim that sense to find our way through all the visualizing tricks and powers of modern sciences and technologies that have transformed the objectivity debates. We need to learn in our bodies, endowed with primate color and stereoscopic vision, how to attach the objective to our theoretical and political scanners in order to name where we are and are not, in dimensions of mental and physical space we hardly know how to name. So, not so perversely, objectivity turns out to be about particular and specific embodiment and definitely not about the false vision promising transcendence of all limits and responsibility. The moral is simple: only partial perspective promises objective vision. All Western cultural narratives about objectivity are allegories of the ideologies governing the relations of what we call mind and body, distance and responsibility. Feminist objectivity is about limited location and situated knowledge, not about transcendence and splitting of subject and object. It allows us to become answerable for what we learn how to see.

Many currents in feminism attempt to theorize grounds for trusting especially the vantage points of the subjugated; there is good reason to believe vision is better from below the brilliant space platforms of the powerful. Building on that suspicion, this essay is an argument for situated and embodied knowledges and an argument against various forms of unlocatable, and so irresponsible, knowledge claims. Irresponsible means unable to be called into account. There is a premium on establishing the capacity to see from the peripheries and the depths. But here there also lies a serious danger of romanticizing and/or appropriating the vision of the less powerful while claiming to see from their positions. To see from below is neither easily learned nor unproblematic, even if "we" "naturally" inhabit the great underground terrain of subjugated knowledges. The positionings of the subjugated are not exempt from critical reexamination, decoding, deconstruction, and interpretation; that is, from both semiological and hermeneutic modes of critical inquiry. The standpoints of the subjugated are not "innocent" positions. On the contrary, they are preferred because in principle they are least likely to allow denial of the critical and interpretive core of all knowledge. They are knowledgeable of modes of denial through repression, forgetting, and disappearing acts—ways of being nowhere while claiming to see comprehensively. The subjugated have a decent chance to be on to the god trick and all its dazzling—and, therefore, blinding—illuminations. "Subjugated" standpoints are preferred because they seem to promise more adequate, sustained, objective, transforming accounts of the world. But *how* to see from below is a problem requiring at least as much skill with bodies and language, with the mediations of vision, as the "highest" technoscientific visualizations.

Such preferred positioning is as hostile to various forms of relativism as to the most explicitly totalizing versions of claims to scientific authority. But the alternative to relativism is not totalization and single vision, which is always finally the unmarked category whose power depends on systematic narrowing and obscuring. The alternative to relativism is partial, locatable, critical knowledges sustaining the possibility of webs of connections called solidarity in politics and shared conversations in epistemology. Relativism is a way of being nowhere while claiming to be everywhere equally. The "equality" of positioning is a denial of responsibility and critical inquiry. Relativism is the perfect mirror twin of totalization in the ideologies of objectivity; both deny the stakes in location, embodiment, and partial perspective; both make it impossible to see well. Relativism and totalization are both "god tricks" promising vision from everywhere and nowhere equally and fully, common myths in rhetorics surrounding Science. But it is precisely in the politics and epistemology of partial perspectives that the possibility of sustained, rational, objective inquiry rests.

So, with many other feminists, I want to argue for a doctrine and practice of objectivity that privileges contestation, deconstruction, passionate construction, webbed connections, and hope for transformation of systems of knowledge and ways of seeing. But not just any partial perspective will do; we must be hostile to easy relativisms and holisms built out of summing and subsuming parts. "Passionate detachment" requires more than acknowledged and self-critical partiality. We are also bound to seek perspective from those points of view, which can never be known in advance, that promise something quite extraordinary, that is, knowledge potent for constructing worlds less organized by axes of domination. From such a viewpoint, the unmarked category would *really* disappear—quite a difference from simply repeating a disappearing act. The imaginary and the rational—the visionary and objective vision—hover close together. I think Harding's plea for a successor science and for postmodern sensibilities must be read as an argument for the idea that the fantastic element of hope for transformative knowledge and the severe check and stimulus of sustained critical inquiry are jointly the ground of any believable claim to objectivity or rationality not riddled with breathtaking denials and repressions. It is even possible to read the record of scientific revolutions in terms of this feminist doctrine of rationality and objectivity. Science has been utopian and visionary from the start; that is one reason "we" need it.

A commitment to mobile positioning and to passionate detachment is dependent on the impossibility of entertaining innocent "identity" politics and epistemologies as strategies for seeing from the standpoints of the subjugated in order to see well. One cannot "be" either a cell or molecule—or a woman, colonized person, laborer, and so on—if one intends to see and see from these positions critically. "Being" is much more problematic and contingent. Also, one cannot relocate in any possible vantage point without being accountable for that movement. Vision is *always* a question of the power to see—and perhaps of the violence implicit in our visualizing practices. With whose blood were my eyes crafted? These points also apply to testimony from the position of "oneself." We are not immediately present to ourselves. Self-knowledge requires a semiotic-material technology to link meanings and bodies. Self-identity is a bad visual system. Fusion is a bad strategy of positioning. The boys in the human sciences have called this doubt about self-presence the "death of the subject" defined as a single ordering point of will and consciousness. That judgment seems bizarre to me. I prefer to call this doubt the opening of nonisomorphic subjects, agents, and territories of stories unimaginable from the vantage point of the cyclopean, self-satiated eye of the master subject. The Western eye has fundamentally been a wandering eye, a traveling lens. These peregrinations have often been violent and insistent on having mirrors for a conquering self—but not always. Western feminists also *inherit* some skill in learning to participate in revisualizing worlds turned upside down in earth-transforming challenges to the views of the masters. All is not to be done from scratch.

The split and contradictory self is the one who can interrogate positionings and be accountable, the one who can construct and join rational conversations and fantastic imaginings that change history. Splitting, not being, is the privileged image for feminist epistemologies of scientific knowledge. "Splitting" in this context should be about heterogeneous multiplicities that are simultaneously salient and incapable of being squashed into isomorphic slots or cumulative lists. This geometry pertains within and among subjects. Subjectivity is multidimensional; so, therefore, is vision. The knowing self is partial in all its guises, never finished, whole, simply there and original; it is always constructed and stitched together imperfectly, and *therefore* able to join with another, to see together without claiming to be another. Here is the promise of objectivity: a scientific knower seeks the subject position, not of identity, but of objectivity, that is, partial connection. There is no way to "be" simultaneously in all, or wholly in any, of the privileged (i.e., subjugated) positions structured by gender, race, nation, and class. And that is a short list of critical positions. The search for such a "full" and total position is the search for the fetishized perfect subject of oppositional history, sometimes appearing in feminist theory as the essentialized Third World Woman. Subjugation is not grounds for an ontology; it might be a visual clue. Vision requires instruments of vision; an optics is a politics of positioning. Instruments of vision mediate standpoints; there is no immediate vision from the standpoints of the subjugated. Identity, including self-identity, does not produce science; critical positioning does, that is, objectivity. Only those occupying the positions of the dominators are self-identical, unmarked, disembodied, unmediated, transcendent, born again. It is unfortunately possible for the subjugated to lust for and even scramble into that subject position—and then disappear from view. Knowledge from the point of view of the unmarked is truly fantastic, distorted, and irrational. The only position from which objectivity could not possibly be practiced and honored is the standpoint of the master, the Man, the One God, whose Eye produces, appropriates, and orders all difference. No one ever accused the God of monotheism of objectivity, only of indifference. The god trick is self-identical, and we have mistaken that for creativity and knowledge, omniscience even.

Positioning is, therefore, the key practice in grounding knowledge organized around the imagery of vision, and much Western scientific and philosophic discourse is organized in this way. Positioning implies responsibility for our enabling practices. It follows that politics and ethics ground struggles for and contests over what may count as rational knowledge. That is, admitted or not, politics and ethics ground struggles over knowledge projects in the exact, natural, social, and human sciences. Otherwise, rationality is simply impossible, an optical illusion projected from nowhere comprehensively. Histories of science may be powerfully told as histories of the technologies. These technologies are ways of life, social orders, practices of visualization. Technologies are skilled practices. How to see? Where to see from? What limits to vision? What to see for? Whom to see with? Who gets to have more than one point of view? Who gets blinded? Who wears blinders? Who interprets the visual field? What other sensory powers do we wish to cultivate besides vision? Moral and political discourse should be the paradigm for rational discourse about the imagery and technologies of vision. Sandra Harding's claim, or observation, that movements of social revolution have most contributed to improvements in science might be read as a claim about the knowledge consequences of new technologies of positioning. But I wish Harding had spent more time remembering that social and scientific revolutions have not always been liberatory, even if they have always been visionary. Perhaps this point could be captured in another phrase: the science question in the military. Struggles over what will count as rational accounts of the world are struggles over *how* to see. The terms of vision: the science question in colonialism, the science question in exterminism, the science question in feminism.

Patricia Hill Collins

Though Patricia Hill Collins's *Black Feminist Thought: Knowledge, Consciousness and the Politics of Empowerment* (1990/2000) has become synonymous with the term "intersectionality," her contributions to the field extend far beyond the pages of that landmark text. In *Fighting Words: Black Women and the Search for Justice* (1998), for example, Collins tackles the messy domain of postmodern theory to explore its consequences for Black feminist epistemology and politics. Her conclusions, featured below, suggest that the rhetoric of much of what is called "postmodernism" may be more powerful than its actual ability to catalyze justice and promote social change. Collins's book *Black Sexual Politics: African Americans, Gender, and the New Racism* (2005) was widely acclaimed for its foregrounding of sexuality in Black feminist cultural criticism, which has been criticized for ignoring sexuality, generally, and nonnormative (i.e., nonheterosexual) sexualities, in particular. Her seminal *Race,*

Class, and Gender: An Anthology (coedited with Margaret L. Andersen) is in its eighth edition. Collins is the past president of the American Sociological Association and the former head of the Department of African American Studies at the University of Cincinnati, and she is currently a Distinguished University Professor of Sociology at the University of Maryland, College Park. Her work continues to push sociology, women's studies, and the field of intersectionality more broadly in important new directions, but in this (relatively) older writing below, Collins explains the importance of always being critical—suspicious, even—of the next "big idea" in social theory. New does not always mean better, and *expressing* a commitment to emancipatory politics is not the same as creating knowledge that can actually *produce* justice.

7. The Trouble with Postmodernism*

Like other oppositional discourses, Black feminist thought can never remove itself totally from the ideas expressed by more powerful groups. Although it challenges social theories dominant to itself, in order to be both comprehensible and legitimated it must use the constructs, paradigms, and epistemologies of these discourses. These tensions become apparent in the relationship of Black feminist thought to a loose constellation of academic discourses in the United States best known as postmodernism. On the one hand, postmodernism opposes some of the core tenets of positivist science, structuralist literary criticism, and other discourses of modernity. Thus, postmodernism can foster a powerful critique of existing knowledges and the hierarchical power relations they defend. For example, postmodernism questions the taken-for-granted nature of categories such as race, gender, and heterosexuality and suggests that these seeming "biological truths" constitute social constructions. By focusing on marginalized, excluded, and silenced dimensions of social life, postmodernism destabilizes what has been deemed natural, normal, normative, and true. Overall, postmodernism rejects notions of epistemological and methodological certainty provided by the natural sciences, social sciences, and other discourses of modernity that have been used to justify Black women's oppression (Best and Kellner 1991; McGowan 1991; Rosenau 1992).

On the other hand, postmodernism undercuts selected dimensions of African-American women's political activism. For example, postmodernism rejects ethical positions that emerge from absolutes such as faith. It also eschews social policy recommendations—to make such recommendations requires advancing truth claims and advocating specific political actions stemming from

---

* Excerpted from P. H. Collins, *Fighting Words: Black Women and the Search for Justice* (Minneapolis: University of Minnesota Press, 1998).

those claims (McGowan 1991; Rosenau 1992). This absence of responsibility grounded in some sort of ethical stance is at odds with African-American women's long-standing contributions to Black civil society. Thus, although postmodernism provides a plausible response to dominant discourses and the politics they promote, it fails to provide direction for constructing alternatives.

Postmodern claims to decentering introduce one important question: who might be most likely to care about decentering—those in the centers of power or those on the margins? By legitimating marginality as a potential source of strength for oppressed groups, the postmodern rubric of decentering seemingly supports Black women's longstanding efforts to challenge false universal knowledge that privileged Whiteness, maleness, and wealth. However, as with the changing interpretations associated with Black women's "coming to voice," current meanings attached to decentering as a construct illustrate how terms can continue to be used yet can be stripped of their initial oppositional intent (Winant 1994).

Tracing the changing interpretations attached to the center/margin metaphor from its initial affiliation with global postcolonial struggles and social movements of the 1960s and 1970s in the United States reveals a dramatic shift in meaning. As a literary metaphor, the language of centers and margins emerged in tandem with similar social-science emphases on core and periphery power relations. Designed to describe a range of unequal, exploitive political and economic relationships, these include the classical colonialism that characterized modern European nations' dominion over their oriental and African colonies (Said 1978; 1993); neocolonial relationships that juxtaposed the wealth of core industrial, developed nations of Europe and North America to that of the poverty of the largely colored Third World on the periphery (Said 1990); the geographic reversal of internal colonial relationships that viewed the affluence of White suburban communities in the United States as intimately linked to the poverty of Black inner-city neighborhoods (Blauner 1972); and the core and periphery industrial sectors that separated workers by race, class, and gender into segmented labor markets (Edwards 1979; Gordon et al. 1982; Bonacich 1989). In all of these cases, the construct of core/periphery relationships and its closely affiliated center/margin literary metaphor signaled unjust, hierarchal power relationships.

When embedded in an understanding of core/periphery relationships, this center/margin metaphor became a useful way of viewing Black women's experiences within hierarchical power relations in the United States (see, e.g., Glenn 1985; Dill 1988b; and Amott and Matthaei 1991). Within power relations that constructed Whiteness, maleness, and wealth as centers of power, African-American women were relegated to positions of marginalized Others. One "decentered" hierarchical power relations by claiming the marginalized and devalued space of Black womanhood not as one of tragedy but as one of creativity and power. For African-American women as a collectivity, redefining marginality as a potential source of strength fostered a powerful oppositional knowledge (Collins 1990). Moreover, the work of Black women and other similarly situated groups participated in a much larger project that used the margins as a source of intellectual freedom and strength (see, e.g., Anzaldúa 1987 and Awkward 1995).

Despite these contributions, the continued efficacy of marginality as a space of radical openness remains questionable. Over time, the connections between the center/margin metaphor as a heuristic device and actual core/periphery relations became less clear. While continuing to reference power relations, talk of centers and margins became increasingly distanced from its initial grounding in structural, group-based power relations. Old centers of Whiteness, maleness, and wealth attached to core/periphery relationships in industrial sectors, labor markets, and among the colonial powers and their former colonies persisted. The center/margin metaphor, however, increasingly became recast as yet another ahistorical, "universal" construct applied to all sorts of power relations. Conceptions of power shifted—talk of tops and bottoms, long associated with hierarchy, was recast as flattened geographies of centers and margins.

Once decontextualized in this fashion, because all groups now occupied a flattened theoretical space of shifting centers and margins, decentering as a strategy could be more easily appropriated by groups situated anywhere within real-world hierarchical power relations. Decentering as a resistance strategy was no longer reserved for those actually oppressed within hierarchical power relations of race, class, and gender. Decentering increasingly became recast as a literary term, a decontextualized, abstract construct immersed in representations, texts, and intertextuality.

In this academic context, postmodern treatment of power relations suggested by the rubric of decentering may provide some relief to intellectuals who wish to resist oppression in the abstract without decentering their own material privileges. Current preoccupations with hegemony and microlevel, local politics—two emphases within postmodern treatments of power—are revealing in this regard. As the resurgence of interest in Italian Marxist Antonio Gramsci's work illustrates (Forgacs 1988), postmodern social theorists seem fascinated with the thesis of an all-powerful hegemony that swallows up all resistance except that which manages to survive within local interstices of power. The ways in which many postmodernist theorists use the heterogeneous work of French philosopher Michel Foucault illustrate these dual emphases. Foucault's sympathy for disempowered people can be seen in his sustained attention to themes of institutional power via historical treatment of social

structural change in his earlier works (see, e.g., Foucault's analysis of domination in his work on prisons [1979] and his efforts to write a genealogy linking
sexuality to institutional power [1980a]). Despite these emphases, some interpretations of his work present power as being everywhere, ultimately nowhere,
and, strangely enough, growing. Historical context is minimized—the prison,
the Church, France, and Rome all disappear—leaving in place a decontextualized Foucauldian "theory of power." All of social life comes to be portrayed as
a network of power relations that become increasingly analyzed not at the level
of large-scale social structures, but rather at the local level of the individual
(Hartsock 1990). The increasing attention given to micropolitics as a response
to this growing hegemony, namely, politics on the local level that are allegedly
plural, multiple, and fragmented, stems in part from this reading of history
that eschews grand narratives, including those of collective social movements.
In part, this tendency to decontextualize social theory plagues academic social
theories of all sorts, much as the richly textured nuances of Marx's historical
work on class conflict (see, e.g., *The Eighteenth Brumaire of Louis Bonaparte*
[1963]) become routinely recast into a mechanistic Marxist "theory of social
class." This decontextualization also illustrates how academic theories "empty
out the more political and worldly substance of radical critiques" (West 1993,
41) and thus participate in relations of ruling.

In this sense, postmodern views of power that overemphasize hegemony
and local politics provide a seductive mix of appearing to challenge oppression while secretly believing that such efforts are doomed. Hegemonic power
appears as ever expanding and invading. It may even attempt to "annex" the
counterdiscourses that have developed, oppositional discourses such as Afro-
centrism, postmodernism, feminism, and Black feminist thought. This is a
very important insight. However, there is a difference between being aware
of the power of one's enemy and arguing that such power is so pervasive that
resistance will, at best, provide a brief respite and, at worst, prove ultimately
futile. This emphasis on power as being hegemonic and seemingly absolute,
coupled with a belief in local resistance as the best that people can do, flies
in the face of actual, historical successes. African-Americans, women, poor
people, and others have achieved results through social movements, revolts,
revolutions, and other collective social action against government, corporate,
and academic structures. As James Scott queries, "What remains to be explained . . . is why theories of hegemony . . . have . . . retained an enormous
intellectual appeal to social scientists and historians" (1990, 86). Perhaps for
colonizers who refuse, individualized, local resistance is the best that they can
envision. Overemphasizing hegemony and stressing nihilism not only does not
resist injustice but participates in its manufacture. Views of power grounded
exclusively in notions of hegemony and nihilism are not only pessimistic, they

can be dangerous for members of historically marginalized groups. Moreover, the emphasis on local versus structural institutions makes it difficult to examine major structures such as racism, sexism, and other structural forms of oppression.

Social theories that reduce hierarchical power relations to the level of representation, performance, or constructed phenomena not only emphasize the likelihood that resistance will fail in the face of a pervasive hegemonic presence, they also reinforce perceptions that local, individualized micropolitics constitutes the most effective terrain of struggle. This emphasis on the local dovetails nicely with increasing emphasis on the "personal" as a source of power and with parallel attention to subjectivity. If politics becomes reduced to the "personal," decentering relations of ruling in academia and other bureaucratic structures seems increasingly unlikely. As Rey Chow opines, "What these intellectuals are doing is robbing the terms of oppression of their critical and oppositional import, and thus depriving the oppressed of even the vocabulary of protest and rightful demand" (1993, 13). Viewing decentering as a strategy situated within a larger process of resistance to oppression is dramatically different from perceiving decentering as an academic theory of how scholars should view all truth. When weapons of resistance are theorized away in this fashion, one might ask, who really benefits?

Unless they explicitly deal with structural power relations and wealth, expressions of the rubric of difference within postmodernism present a conflictual terrain for Black feminist thought. The belief that people are all the same under the skin and that difference is a matter of superficial commodified style meshes with long-standing beliefs that attribute differences of power and wealth among Blacks, women, and other historically oppressed groups as being their own fault. Hazel Carby queries, "At what point do theories of 'difference,' as they inform academic practices, become totally compatible with, rather than a threat to, the rigid frameworks of segregation and ghettoization at work throughout society?" (1992, 193). To the end of this question, I might add, "and within academia itself."

Moving beyond difference (with its assumed question, difference from what?) to the conceptual terrain of intersectionality creates new conceptual space. By jettisoning the implicit assumption of a normative center needed for both oppositional difference and reconstructive postmodern tolerance for difference, intersectionality provides a conceptual framework for studying the complexities within historically constructed groups as well as those characterizing relationships among such groups. Drawing from the strengths of decentering and constructionist approaches to difference, the historical realities that created and maintain African-American women's particular history can be acknowledged, all the while recognizing the complexity that operates within the term *Black women*. Moreover, moving beyond difference to intersectionality may shed light on the mutually constructing nature of systems of oppression, as well as social locations created by such mutual constructions. In this sense, the postmodern legitimation of ongoing projects of oppressed groups to decenter power, deconstruct Western metanarratives, and rethink differences legitimates efforts to understand race, class, and gender intersectionality.

Despite these potential contributions, some might question whether postmodernism itself is part of the new politics of containment dedicated to maintaining hierarchy in desegregated spaces. In his essay "The New Politics of Difference," African-American philosopher Cornel West examines the oppositional nature not only of difference but of postmodernism overall:

> The new cultural politics of difference are neither simply oppositional in contesting the mainstream . . . for inclusion, nor transgressive in the avant-guardist sense of shocking conventional bourgeois audiences. Rather, they are distinct articulations of talented (and usually privileged) contributors to culture who desire to align themselves with demoralized, demobilized, depoliticized and disorganized people in order to empower and enable social action and, if possible, to enlist collective insurgency for the expansion of freedom, democracy and individuality. . . . For these critics of culture, theirs is a gesture that is simultaneously progressive and co-opted. (1990, 19–20)

Thus, the essential irony of the postmodern rubrics of decentering, deconstruction, and difference stems from the type of politics they suggest. Political struggles by people of color against racism, by women against patriarchy, and by gays, lesbians, and bisexuals against heterosexism fostered the decentering of Western beliefs about modernity. Yet the main ideas that grow from these struggles have been appropriated by a class of intellectuals who keep the language of resistance yet denude the theory of actual political effectiveness. This theory is then given back to people in a form that, because of the language used, becomes unusable for political struggle and virtually unrecognizable. The result is a discourse critical of hierarchical power relations that simultaneously fosters a politics of impotence.

Postmodernism neither gave African-American women license to decenter the authority of privileged White males nor planted the idea to do so. Rather, postmodernism provides powerful analytical tools and a much-needed legitimation function for those Black women and similarly situated intellectuals whose struggles take place in academic arenas. Thus, postmodernism can be a potentially powerful means for all of us who wish to challenge not just the results of dominant discourses but the rules of the game itself.

Philip Brian Harper

Philip Brian Harper is not a social scientist, but his work has tremendous import for social theorists invested in understanding and critiquing the interlocking relationships between systems of knowledge and power. Harper is a professor of literature and social and cultural analysis at New York University and the author of several books that explore the intersections of race, gender, and sexuality in African American life and culture. The accessible language and inviting style of Harper's writing should not be confused with simplicity of ideas. Indeed, the questions raised in Harper's essay below are among the most difficult to answer in this entire book; perhaps they are even among the most pressing questions facing intersectionality as a field. Whereas the legacy of positivism in the social sciences (and arguably the humanities, as well) necessitates data, fact, and proof—in other words, material *evidence*—for all claims to knowledge and truth, experiences of intersectional oppression do not always leave behind evidence that counts as truthful, reliable, or valid in traditional forms of academic research. What do we do with the affective (i.e., emotional) dimensions of *intuition,* which is particularly difficult to pinpoint, prove, or even explain, and yet which possesses tremendous explanatory power in the lives of multiply marginalized peoples, such as Black queer men? What might intuition illuminate that data (e.g., historical archives, demography, survey research, etc.) cannot? Harper pushes us to reconsider what counts as useful forms of knowledge, and he points in the direction of speculative reasoning as a potent kind of social theoretical tool with which to explore the complexities of intersectionality.

8. Felt Intuition*

Before I go too far in a direction that so clearly could lead to tiresome complaint, I should explicitly acknowledge that I have been extremely fortunate—not only in the results of my queer studies work but in my overall professional-academic positioning—and I am very grateful for my indisputable good luck. For a long time, however, I used to joke to friends that the basis for my success lay in a combination of tokenism and hackwork, forwarded through a sort of intellectual and professional promiscuity whereby I simply

---

* Excerpted from P. B. Harper, "The Evidence of Felt Intuition: Minority Experience, Everyday Life, and Critical Speculative Knowledge," *GLQ: A Journal of Lesbian and Gay Studies* 6 (2000): 641–657. Copyright, 2000, Duke University Press. All rights reserved. Republished by permission of the copyright holder, Duke University Press. www.dukeupress.edu.

never said no to a particular type of proposition—a proposition that generally sounded something like this, as it came to my ear from the far end of a phone line: "Hi, we've never met, but I got your name from X, who met you through Y when you were at a conference with Z and who suggested I give you a call because I'm editing a book volume [or special journal issue] on queer sexuality [or racial politics] that's almost ready to go to press except for the fact that we don't yet have in it any pieces addressing racial politics [or queer sexuality], and X said you'd be the perfect person to contribute something, which I hope you can do because it would really round out the collection, and since all the other authors are already finished with their pieces because they were solicited well over a year ago we really need to have received this essay by our deadline of last Tuesday but if you absolutely have to have more time then I can probably negotiate with the press editor for an extra two weeks, but no more, and can you do it, are you interested, aren't you grateful that I called?" And yes, I always said, yes, oh yes, like some pathetically obsequious version of Molly Bloom, and cleared my schedule for the next two weeks, and installed myself in front of my keyboard, and hammered out an essay at such a furious pace that I didn't have time to worry that it was bad or to double-check the argument or to have second thoughts about submitting it to press—and so on and so on, until the next thing I knew, voilà! I had a c.v., I had a publication record, I seemed to have what we could call a *career,* and that career, moreover, seemed to implicate a profile in what we've all learned to refer to as the field of queer studies.

This was not necessarily a bad development, mind you, especially with respect to my material well-being. It's just that I didn't quite realize that it was happening—or, to be more precise about it, I didn't quite realize what it actually *meant,* since I didn't feel at all certain what queer studies—or, as it was generally and much more problematically called at that relatively early date, queer theory—*was.* But then, who did? We are, after all, talking about an extremely new framework for cultural criticism and social analysis, one that was only just emerging and consolidating—if, indeed, it *has* consolidated, itself a questionable proposition—at the time when I first began working in the area in 1988, a mere twelve years ago. In fact, within the few years after that date, the very definition of the enterprise began to be publicly discussed and debated, with no certain outcome except contestation itself. This unsettled state of affairs has since been assimilated as a signal constituent within queer critique, which during the last five to seven years or so has been characterized by numerous commentators as fundamentally provisional, anticipatory, and incomplete—and thus properly irreducible to a coherent singular project. I actually feel no reason whatsoever to protest on this score, since it seems to me—as to many others—that it is precisely the indeterminate character of queer critique that predicates its analytic force. On the other hand, while that indeterminacy—and here I am using the word in its most literal sense— is frequently cited as a positive attribute of queer analysis, it is much more rarely manifested in the actual critical work that aspires to the rubric, or—and this latter fact constitutes a primary reason for the former—in the contexts in which that work emerges and circulates.

This claim itself is by now a commonplace, and yet this doesn't mean that its full significance has been adequately elaborated. That significance extends far beyond the objection—as valid and urgent as it is—that what is currently recognized as queer studies is, for instance, unacceptably Euro-American in orientation, its purview effectively determined by the practically invisible— because putatively nonexistent—bounds of racial whiteness. It encompasses as well (to continue for the moment with the topic of whiteness) the abiding failure of most supposed queer critique to subject whiteness itself to sustained interrogation and thus to delineate its import in sexual terms, whether con- ceived in normative or nonnormative modes. In other words, to speak per- sonally, it bothers me less that white practitioners of queer critique tend not to address the significance of racial nonwhiteness in the phenomena of sex and sexuality they explore (though one often wishes they would, and, indeed, some do) than that they tend not to address the effect of racial *whiteness* on the very manifestations of those phenomena and on their understanding of them; for the upshot of this failure—somewhat paradoxically, given the interest of queer criticism in definitional fluidity—is an implicit acquiescence to received notions of what constitutes *sex and sexuality,* however nonnormative, as though the current hegemony in this regard were not thoroughly imbricated with the ongoing maintenance of white supremacist culture.

At the same time (for as I have indicated, I am positing this critical short- coming as only one example of the practical limitations that queer studies has both expressed and suffered), it is just as easy—and just as valid—to note that the vast majority of work in black studies (and I'm confining my observations to that field both because it's the one I know best and because such a focus is demanded by the occasion) has similarly failed to interrogate how conven- tional ideas of racial blackness—however variously they may be valued—are themselves conditioned by disparate factors of sex and sexuality, mobilized in myriad ways that may or may not be recognizable as "proper," the consider- ation of which is crucial to fully understanding the social and cultural signifi- cances of blackness itself.

Now, the silence on this score that I perceived within the precincts of African American studies would not, I imagine, have seemed unfamiliar to any number of black people who identify even slightly with any of the subject positions potentially connoted by the term *queer sexuality.* It certainly did not seem unfamiliar to this particular black faggot. I had encountered it before, and so I felt quite sure about what it meant, what tense and admonitory message was conveyed in the very form of implacable muteness. It said: "Now this cannot be, for while all sorts of interpersonal activity might be forwarded by individuals bearing to differing degrees the phenotypical signs of racial blackness and indeed consciously and explicitly subscribing to the identity, the significance of the deed—which may even be pleasurable in its power—must not in all cases be rendered as word—which is undeniably powerful in its punch, which affords us the terms of our life and our death, and by which we have strived to wrest our survival from the teeth of a world that would have us forlorn. Because propriety is requisite for success in this vein, we simply cannot acknowledge what you would have us acknowledge, as upon consideration you surely must see."

As a matter of fact, however, I *don't* at all see, which, as it happens, is very much to the point, since the majority of what occupies me here concerns the status of that which is not readily perceptible by conventional means. After all, one of the most intractable and infuriating problems met with by the would-be commentator on dissident sexual practices is the charge that the *evidence* for our arguments is not solid—which, indeed, it often is not, in literal terms. But what does this mean, really? It means (for instance) that sex and sexuality are by definition evanescent experiences, made even more so in our sociocultural context by the peculiar ways that we negotiate them verbally. It isn't exactly that we don't talk about them, as Foucault famously demonstrated in *The History of Sexuality,* vol. 1, but rather that the *modes* through which we talk about them displace them ever further from easy referential access: we exaggerate; we obfuscate; we tease and we hint; we mislead by indirection; and in fact we outright *lie*—and I don't mean merely with respect to our own personal practices, though I do indeed mean that in part. More than this, though, I mean that we, as a social collectivity, routinely deceive ourselves about the character and the extent of the sexual activity engaged in by human beings in general, and most especially by those in our own extended cultural context. In other words, we most certainly do not "see" dissident sexuality—queer sexuality—evidenced in the ways conventionally called for by the more positivist-minded folk whom we encounter in our professional activity; and it is precisely for this reason that I do not at all "see" that we should refrain from discussing it—as a thankfully growing number of us are proceeding to do—for we have to take our objects of analysis on the terms that define them, if we hope to make any headway whatever toward the increased understanding we supposedly seek.

What this means, it seems to me, for black queer studies, is that we must necessarily take recourse—for the umpteenth time in the history of our extended endeavor—to the evidence of things not seen and, further, to a particular subcategory within this genre, what I call in the title of this lecture the evidence of felt intuition.

So, then, how to proceed? (For not to proceed is not an option, unless one actually approves of the status quo, and given that we are all human and not yet dead, I assume that none of us does.) How to consider the meaning of an experience no concrete evidence of which exists, and of which we can therefore claim no positive knowledge?

One might well worry, however, that we won't always have the benefit—as dubious as that benefit was in the instance at hand—of such a definitive counterphenomenon against which we can gauge the possible meanings of a sexuality that remains almost entirely unarticulated, and what then? Well, to be quite frank, I don't think that we are at risk of ever facing that scenario, for reasons that I will elucidate shortly. Leaving that point aside for the moment, though, let us simply consider what might happen in the instances (whose number and frequency will certainly increase the more we pursue critical consideration of black queer sexuality) where the objects of our analysis are so ethereal that they appear to offer us no hard evidence at all. Well, in those cases, we will doubtless have to take recourse in a direction to which I have already alluded and rely on the evidence of felt intuition. Immediately upon invoking it, of course, I realize that this phrase may strike some as worrisome, for it seems conventionally to refer to mere instinctive emotion, rather than to the engagement with external factors that is understood to be the rightful province of critical thought. On consulting the dictionary in order to settle my own fears on this score, however, I discovered that intuition is *exactly* the word I want, etymologically speaking, since in its root meaning it connotes precisely such outward engagement, signifying contemplation, or the practice of *looking* (Latin *tuērī*, to look [at]) *upon* (Latin *in*, on) some entity or another—and, by extension, coming to some speculative conclusion about it.

This process seems to me to characterize a significant portion of our lives, and most assuredly a large percentage of minority experience, given the uncertainty that I have already suggested defines the latter. In fact, I remember a train trip from Madison to Syracuse during which I rebuffed a white man who approached me. He'd asked if I'd join him in a game of cards, but I surmised that he was sexually attracted to me. Now, for a long time, from the late 1970s through the early 1990s, I used to lead educational workshops on "lesbian and gay lifestyles" in various institutional settings—schools, social-service centers, halfway houses for young offenders. Like many people, members of these audiences often wanted to know whether gay men could identify others of our kind by the way they looked; I generally said that I could, but not by the way they looked *to* me so much as the way they looked *at* me, and this is what I noticed about the man on the train—the way he looked *at* me as he stood over my seat, asking me whether I'd like to play cards. I don't know for a fact that he was attracted to me; I only know that look and the sensation in my face when I'm giving the same look to somebody else.

Does this look—and the knowledge of it that I have accumulated over the years—constitute sex? It well might. Does it constitute *sexuality*? I have no doubt that it does. Am I ineluctably compelled to speculate about it, so as to arrive at some judgment that has its own consequences? I believe that I am, or else how would I get through the day, as fraught as it is with the possibility of danger? The man might just as easily have been an ax murderer, which would certainly have put a damper on things had I decided to follow through on what seemed to me his flirtatious inquiries. Or he might even have been a rather more run-of-the-mill homophobe, out to victimize gay men by queer-baiting them first. In any case, we necessarily adjudicate such situations on the fly every single day of our natural lives, and some of us much more frequently than others. Precisely because minority experience is characterized by the uncertainty I have already referenced, we basically stake our lives and we take our chances, hoping that we haven't miscalculated the risk. Things could go deadly wrong, as I am frequently reminded; after all, judging from photographs I've seen in the news, I probably would have gone home with Jeffrey Dahmer if he'd asked me, and we all know what the result of *that* gamble would have been. The point, however, is not the peril, but rather the fact that we cannot not test it, for not to proceed speculatively is, to speak plainly, not to live. And it certainly is not to perform critical analysis, which incontrovertibly *depends upon* speculative logic for the force of its arguments, as we all know deep down.

Indeed, the whole metaphorics of "seeing" that I elaborated a minute ago is the product entirely of my own surmisings, however much it helps me in plotting my next analytic move amid the critical context that I want to help transform. One hopes my conclusions are not wholly off mark, for a great deal of what I propose here is predicated on them. And, of course, that would be the objection to speculative knowledge—that it potentially leads us astray from known data, from the concrete reality of worldly existence (as if entire disciplines weren't based on speculation; as if we didn't credit those disciplines with the discovery of truth), and indeed it might do so, but then what's wrong with that?

This, I guess, explains why I harbor no reservations about theory, because I don't see it as ever being "merely" theoretical. Moreover, as far as queer studies is concerned, theory may in some respects be all that we have, if by theory we mean (to be etymological again) *a way of seeing* that allows us to apprehend our world in different and potentially productive ways.

Roderick Ferguson

Roderick Ferguson, a leader in the fields of sociology, queer studies, gender studies, African American studies, and their various convergences, is a professor of American Studies at the University of Minnesota. Though he is a prolific scholar whose publications include a recent treatise of the politics of multiculturalism in higher education (*The Reorder of Things: The University and Its Pedagogies of Minority Difference,* 2012) and an edited anthology on the cultural politics of neocolonialism and neoliberalism (*Strange Affinities: The Gender and Sexual Politics of Comparative Racialization,* coedited with Grace Hong, 2011), his *Aberrations in Black: Toward a Queer of Color Critique* (2004), is his most celebrated and well known. Ferguson is sometimes difficult to read, because he simultaneously attends to uncharted frontiers in social theory while engaging the most "classic" and traditional theorists that serve as the foundations of sociology (e.g., Marx, Durkheim, Weber, etc.). The excerpt below is no exception, as Ferguson explains what the emerging queer of color critique does to the canon of sociology, particularly historical materialism (from Marx) and other forms of "classical" (also called "modern") sociology in the United States. Readers unacquainted with Marxism may perhaps find themselves in unfamiliar territory here, but can think of "historical materialism" as an approach that seeks to explain social phenomena—including racism and sexism—through the study and criticism of class conflict, particularly class conflict as understood by Marx to be the inevitable product of capitalism. Ferguson has importantly showcased how the intersections of queer studies and African American studies mean much more than Black + gay; indeed, the epistemological calculus of such a project is infinitely more complicated and consequential. Black queer studies and the queer of color critique differentially advanced by Harper (see reading 8), Ferguson, José Esteban Muñoz, Kara Keeling (Unit V, reading 20), Chandan Reddy (Unit I, reading 4), and others is an epistemological turning point for intersectionality that demands reconsideration of the assumptions that undergird even the metaphor of "intersection." These are not the first arguments about sexuality to be made in the discourse on intersectionality, but they have been taken up differently than Audre Lorde, Barbara Smith, and the Combahee River Collective, whose arguments about lesbian sexualities were often overlooked in the normative race, class, gender paradigm of intersectionality. Like Patricia Hill Collins insisted earlier in this unit (see reading 7), one of the first steps in going forward (in terms of theory and politics) is to look backward and inward to interrogate the root metaphors, origin stories, and founding narratives of our fields that may have produced heterogeneous sites of silence in which oppression hides.

9. Queer of Color Critique and the Canon*

By relating queer of color subjects and practices to marxism and liberal pluralism, Reddy suggests that queer of color analysis must critically engage the genealogy of materialist critique. In his book, *Disidentifications: Queers of Color and the Performance of Politics,* José Esteban Muñoz argues, "Disidentification is the hermeneutical performance of decoding mass, high, or any other cultural field from the perspective of a minority subject who is disempowered in such a representational hierarchy." As Muñoz suggests, queer of color critique decodes cultural fields not from a position outside those fields, but from within them, as those fields account for the queer of color subject's historicity. If the intersections of race, gender, sexuality, and class constitute social formations within liberal capitalism, then queer of color analysis obtains its genealogy within a variety of locations. We may say that women of color feminism names a crucial component of that genealogy as women of color theorists have historically theorized intersections as the basis of social formations. Queer of color analysis extends women of color feminism by investigating how intersecting racial, gender, and sexual practices antagonize and/or conspire with the normative investments of nation-states and capital.

As queer of color analysis claims an interest in social formations, it locates itself within the mode of critique known as historical materialism. Since historical materialism has traditionally privileged class over other social relations, queer of color critique cannot take it up without revision, must not employ it without disidentification. If to disidentify means to "[recycle] and [rethink] encoded meaning" and "to use the code [of the majority] as raw material for representing a disempowered politics of positionality that has been rendered unthinkable by the dominant culture," then disidentification resembles Louis Althusser's rereading of historical materialism. Queer of color analysis disidentifies with historical materialism to *rethink* its categories and how they might conceal the materiality of race, gender, and sexuality. In this instance, to disidentify in no way means to discard.

Addressing the silences within Marx's writings that enable rather than disturb bourgeois ideology, silences produced by Marx's failure to theorize received abstractions like "division of labor, money, value, etc.," Althusser writes in *Reading Capital,*

---

* Excerpted from R. Ferguson, *Aberrations in Black: Toward a Queer of Color Critique* (Minneapolis: University of Minnesota Press, 2004).

This silence is only "heard" at one precise point, just where it goes unperceived: when Marx speaks of the initial abstractions on which the work of transformation is performed. What are these initial abstractions? By what right does Marx accept in these initial abstractions the categories from which Smith and Ricardo started, thus suggesting that he thinks in continuity with their object, and that therefore there is no break in object between them and him? These two questions are really only one single question, precisely the question Marx does not answer, simply because he does not pose it. Here is the site of his silence, and this site, being empty, threatens to be occupied by the "natural" discourse of ideology, in particular, of empiricism. . . . An ideology may gather naturally in the hollow left by this silence, the ideology of a relation of real correspondence between the real and its intuition and representation, and the presence of an "abstraction" which operates on this real in order to disengage from it these "abstract general relations," i.e., an empiricist ideology of abstraction.

As empiricism grants authority to representation, empiricism functions hegemonically, making representations seem natural and objective. To assume that categories conform to reality is to think with, instead of against, hegemony. As he uncritically appropriated the conceptions of political economy formulated by bourgeois economists, Marx abetted liberal ideology. He identified with that ideology instead of disidentifying with it. Disidentifying with historical materialism means determining the silences and ideologies that reside within critical terrains, silences and ideologies that equate representations with reality. Queer of color analysis, therefore, extends Althusser's observations by accounting for the ways in which Marx's critique of capitalist property relations is haunted by silences that make racial, gender, and sexual ideologies and discourses commensurate with reality and suitable for universal ideals.

Historical materialism is not the only inquiry into social formations characterized by investments in normative epistemes. Canonical American sociology betrays those investments as well. Canonical sociology denotes a discursive formation that emerges out of Enlightenment claims to rationality and scientific objectivity. These claims entail an investment in heterosexual patriarchy as the appropriate standard for social relations and the signature of hegemonic whiteness. As canonical sociology has racialized heteropatriarchy through whiteness, the discipline has excluded and disciplined those formations that deviate from the racial ideal of heteropatriarchy.

We can see the exclusionary and disciplinary techniques at work in the discipline's engagement with African American culture. American sociology has historically understood civilization as the production of wealth and order and as the spread of disorder and dehumanization. American sociology, like historical materialism, has proffered heteronormativity as the scene of order and rationality and nonheteronormativity as the scene of abandonment and dysfunction. In doing so, the discipline has contributed to the discursivity of capital. I turn now to canonical sociology because it has contributed to that discursivity as it has produced racial knowledge about African American culture. Indeed, sociology has been a hegemonic site of reflection about African American culture and has read that culture consistently through a heteronormative lens. American sociology has deployed liberal ideology as the main paradigm through which to read American racialization. Historical materialism has provided the means by which canonical sociology could translate processes of state and capital into a narrative of African American racial formation and disruptions to gender and sexual ideals. In fact, universalizing heteropatriarchy and understanding that universalization as whiteness and through American citizenship defined the core of sociological reflection about African American culture. As it has done so, formations like the drag-queen prostitute have been a constant preoccupation that canonical sociology has constructed as pathologies emblematic of African American culture. Looking at canonical sociology's relationship to African American nonheteronormative formations can help us see how U.S. capital has also been regarded as a site of pathologies and perversions that have designated racialized nonwhite communities as the often ominous outcome of capital's productive needs. As I stated earlier, queer of color analysis attempts to explain how gender and sexuality variegate racial formations and how that variety indexes material processes. We must engage racial knowledge about African American culture as it was produced by sociology if we are to understand the gender and sexual variation within African American culture as the outcome of material and discursive processes.

In *Modernity and Self-Identity,* Anthony Giddens argues that reflection is one of the institutional traits of modernity and that "[sociology], and the social sciences more widely conceived, are inherent elements of the institutional reflexivity of modernity." We can see American sociology's interest in difference in the discipline's fascination with the social conditions of African American existence. For early American sociologists of racial relations, the question of African American culture became the location within which sociologists could speculate about the relationships between modernization and cultural difference. American sociology began as a way to reflect on "the vast dislocations from extremely rapid urbanization and industrialization. [It] was shaped from the start by a *moral response to immediate national social problems—racial and cultural concerns prominent among them.*" Often sociologists explained African American poverty and upheaval through what was considered African American gender, sexual, and familial eccentricity. Sociological arguments about

African American cultural inferiority were racialized discourses of gender and sexuality. As Kobena Mercer argues, "[A]ssumptions about black sexuality lie at the heart of the ideological view that black households constitute deviant, disorganized and even pathological familial forms, that fail to socialize their members into societal norms."

At the base of sociological arguments about African American cultural inferiority lay questions about how well African Americans approximated heteronormative ideals and practices embodied in whiteness and ennobled in American citizenship. African American culture has historically been deemed contrary to the norms of heterosexuality and patriarchy. As its embodiment in whiteness attests, heteronormativity is not simply articulated through inter-gender relations, but also through the racialized body. Sociology helped to establish African American corporeal difference as the sign of a nonhetero-normativity presumed to be fundamental to African American culture. Marking African Americans as such was a way of disenfranchising them politically and economically. In sum, the material and discursive production of African American nonheteronormativity provided the interface between the gendered and eroticized properties of African American racial formation and the material practices of state and civil society.

I theorize African American nonheteronormative difference as a way of thinking discourse and contradiction in tandem. Foucault argues against the presumption that the modern age was simply about the repression of sexuality, arguing instead that scientific discourses have produced a multiplicity of sexual perversions. Foucault is also arguing against narratives that locate the age of repression within the development of capitalism and bourgeois order. We may extend and revise Foucault's argument by addressing the ways in which sociological discourse produced multiple sexual and gender perversions coded as nonwhite racial difference and as the study of African American culture. By engaging capital as a site of contradictions that compels racial formations that are eccentric to gender and sexual normativity, I have also attempted to revise the presumption that capital is the site of gender and sexual uniformity.

IDENTITIES

The (Intersectional) Self and Society
Patrick R. Grzanka

Though the word itself sounds relatively innocuous, "identity" is one of the most contentious concepts in intersectionality, and not for the reasons one might expect. Certainly, social "identity" is complicated and consequential to the extent that it is an organizing element of social life and one of the key factors that predicts life chances, including education, income, mental and physical health, access to institutional resources, and so on—this much we know. But identity in intersectionality is a hotly contested construct, because many intersectional theorists insist that intersectionality is actually *not about* identity. Rather than seek resolution over this multifaceted debate, this unit takes up these controversies and offers numerous perspectives on the theorization and examination of social, cultural, and personal identities in the interest of keeping the controversy over identity front and center.

In his recent attempt to summarize major criticisms of intersectionality as a research paradigm, legal scholar Devon Carbado summarizes the trouble over identity thusly:

> Three criticisms of intersectionality (that the theory is identitarian, static, and invested in subjects) are curious given the theory's genesis in law and critical race theory. Intersectionality reflects a commitment neither to subjects nor to identities per se but, rather, to marking and mapping the production and contingency of both. Nor is the theory an effort to identify, in the abstract, an exhaustive list of intersectional social categories and to add them up to determine—once and for all—the different intersectional configurations those categories can form. (2013, 815)

Cho, Crenshaw, and McCall (2013) articulate the debate similarly:

> Intersectionality is inextricably linked to an analysis of power, yet one challenge to intersectionality is its alleged emphasis on categories of identity versus structures of inequality. While this theme has surfaced in a variety of texts, particularly those that might be framed as projects that seek intersectionality's rescue . . . we emphasize an understanding of intersectionality that is not exclusively or even primarily preoccupied with categories, identities, and subjectivities. (797)

Accordingly, to legal scholars and sociologists whose political and intellectual investments lie in the interrogation of social structures or "systems of oppression" (see my introduction to Unit I), the appraisal that intersectionality is preoccupied with identity or subjectivity (i.e., the construction and experience of personhood) is misguided at best and wholly inaccurate at worst. Intersectionality, by this account, has always been about structural dynamics and the critique thereof. If identity matters, it is because social identity categories are the products of these systems, such as racism, sexism, heterosexism, and capitalism, and are one especially efficacious way of recognizing and measuring the inequalities produced by such systems. From this perspective, even the phrase "identity-based inequalities" is an insufficient compromise and a mischaracterization of the systemic organization of intersectional oppression. The inequality is not based in identity; but rather inequalities produce social identities. For example, racist, xenophobic immigration laws produce "aliens," "illegals," and "noncitizens," and not the other way around. Heterosexist ideologies shaped the science that taxonomized "deviant" sexual behaviors and organized them into a category of personhood: the homosexual. These identities are not *essential,* but socially and historically produced by large-scale ideological and institutionalized systems. As Catherine MacKinnon (2013) puts it, "[Categories] are the ossified outcomes of the dynamic intersection of multiple hierarchies, not the dynamic that creates them. They are there, but they are not the reason they are there" (1023). "Inequality-based identities," therefore, might be a better way to put it.

The concern over a focus on identity comes from an epistemological and arguably disciplinary-informed position that anchoring social and cultural critique in subjects and identities obfuscates the structural realities that engender social injustices. In sociology, we might compare this to the micro/macro and agency/structure debates. They sound something like: if you pay too much attention to the microsociological elements of life, then you'll miss the macrosociological dynamics that make microsociological interactions possible. Likewise, if you overemphasize the role of agency, choice, and self-determination, all life outcomes will be attributed to decisions made by subjects, rather than the social forces that limit the universe of possible choices and produce socially acceptable and unacceptable behaviors. As Patricia Hill Collins (2009) reflects:

> In recent years, intersectional analyses have far too often turned inward, to the level of personal identity narratives, in part, because intersectionality can be grasped far more easily when constructing one's own autobiography. This stress on identity narratives, especially individual identity narratives, does provide an important contribution to fleshing out our understandings of how people experience and construct identities within intersecting systems of power. Yet this turning inward also reflects the shift within American society away from social structural analyses of social problems, for example, the role of schools, prisons, and workplace practices in producing poverty, and the growing rejection of institutional responses to social inequalities, e.g., how governmental social policies might address this intractable social problem. (ix)

Fixation on agency, identities, and microsociological dynamics promotes, from this perspective, a kind of tunnel vision that encourages researchers to miss the bigger picture of society at work. If we imagine a spectrum of academic disciplines, sociology and the law would sit at one end with a focus on structures, and most of the humanities and psychology would be at the other end studying subjective experiences and the capacity of the mind to influence behavior.

This, of course, is a gross simplification of what both scholars of intersectionality who study structures and those who study identity actually do. Surely, some scholars and even some areas of study within intersectionality likely do emphasize one end of the spectrum to the extreme and at the expense of all other considerations (and this is certainly true outside of intersectionality and is exemplified by rational choice theorists in economics, as well as "evolutionary" strands of social psychology), but I would posit that the study of intersectionality generally does involve attention to both identity and structure, and that to position the two as "opposites" or as fundamentally competing interests is a false dichotomization of two deeply intertwined facets of social life and inquiry. Black lesbian women, for example, as a social group the boundaries of which are constituted by the intersection of Blackness, womanhood, and lesbian identities, were the foundational launching pad for intersectional analyses of inequality. Black feminists in the Combahee River Collective were not just making the point that scholars and institutions must recognize how some Black people are women, some women are Black, and some Black women are lesbians. Intersectionality's exigencies lie in the need for a political agenda, a social critique, and research methods that could better attend to the experiences of Black lesbian women—the extant "tools," as Audre Lorde (1984) named them, were just not cutting it and were mostly doing more harm than good. Intersectionality, as manifest in the writing of Lorde, Barbara Smith, Bonnie Thornton Dill, Gloria Anzaldúa, Chandra Talpade Mohanty, and other women of color feminists in the early stages of the movement, made claims about macrosociological structures that were derived from the *lived experiences* of multiply marginalized peoples that could not be explained by the dominant single-axis paradigms in research and political activism (i.e., White Western feminism or male-dominated forms of Black nationalism, for example). Likewise, the critical study of *institutions* such as education, medicine, government, and the law were used to examine, predict, and fight the material consequences of structural oppression on the *lives* of actual women of color trying to negotiate classism, racism, sexism, xenophobia, and homophobia simultaneously. While the traditional centers of social science disciplines were caught up in reductive, pedantic, and esoteric debates about structure versus agency, quantitative versus qualitative, and micro versus macro, intersectional scholars were crafting new methods and new theories that creatively negotiated artificial disciplinary and paradigmatic boundaries.

The potential for intersectional criticism to subvert, undermine, and destabilize the binary of structure/identity is indeed one of its most potent analytic and political strengths. In sociology, which could be caricaturized as obsessed with structure above all else, intersectionality has pushed segments of the discipline, including the study of deviance, labor economics, and demography, to confront the nuances of identity and the significance of lived experiences in understanding structural dynamics (e.g., Frankenberg 1993; Daniels 1997). Qualitative methods, accordingly, have dominated intersectional sociological inquiry because they are often more adept at capturing these kinds of social complexities and personal subjectivities than demographic questionnaires and census-derived datasets that rely on preexisting frameworks to group and order individuals (Dill, McLaughlin, and Nieves 2007). Likewise, to characterize intersectional psychologists as overly invested in identity and subjectivity is a great mischaracterization of the work being done in that discipline, where scholars such as Michelle Fine (Unit VI, reading 24), Elizabeth Cole (Unit X, reading 41), and Lisa Bowleg (Unit X, reading 40) have thoroughly complicated how social identity categories can be understood in psychological research and have advocated a deeper attention to structural dynamics in both qualitative *and* quantitative inquiry. Finally, to claim that intersectionality *is not* or *should not* be about identity—because to be concerned with identity is supposedly a bad thing—betrays an assumption that structures are complicated and consequential while identities are neither. If the intersectional projects of Black queer studies (e.g., Keeling 2009, Unit V, reading 20) and transnational feminisms (e.g., Mohanty 1993/2008, reading 11), for example, have shown us nothing else, it is that identities are neither inert forms of group membership, nor easily pinpointed markers of difference. Surely some social identity categories and their attendant stereotypes may be "static and hard to move," as MacKinnon writes, but many identities are hard to find, and some are engaged in perpetual disappearing acts (2013, 1023). Consider the politics of the closet, which are constantly changing even after one "comes out" of it (Sedgwick 1990), and the landscape of contemporary sexual politics in which identity categories (e.g., butch, femme, metrosexual, queer, LGBT) are frequently being crafted, modified, forgotten, abandoned, and resuscitated (Gamson 1996; Ghaziani 2011). Identity for those who live in a diaspora, as an immigrant or as a refugee seeking asylum, may also be distinguished by perpetual transformations determined by the state and other institutions that have the power to give identity and take it away (Decena 2011; Mohanty 1993/2008, reading 11; Sengupta 2006, reading 12). "Identity politics" remains a dirty word even twenty years after the 1990s' "Culture Wars" in which contestations over identity were often lampooned as unproductive and fatalistic boundary-policing and/or oppression-measuring contests in which groups vied for the right to claim Most Marginalized. We should remember, though, that while some of the criticisms of identity politics came from within Left progressive movements, most came from those on the conservative Right seeking to trivialize the claims of "special interest groups," which was the catchall code word for social minorities who want equality (Duggan 1994). Anna Carastathis (2013) has recently considered how identity categories may remain "a useful basis for political organizing, as long as identity categories are conceptualized as coalitions" and move beyond the restricting pitfalls of essentialist renderings of identity that stress in-group homogeneity (941).

At a dinner with two of my dear friends and colleagues a few years ago during an academic conference, we got into it over "identity." I found myself on the defensive over my use of the word "identity" in the context of teaching intersectionality. My friends—both sociologists who study intersectionality—insisted that identity was one of the most dangerous terms to use in a classroom when trying to explain Patricia Hill Collins's and other Black feminist sociologists' work. They said something like, "If you say 'identity,' students will immediately assume that intersectionality comes down to a matter of 'who I am' or 'how I identify,' and it will become narcissistic and superficial. 'Identity' makes it too easy to reduce the whole thing to individuals and choice. They'll miss the whole point." I agreed, somewhat, and there are ways in which they were both probably right, because thinking inward and focusing on the self is not the same as becoming critical about one's positions of privilege or disadvantage within communities, organizations, groups, and society. Nonetheless,

I argued back and we went at it for a bit through a spirited debate about identity in teaching and research. We reached no resolution, though we got each other to think. I do not have a silver bullet to offer, and I am suspicious of anyone who claims to have the smoking gun that will close the case on identity in intersectionality once and for all. I suggest that we keep thinking about it.

References and Further Reading

Anchisi, L. 2009. "One, No One, and a Hundred Thousand: On Being a Korean Woman Adopted by European Parents." In *The Intersectional Approach: Transforming the Academy Through Race, Class, & Gender,* edited by M. T. Berger and K. Guidroz, 290–299. Chapel Hill, NC: University of North Carolina Press.

Bowleg, L. 2013. "'Once You've Blended the Cake, You Can't Take the Parts Back to the Main Ingredients': Black Gay and Bisexual Men's Descriptions and Experiences of Intersectionality." *Sex Roles* 68: 754–767.

Carastathis, A. 2013. "Identity Categories as Potential Coalitions." *Signs: The Journal of Women in Culture and Society* 38: 941–965.

Carbado, D. W. 2013. "Colorblind Intersectionality." *Signs: The Journal of Women in Culture and Society* 38: 811–845.

Cho, S., K. W. Crenshaw, and L. McCall. 2013. "Intersectionality Studies: Theory, Applications, and Praxis." *Signs: The Journal of Women in Culture and Society* 38: 785–810.

Collins, P. H. 2009. "Foreword: Emerging Intersections—Building Knowledge and Transforming Institutions." In *Emerging Intersections: Race, Class, and Gender in Theory, Policy, and Practice,* edited by B. T. Dill and R. E. Zambrana, vii–xiii. New Brunswick, NJ: Rutgers University Press.

Daniels, J. 1997. *White Lies: Race, Class, Gender, and Sexuality in White Supremacist Discourse.* New York: Routledge.

Decena, C. U. 2011. *Tacit Subjects: Belonging and Same-Sex Desire Among Dominican Immigrant Men.* Durham, NC: Duke University Press.

Dill, B. T., A. E. McLaughlin, and A. D. Nieves. 2007. "Future Directions of Feminist Research: Intersectionality." In *Handbook of Feminist Research: Theory and Praxis,* edited by S. N. Hesse-Biber, 629–638. Thousand Oaks, CA: Sage Publications.

Duggan, L. 1994. "Queering the State." *Social Text* 39: 1–14.

Frankenberg, R. 1993. *The Social Construction of Whiteness: White Women, Race Matters.* Minneapolis, MN: University of Minnesota Press.

Gamson, J. 1996. "Must Identity Movements Self-Destruct?: A Queer Dilemma." In *Queer Theory/Sociology,* edited by S. Seidman, 395–420. Cambridge, MA: Blackwell.

Ghaziani, A. 2011. "Post-Gay Collective Identity Construction." *Social Problems* 58: 99–125.

Gines, K. 2011. "Being a Black Women Philosopher: Reflections on Founding the Collegium of Black Women Philosophers." *Hypatia* 26: 429–437.

Hancock, A.-M. 2011. *Solidarity Politics for Millennials: A Guide to Ending the Oppression Olympics.* New York: Palgrave Macmillan.

Keeling, K. 2009. "Looking for M—: Queer Temporality, Black Political Possibility, and Poetry from the Future." *GLQ: A Journal of Lesbian and Gay Studies* 15: 565–582.

Lorde, A. 1984. *Sister Outsider: Essays and Speeches.* Berkeley, CA: The Crossing Press.

MacKinnon, C. 2013. "Intersectionality as Method: A Note." *Signs: The Journal of Women in Culture and Society* 38: 1019–1030.

Mohanty, C. T. (1993) 2008. "Defining Genealogies: Feminist Reflections on Being South Asian in North America." In *Our Feet Walk the Sky, Writings by Women of the South Asian Diaspora,* edited by S. Bhatt, P. Kaira, A. Kohli, L. Malkani, and D. Rasiah, 351–358. Aunt Lute Books.

Sedgwick, E. K. 1990. *Epistemology of the Closet.* Berkeley: University of California Press.

Sengupta, S. 2006. "I/Me/Mine: Intersectional Identities as Negotiated Minefields." *Signs: The Journal of Women in Culture and Society* 31: 629–639.

Shields, S. 2008. "Gender: An Intersectionality Perspective." *Sex Roles* 59: 301–311.

Angela Y. Davis

It is difficult to sufficiently capture Angela Davis's influence on social justice politics and activism in the United States and worldwide since the 1960s. She has been one of the most recognized activists in the world since at least 1969, when she came to national attention after being removed from her teaching position in UCLA's philosophy department because of politics, namely her membership in a US communist party. In 1970, she was famously placed on the FBI's Ten Most Wanted Fugitives list on false charges, and was ultimately captured and imprisoned for sixteen months before being acquitted in 1972. Since then, she has become an internationally renowned advocate for the abolition of the "prison industrial complex" and continues to write extensively on racism in the criminal justice system and political life in the United States and worldwide. Davis is currently Distinguished Professor Emerita in the History of Consciousness and Feminist Studies departments at the University of California, Santa Cruz, where she taught for decades despite former California Governor Ronald Reagan's earlier vow that Davis would never again teach in the venerable University of California system.

In the excerpt from *Women, Culture, and Politics* featured here, Davis uses the "feminization of poverty" and the cultural archetype of the "welfare queen" to examine the intersection of race, gender, and class in the lives of US Black women and women of color more broadly during the Reagan era. Her critique here is at least twofold. First, she argues that to understand the effects of capitalism on women of color in the United States, we need to consider the co-constitution of gender and race in diverse women's lives. Second, she compels White women—and members of the US women's movement in particular—to face the racism implicit in their elision of race and class issues that disproportionately affect and marginalize women of color. From her analysis of what Patricia Hill Collins will later call "controlling images" in the public sphere, to her careful investigation of the demographics of poverty, to her interrogation of intersectional dimensions of reproductive health and justice, the breadth of Davis's insight is at once profound and sobering. Contemporary readers will note that many of the same issues Davis writes about here continue to plague contemporary social life and politics today.

10. Black Women and Welfare*

The concept of the "feminization of poverty" must not be allowed to obscure the extent to which the entire Black community has suffered grave economic setbacks as a direct consequence of the domestic policies framed by the Reagan administration. The government's budget and tax policies have brought about a decline in income and in the standard of living for the average Black family in virtually every income stratum. In 1983, nearly 36 percent of all Black people lived in poverty—the highest percentage since the Census Bureau began collecting data on Black poverty in 1966. From 1980 to 1983, an additional 1.3 million Black people fell into the ranks of the officially poor. While white unemployment is lower now than at the beginning of Reagan's term of office—according to government statistics, that is—Black unemployment is now higher—16 percent, as compared to 14.4 percent when Reagan took office in 1981. The racial gap in unemployment has increased across the board—between black and white men, black and white women, and black and white youth.

George Gilder, one of the foremost philosophers of Reaganism, sophistically argues in his book *Wealth and Poverty* that Black women bear substantial responsibility for the impoverishment of the Black community. Challenging the notion that Black women are targets of double discrimination, he states that "[t]here is little evidence that black women suffer any discrimination at all, let alone in double doses." Resurrecting the myth of the Black matriarchy, he suggests that Black women are intellectually and occupationally more advanced than their male counterparts. Moreover, he fallaciously reasons, their welfare benefits allow them special access to money—money that Black men do not have.

> Nothing is so destructive to . . . male values (such as male confidence and authority, which determine sexual potency and respect from the wife and children) as the growing, imperious recognition that when all is said and done, his wife can do better without him. The man has the gradually sinking feeling that his role as provider, the definitive male activity from

---

* Excerpted from A. Y. Davis, *Women, Culture, and Politics* (New York: Vintage, 1990).

the primal days of the hunt, through the industrial revolution and into modern life, has been largely seized from him, he has been cuckolded by the compassionate state.

"In the welfare culture," Gilder more explicitly argues,

> money becomes not something earned by men through hard work, but a right conferred on women by the state. Protest and complaint replace diligence and discipline as the sources of pay. Boys grow up seeking support from women, while they find manhood in the macho circles of the street and the bar or in the irresponsible fathering of random progeny.

Gilder contends that men who live with welfare mothers move from one woman to another and are both "beneficiaries and victims" of the welfare system. He suggests that hundreds of thousands of Black men do not marry and do not work because they are able to live off the benefits received by Black women, and that at the same time, the welfare system incites young Black women to become pregnant before they are in a position to raise a family.

> AFDC . . . offers a guaranteed income to any child-raising couple in America that is willing to break up, or to any teenaged girl over sixteen who is willing to bear an illegitimate child.

If welfare benefits were anywhere as abundant as ideologues like Gilder make them out to be, acquiring the primary necessities of life for themselves and their children would not constitute such an arduous task for welfare mothers. Average AFDC benefits do not provide enough to raise a mother and her children above the poverty level, much less to support a man. Yet thanks to ideologues like Gilder, the myth persists that welfare mothers squander taxpayers' hard-earned money on Cadillacs and fur coats. Reagan himself has been known to fabricate stories about welfare fraud. "There's a woman in Chicago," he once said.

> She has eight names, thirty addresses, twelve social security cards. . . . She's got Medicaid, is getting food stamps, and she is collecting welfare under each of her names. Her tax-free cash income is $150,000.

What Reagan was actually referring to was a case of welfare fraud in which a Chicago woman used *four* aliases, with which she managed to acquire about eight thousand dollars. Even though she did commit fraud, she nonetheless remained well below the income level required to lead a comfortable life in this country. Reagan concocted this lie for the purpose of publicly discrediting people—especially Black women—on welfare.

Media propagandists are now attributing a significant portion of the blame for poverty in the Black community to unmarried mothers—and particularly to teenagers who bear children. As James McGhee points out in the Urban League's 1984 *State of Black America* report:

> It is almost as if these observers propose that black families headed by females are subject to some inexorable law of nature that dictates that the heads of such families will be poor and their children disadvantaged, and that this same law does not apply to other blacks and other females.

Media mystifications should not obfuscate a simple, perceivable fact: Black teenage girls do not create poverty by having children. Quite the contrary, they have babies at such a young age precisely because they are poor—because they do not have the opportunity to acquire an education, because meaningful, well-paying jobs and creative forms of recreation are not accessible to them. They have children at such a young age because safe, effective forms of contraception are not available to them.

In order for the women's movement to meet the challenges of our times, the special problems of racially oppressed women must be given strategic priority. During the early phases of the contemporary women's movement, women's liberationist issues were so narrowly construed that most white women did not grasp the importance of defending Black women from the material and ideological assaults emanating from the government. White women who were then primarily involved in the consciousness-raising process failed to comprehend the relationship between the welfare rights movement and the larger battle for women's emancipation. Neither did they understand the importance of challenging the propagandistic definition of Black women as "emasculating matriarchs" as a struggle in which all women who identified with women's liberation ought to have participated. Today, we can no longer afford to dismiss the racist influences that pervade the women's movement, nor can we continue to succumb to the belief that white women will be unable eternally to grasp the nature of the bonds that link them to their sisters of color.

It is no longer permissible for white women to justify their failure to struggle jointly with women of color by offering such frail excuses as, "We invited them to our meeting, but they just don't seem to be interested in women's issues." During the late 1960s and early 1970s, it was frequently suggested in women's liberation circles that Black, Chicana, and Puerto Rican women were not interested in feminist issues because our awareness of male supremacy was not so advanced as that of the white women who hastened to participate in the antisexist consciousness-raising process. However, their articulation of the problem in these terms reflected their own particular class and racial backgrounds. Women of color—and white working-class women as well—suffered the effects of sexism in different ways than their sisters associated with the women's liberation movement and consequently felt that middle-class white women's issues were largely irrelevant to their own lives.

Economic issues certainly may not seem as central to white middle-class women as to women whose children may become irreparably malnourished if they are unable to find a job—or if they do not receive the welfare subsidies or food stamps so drastically reduced by the Reagan administration. The demand for jobs, the fight against plant shutdowns and against union-busting—these are women's struggles. While these struggles are waged by the labor movement as a whole, women have a special interest in them because we have been most severely hurt—particularly if we happen to be Black or Brown—by the Reagan administration's economic policies.

In order to cultivate a strong women's presence in our movements against racism, women must resolutely defend affirmative action from such callous attacks as those mounted by the Reagan administration. Women and men of all racial and economic backgrounds should remember that the Black liberation movement formulated the strategy of affirmative action for the purpose of furthering the struggle against racism—and that this strategy was subsequently taken up by the women's movement as a means of facilitating the campaign against sexist discrimination. Affirmative action on the job as well as on the campus must not only be defended, but ultimately must be expanded so that it will assist all who currently suffer the discrimination wrought by our racist, sexist, capitalist society and government.

We must not presume that authentic solidarity will automatically flow from the recognition of the simple fact that women of color are the most oppressed human beings in our society. Certainly, white women *should* feel compelled to lend their support to our struggles, but if they do not understand how their causes are substantially advanced by the victories won by women of color, they may inadvertently fall into ideological traps of racism even as they honestly attempt to challenge racist institutions. White women who labor under the illusion that only with their assistance will their "poor Black sisters" rise out of their deprivation—as if we need a Great White Sister Savior—have fallen prey to prevailing racist attitudes, and their activism could well prove more detrimental to our cause than beneficial. White women activists in the battered women's movement must especially beware of racist overtones in their conduct, of which they may be entirely unaware but to which women of color are highly sensitized. Lesbian organizations that are predominantly white should strive to understand the special impact of homophobia on women of color.

For the purpose of clarifying how middle-class white women benefit from the gains of their working-class sisters and sisters of color, try to visualize a simple pyramid, laterally divided according to the race and social class of different groups of women. White women are situated at the top—the bourgeoisie first, under which we place the middle classes and then white working-class women. Located at the very bottom are Black and other racially oppressed women, the vast majority of whom come from working-class backgrounds. Now, when those at the very apex of the pyramid achieve victories for themselves, in all likelihood the status of the other women remains unchanged. This dynamic has proven true in the cases of Sandra Day O'Connor and Jeane Kirkpatrick, who both achieved "firsts" as women in their respective fields. On the other hand, if those at the nadir of the pyramid win victories for themselves, it is virtually inevitable that their progress will push the entire structure upward. The forward movement of women of color almost always initiates progressive change for all women.

Working-class women, and women of color in particular, confront sexist oppression in a way that reflects the real and complex objective interconnections between economic, racial, and sexual oppression. Whereas a white middle-class woman's experience of sexism incorporates a relatively isolated form of this oppression, working-class women's experiences necessarily place sexism in its context of class exploitation—and Black women's experiences further contextualize gender oppression within the realities of racism.

Let us consider one of the most visible issues associated with the women's movement today within the framework of its relationship to the campaign against racism—the attempt to force women to surrender the right to control their bodies. Not only does the "pro-life" movement oppose the constitutional amendment that would guarantee women equal rights, they are pushing for a constitutional ban on abortions that, in effect, would extinguish women's most fundamental—and, ironically, most sacred—right: to determine what comes of and from their own bodies.

In considering the issue of abortion from a progressive vantage point, it is not enough to challenge the conservative factions that would deny women the right to control the biological processes of their bodies. It is also incumbent upon us to carefully examine the strategical and tactical approaches of the movement that strive to defend this basic right of all women. We must first ask why there have been so few women of color in the ranks of the abortion rights movement. And we must go on to consider a related issue: Why, with all the raging controversy surrounding women's right to abortion, has an equally burning question—that of women's right to be free of sterilization abuse—been virtually ignored? As a result of the 1977 Hyde Amendment, which withdrew federal funding for abortions, the likelihood that poor women will be forced to submit to sterilization surgery—knowingly or unknowingly—has increased, in spite of the fact that they may wish to remain capable of bearing children in the future. And how can we explain the fact that while there is presently no federal funding for abortions, over 90 percent of the cost of sterilization surgery is covered by the federal government? Sterilization abuse is sometimes blatant, but usually it occurs in more subtle ways, and its victims are most often Puerto Rican, Chicana, Native American, Black, and poor white women. One advocate of involuntary sterilization, the Nobel Prize–winning physicist William Shockley, has deemed 85 percent of Black Americans "genetically disadvantaged" and thus candidates for sterilization. Such policies must be challenged because we must protect not only women's right to limit the size of their families, but also their right to *expand* their families if and when they so desire.

This is only one example of the many ways in which we must formulate issues so as to ensure that they reflect the experiences of women of color. Certainly, there are many more issues related to the women's movement that, if explored, would demonstrate the extent to which racism often influences the way those issues are framed and publicly articulated. Such racist influences, as long as they pervade the women's movement, will continue to obstruct the building of multiracial organizations and coalitions. Thus, the *eradication* of those influences is a fundamental prerequisite to all endeavors undertaken by the women's movement. This process of exorcising racism from our ranks will determine whether the women's movement will ultimately have a part in bringing about radical changes in the socioeconomic structures of this country.

Chandra Talpade Mohanty

Since at least the publication of her celebrated essay "Under Western Eyes: Feminist Scholarship and Colonial Discourses" (1984, Unit VII, reading 26) in the cultural studies journal *boundary 2*, Chandra Talpade Mohanty has been recognized as a leading scholar-activist in women of color feminism and transnational approaches to cultural studies. She is currently a Dean's Professor of women's studies, sociology, and cultural foundations of education at Syracuse University, and she has published several notable books, including *Feminism Without Borders: Decolonizing Theory, Practicing Solidarity* (2003) and *The Sage Handbook of Identities* (2010, coedited with Margaret Wetherell).

The concept of "home"—homeland, coming home, creating new homes, being pushed out of homes—reverberates throughout the genealogy of intersectional theory and research. Here, Mohanty considers the cultural and spatial politics of "home" through personal narrative and historico-political analyses. "Identity" and "home" are inextricable to Mohanty and are cocreated through complex processes of geography, politics, and life histories. Both identity and home are highly unstable, dynamic constructs in Mohanty's writing, but she does not render them into nothingness. To the contrary, she posits a framework for thinking about identity—in relationship to home—that recognizes both personal, agentic processes (i.e., this is how I choose to identify) *and* structural, institutional dynamics (i.e., this is how others, including the State, identify me). Nonetheless, Mohanty's writing is hardly a tacit synthesis of psychological and sociological approaches to identity that might differentially emphasize the personal over the social and vice versa. Likewise, Mohanty elaborates how traditional (read: White, Western, middle-class) feminist theories of identity failed to account for the heterogeneity of women's lives at least in part because of a pervasive emphasis on the allegedly universal identity category of "woman." Mohanty's version of intersectionality keeps personal and macrolevel social dynamics in productive tension, and her writing cuts across broad colonial genealogies, lived experiences, and political critique, always linking "gender, race, and class in their US manifestations" and transnational elaborations. Her concluding lines here point toward a robust understanding of intersectional oppression that necessitates a kind of social theory that embraces the complexities of the experiences of immigrant women of color without imposing linear, Western narratives and theories upon these lives and identities. Only by rethinking what identity means can we, according to Mohanty, get a better sense of the power, politics, and possibilities of "home."

11. The "Home" Question*

On a TWA flight on my way back to the U.S. from a conference in the Netherlands, the professional white man sitting next to me asks: a) which school do I go to? and b) when do I plan to go home?—all in the same breath. I put on my most professorial demeanor (somewhat hard in crumpled blue jeans and cotton T-shirt—this uniform only works for white male professors, who of course could command authority even in swimwear!) and inform him that I teach at a small liberal arts college in upstate New York, and that I have lived in the U.S. for fifteen years. At this point, my work is in the U.S., not in India. This is no longer entirely true—my work is also with feminists and grassroots activists in India, but he doesn't need to know this. Being "mistaken" for a

---

* Excerpted from C. T. Mohanty, "Defining Genealogies: Feminist Reflections on Being South Asian in North America," in *Our Feet Walk the Sky, Writings by Women of the South Asian Diaspora,* edited by S. Bhatt, P. Kaira, A. Kohli, L. Malkani, and D. Rasiah (San Francisco, CA: Aunt Lute Books, 1993/2008), 351–358. Copyright © 1993, 2008. Reprinted by permission of Aunt Lute Books. www.auntlute.com.

graduate student seems endemic to my existence in this country—few Third World women are granted professional (i.e. adult) and/or permanent (one is always a student!) status in the U.S., even if we exhibit clear characteristics of adulthood, like grey hair and facial lines. He ventures a further question: what do you teach? On hearing "women's studies," he becomes quiet and we spend the next eight hours in polite silence. He has decided that I do not fit into any of his categories, but what can you expect from a *Feminist* (*an Asian* one!) anyway? I feel vindicated and a little superior—even though I know he doesn't really feel "put in his place." Why should he? He has a number of advantages in this situation: white skin, maleness and citizenship privileges. From his enthusiasm about expensive "ethnic food" in Amsterdam, and his J. Crew clothes, I figured class difference (economic or cultural) wasn't exactly an issue in our interaction. We both appeared to have similar social access as "professionals."

I have been asked the "home" question (when are you going home) periodically for fifteen years now. Leaving aside the subtly racist implications of the question (go home—you don't belong), I am still not satisfied with my response. What is home? The place I was born? Where I grew up? Where my parents live? Where I live and work as an adult? Where I locate my community—my people? Who are "my people"? Is home a geographical space, an historical space, an emotional, sensory space? Home is always so crucial to immigrants and migrants—I even write about it in scholarly texts, perhaps to avoid addressing it as an issue that is also very personal. Does two percent of the world's population think about these questions pertaining to home? This is not to imply that the other ninety-eight percent does not think about home. What interests me is the meaning of home for immigrants and migrants. I am convinced that this question—how one understands and defines home—is a profoundly political one.

Since settled notions of territory, community, geography, and history don't work for us, what does it really mean to be "South Asian" in the USA? Obviously I was not South Asian in India—I was Indian. What else could one be but "Indian" at a time when a successful national independence struggle had given birth to a socialist democratic nation-state? This was the beginning of the decolonization of the Third World. Regional geographies (South Asia) appeared less relevant as a mark of identification than citizenship in a postcolonial independent nation on the cusp of economic and political autonomy. However, in North America, identification as South Asian (in addition to Indian, in my case) takes on its own logic. "South Asian" refers to folks of Indian, Pakistani, Sri Lankan, Bangladeshi, Kashmiri, and Burmese origin. Identifying as South Asian rather than Indian adds numbers and hence power within the U.S. State. Besides, regional differences among those from different South Asian countries are often less relevant than the commonalities based on our experiences and histories of immigration, treatment and location in the U.S.

Let me reflect a bit on the way I identify myself, and the way the U.S. State and its institutions categorize me. Perhaps thinking through the various labels will lead me back to the question of home and identity. In 1977, I arrived in the USA on an F1 visa—a student visa. At that time, my definition of myself—a graduate student in Education at the University of Illinois, and the "official" definition of me (a student allowed into the country on an FI visa) obviously coincided. Then I was called a "foreign student," and expected to go "home" (to India—even though my parents were in Nigeria at the time) after getting my Ph.D. Let's face it, this is the assumed trajectory for a number of Indians, especially the post-independence (my) generation, who come to the U.S. for graduate study.

However, this was not to be my trajectory. I quickly discovered that being a foreign student, and a woman at that, meant being either dismissed as irrelevant (the quiet Asian woman stereotype), treated in racist ways (my teachers asked if I understood English and if they should speak slower and louder so that I could keep up—this in spite of my inheritance of the Queen's English and British colonialism!), or celebrated and exoticized (you are so smart! your accent is even better than that of Americans—a little Anglophilia at work here, even though all my Indian colleagues insist we speak English the Indian way!).

The most significant transition I made at that time was the one from "foreign student" to "student of color." Once I was able to "read" my experiences in terms of race, and to read race and racism as it is written into the social and political fabric of the U.S., practices of racism and sexism became the analytic and political lenses through which I was able to anchor myself here. Of course, none of this happened in isolation—friends, colleagues, comrades, classes, books, films, arguments, and dialogues were constitutive of my political education as a woman of color in the U.S.

In the late 1970s and early 1980s feminism was gaining momentum on American campuses—it was in the air, in the classrooms, on the streets. However, what attracted me wasn't feminism as the mainstream media and white Women's Studies departments defined it. Instead, it was a very specific kind of feminism, the feminism of U.S. women of color and Third World women, that spoke to me. In thinking through the links between gender, race and class in their U.S. manifestations, I was for the first time enabled to think through my own gendered, classed post-colonial history. In the early 1980s, reading Audre Lorde, Nawal el Sadaawi, Cherrie Moraga, bell hooks, Gloria Joseph, Paula Gunn Allen, Barbara Smith, Merle Woo and Mitsuye Yamada, among others, generated a sort of recognition that was intangible but very inspiring. A number of actions, decisions and organizing efforts at that time led me to a sense of home and community in relation to women of color in the U.S. Home not as a comfortable, stable, inherited and familiar space, but instead as an imaginative, politically charged space where the familiarity and sense of affection and commitment lay in shared collective analysis of social injustice, as well as a vision of radical transformation. Political solidarity and a sense of family could be melded together imaginatively to create a strategic space I could call "home." Politically, intellectually and emotionally I owe an enormous debt to feminists of color—and especially to the sisters who have sustained me over the years. Even though our attempt to start the Women of Color Institute for Radical Research and Action fell through, the spirit of this vision, and the friendships it generated, still continue to nurture me. A number of us, including Barbara Smith, Papusa Molina, Jacqui Alexander, Gloria Joseph, Mitsuye Yamada, Kesho Scott, and myself, among others met in 1984 to discuss the possibility of such an Institute. The Institute never really happened, but I still hope we will pull it off one day.

For me, engagement as a feminist of color in the U.S. made possible an intellectual and political genealogy of being Indian that was radically challenging as well as profoundly activist. Notions of home and community began to be located within a deeply political space where racialization and gender and class relations and histories became the prism through which I understood, however partially, what it could mean to be South Asian in North America. Interestingly, this recognition also forced me to re-examine the meanings attached to home and community in India.

Rather obstinately, I have refused to give up my Indian passport and have chosen to remain as a resident alien in the U.S. for the last decade or so. Which leads me to reflect on the complicated meanings attached to holding Indian citizenship while making a life for myself in the USA. In India, what does it mean to have a green card—to be an expatriate? What does it mean to visit Bombay every two to four years, and still call it home? Why does speaking in Marathi (my mothertongue) become a measure and confirmation of home? What are the politics of being a part of the majority and the "absent elite" in India, while being a minority and a racialized "other" in the U.S.? And does feminist politics, or advocating feminism, have the same meanings and urgencies in these different geographical and political contexts?

Some of these questions hit me smack in the face during my last visit to India, in December 1992—post-Ayodhya (the infamous destruction of the Babri Masjid in Ayodhya by Hindu fundamentalists on 6 December 1992). In earlier, rather infrequent visits (once every four or five years was all I could afford), my green card designated me as an object of envy, privilege and status within my extended family. Of course the same green card has always been viewed with suspicion by left and feminist friends who (quite understandably) demand evidence of my ongoing commitment to a socialist and democratic India. During this visit, however, with emotions running high within my family, my green card marked me as an outsider who couldn't possibly understand the "Muslim problem" in India. I was made aware of being an "outsider" in two profoundly troubling shouting matches with my uncles, who voiced the most incredibly hostile sentiments against Muslims. Arguing that India was created as a secular state and that democracy had everything to do with equality for all groups (majority and minority) got me nowhere. The very fundamentals of democratic citizenship in India were/are being undermined and redefined as "Hindu."

Although born a Hindu, I have always considered myself a non-practicing one—religion had always felt rather repressive when I was growing up. I enjoyed the rituals but resisted the authoritarian hierarchies of organized Hinduism. However, the Hinduism touted by fundamentalist organizations like the RSS (Rashtriya Swayamsevak Sangh, a paramilitary Hindu fundamentalist organization founded in the 1930s) and the Shiv Sena (a Maharashtrian chauvinist, fundamentalist, fascist political organization that has amassed a significant voice in Bombay politics and government) was one that even I, in my ignorance, recognized as reactionary and distorted. But this discourse was real—hate-filled rhetoric against Muslims appeared to be the mark of a "loyal Hindu." It was unbelievably heart-wrenching to see my hometown become a war zone with whole streets set on fire, and a daily death count to rival any major territorial border war. The smells and textures of Bombay, of home, which had always comforted and nurtured me, were violently disrupted. The scent of fish drying on the lines at the fishing village in Danda was submerged in the smell of burning straw and grass as whole bastis (chawls) were burned to the ground. The very topography, language and relationships that constituted "home" were quietly but surely exploding. What does community mean in this context? December 1992 both clarified as well as complicated for me the meanings attached to being an Indian citizen, a Hindu, an educated woman/feminist, and a permanent resident in the U.S. in ways that I have yet to resolve. After all, it is often moments of crisis that make us pay careful attention to questions of identity. Sharp polarizations force one to make choices (not in order to take sides, but in order to accept responsibility) and to clarify our own analytic, political and emotional topographies.

I learned that combating the rise of Hindu fundamentalism was a necessary ethical imperative for all socialists, feminists and Hindus of conscience. Secularism, if it meant absence of religion, was no longer a viable position. From a feminist perspective, it became clear that the battle for women's minds and hearts was very much center-stage in the Hindu fundamentalist strategy.

Religious fundamentalist constructions of women embody the nexus of morality, sexuality and Nation—a nexus of great importance for feminists. Similar to Christian, Islamic and Jewish fundamentalist discourses, the construction of femininity and masculinity, especially in relation to the idea of the Nation, are central to Hindu fundamentalist rhetoric and mobilizations. Women are not only mobilized in the "service" of the Nation, but they also become the ground on which discourses of morality and nationalism are written. For instance, the RSS mobilizes primarily middle-class women in the name of a family-oriented, Hindu nation, much like the Christian Right does in the U.S. But discourses of morality and nation are also embodied in the normative policing of women's sexuality (witness the surveillance and policing of women's dress in the name of morality by the contemporary Iranian State). Thus, one of the central challenges Indian feminists face at this time is how to rethink the relationship of nationalism and feminism in the context of religious identities. In addition to the fundamentalist mobilizations tearing the country apart, the recent incursions of the International Monetary Fund and the World Bank with their structural adjustment programs which are supposed to "discipline" the Indian economy, are redefining the meaning of post-coloniality and of democracy in India. Categories like gender, race, caste/class are profoundly and visibly unstable at such times of crisis. These categories must thus be analyzed in relation to contemporary reconstructions of womanhood and manhood in a *global* arena increasingly dominated by religious fundamentalist movements, the IMF and the World Bank, and the relentless economic and ideological colonization of much of the world by multinationals based in the U.S., Japan and Europe. My responsibility to combat and organize against the regressive and violent repercussions of Hindu fundamentalist mobilizations in India extends to my life in North America. After all, much of the money which sustains the fundamentalist movement is raised and funnelled through organizations in the U.S.

Let me now circle back to the place I began: the meanings I have come to give to home, community and identity. By exploring the relationship between being a South Asian immigrant in America and an expatriate Indian citizen in India, I have tried, however partially and anecdotally, to clarify the complexities of home and community for this particular feminist of color/South Asian in North America. The genealogy I have created for myself here is partial, interested and deliberate. It is a genealogy that I find emotionally and politically enabling—it is part of the genealogy that underlies my self-identification as an educator involved in a pedagogy of liberation. Of course, my history and experiences are far messier and not at all as linear as this narrative makes them sound. But then the very process of constructing a narrative for oneself—of telling a story—imposes a certain linearity and coherence that is never entirely there. But that is the lesson, perhaps, especially for us immigrants and migrants: i.e., that home, community and identity all fall somewhere between the histories and experiences we inherit and the political choices we make through alliances, solidarities and friendships.

Shuddhabrata Sengupta

Shuddhabrata Sengupta is an artist and writer, and he is a member of the Raqs Media Collective, a New Delhi–based group of media practitioners who work in new media and digital art practice while integrating research, philosophical-historical inquiry, and art. In this essay, published in the premier women's studies journal *Signs*, Sengupta integrates performative writing and social theory to explore "identity" within an intersectional framework that stresses the structural dimensions of oppression. Sengupta appears to reject the typically positive valence of "identity" as something to be celebrated, liberated, emancipated, and so forth, instead constituting *identities* (plural) as mines and identity politics as a kind of war zone. Somewhat paradoxically, Sengupta's larger agenda appears to be coalition-building among diverse oppressed groups whose marginalization is organized by intersecting, marginalized identities. Through accessible prose, Sengupta invites his readers to consider the "algebra" of identity and the cultural politics of oppression and resistance. His attempt to envision a new arithmetic of social justice is as provocative as it is beautiful: "Pardon the military metaphor, but how can we clear the minefield without detonating a tactical nuclear weapon that clears the mines by creating a wasteland? In fact, perhaps the question should be, How can we disarm ourselves?" His thoroughly philosophical and creative approach to doing and thinking intersectionality is epistemologically miles away from Stephanie Shields's psychological approach to intersectional identities, and yet Sengupta's writing provides a robust framework for considering identity as something much more than a series of intersecting variables. Pardon my continuation of the military metaphor, but perhaps our question should be: after we explode identity, what remains?

12. **Identity as a Weapon of Mass Destruction***

Identities can occasionally be weapons of mass destruction (lite). They can be invading armies and besieged cities. They can be maps waiting to be redrawn. Or a people, anticipating measures of "freedom" and "occupation" to come their way from an armored vehicle, or a cluster bomb, or depleted uranium.

To speak of identities in times of war and in the aftermath of war is to be compelled to recognize how certain methods of identification—the ascription of citizenship to a subject of a nation-state, for instance—also automatically

---

* Excerpted from S. Sengupta, "I/Me/Mine: Intersectional Identities as Negotiated Minefields." *Signs: The Journal of Women in Culture and Society* 31 (2006): 629–39.

confers on the being so described partisanship vis-à-vis one or the other forces engaged in the battle. The same could be said of religious or ethnic identity, or color, and in some cases of gender, and the battlefields that lie on the terrain within and between these categories. Let me sketch a few scenarios for you, to make all my dilemmas when talking about identities explicit.

Are you the internationally recognized and fêted artist or academic woman of color who considers herself to be more oppressed than the working-class Caucasian woman in prison—let's say a blonde Bosnian Muslim immigrant sex worker who happens to have charges of manslaughter against her for killing her abusive Jamaican pimp? Here, the index of oppression is melanin, not life.

Are you a Caucasian, which translates as "black" in Russia?

Or are you the African American man in prison who considers himself to be less oppressed, because he is a man, than the African American woman on the street, whom he is happy to call a "ho"?

Are you the African American GI in Iraq, sucked into a war by the poverty draft at home and face to face with the anger of a subject population that considers you to be the brutal enforcer of an occupying army that possesses the greatest number of weapons of mass destruction on earth? In combat fatigues, and under camouflage striping, white shades into dark, and dark can pale to white.

Are you the white working-class woman, perhaps a single mother, who is herself a victim of insidious sexism within the military and within working-class subcultures, who nevertheless becomes a willing enforcer of the apparatus of humiliation in the Abu Ghraib prison?

Are you the South Asian illegal alien in New York who washes dishes in a restaurant, is hoping to be a taxi driver, and really wishes he could be a Chinese grocer on the make?

Are you the recently arrived, already battered, non-English-speaking Indian or Pakistani "passport bride" caught between her aggressive husband, notions of community honor, shame, and the (amended) marriage fraud provisions of the 1952 Immigration and Naturalization Act of the United States?

Are you the Palestinian teenager throwing rocks at an Israeli military bulldozer who wishes he were a black rap artist from the Bronx with a Jewish record producer?

Are you the Iraqi woman, relieved that Saddam Hussein is no more, angry about U.S. bombs landing in her neighborhood, worried about the calls for the veil that emanate from Shiite clerics asserting their long oppressed identities by demanding a Shiite Islamic state in Iraq, and equally worried about having been "liberated" from a dictator only to be delivered as a subject to a convicted fraudster, all in the name of her freedom, her honor, and her dignity as an Iraqi?

Are you the rich Indian racist who thinks that white women were made white in order for him to harass them on the streets of New Delhi? Are you the

British exchange student of Nigerian origin in an Indian city who can't find a room to rent because of her color and who listens patiently to stories about how Indians suffer racism in the city where she grew up?

Are you one of the 15 million Bangladeshi illegal immigrants whom the Indian government now plans to identify and deport? Have you given thought to how you might change your accent, or your name, or adjust a few facts in your biography, and tell your children a few stories so that they don't let slip that you walked across the border when the police, accompanied by ethnographers, come knocking on your shack in New Delhi for an interview? Can you exchange one biography of oppression for another that might be more suitable for survival under the present circumstances?

Are you the anti-Semitic black Muslim descendent of slaves? Are you the racist Jewish granddaughter of concentration camp survivors? Are you the white supremacist descendent of refugees from the potato famine in Ireland? Are you the Hindu fundamentalist who has fantasies of raping Muslim women and who will defend the honor of his sister with an automatic weapon? Are you the Kashmiri Muslim woman suicide bomber with a sharp memory of being raped by an Indian army major when you were a teenager?

Is what you call your identity a weapon, a shield, a fortress, a battering ram, an unexploded land mine? The trouble with the deployment of identities as means of offense or defense is that, given a change in the equations of violence in any instance, which may have to do with anything from local politics to broader geopolitical crosscurrents, the victim very quickly becomes the oppressor. And so the idealist builder of Zion becomes a tyrant. Yesterday's Kurdish *peshmarga* (guerrilla fighter), forgotten by the world, becomes today's policeman for an occupying power because of the way the cartographic dice happen to be loaded at present. The players in the game may change; the Kurd may well go back up the mountain, fleeing like he had to the last time Saddam Hussein gassed him with helicopters that were bought with the help of today's "liberators."

The history of the twentieth century bears witness to the fact that the project of national liberation has inevitably turned the dream of freedom into the nightmare of refugee and prison camps and exile. The victims have changed; the rules haven't. And the assertion of the identity of an oppressed people becomes the excuse for silencing any question about the networks of power and privilege within the community.

It is only when we examine identities as fields of intersection and therefore always of contestation that we can imagine possibilities other than the binaries of "Are you with the besieged dictator or are you with the invading army?" It is possible to be neither. Or in the case of another example, "Are you critical of patriarchy within the African American community and of racism in the

United States?" or "Can you be critical of patriarchy in the minority Muslim community in India and be critical at the same time of the anti-Muslim prejudices of Hindu fundamentalists?" It is possible to be both. And can you break your silences about being neither, in the first instance, and about being both in the latter two instances? Or will you choose to voice one opposition and be silent about another because of fears of betrayal, of letting who you are in one sense be held against who you are in another? Being neither in the first instance and being both in the second are concomitant to our admitting to our identities as force fields of different kinds of motivations, of different and sometimes conflicting intersections, of varied yet interlinked trajectories and histories of power and powerlessness.

Identities are minefields, and the mines have been lain by armies that have forgotten the map. The arsenal is familiar; it's just that we don't know which mine (as in "weapon" and as in "first-person possessive singular personal pronoun") will claim which part of me. I negotiate them at my peril, never very sure about what I am stepping on and which aspect of my beings will blow up in my face or what will injure whom.

You may well ask if I am arguing for some form of faded universalism, some cheap bauble left over from the European Enlightenment project, which, as any self-respecting scholar of postmodernism will tell us, is only an index of my discursive power, my deracination, and my postcolonial self-hatred as a non-European man. A universalism that, we already know, is actually the privileged view of the Eurocentric white Judeo-Christian male heterosexual Hegemon who pretends that everything other than what he holds dear is an identity—blackness, femaleness, queerness, or even *Hindutva* and *Islamiyat*—that only needs to be jettisoned for some kind of pale Kantian universal harmony and peace to descend upon us. There is a critique of identity politics that comes quite close to this caricature, and we are familiar with its shades, but I would argue that to say that all critiques of identity politics are something akin to this is a bit in the "Are you with the besieged dictator or with the invading army?" league as an argument.

Pardon the military metaphor, but how can we clear the minefield without detonating a tactical nuclear weapon that clears the mines by creating a wasteland? In fact, perhaps the question should be, How can we disarm ourselves?

My intent is to examine the locus of power, and I am very well aware of the enormous hegemonic power of the misogyny, heterosexism, whiteness, and Eurocentrism at the foundations of the world we live in today We cannot pretend that they do not exist.

But what if we vacate the hollow assumptions of each of these particular forms of violence, not because of who dominates whom but because we find the fact of domination itself repugnant? A world in which people of color oppressed or enslaved others, or where women battered men, or where women who desired men were discriminated against would be no better than the one we have today. To even bring up such a thought seems ridiculous, but it seems ridiculous because it bases itself on falsely essentialist categories. Men do not oppress women because they are men; they do so because one of the forms in which oppression gets articulated happens to be patriarchy, which in turn has relationships with the ways in which forms of control over sexual or reproductive agency are tied to patterns of control over scarce resources. The factors that impel patriarchy are not unrelated to the factors that control other forms of agency in other resource and energy allocation and distribution scenarios in the material world; these can be and are inflected with the tropes of ethnicity, race, caste, and the one that we most often forget to mention these days—class.

It is no wonder, then, that there need not be any distinction between the way in which domination is deployed within groups and the way it may be deployed across groups. Thus, if the power of the plantation owner over the indentured laborer within the arena of formal production produces one set of equations according to who compels whom to do what, then the power of the indentured worker over his wife in the home produces another set of equations that mirrors the first, again in terms of who compels whom to do what. Further down the line, the internalization of what it is to be a black woman, a notion generated over generations of servitude, may provoke some South Asian women to oppress other South Asian women by saying that they are crossing the line of what is acceptable for South Asian women. So a South Asian woman who blows a whistle about violence within her family or is sexually assertive may be shamed by other South Asian women, and men, for bringing dishonor to her community and to her family name.

Once again, we find an equation about who can compel whom to do or not do something. The arithmetic may be different, but the algebra is the same. Once we understand that the underlying mathematics is similar, we also understand that the equation stands no matter what the variables are. So you can replay the scenarios that I sketched out earlier to see exactly which directions power flows in. It flows from black to white, from white to black, from man to man, from woman to woman, from woman to man, and man to woman, depending on who in each instance can call the shots.

An understanding of the networked nature of the contemporary world and of the history of this world will help us understand that there are crosscutting histories of oppression and violence, that no one is innocent, and that all of us are implicated somewhere in our histories or in the histories of our ancestors as victims and as aggressors.

Can we then imagine a nonspecific, tentative universalism that arises when we see the impossibility of vacating specific identity constructs in terms of any privileged moral or epistemic valence? I think we can. The negation of identities is simultaneously the affirmation of what lies between the classificatory categories. It is the cipher, the nought, if you like, which, by denying itself a substance, is nevertheless able to be the great multiplier and divider. It is what makes the hyphenation in the term *African-American-Working-Woman* respond to the hyphenation in the term *Unemployed-Argentinian-Shadow-Working-Woman* and at the same time see itself in contrast to the Teflon-coated figure of Condoleezza Rice.

A recognition of the resonances of the experiences of oppression in each instance is a function of our desire to connect with or to be curious about others and to try to see how those who might appear to share our color or our sex can still speak to us in the language of mastery. This, too, is a function of our ability to be skeptical about familiar assumptions, as in, "How come she looks like me and yet wields so much power over my destiny that she can send my son to war in a way that I thought only people who did not look like me could do?" (This is the hypothetical African American female janitor thinking about the very real Condoleezza Rice.)

This recognition is also an attempt to understand how, in a networked world, each of our individual circumstances connects to form larger patterns of oppression and liberty. Too often when we agonize over our identities, our sufferings preclude an understanding of the predicaments of others, and, too often, this blinds us to potential solidarities and to an attempt to insert some new terms in the algebra of our world.

Stephanie Shields

In this introduction to a special issue of *Sex Roles* on intersectionality, Penn State University social psychologist of gender and emotions Stephanie Shields begins to tackle the enormous task of theorizing intersectionality from a psychological perspective. Note that "theorizing" to psychologists (and indeed most traditionally trained social scientists) is an empirical process, not necessarily an imaginative or "creative" practice as in the humanities. Theory in psychology is built from the "ground up," insomuch as claims to how things work psychologically are based on systematically accumulated empirical evidence. Of course, as Donna Haraway (reading 6) and others have already shown in this volume, the process of theory-building is hardly a value-neutral one, and the scientific method is no guarantee of accuracy or truthfulness. Nonetheless, Shields attempts to cogently articulate intersectional approaches to gender in psychology by reviewing the extant literature that has slowly but surely pushed some domains of psychology toward an intersectional turn. As of 2008, there was relatively little attention to intersectionality in psychology broadly speaking, and Shields does some thinking here about why that might be and why it is so critical for feminist psychologists in particular to challenge themselves to learn and innovate intersectional perspectives (i.e., methodologies and methods). Shields does much in this short piece, but two things are of particular import to the intersectional discourse on identity. First, she begins by positing a scientifically derived definition of identity that may strike some readers as thoroughly reductive; nevertheless, I caution readers to take Shields on her own terms and to consider the value of psychological perspectives on the study of identity. As Shields explains, antiracist, feminist psychologists face tremendous pushback from the "center" of the discipline, and their continued resistance of masculinist, racist psychology has produced robust theory and methods despite persistent disciplinary marginalization and the risk of total professional isolation. Second, Shields's intersectionality here is anchored in gender and the study thereof. What are the consequences of such a decision, and how might this reflect an implicit bias of the extant literature in feminist psychology? Where, accordingly, might Shields's "activist scientists" need to go when we move "beyond one's own research comfort zone"?

13. "It's Not Psychology": Gender, Intersectionality, and Activist Science[*]

Most important, by *identity* I mean social categories in which an individual claims membership as well as the personal meaning associated with those categories (Ashmore et al. 2004). Identity in psychological terms relates to awareness of self, self-image, self-reflection, and self-esteem. In contemporary American society, identity is emphasized as a quality that enables the expression of the individual's authentic sense of self. The specific definition of *intersectionality* varies by research context, but a consistent thread across definitions is that social identities which serve as organizing features of social relations, mutually constitute, reinforce, and naturalize one another. By *mutually constitute* I mean that one category of identity, such as gender, takes its meaning as a category in relation to another category. By *reinforce* I mean that the formation and maintenance of identity categories is a dynamic process in which the individual herself or himself is actively engaged. We are not passive "recipients" of an identity position, but "practice" each aspect of identity as informed by

* Excerpted from S. Shields, "Gender: An Intersectionality Perspective." *Sex Roles* 59 (2008): 301–11. Reprinted with permission from Springer Science+Business Media B.V.

other identities we claim. By *naturalize* I mean that identities in one category come to be seen as self-evident or "basic" through the lens of another category. For example, in the contemporary U.S., racial categories are construed as containing two genders. This suggests that gender categories are always and everywhere similarly understood and employed, thus "natural" and without other possibilities (e.g., multiple genders; "temporary" gender categories). To this definition we might add the acknowledgment that these meanings are historically contingent.

It is also widely agreed that intersections create both oppression and opportunity (Baca Zinn and Thornton Dill 1996). In other words, being on the advantaged side offers more than avoidance of disadvantage or oppression by actually opening up access to rewards, status, and opportunities unavailable to other intersections. Furthermore, an intersectional position may be disadvantaged relative to one group, but advantaged relative to another. The White lesbian may be disadvantaged because of divergence from the heterosexual norm and standard, but relative to other lesbians she enjoys racial privilege. Last and not least, identities instantiate social stratification. That is, identity, such as gender or social class, may be experienced as a feature of individual selves, but it also reflects the operation of power relations among groups that comprise that identity category.

Some social sciences have been more open to the transformative effects of an intersectionality perspective than others. The intersectionality perspective has had more impact in academic specializations already concerned with questions of power relations between groups. Disciplines/specializations whose conventional methodologies embrace multidimensionality and the capacity to represent complex and dynamic relationships among variables are more open to the intersectionality perspective. Psychology, which as a discipline and as a subject matter *should* be fundamentally concerned with intersections of identity, has lagged behind. There are, however, some signs of forward momentum. There is growing interest in employing the intersectionality perspective to transform and advance empirically based research in psychology and allied disciplines, especially through using conventional empirical strategies in innovative ways to investigate intersectionality (e.g., Settles 2006).

The theoretical foundation for intersectionality grew from study of the production and reproduction of inequalities, dominance, and oppression. The evolution of intersectionality as a theoretical framework has been traced to Black feminist responses to the limitations of the accumulated disadvantage model (e.g., Mullings 1997; Nakano Glenn 1999) and the recognition that the intersections of gender with other dimensions of social identity are the starting point of theory (Crenshaw 1994/2005). A fundamental assumption in every influential theoretical formulation of intersectionality is that intersectional identities are defined in relation to one another. That is, intersectional identities, as Spelman (1988) famously observed, are not a "pop bead metaphysics," that is, not a set of discrete identities like beads on a string, but, rather, they are relationally defined and emergent (e.g., Anthias and Yuval-Davis 1983; Collins 1990). In contrast to models that suggest for each minority status there is a simple accumulation of disadvantage, such that the Black woman is doubly disadvantaged compared to the Black man, the intersectionality framework emphasizes the qualitative differences among different intersectional positions.

In sum, the construct of intersectionality has assumed a significant position in thinking about gender. As the foundation for theory it promised a more accurate and tractable way of dealing with two issues. First, it promised a solution, or at least a language for the glaring fact that it is impossible to talk about gender without considering other dimensions of social structure/social identity that play a formative role in gender's operation and meaning. In the U.S., the most obvious, pervasive, and seemingly unalterable are race and social class. Second, intersectionality seemed a generally applicable descriptive solution to the multiplying features that create and define social identities. It is not race-class-gender, but also age, ableness, sexual orientation, to name the most salient.

The intellectual and moral imperatives of intersectionality notwithstanding, the prevailing approach to understanding individuals in the context of groups is to focus on comparison of group differences and similarities. The naturalization of gender categories has fostered an approach to gender research in psychology in which the goal is to identify gender differences (and occasionally, similarities). Within this gender-as-difference framework, the status of gender as a category remains outside the spotlight. The question "In what ways do women and men differ?" does not seem that it will ever go away. Simplistic catalogs of difference resist theory's demonstration that focus on the descriptions of difference and similarity do not aid us in understanding when and how gender operates as a system of oppression or as an aspect of identity.

We have long known that "difference" is a seductive oversimplification. Gender-as-difference predominates in lay and popular culture discourse on gender and thereby demands its attention and inclusion in scientific and scholarly discourse. The end result is further reification of gender-as-difference which, in turn, endows it with the status of explanation (difference-as-explanation). One need look no further than recent neuroscience publications on gender differences in fMRI responses for examples of this process. Difference-as-explanation, in turn, reaffirms the legitimacy of gender stereotypes. In the case of racial categories, a similar misattribution to the category occurs. For example, Helms et al. (2005) point out that the combination of imprecise definition of racial categories with their easy quantification leads researchers to attribute more meaning to race categories than is merited.

Moving from the description of difference/similarity to explanation of processes is a challenge for most researchers. In adopting an intersectionality perspective, the question of how to approach empirical work without falling back into the *status quo* approach of testing for difference takes enormous effort. After all, conventional quantitative research designs and statistical analyses are constructed to test for differences between groups. It is neither an automatic nor easy step to go from *acknowledging* linkages among social identities to *explaining* those linkages or the processes through which intersecting identities define and shape one another.

It's Not Psychology

The simplest and least tenable way that intersectionality has been dealt with is to define it as outside disciplinary boundaries. Intersectionality is excluded by defining questions of interlinking identities as sociological, as being about social stratification rather than the psychology of individual experience.

This "solution" is not taken defensively, but as a kind of naive circling of the disciplinary wagons. If we say "yes, but that's not psychology" it is unnecessary to recognize that in defining the subject population in one way, "college students," for example, that it might make a difference who those college students are. In some ways, psychology's solution is to add categories of "special" subject populations. Early on, the solution was to add women to the sample and leave race unspecified—why? Because the college student population from which most research participants were drawn was predominantly White. When specific populations are studied, they are identified as nonnormative (Reid 1993).

Not Enough Information

The social/developmental/personality/clinical psychologist who does see the need to acknowledge intersectionality has found little theory or empirical work within psychology to serve as a guide or resource. So the second strategy is to defer the question to a future day because relevant data/theory does not yet exist. I know I am not alone among feminist psychologists who have relied on inserting a self-excusing paragraph that simultaneously acknowledges the central significance of intersectionality and absolves oneself of responsibility for attempting to incorporate it into the work. The paragraph typically goes something like this:

> In this book I limit my discussion to the contemporary U.S., a westernized post-industrial society. There are important limitations in how I can represent "contemporary westernized post-industrial society." . . . My goal is to move the discussion about gender and emotion beyond

the discussion of differences, not only to advance theory on gender and emotion, but also to set the stage for a more sophisticated discussion of the intersections of gender and emotion with racial ethnicity, historical period, culture, and social class. That said, I can be only partially successful; real progress would require placing these variables at the center, not the periphery, of the inquiry. (Shields 2002, p. 25)

I'm particularly discomfited by the passage's tone of apology loaded with self-justification because I wrote it; it is taken from my book on gender and the social meaning of emotion! Maybe apologies were still acceptable at the turn of the 21st Century, but now, nearly 10 years along, the bar should be set higher.

Knapp (2005) takes us to task for settling for mention of race-class-gender as opposed to actually using it. Mentioning, she notes, offers the dual message of being well-informed and politically correct. Yet, mentioning alone leaves the work of actually incorporating intersectionality into one's work to others (or "others," in Knapp's terms). The end result is to mention the newer view of difference, but to continue to work in the same way as always, not to change a thing about how difference is theorized or studied. The introduction of intersectionality, Knapp argues, changes all of that—now the gaps are revealed and one cannot successfully continue in old ways simply by acknowledgement in passing.

A Perspective in Search of a Method

A third strategy is to view intersectionality in limited terms, such as a 2x2 study of sexual orientation and gender. Within the analysis of variance framework we can get a picture of how one variable (gender, for example) influences and is influenced by the effects of another variable, such as age or social class. The problem is that it does not go far enough and we settle for identification of points of mutual effect without appreciation of the dependence of one category's very definition on the other and vice versa. In psychological research, intersectionality often simply takes the form of predicted interactions in additive-model analysis of variance designs. That is, for example, the gender comparison becomes the gender X race (or sexual orientation or cross-national cultural comparison), which requires the assumption that gender and race are independent of one another. At the level of the category, yes, the assumption of independence is warranted. At the political, interpersonal, and experiential levels, however, it is not. The limits of a highly constrained approach as an end in itself become more apparent when we move beyond basic demographic categories. For example, intersections with immigrant status are complicated by the ways in which the network of related identity categories (e.g., legal/illegal, culture of origin) define it.

The elephant in the room, of course, is the question of the match between research methods and research goals. Can a quantitative approach ever work? And what would that look like that would not simultaneously oversimplify or disaggregate the very relational, emergent properties of identity that intersectionality theory captures? Audre Lorde famously asserted that you cannot dismantle the master's house with the master's tools, which has spurred ongoing debate, not only in psychology (e.g., Unger 1983; Riger 2000), but in all areas of the social and behavioral sciences that have a strong tradition of relying on quantitative methods (e.g., McCall 2005; Walker 2003).

In general, feminist theory that is the most fully developed theoretical orientation to intersectionality has a more comfortable relation to qualitative than quantitative work, particularly when that quantitative work is grounded in experimental method and hypothesis testing. That said, in psychology, at least, it is difficult for qualitative work to find entry into the top "mainstream" journals which, for better or worse, are the benchmarks of quality required for professional advancement. Only a very small proportion of qualitative research is published in psychology journals, a fact that led Marchel and Owens (2007) only half facetiously to title their article "Qualitative Research in Psychology: Could William James Get a Job?"

There is clearly no one-size-fits-all methodological solution to incorporating an intersectionality perspective. A both/and strategy both pragmatically and conceptually seems the best way forward (Collins 1998; Risman 2004). The both/and strategy entails both comparing individual identities to each other as well as considering intersections and their emergent properties. An intersectionality perspective requires that identity categories be studied in relation to one other—the facts of intersectionality at the individual, interpersonal, and structural level compel us to. At the same time, however, we must be mindful of the specific historical and contextual features of individual identity categories.

Naomi Weisstein is a psychologist whose work on the basic processes of visual perception is highly regarded by peer scientists. Among feminists, however, she is far better known for her influential paper, first delivered in 1968, which jump-started contemporary feminist psychology. "Kinder, Küche, Kirche, The Fantasy Life of the Male Psychologist" (Weisstein 1968) was an exposé of experimental psychology's reliance on androcentric theory and white, male college student research participants to map the "facts" of human behavior. Her paper was a powerful call to change fundamentally the questions that academic psychology identified as important. Nearly 25 years later she lamented that the wave of feminist research of the 1970s had been tamed (Weisstein 1993). Adopting an unreformed feminist empiricist position she argued for the revival of feminist activist science (Shields 1998). Asserting that good scientific method *is* the way forward, she urged a "return to an activist, challenging, badass feminist psychology" (1993, p. 244). Intersectionality is an urgent issue because it is critical to the effective, activist science that feminist psychology should be.

The goal of activist science itself is not to create policy, but to inform it. Research undertaken from an intersectionality perspective does originate from a point of view which includes an agenda for positive social change, but the agenda requires data to support it. This approach reflects a belief that science can be beneficial to society and that it is our obligation to study scientifically those problems and issues that bear on real people's lived experience. Intersectionality has consequences for how social issues are construed and the construction of systematic explanation, including empirical strategies with a foundation in scientific method. Bograd (1999), for example, describes how focusing on gender alone as the central issue in domestic violence hindered theory development and empirical research. In another vein, Burman (2005) shows how prevailing research approaches to cultural psychology, such as multiculturality, each in their own way marginalize or erase gender.

Intersectionality is urgent because it gets us as researchers to go beyond the individually informed perspective that we each inevitably bring to our scholarship and science. Walker (2003) points out that "the attempt to understand intersectionality is, in fact, an effort to see things from the worldview of others and not simply from our own unique standpoints" (p. 991). The intersectionality perspective is thus an invitation to move beyond one's own research comfort zone.

The intersectionality perspective is especially relevant to enhancing those research methods that seem to be least amenable to adopting it. Laboratory experiment and large-scale survey research, as removed as they are from tapping the subjectivity of participants, can benefit from ways to formulate research questions that allow for and can reveal the responses of individuals as a reflection of the identities that form them. If one adopts an intersectional perspective, one will look at research problems from that perspective and not be satisfied until some sort of research strategy is developed that enables one to answer the question. That's what scientists do.

SPACE, PLACE, COMMUNITIES, AND GEOGRAPHIES

The Cartographic Imagination
Patrick R. Grzanka

Oppression has not only a when, but a where.

As was stressed in Unit I on the law, history is an essential tool for intersectional analysis, because history facilitates the tracing of how systems of oppression have formed, shifted, and transformed across time. But the work of situating and specifying social phenomena includes another dimension that is sometimes overlooked, particularly in the social sciences, in the interest of describing generalizable phenomena: place. In survey research, for example, one finds that limited samples collected in particular states come to represent "American attitudes." Comparative analyses of international differences in economy, religion, politics, and education become "the United States" and "everyone else." And terms such as "popular" are applied to cultural production that may have limited import outside of a specific community or region. Even critical attempts to map the distribution of poverty and to highlight inequality across regions may deny the role that particular environments play in engendering privilege and disadvantage. This flattening of spatial dynamics denies the paramount function of the politics of place and space in the production of social life and, therefore, inequality. Namely, this includes the ways in which the particulars of landscapes and geographies create sites of oppression and activism that are inextricable from racial, class, gender, and sexual dynamics. Consider, for example, how important space and place are to the following major historical events. Can we even imagine divorcing these recent events and social problems from their locations?

- The terrorist attacks of September 11, 2001
- Hurricane Katrina
- The 2013 bombing of the Boston Marathon
- The home foreclosure epidemic of the Great Recession
- The first inauguration of Barack Obama
- The attempted assassination of US Congresswoman Gabrielle Giffords
- The ouster of Egyptian President Hosni Mubarak

The New York City streetscape covered in dust and debris, the thousands of people crammed into Tahrir Square, and the rows of abandoned tract homes across decaying American suburban neighborhoods are the cultural landscapes that give meaning to the phrases 9/11, Arab Spring, and subprime mortgage crisis. Likewise, consider the centrality of space in the ordinary occurrences that shape everyday life, such as the settings in which people worship, eat, socialize, and learn. Space and place are integral to how social interactions and behaviors are encouraged and discouraged, sanctioned and condoned, celebrated or castigated, and the meanings and norms attached to spaces help to signal who "belongs" in certain places, and who does not. An exclusive country club, for example, demands a different performance of social class, gender, and race than a corner dive bar where those same behaviors that previously signaled sophistication and refinement may be interpreted as elitism or snobbery (c.f., Sherwood 2010).

In intersectionality theory and research, space and place can be conceptualized and treated in multiple ways that can be grouped into three broad categories: 1) space/place may be figured as another dimension of difference, like race, class, and gender, through which inequality is organized; 2) space/place is the context or setting in which intersectional oppression happens, so it functions analytically as a framing device for the object of study or situation of inquiry and is incorporated into the analysis like other social details, such as demographics; or 3) space/place becomes a kind of method or tool, like history or visual studies, by which to investigate intersectional dynamics. The readings in this unit contain elements of all three approaches, and treat space and place differently, but the politics and social dimensions of space are the locus of analysis throughout.

It is not easy to settle on a strict definition of space and place, and various geographers and sociologists have debated over proper uses of both terms; like most academic debates, this one appears to have no end (see Agnew 2011 and Gieryn 2000 for an overview). Here, we can consider both space and place as concepts meant to capture the meanings given to environments, from the most mundane of locations (e.g., a kitchen) to the grandest and large-scale (e.g., a country). If location denotes a *there* in the strictest geometric sense, then space and place can be thought of as wholly social constructs. Space is the social product of human interactions with the built and natural environment, as well as among each other. In social science disciplines such as anthropology, sociology, and especially geography, the study of space may be driven by research questions such as: "How do people negotiate this space (e.g., an airport, coffee shop, nightclub, sporting venue, hospital, prison, etc.)?" "Why are people leaving or coming to this place?" as in studies of gentrification, housing booms, economic crises, or regional disinvestment. "How is this space being re-created and used in unexpected ways?" may be asked in studies of protest activities (e.g., Arab Spring, Occupy Wall Street), public art, abandoned buildings, and "urban renewal." "How is community being created here, and what are the boundaries of that community?" is often the kind of question at the heart of inquiry into neighborhood formation and transformation, coalition-building within oppressive institutions (e.g., minority groups in historically and predominantly White organizations, prisons) and studies of cyberspace, including online gaming, support groups, and dating, that transcend traditional, corporeal understandings of place. All of these are questions about location(s), but the meanings locations possess are created in social interaction and therefore come to be something more than just a geographic locale, a dot on a map: they become space.

Intersectionality must and has taken spatial dynamics seriously for many reasons, not the least of which is that space is a resource that is created and distributed unevenly across populations. Geography as a discipline has, not unlike many traditional social sciences, been slow to integrate intersectionality widely, but feminist geographers have increasingly recognized the theoretical and pragmatic utility of intersectionality. In a much-cited article, geographer Gill Valentine (2007, 91) reflects that "through rigorous empirical work, [intersectionality] offers an important potential tool for geography to understand the intimate connections between the production of space and the systematic production of power, thereby increasing its effectiveness to develop and employ its critical insights within and beyond the academy." Reflecting back on the lack of sustained attention to space in certain domains of feminist social science, she concludes that "an appreciation of intersectionality as spatially constituted and experienced offers feminists a way of addressing the tension between the fluidity and multiplicity of individual identities and the continued importance and necessity of group politics" (19). To Valentine, intersectionality is social phenomena *constituted* by spatiality, and thinking spatially affords an access point through which to investigate and complicate research and activism about group identities and politics. Valentine reminds us that contests over power not only happen *in* space, but *over* space—who can use it, who can have it, who has rights to it, who is changing it. For example, Nan Alamilla Boyd's

(2008, reading 16) scholarship explores how cities, regions, and countries market themselves to gay tourists who either possess or are imagined to possess disposable income and purchasing power. Because class is a highly racialized and gendered marker of difference, the marketing of cities as "gay friendly" or as "gay destinations" means that cities project images of themselves onto imagined consumers who are racialized, gendered, and sexualized in particular ways. The ideal targets of the gay tourism market become, then, an upper-middle-class White gay-identified man seeking potential (sex) partnership or a couple who might get married, honeymoon, or vacation in a place that reflects and celebrates their identity. Tourism—the movement of bodies through space for leisure and recreation—is fashioned by race, gender, sexuality, and class, according to Boyd.

Since at least the development of the urban sociology approach of the Chicago School, led by founder Robert Park in the early twentieth century, ethnographers have targeted the city itself as an object of study. What critical intersectional studies of the city do—and what earlier urban sociologists generally did not—is a) map out the intersecting patterns of inequality that produce urban spaces, and b) identify and critique the institutions and systems that catalyze and buttress these inequalities. The hallmark of the intersectional approach to urban studies, beyond its critical activist orientation, is the incorporation of multiple axes of inequality. For example, Arlene Dávila, a cultural anthropologist and pioneer of intersectional analyses of cities, has written extensively on the complex social and economic forces driving the development of transformation of urban spaces, especially Latino neighborhoods. In *Barrio Dreams* (2004), she explores how "neoliberal" policies and corporate agendas have reshaped Spanish Harlem in New York City, promising opportunities for upward socioeconomic mobility for some while contradictorily forcing out long-time neighborhood residents. Her work has been influential for how she characterizes the paradoxes of neoliberalism (which is explored in greater depth in Unit VIII) as they affect social environments: finite economic opportunity amid fierce, unregulated competition; marketing of racial and ethnic diversity concurrent with the absence of actual demographic multiculturalism; and the market forces that value the appearance of difference while simultaneously encouraging racial and ethnic homogeneity. Similarly, sociologist Mary Pattillo's (1999, 2008) scholarship on race, class, and the city examines how processes that are often rhetorically framed as "revitalization" or "renewal" have the intended consequence of transforming the social, as well as the physical, terrain of neighborhoods. In *Black on the Block* (2007, reading 17), she explains the stakes of North Kenwood-Oakland's "rebirth" in Chicago, in which the relative racial homogeneity of the neighborhood hardly guarantees the absence of class conflict. Dávila and Pattillo's work illustrate how spatial phenomena both work through and are productive of racial and ethnic formations, such as the Black middle-class of North Kenwood-Oakland and the largest minority group in New York City (i.e., Latinos), as well as class stratifications that cut across racial groups but are never not racialized.

Like Dávila, Christina Hanhardt has also studied New York City, but she focuses on the other end of town and foregrounds a different configuration of intersectional identities. Her work (2008, 2013) explores the sexual, racial, and class politics of gay neighborhoods in New York (e.g., Chelsea) and San Francisco (e.g., the Castro District), where neighborhood patrols and calls for "safe streets" were choreographed along highly unequal dimensions of race, sexuality, class, *and* gender, and ultimately remapped neighborhoods along these registers. As Hanhardt (2008) elaborates:

> The debates in Greenwich Village show the contradictions of postwar urban politics, in which neighborhood activists cast racial, sexual, and gender identities, as well as economic diversity, as "liabilities" of a community best known for its gay populations and bohemianism. Moreover, in residents', gay activists', and developers' shared investment in the assessment of *risk*, the debates show the discursive construction of antigay violence as part of the history of real estate speculation fueling gentrification and gay enclave formation. Here violence is imagined as the risk of gay visibility—the dominant trope of mainstream LGBT politics since the 1970s. Yet in naming the solution to be the settling of gay identity in place, LGBT politics and urban developers invest in the race and class stratification of postwar urban space. (64)

Hanhardt's work contributes to a robust body of scholarship on the sexual and racial politics of space, here exemplified by Charles Nero's (2005) work on a "gay ghetto" in New Orleans (reading 15). Along with Judith Halberstam (2005), Karen Tongson (2011), Mary Gray (2009) and others (e.g., Delaney 1999; Sloop 2004), Hanhardt is crafting an archive of spatial politics that offers insight into how race, class, gender, and sexuality are figurative and material dividing lines that create *and* carve up space.

Intersectionality's potential insights are hardly limited to urban studies, and extend to other spaces and into other ways of thinking about space and place. Historic preservation and architecture have different concerns and methods than sociology or anthropology, but work in these domains has likewise considered the intersectional dynamics of built environments (e.g., Nieves 2008; Nieves and Alexander 2008). Cultural geographer Ruth Wilson Gilmore (2007), whose work is featured in Unit VIII (reading 32), centers her analysis on the prison industrial complex as a site whose social cartography is dependent upon intersecting oppressions. Pamela Perry (2002) takes up two high schools in two different neighborhoods to explore how the literal halls of education engender symbolic fences among White youth from different social classes. In disability studies, the built environment is theorized as social architecture that produces bodily differences and embodied inequalities (e.g., Thomson 1997; see also Hirschmann 2012, Unit IX, reading 38). Furthermore, the well-tread concept of "home" has been a powerful metaphor in intersectional scholarship that seeks to theorize, imagine, and create new spaces of empowerment and resistance. Space and place are not always literal, and may signal imaginative terrains of community-making and coalition-building among multiply marginalized, dispersed, or otherwise displaced groups (see Anzaldúa 1987, reading 14; Mohanty 1993, reading 11; Morrison 1998).

American sociologist C. Wright Mills (1959) famously encouraged the propagation of critical, sociological thinking across the disciplines and professions, because, to him, a "sociological imagination" was the indispensible tool for the negotiation of social life in the second half of the twentieth century. The sociological imagination has become a calling card of sociology and remains one of its most treasured concepts; it is in many ways the promise of a higher education in sociology and the discipline's defense of its continued relevance. If the pieces in this unit have a collective message, it is the necessity of critical, spatially attuned thinking in the execution of intersectional theorizing, research, and activism. Thomas Gieryn (2000) argues that *all* sociology is essentially the sociology of place, because: "place matters for politics and identity, history and futures, inequality and community. Is there anything sociological not touched by place? Probably not" (483). Though we might not ultimately consider space and place to be a dimension of difference per se (i.e., another axis, like race, gender, or class, on which to conduct intersectional analysis), the politics of space and place are the terrain on which racism, sexism, classism, heterosexism, and other systems of oppression are elaborated, produced, and reinforced. From these texts, we learn that critical sensitivity to space, place, and geography—a cartographic imagination—is another potential tool for social justice.

References and Further Reading

Agnew, J. 2011. "Space and Place." In *The SAGE Handbook of Geographical Knowledge*, edited by J. Agnew and D. Livingstone, 316–330. London: Sage.

Anzaldúa, G. (1987) 1999. *Borderlands/La Frontera: The New Mestiza*. Second edition. San Francisco: Aunt Lute Books.

Boyd, N. A. 2003. *Wide Open Town: A History of Queer San Francisco to 1965*. Berkeley, CA: University of California Press.

Boyd, N. A. 2008. "Sex and Tourism: The Economic Implications for the Gay Marriage Movement." *Radical History Review* 100: 223–235.

Dávila, A. 2004. *Barrio Dreams: Puerto Ricans, Latinos and the Neoliberal City.* Berkeley, CA: University of California Press.

Delaney, S. 1999. *Times Square Red, Times Square Blue.* New York: New York University Press.

Gieryn, T. F. 2000. "A Space for Place in Sociology." *Annual Review of Sociology* 26: 463–496.

Gilmore, R. W. 2007. *Golden Gulag: Prisons, Surplus, Crisis, and Opposition in Globalizing California.* Berkeley: University of California Press.

Gray, M. L. 2009. *Out in the Country: Youth, Media, and Queer Visibility in Rural America.* New York: New York University Press.

Halberstam, J. 2005. *In a Queer Time and Place.* New York: New York University Press.

Hanhardt, C. B. 2008. "Butterflies, Whistles, and Fists: Gay Safe Street Patrols and the New Gay Ghetto, 1976–1981." *Radical History Review* 100: 60–85.

Hanhardt, C. B. 2013. *Safe Space: Gay Neighborhood History and the Politics of Violence.* Durham, NC: Duke University Press.

Hirschmann, N. J. 2012. "Disability as a New Frontier in Feminist Intersectionality Research." *Politics & Gender* 8: 396–405.

Manalansan, M. 2005. "Race, Violence, and Neoliberal Spatial Politics in the Global City." *Social Text* 23: 141–155.

Mendieta, E. 2012. "Mapping the Geographies of Social Inequality: Patricia Hill Collins's Intersectional Critical Theory." *Journal of Speculative Philosophy* 26: 458–465.

Mills, C. W. (1959) 2000. *The Sociological Imagination.* New York: Oxford University Press.

Mohanty, C. T. (1993) 2008. "Defining Genealogies: Feminist Reflections on Being South Asian in North America." In *Our Feet Walk the Sky, Writings by Women of the South Asian Diaspora,* edited by S. Bhatt, P. Kaira, A. Kohli, L. Malkani, and D. Rasiah, 351–358. Aunt Lute Books.

Morrison, T. (1993) 1998. "Home—the Nobel Lecture." In *The House That Race Built,* edited by W. Lubiano, 3–12. New York: Vintage.

Nero, C. I. 2005. "Why Are the Gay Ghettoes White?" In *Black Queer Studies,* edited by E. P. Johnson and M. G. Henderson, 228–245. Durham, NC: Duke University Press.

Nieves, A. D. 2008. "Place of Pain as Tools for Social Justice in the 'New' South Africa: Black Heritage Preservation in the 'Rainbow' Nation's Townships." In *Place of Pain and Shame: Dealing with Difficult Heritage,* edited by W. Logan and K. Reeves, 198–214. London: Routledge.

Nieves, A. D., and L. M. Alexander. 2008. *"We Shall Independent Be:" African American Place-Making and the Struggle to Claim Space in the United States.* Boulder: University Press of Colorado.

Pattillo, M. 2007. *Black on the Block: The Politics of Race and Class in the City.* Chicago: University of Chicago Press.

Pattillo-McCoy, M. 1999. *Black Picket Fences: Privilege and Peril Among the Black Middle Class.* Chicago: University of Chicago Press.

Perry, P. 2002. *Shades of White: White Kids and Racial Identities in High School.* Durham, NC: University of North Carolina Press.

Puar, J. K. 2002. "Circuits of Queer Mobility: Tourism, Travel and Globalization." *GLQ: A Journal of Lesbian and Gay Studies* 8: 100–137.

Sherwood, J. H. 2010. *Wealth, Whiteness and the Matrix of Privilege: The View from the Country Club*. Lanham, MD: Lexington Books.

Sloop, J. 2004. "Disciplining the Transgendered: Brandon Teena, Public Representation, and Normativity." In *Disciplining Gender: Rhetorics of Sex Identity in Contemporary U.S. Culture,* 50–82. Amherst: University of Massachusetts Press.

Thomson, R. G. 1997. *Extraordinary Bodies: Figuring Physical Disability in American Culture and Literature*. New York: Columbia University Press.

Tongson, K. 2011. *Relocations: Queer Suburban Imaginaries*. New York: New York University Press.

Valentine, G. 2007. "Theorizing and Researching Intersectionality: A Challenge for Feminist Geography." *The Professional Geographer* 59: 10–21.

Gloria Anzaldúa

With the exception of Kimberlé Crenshaw, few authors have had the kind of impact Gloria Anzaldúa has had on how we imagine the literal and metaphorical terrain of intersectionality. Anzaldúa taught and wrote extensively during her esteemed career as a writer, artist, teacher, and activist. Born in 1942 in South Texas's Rio Grande Valley, Anzaldúa worked in the fields of Texas and the Great Plains as a child and teenager to support her family while also pursuing her education. She ultimately earned degrees in English, art, and secondary education, and she taught feminism, Chicana/o studies, and creative writing at several US universities while lecturing around the world. She died in 2004 from diabetes complications after decades of provocative scholar-activism that changed the face of women of color feminism, sexuality studies, and Latina/o studies, among other fields. Her "borderlands"—articulated in a genre-busting work of creative nonfiction and poetry now widely recognized by academics as an invaluable contribution to social theory—signify a geographic, affective, cultural, and political landscape that cannot be explained by binary logic (black/white, gay/straight, Mexican/American, etc.) or even the notion of liminality, that is, *the space between*. Anzaldúa's borderlands are a very *real* space of cutting, overlap, collision, violence, resistance, blending, and complexity; simultaneously, the borderlands are nearly unrepresentable insomuch as no singular scientific, geometric, or cartographic framework can adequately capture the dynamic, co-constitutive processes that characterize life in the borderlands. In this sense, Anzaldúa's work exemplifies the concept of intersectionality perhaps better than the traffic intersection metaphor so central to the field and to Crenshaw's initial articulation of the concept, because Anzaldúa denies any logic that presumes there were ever discreet dimensions of difference that collided at some particular point: in the borderlands, mixing, hybridity, unfinished synthesis, and unpredictable amalgamation were always already happening, and are forever ongoing.

In this excerpt from *Borderlands/La Frontera* (1987), Anzaldúa offers a window into the spatial dimensions of her borderlands theory; to her, space and place are integrally implicated in the structural elements of intersectional oppression. Though we typically consider intersecting dimensions of difference to reflect structures of inequality that manifest in the politics of identity (e.g., race, gender, sexuality, class, nation), Anzaldúa's work suggests that place/space itself is fundamental to understanding the experience and organization of oppressions. Finally, Anzaldua's space is much more than simply location. Indeed, her use of the term "feminist architecture" suggests that space and place convey an epistemology, or a way that knowledge and politics are purposefully configured and deployed. Such a notion of "architecture" implies that the politics of space can be marginalizing and violent, as in the case of White European colonists, but also contains the possibility for creative, imaginative forms of potent resistance, such as those embodied in Anzaldúa's *mestizaje*.

14. **Feminist Architecture**[*]

I have a vivid memory of an old photograph: I am six years old. I stand between my father and mother, head cocked to the right, the toes of my flat feet gripping the ground. I hold my mother's hand.

To this day I'm not sure where I found the strength to leave the source, the mother, disengage from my family, *mi tierra, mi gente,* and all that picture stood for. I had to leave home so I could find myself, find my own intrinsic nature buried under the personality that had been imposed on me.

I was the first in six generations to leave the Valley, the only one in my family to ever leave home. But I didn't leave all the parts of me: I kept the ground of my own being. On it I walked away, taking with me the land, the Valley, Texas. *Gané mi camino y me largué. Muy andariega mi hija.* Because I left of my own accord *me dicen, "¿Cómo te gusta la mala vida?"*

At a very early age I had a strong sense of who I was and what I was about and what was fair. I had a stubborn will. It tried constantly to mobilize my soul under my own regime, to live life on my own terms no matter how unsuitable to others they were. *Terca.* Even as a child I would not obey. I was "lazy." Instead of ironing my younger brothers' shirts or cleaning the cupboards, I

---

[*] Excerpted from G. Anzaldúa, *Borderlands/La Frontera: The New Mestiza* (San Francisco: Aunt Lute Books, 1987). Copyright © 1987, 1999, 2007, 2012. Reprinted by permission of Aunt Lute Books. www.auntlute.com.

would pass many hours studying, reading, painting, writing. Every bit of self-faith I'd painstakingly gathered took a beating daily. Nothing in my culture approved of me. *Había agarrado malos pasos.* Something was "wrong" with me. *Estaba más allá de la tradición.*

There is a rebel in me—the Shadow-Beast. It is a part of me that refuses to take orders from outside authorities. It refuses to take orders from my conscious will, it threatens the sovereignty of my rulership. It is that part of me that hates constraints of any kind, even those self-imposed. At the least hint of limitations on my time or space by others, it kicks out with both feet. Bolts.

There was a *muchacha* who lived near my house. *La gente del pueblo* talked about her being *una de las otras,* "of the Others." They said that for six months she was a woman who had a vagina that bled once a month, and that for the other six months she was a man, had a penis and she peed standing up. They called her half and half, *mita'y mita',* neither one nor the other but a strange doubling, a deviation of nature that horrified, a work of nature inverted. But there is a magic aspect in abnormality and so-called deformity. Maimed, mad, and sexually different people were believed to possess supernatural powers by primal cultures' magico-religious thinking. For them, abnormality was the price a person had to pay for her or his inborn extraordinary gift.

There is something compelling about being both male and female, about having an entry into both worlds. Contrary to some psychiatric tenets, half and halfs are not suffering from a confusion of sexual identity, or even from a confusion of gender. What we are suffering from is an absolute despot duality that says we are able to be only one or the other. It claims that human nature is limited and cannot evolve into something better. But I, like other queer people, am two in one body, both male and female. I am the embodiment of the *hieros gamos:* the coming together of opposite qualities within.

For the lesbian of color, the ultimate rebellion she can make against her native culture is through her sexual behavior. She goes against two moral prohibitions: sexuality and homosexuality. Being lesbian and raised Catholic, indoctrinated as straight, I *made the choice to be queer* (for some it is genetically inherent). It's an interesting path, one that continually slips in and out of the white, the Catholic, the Mexican, the indigenous, the instincts. In and out of my head. It makes for *loquería,* the crazies. It is a path of knowledge—one of knowing (and of learning) the history of oppression of our *raza.* It is a way of balancing, of mitigating duality.

In a New England college where I taught, the presence of a few lesbians threw the more conservative heterosexual students and faculty into a panic. The two lesbian students and we two lesbian instructors met with them to discuss their fears. One of the students said, "I thought homophobia meant fear of going home after a residency."

And I thought, how apt. Fear of going home. And of not being taken in. We're afraid of being abandoned by the mother, the culture, *la Raza,* for being unacceptable, faulty, damaged. Most of us unconsciously believe that if we reveal this unacceptable aspect of the self our mother/culture/race will totally reject us. To avoid rejection, some of us conform to the values of the culture, push the unacceptable parts into the shadows. Which leaves only one fear—that we will be found out and that the Shadow-Beast will break of its cage. Some of us take another route. We try to make ourselves conscious of the Shadow-Beast, stare at the sexual lust and lust for power and destruction we see on its face, discern among its features the undershadow that the reigning order of heterosexual males project on our Beast. Yet still others of us take it another step: we try to waken the Shadow-Beast inside us. Not many jump at the chance to confront the Shadow-Beast in the mirror without flinching at her lidless serpent eyes, her cold clammy moist hand dragging us underground, fangs bared and hissing. How does one put feathers on this particular serpent? But a few of us have been lucky—on the face of the Shadow-Beast we have seen not lust but tenderness; on its face we have uncovered the lie.

The world is not a safe place to live in. We shiver in separate cells in enclosed cities, shoulders hunched, barely keeping the panic below the surface of the skin, daily drinking shock along with our morning coffee, fearing the torches being set to our buildings, the attacks in the streets. Shutting down. Woman does not feel safe when her own culture, and white culture, are critical of her; when the males of all races hunt her as prey.

Alienated from her mother culture, "alien" in the dominant culture, the woman of color does not feel safe within the inner life of her Self. Petrified, she can't respond, her face caught between *los intersticios,* the spaces between the different worlds she inhabits.

The ability to respond is what is meant by responsibility, yet our cultures take away our ability to act—shackle us in the name of protection. Blocked, immobilized, we can't move forward, can't move backwards. That writhing serpent movement, the very movement of life, swifter than lightning, frozen.

We do not engage fully. We do not make full use of our faculties. We abnegate. And there in front of us is the crossroads and choice: to feel a victim where someone else is in control and therefore responsible and to blame (being a victim and transferring the blame on culture, mother, father, ex-lover, friend, absolves me of responsibility), or to feel strong, and, for the most part, in control.

My Chicana identity is grounded in the Indian woman's history of resistance. The Aztec female rites of mourning were rites of defiance protesting the cultural changes which disrupted the equality and balance between female and male, and protesting their demotion to a lesser status, their denigration. Like *la Llorona,* the Indian woman's only means of protest was wailing.

So *mamá, Raza*, how wonderful, *no tener que rendir cuentas a nadie*. I feel perfectly free to rebel and to rail against my culture. I fear no betrayal on my part because, unlike Chicanas and other women of color who grew up white or who have only recently returned to their native cultural roots, I was totally immersed in mine. It wasn't until I went to high school that I "saw" whites. Until I worked on my master's degree I had not gotten within an arm's distance of them. I was totally immersed *en lo mexicano*, a rural, peasant, isolated, *mexicanismo*. To separate from my culture (as from my family) I had to feel competent enough on the outside and secure enough inside to live life on my own. Yet in leaving home I did not lose touch with my origins because *lo mexicano* is in my system. I am a turtle, wherever I go I carry "home" on my back.

Not me sold out my people but they me. So yes, though "home" permeates every sinew and cartilage in my body, I too am afraid of going home. Though I'll defend my race and culture when they are attacked by non-*mexicanos, conozco el malestar de mi cultura*. I abhor some of my culture's ways, how it cripples its women, *como burras,* our strengths used against us, lowly *burras* bearing humility with dignity. The ability to serve, claim the males, is our highest virtue. I abhor how my culture makes *macho* caricatures of its men. No, I do not buy all the myths of the tribe into which I was born. I can understand why the more tinged with Anglo blood, the more adamantly my colored and colorless sisters glorify their colored culture's values—to offset the extreme devaluation of it by the white culture. It's a legitimate reaction. But I will not glorify those aspects of my culture which have injured me and which have injured me in the name of protecting me.

So, don't give me your tenets and your laws. Don't give me your lukewarm gods. What I want is an accounting with all three cultures—white, Mexican, Indian. I want the freedom to carve and chisel my own face, to staunch the bleeding with ashes, to fashion my own gods out of my entrails. And if going home is denied me then I will have to stand and claim my space, making a new culture—*una cultura mestiza*—with my own lumber, my own bricks and mortar and my own feminist architecture.

Charles I. Nero

Charles Nero is a cultural critic and professor of rhetoric at Bates College whose work sits at the intersection of communication studies, film and literary criticism, African American studies, and cultural studies. Notably, Nero's work also deeply engages the place of sexuality in African American studies and African American culture, and his essay is a noteworthy example of queer of color criticism that illuminates the weaknesses of queer studies and Black studies when positioned and conducted in isolation. The essay excerpted here initially appeared in Henderson and Johnson's landmark *Black Queer Studies* (2005) anthology and represents a thoroughly interdisciplinary approach to intersectional analysis, as Nero weaves together personal narrative of his life in New Orleans with history, geography, and film criticism. The intersections of difference most central in this piece are race, gender, class, and sexuality; but, once again, the cartography of space and place—specifically gentrified urban space—is a requisite element of the story. The Faubourg Marigny neighborhood is less the backdrop or setting in this piece and more the locus of Nero's intersectional analysis. The ways in which Whiteness, Blackness, and queer sexualities interface to produce racialized gay ghettoes and controlling images of Black queer "imposters" in film are all co-productive phenomena. That is to say that being a gay man in New Orleans is at least partially created by the Marigny, which is materially and symbolically transformed by White, upwardly mobile gay men, whose popular culture foil may very well not be their straight counterparts but the Black queer imposter figure. From screen to street, bank office to local bar, Nero asks us to see the elusive but consequential connections between popular culture and cultural geography that distribute resources, housing opportunities, and life chances along intersectional networks of inequality.

15. Why Are the Gay Ghettoes White?*

San Francisco's Castro District is perhaps the most well-known gay community in the world. The creation of the Castro is an oft-repeated narrative that sometimes assumes mythic dimensions. Gay men fleeing oppression in small towns across North America arrived in San Francisco. Finding anonymity in the city and the ability to derive an income apart from a familial structure, these men created "a gay Israel" in San Francisco. Once established, gay men initiated community renewal projects, which "helped to make the city beautiful and alive."

Lawrence Knopp's study of gentrification in the Faubourg Marigny in New Orleans, a small but densely populated area adjacent to the famous French Quarter, presents rigorous and innovative research that sheds much-needed light on gay neighborhood formation. Knopp's research includes a doctoral dissertation in geography and several articles in refereed journals and anthologies. Not only is Knopp's research rigorous, it is also innovative because of its interdisciplinary approach. He uses the methods of geography and demography, as well as methods more often associated with sociology, journalism, and history. The result is that his studies are exacting in their precision and also highly engaging.

Knopp's study is particularly interesting for me because I grew up, attended school and college, and worked in New Orleans. Having come out as a gay man in New Orleans, I was familiar with the neighborhood and surrounding environs that Knopp describes. Perhaps my familiarity with the city led me to notice that Knopp was not particularly adept at explaining the racial homogeneity of the Faubourg Marigny. When I lived in New Orleans, particularly during the years between 1974 and 1983, the Faubourg Marigny appeared to be almost exclusively comprised of white gay men. In his research Knopp confirms my memories about the racial and gender homogeneity of the Faubourg Marigny.

Given that Knopp is such a sophisticated scholar, it is somewhat surprising that he is unable to satisfactorily explain the racial and gender makeup of the Faubourg. Rather than offering an explanation, Knopp merely restates the paradox that gayness is multicultural yet gay neighborhoods are overwhelmingly white and male. As Knopp explains: "Gay identity in the United States is skewed in terms of class, race, and gender, i.e., that while homosexual desire and behaviors are multiclass and multiracial phenomena involving both women and men, the self-identification of individuals as gay is more of a white, male, and middle-class phenomenon. This is because it is easier, economically and otherwise, for middle-class white males to identify and live as openly gay people than it is for women, non-whites, and nonmiddle-class people." Needless to say, my initial reaction to this explanation was one of astonishment at its lack in exploring in complex ways the relationship between wealth, gender, and race. Although Knopp hints at this complicated relationship in his own research, especially when he shows how the accumulation of wealth through the acquisition of real estate is socially constructed and manipulated, it appears that he is not willing to think in complicated ways about the intersection of race and homosexuality.

On further reflection about Knopp's explanation, it dawned on me that it is possible that he conceives of race in traditional terms that focus solely on difference. For instance, one case where race becomes important in his studies is when he points out that the gays in the Faubourg often interacted violently with African Americans in adjacent communities. In order to address this issue and to offer a critique of Knopp's work that takes race into account in discussing gay neighborhood formation in the Faubourg Marigny, I have used my own knowledge about New Orleans, supplemented by further research. What follows is thus a racially conscious engagement with Knopp's research that points out some of the ways in which race matters as a factor in creating a white and male gay ghetto.

Knopp attributes the gentrification of the Faubourg Marigny to three events: "The movement of a small number of predominantly gay middle-class professionals to Marigny during the 1960s"; "a movement for historic preservation in the neighborhood, organized primarily by gay men"; and "the arrival of speculators and developers, who again were mostly gay, in the mid-to-late 1970s" (46). Although Knopp does not state as much, whiteness (and concomitantly the exclusion of black men and to a significant extent lesbians) mattered in all three events.

First, the gay middle-class professionals who moved to the Faubourg Marigny in the 1960s were men hired to work at the newly created University of New Orleans (UNO). Knopp does not identify them racially, but at that time whiteness was an implicit criterion for employment at UNO, which was founded, during the last days of legalized segregation in 1958, as Louisiana State University at New Orleans. Until the late 1980s, most black professionals in higher education worked at one of the three historically black universities in the city—Dillard University, Xavier University, and Southern University of New Orleans—rather than at UNO. This fact of employment segregation is important for Knopp to consider because informal networks were to play a crucial role in the gentrification of the Marigny. Racially segregated workplaces made it highly unlikely that middle-class black and white gay males would create racially integrated informal networks.

Second, by emphasizing historical preservation, white gays practiced racial and class "tribalism" whereby they identified their interests with those of other middle- and upper-class whites. Historical preservation has a long history in New Orleans that is very much associated with local white elites. The Vieux Carre Commission, which regulated development in the French Quarter, was established by local white elites in 1936. The initiator of the gay housing movement in the Faubourg Marigny was a white gay architect who lived part of the year in San Francisco's gay Castro. According to Knopp, this architect purchased property in the Faubourg in 1971 and used his connections with other white middle- and upper-class gay men to encourage gay gentrification there. These men created the Faubourg Marigny Improvement Association (FMIA) and they emphasized historic preservation. The FMIA cultivated their connections with city officials, successfully lobbied the mayor and city council for land use regulations, and held candidate forums at election time. The success of the FMIA had notable consequences beneficial to middle- and upper-class whites. Local politicians and new zoning regulations made historical preservation a priority in the Faubourg, which had the very practical effect that bank financing and insurance became easier for single men to get.

These middle-class white gay men extended their successes to work-ing-class white gay men when the speculators and developers who brought about the gay gentrification of the Faubourg focused on creating a market for all kinds of housing in the neighborhood among gays. Knopp observes that one real estate broker in particular encouraged "as much in-migration, home-ownership, and renovation in Marigny as was humanly possible, regardless of the in-migrant's class status" (53). His targets included gay men employed in the low-wage service sector who otherwise would not have had access to the housing market. One of Knopp's interviewees recalled that this group included "all the waiters and all the gay people and all the people that were his friends in the Quarter that always wanted houses. . . . Just nobody was ever going to look for that type of person. It was a natural! . . . He was the first person to go after that market" (53). Neither the interviewee nor Knopp, however, address the racial composition of the gay men in the low-wage service sector. My own ex-perience and engagement with gay businesses during this time period informs me that most of these men were, in fact, white.

Exploiting personal and friendship networks that had been established because of shared sexual—and racial and gender—identities was crucial at this stage of gentrification in the Marigny because real estate firms and other spec-ulators resorted to using illegal maneuvers. These schemes allowed members of the local gay community to secure financing for virtually the entire purchase price of the home and enabled first-time home buyers and others of relatively modest means to avoid down payments and invest instead in renovations. Most of these first-time buyers were young gay men who had been recruited into the housing market by other gay men involved in the real estate busi-ness. Knopp points out that one real estate firm employed at its peak fifty-two agents, "nearly all of whom were gay" (84). Once again, Knopp is silent about the racial composition of this group.

The consequence of these schemes was that gay men, regardless of social class, received access to housing and the wealth that accrues from home own-ership. One interviewee told Knopp: "I was a schoolteacher and I was making $400 a month . . . I saved $1200. The biggest savings of my life! . . . I bought [my first] house for $7500" (83). Knopp estimates that these schemes enabled "hundreds of gay first-time home buyers to enter the housing market" in what was essentially "a conscious and deliberate project of developing social and eco-nomic resources with New Orleans and Marigny's gay community" (87). Black gay men and women were excluded from participating in home ownership in the Faubourg Marigny because they were neither a part of the informal net-works of middle-class gay men nor were they employed in the low-wage service sector of gay-owned businesses.

One reason for the exclusion of black gay men that I would like to explore further is the historical meaning of the hostility of whites toward African Americans. Since emancipation, white racial hostility toward blacks has had a material dimension. At the end of the nineteenth century the black journalist and activist Ida B. Wells-Barnett pointed out how lynching benefited whites when she carefully demolished the image of the black male rapist of white women. According to Wells, lynching was nothing more than an "excuse to get rid of Negroes who were acquiring wealth and property and thus keep the race terrorized and 'keep the nigger down.'" More recent pioneering scholarship in "white studies" confirms Wells's view. For instance, Thomas A. Guglielmo has shown that in the 1940s and 1950s Chicago's Italians became increasingly anti-black as they learned to emphasize their identities as "whites" and that "whiteness was not some meaningless social category, but something that carried considerable power and provided them with innumerable resources." In their particular case, the resources included low-interest loans, backed by the Federal Housing Authority, to purchase homes in neighborhoods whose alleged value rested on excluding blacks.

Admittedly, white hostility takes a particular form when directed at black gay men. In the next section, I address a hostile representation that I observe in the American media. The sheer repetition of this image points to the racialization of gay identity and requires us to ask questions about the role that this form of media hostility plays in the distribution of material resources among gays.

Here, I borrow Patricia Hill Collins's term "controlling images" to illuminate the continuing explanations for the existence of black gay men in white discourses. Collins points out that in white discourses about black women, controlling images help "to make racism, sexism, and poverty appear to be natural, normal, and an inevitable part of everyday life." The impostor—which also includes the sexually voracious black stud who is not really a gay man since he exists only to satiate white male desire—is the predominate controlling image of black gay men. HBO's *Six Feet Under* is the latest entry to perpetuate the image of black gay men as impostors. The postmodern ironic sensibility of *Six Feet Under* seems to challenge prevailing conventions, but the show's African American gay male character has been transformed from the soul of the show into its lost soul. In the show's first season the African American Keith Charles (Matthew St. Patrick) appeared to be the show's moral center—the equivalent of a gay role model. Keith was completely comfortable with being "out." Further, Keith's ethical standards led him to break off a relationship with his closeted love interest, the show's costar David Fisher (Michael C. Hall) who was, for all intents and purposes, the white equivalent of a black buck: a brutal, irresponsible, sexual adventurer.

As the show developed over four seasons, Keith seemed to become "blacker." This transformation is significant for Keith's character for two reasons. First, Keith's blackness seems to mean an incompatibility with gayness to the show's writers and creators. This point was made quite clear in the third-season episode "Timing and Space," in which Keith became the source of humor at a gay party because he was completely ignorant about camp sensibility. Since Keith was the only black gay man present, the show seemed to support the belief that blacks are alien to gay sensibilities, such as camp. Moreover, Keith's complete ignorance about gay forms of culture seemed incongruous with the persona that had been established in the first season when the show implied that Keith belonged to a sizable network of gay men because he was active in queer social, religious, and political organizations.

Second, the show presents blackness as savage and unredeemable. In a series that is about family dysfunction, the writers reveal a distressing double standard. White families have eccentricities, but black families are violent and criminal. In fact, in the opening episode of the third season, "Perfect Circles," Keith explains that his violent, threatening behavior is just his way of showing that he is comfortable with his lover! As Keith is more associated with blackness, he retreats further and further from the first season's out and proud character. In season four, Keith, who has been fired from his job as a policeman and who works for a private security firm, now pretends to be straight to his coworkers. Keith's character may morph (as is the nature of an ongoing television series), but at the time of this writing his character continues the controlling image of black gay men as fraudulent.

This controlling image of black gay men, which is produced by straights and gays, provides ideological support for the exclusion of black gay men from full participation in queer cultures. Anecdotal evidence suggests that this exclusion is widespread. Bars have been especially notorious for excluding black men through the practice of "carding," in which doormen and bouncers request an unreasonable amount of identification as a requirement for admission. Marlon Riggs includes in his brilliant 1989 documentary *Tongues Untied* a sequence in which an African American gay man becomes outraged after a white doorman requests five forms of picture identification to enter a bar. Interestingly, this belief that the admission of too many black men will cause a bar to lose its desirability for white patrons mirrors the social reality of housing. Sheryll Cashin, in *The Failures of Integration,* repeatedly observes that in housing "whites place a premium on homogeneity," and, further, that "where blacks or Latinos exist in large numbers, whites flee." This practice of white separatism led Marlon Riggs to conclude that while living in San Francisco's overwhelmingly white and gay male Castro District, he became "an invisible man," possessing "no shadow, no substance. No history, no place. No reflection." Riggs surmised that for all intents and purposes, in the gay Castro he had become "an alien, unseen, and seen, unwanted."

The persistence of controlling images of black gay male fraudulence in white discourse reveals white hostility toward black gay men. Racial hostility is important to consider in light of the pivotal role it has played in housing. As I show in the next section, white racial hostility has material benefits.

Race, Racism, Class, and Housing

Historically, housing has been a major site for racial formation in the United States. Melvin Oliver and Thomas Shapiro, in their impressive volume *Black Wealth/White Wealth,* identify with precision the race-based policies of the state that "collectively enabled over thirty-five million families between 1933 and 1978 to participate in homeowner equity accumulation" but also "had the adverse effect of constraining black Americans' residential opportunities to central-city ghettos of major U.S. metropolitan communities." The story begins during the Great Depression with the creation of the Home Owners Loan Corporation (HOLC), which refinanced tens of thousands of mortgages in danger of default or foreclosure. Of more importance, the HOLC introduced standardized appraisals of the fitness of properties for financing, and government agents used racial criterion that negatively impacted black people. Oliver and Shapiro state that

> government agents methodically included in their procedures the evaluation of the racial composition or potential racial composition of the community. Communities that were changing racially or were already black were deemed undesirable and placed in the lowest category. The categories, assigned various colors on a map ranging from green for the most desirable, which included new, all-white housing that was always in demand, to red, which included already racially mixed or all-black, old, and undesirable areas, subsequently were used by Federal Housing Authority (FHA) loan officers who made loans on the basis of these designations. (17)

The FHA was inaugurated in 1934 to bolster the economy and increase employment by aiding the construction industry. The FHA ushered in the modern mortgage system, which enabled people to buy homes on small down payments and at reasonable interest rates with lengthy repayment periods. The FHA's success was immediate and remarkable as housing starts doubled in the seven years after it was inaugurated. However, the FHA's policies worked against black people. Some policies indirectly impacted black people by favoring the financing of houses in suburbs over those in central cities. Other policies, however, were more direct. Notably, in its *Underwriting Manual*, the FHA upheld racial segregation and the use of restrictive covenants because it feared that property values would decline if "a rigid black and white segregation was not maintained" (18).

Contemporary institutional racism in the forms of mortgage lending practices and of redlining solidified segregated housing patterns. Oliver and Shapiro call attention to a 1991 Federal Reserve study of 6.4 million home mortgage applications by race and income that disclosed that "commercial banks rejected black applicants twice as often as whites nationwide," and that "the poorest white applicant . . . was more likely to get a mortgage loan approved than a black in the highest income bracket" (19–20). Discriminatory policies based on exclusion have provided "cumulative advantages" in wealth for white Americans and "cumulative disadvantages" for blacks (51).

The cumulative effect of racial exclusion has been to confine blacks to the bottom of our social hierarchy. The legal scholar Derrick Bell, in *Faces at the Bottom of the Well: The Permanence of Racism*, affirms this view when he states, "Americans achieve a measure of social stability through their unspoken pact to keep blacks on the bottom—an aspect of social functioning that more than any other has retained its viability and its value to general stability from the very beginning of the American experience down to the present day." When white gay men practice this exclusion in housing, they are participating in that "unspoken pact to keep blacks on the bottom."

Conclusion

Oliver and Shapiro consider suburbanization possibly "the greatest mass-based opportunity for home ownership and wealth accumulation in American history" (147). Gay neighborhood formation, Escoffiers "Territorial Economy" of the 1970s, is the "queered" spawn of 1950s suburbanization. Certainly, the example of gay gentrification of the Faubourg Marigny resulted in the equivalent of a queer male Levittown, the Long Island suburb that was built on a mass scale and was eminently affordable thanks to accessible financing, yet as late as 1960 had not a single black resident among its total population of 82,000 (147). Admittedly, differences exist between a suburb like Levittown and an urban neighborhood like the Faubourg Marigny, yet both are outposts of whiteness—one in the city, the other in the suburb—and both came into existence through policies that made the inclusion of whites and the exclusion of people of color appear normal and even natural. It is my view that the widely circulated image of the black gay impostor plays a role in allowing gay and non-gay whites to bond and to exclude black gay men.

Nan Alamilla Boyd

Nan Alamilla Boyd is a professor of women and gender studies at San Francisco State University, where she teaches courses on the history of sexuality, queer theory, historiography, and urban tourism. Her book *Wide Open Town: A History of Queer San Francisco to 1965* (2003) foreshadows some of the concerns centralized in the excerpt here from her later essay on the intersections of race, class, and gender in the new "gay tourism" industry. Boyd's work raises pressing questions, such as: what does it mean to be a "gay-friendly" space, and to whom specifically does this hospitality extend? How do racial and class forces produce different kinds of differently desirable gay subjects? How might gay marriage—the kind that can be marketed as spectacular and like a spectacle—become a tourist attraction in and of itself? History and geography are intertwined to Boyd, because the spatial dynamics of the past choreograph how we remember. As she explores various municipal and national efforts to recruit gay tourists—albeit a particular kind of gay tourist—Boyd uncovers the contradictions in contemporary LGBT politics in which a US state such as Arizona can support vigorous anti-LGBT social movements *and* a pro-gay business agenda. Boyd's work contributes not only to the discourse on neoliberalism explored more extensively in Unit VIII on politics, but also reminds us here of the intersectional dynamics of history and the social construction of space. Her critique implicates how we consider the movement of queer bodies and capital across transnational spaces, and invites a reconsideration of migration, transportation, consumption, and citizenship in the context of dynamic twenty-first-century sexual geopolitics. In recruiting gay tourists, these various cities produce an idea of themselves—a brand, even—in cultural imaginaries. And in the single-axis politics of mainstream gay rights in the United States and other countries worldwide, that can mean that capitalist interests trump all else, especially a substantive critique of heteronormativity and some of its most dangerous bedfellows: racism, classism, and xenophobia.

16. **Sex and Tourism**[*]

The narrative produced by gay and lesbian marketing professionals attaches marketplace activity to political enfranchisement by equating spending with

[*] Excerpted from N. A. Boyd, "Sex and Tourism: The Economic Implications for the Gay Marriage Movement," *Radical History Review* 2008: 223–35. Copyright, 2008, MARHO: The Radical Historians Organization, Inc. All rights reserved. Republished by permission of the copyright holder, and the present publisher, Duke University Press, www.dukeupress.edu.

civil rights. Translating brand loyalty to cities or countries rather than companies or consumer goods demands different strategies, but the basic idea is the same. A March 2004 article in the *Boston Globe* described how some U.S. cities—including Miami, West Hollywood, San Diego, San Francisco, Boston, Washington, DC, and Philadelphia, but also Newport, Milwaukee, and Fort Lauderdale—have begun to market themselves directly to gay travelers. The economic stakes are high. In 2003, for instance, the Greater Fort Lauderdale Convention and Visitor's Bureau spent 7 percent, or $200,000, of its $3 million advertising budget on potential gay tourists, and gay tourists in 2003 accounted for 13 percent, or $700 million, of the $5.3 billion tourist economy there. More recently, Philadelphia completed a three-year, $900,000 campaign to draw gay travelers to that city, and a report reveals that the city has seen a return of $153 in spending for every dollar invested in gay marketing. Philadelphia's branding campaign, which positions the slogan, "Get your history straight and your nightlife gay," alongside images of Benjamin Franklin flying a rainbow kite and Betsy Ross sewing a rainbow flag, has received much press attention. Other cities, seeking similar returns, worked with marketing experts—like those at CMI—to develop gay-friendly slogans to promote their city to gay and lesbian travelers. Boston toyed with the slogan, "Boston Marriages: Invented Here," while Washington, DC, chose, "Celebrate the Freedom to Be" and San Francisco encouraged visitors to "Make a Commitment."

The link between gay marriage and gay tourism is unstable but alluring; it makes for the newest factor in a well-established pattern of gay travel and spending. For instance, even when states ban same-sex marriage, cities within these states continue to vie for gay travel dollars through the production of gay-friendly activities and amenities. In other words, the marketplace activity does not always have to be a destination wedding. A February 2006 *USA Today* article entitled "Cities in Red States Play Ball with Gay Travelers," notes that despite Arizona's proposed ban on gay marriage (which, surprisingly, failed in the November 2006 elections), Phoenix continues to aggressively court gay travelers. Phoenix city and tourism officials met in January 2006 to coordinate their efforts, which resulted in a homoerotic ad featuring a rear-view close-up of a baseball player with the caption, "To the rest of the country, they're the 'Boys of Summer,' to Phoenix, they're the 'Boys of Summer, Spring, Winter, and Fall.'" This ad capitalizes on Arizona's largest tourist draw, major-league baseball's spring training camps, while it advertises the year-round availability of young men to gay travelers. Similarly, Dallas has initiated a marketing campaign to attract gay travelers to a host of activities including the gay volleyball championships and the International Gay Rodeo Association. On the topic of gay tourism, Gregory Pierce, the senior vice president at the Atlanta Convention and Visitors Bureau, states that "around here, we like to say, the color of diversity is green."

The consequence of this economic courtship of the "lavender dollar" is that as the gay tourism industry trumps politics and infuses culturally conservative spaces with new economic interests, the economic implications of same-sex marriage, via its impact on gay tourism, have become increasingly important to thinking about the viability of same-sex marriage as a civil rights issue. Cities like San Francisco with a long history of queer activism can lean on their reputation, but increased competition means smarter business practices. San Francisco now works to expand its share of an increasingly global market, and the February 2004 gay marriages in San Francisco provided a spectacle that no marketing company could dream up: smartly dressed gay and lesbian couples primping inside San Francisco's magnificent City Hall; potential newlyweds waiting patiently with their proud families and, often, small children, in lines that wrapped thickly around an entire city block; and local business owners distributing pizza, cookies, flowers, and balloons to the crowds waiting in the drizzling rain. Journalists documented the stories of gay and lesbian couples waiting to get hitched: one couple had been together for decades; another showed up because their children insisted; a third came all the way from North Dakota. These are compelling images—sincere and heartfelt—and while they demonstrate the complex and often personal meanings swirling around the legal struggle for same-sex marriage, they also secure through reiteration San Francisco's centrality as a gay travel destination. These images cement the link between the idea of San Francisco and the idea of gay and lesbian civil rights, and they insure San Francisco's stake in the increasingly lucrative and globally expanding gay travel market.

Gay marriage can thus be seen as a tourist attraction, an export commodity, and a marketplace activity through which gays and lesbians are schooled in how to participate in consumer culture and be good citizens by a host of teachers, the most familiar of which are celebrities. Rosie O'Donnell's February 26, 2004, marriage to Kelli Carpenter provides a case in point. After a private ceremony in Mayor Newsom's office, the New Yorkers exchanged a kiss on the steps of San Francisco's City Hall while crowds cheered and the San Francisco Gay Men's Chorus serenaded them with show tunes. O'Donnell stated, "I want to thank the city of San Francisco for this amazing stance the mayor has taken for all the people here, not just us but all the thousands and thousands of loving, law-abiding couples."

The U.S. tourist economy is changing to accommodate current U.S. national debates about the legalization of same-sex marriage. As same-sex marriage registers as a tourist attraction and a gay travel indicator—a measure of gay-friendliness—gay marriage becomes part of a larger campaign whereby municipalities market themselves to gay travelers. In 2006, for instance, Tourism Vancouver, which has been working to lure U.S. gay travelers since 2000, offered a "gay-marriage sweepstakes" to Americans. Over four hundred potential gay and lesbian travelers registered to win a $50,000 wedding package that included an Alaskan honeymoon cruise. Municipalities that offer travelers same-sex marriage as part of a travel or tourism package transform that service or civil right into a commodity, but they are also transformed by it.

The commodification of gay marriage via marketplace activity produces a new kind of queer citizen, one that participates in civic life via the social rituals of marriage and the commercial rituals of conspicuous consumption. As M. Jacqui Alexander has argued, gay tourism functions as a neocolonial enterprise that transforms white gay travelers into global citizens whose consuming practices maintain colonial patterns of production, consumption, and service. "[The white gay tourist] brings with him the potential to develop new and perennially changing needs and desires that capitalism alone can satisfy. Although citizenship based in political rights gets forfeited, they do not disappear. Instead, they get reconfigured and restored under the rubric of consumer at this moment in late twentieth-century capitalism." Alexander's insights help us understand the uneven and complex relationship between consumption and civil rights. For instance, municipalities that do not offer gay marriage as a commodity are increasingly aware of the power of marriage or other civil rights protections to pull gay travelers into new kinds of marketplace activity but also to brand the municipality's gay-friendliness. Gay marriage thus serves as a marketplace activity (through the sale of hotel rooms, flowers, and so forth), a marketing strategy (through the production of gay-friendliness), and a behavior, as O'Donnell articulated so clearly, that signifies law-abiding, homonormative citizenship.[*]

The historical dimensions of these commercial transformations raise important questions: when, for example, and for what reasons does a city begin to market itself as a gay travel destination? How do municipal or national investments in gay tourism impact the viability of civil rights protections? In San Francisco's history marketplace activity set the stage for the emergence of nascent political organizations and the eventual assertion of civil rights. The marketability of San Francisco's queer subcultures led to civil rights through the development of a commercial district, a gay spending zone that shifted from San Francisco's North Beach district in the 1940s and 1950s to Polk Street in the 1960s and 1970s to the Castro district—and, to a lesser degree, the Valencia Street corridor where lesbian feminism set up shop—in the late 1970s and 1980s. San Francisco's queer subcultures have historically functioned as a vital aspect of San Francisco's larger tourist culture, and it is this development—in combination with the emergence of early homophile organizations—that

---

[*] For an explanation of "homonormative," see Duggan (2003, Unit VIII, reading 30).

enabled gay and lesbian civil rights movements to coalesce and make viable appeals to city government.

At the same time, it is important to note that the marketplace viability of San Francisco's queer subcultures emerged in the period between the expansion of global markets after World War I and the reorganization of global capital after World War II. San Francisco's queer nightlife, its male and female impersonator shows, emerged as part of a larger process of colonization—making the exotic familiar—that stimulated new tourist and travel markets, and, ultimately involved the reorganization of ideas about political subjectivity and citizenship. For instance, in the adjacent districts of Chinatown and North Beach, racialized and sexualized subcultures were colonized and commodified, that is, transformed into a cultural commodity, for the benefit of a developing tourist economy. Through these marketplace activities, a kind of queer citizenship emerged in the 1960s that transformed queer performers and the communities that coalesced around them into a lesbian and gay constituency—that is, a recognizable and intelligible political body. Through their marketplace activity (their role in the production of new capital via the global expansion of San Francisco's nascent tourist economy), gays and lesbians became citizens recognizable to the state through docile and often desexualized notions of sexual subjectivity. The neoliberal trajectory of the gay marriage movement follows a similar pattern, but the economic stakes are higher.

Saskia Sassen has suggested that the development of global cities, linked by superprofits associated with finance industries and specialty services, may occasion new kinds of citizenship claims that deemphasize nationalism against larger economic forces. "The global city [is] a nexus for new politico-economic alignments," Sassen writes, and the valorization of highly lucrative transnational gay tourist industries, especially when set alongside devalued and often informal "native" or "immigrant" services fits neatly into Sassen's analysis. The catch is: What kind of citizenship claims will be made as a result of the production of new capital, and who will be counted as viable citizens? Sassen's critique of the global city as, on the one hand, "a frontier zone for a new type of engagement," asserts, on the other hand, that the undervalued and informal economies that sustain global cities continue to be discounted in the reconfiguration of globalized political constituencies. That is, women and people of color—often configured as immigrants and thus as outside citizenship claims, despite their economic viability with the feminization of the global labor force—continue to be disregarded as peripheral rather than central to the superprofits of corporate capitalism. As was the case in mid-twentieth-century San Francisco, the kind of citizenship enabled by the new capital developments of gay tourism via same-sex marriage will, no doubt, serve the interests of white capitalists rather than people-of-color workers. Or, as Alexander puts it, "the marriage between white gay citizenship and white gay consumption [will have] been efficiently sealed."

The transmission of gay marriage as a kind of export commodity via the gay travel market has important implications for thinking about the production of global gay and lesbian identities that carry neocolonial messages about sexual liberation and freedom. That is, the globalization of gay tourism has the potential to produce the image and reality of a kind of global queer citizen defined by either erotic consumption that depends on neocolonial and racist sexual services or monogamous, marriagelike pairings with predictable and disciplined spending patterns. As Jasbir Puar explains in her analysis of the globalization of gay tourism, "queer tourism underpins and fuels a gay and lesbian rights agenda that assumes the attainment of 'modern queer sexuality' as its ultimate goal." As gay marriage circulates as a commodity on the global marketplace, it attaches new meanings to same-sex sexuality, and these meanings underscore and insist on the intelligibility of modern gay and lesbian subjectivities. But to read this dynamic in reverse, the assertion of gay and lesbian subjectivity and citizenship may work to produce new marketing possibilities.

In her analysis of the U.S. "Hispanic market," Arlene Dávila notes that mass-produced representations of Latino consumers reflect U.S. social anxieties about its others, and advertisements featuring Latino shoppers produce "an idealized, good, all-American citizenship in the image of the 'ethnic consumer.'" The production of new markets creates new social identities that reflect the desires of the mainstream or dominant culture to put so-called others in their place, that is, in a position that does not fundamentally challenge the inequities and injustices of global capitalism. Similarly, the U.S. gay travel market is a recognized and lucrative market that is changing to accommodate current U.S. national debates about same-sex marriage, but these domestic markets interact with highly competitive global markets that have important implications for thinking about, first, the relationship between travel, tourism, and the production of new transnational and/or diasporic sexual cultures; and second, the production of global gay and lesbian identities that carry neocolonial messages about liberation and sexual freedom. Gay marriage can be seen as an export commodity in that it has the potential to open new markets via gay travel, but it also attaches neoliberal ideologies to the state regulation of same-sex sexuality. What is produced in the end, through commodification, is a set of modern and global sexual identities that suture sexual citizenship to spending.

As Lisa Duggan and others have noted in "Beyond Same-Sex Marriage," a reconsideration of the politics of same-sex marriage involves tackling questions of poverty head-on, rather than buying into the rhetoric of privatization and individual rights that rewards docile (gay and lesbian) bodies with citizenship.

The emergence of gay marriage as yet another fabulous niche market for advertisers to exploit, and the concomitant neocolonial transportation of ideas about gay marriage into globalizing economies via the already fabulously lucrative gay travel and tourism market, add yet more difficult questions to those posed by "Beyond Same-Sex Marriage": Who benefits from the production of ad copy featuring same-sex couples traveling or planning their own wedding ceremony? And what stories are told as marketing professionals increasingly frame the contemporary struggle for justice and civil rights? The stories that are not told are those that frame justice in economic terms and value the integrity of caring relationships—whether they are conjugal, familial, sexual, or not.

Mary Pattillo

Black on the Block: The Politics of Race and Class in the City (2007) is the follow-up to Northwestern University sociologist Mary Pattillo's celebrated *Black Picket Fences* (1999), both of which explore the economic, spatial, and cultural forces that affect African American experiences in Chicago neighborhoods. *Black on the Block* focuses on the intersection of race and class in Chicago's North Kenwood-Oakland (NKO) neighborhood, which experienced "urban revitalization" in the form of the sustained relocation of Black middle-class households into the neighborhood during the 1990s and 2000s. Though "gentrification" today tends to evoke images of White young urban professionals (i.e., "yuppies") or White young urban counterculture twenty-somethings (i.e., "hipsters") moving into neighborhoods historically occupied by working-class people of color, the case of NKO presents a challenge to this dominant logic and a complex investigation of class and cultural dynamics within a single racial group. "The face of racial homogeneity does not," Pattillo explains, "preclude the importance of difference, divisions, and distinctions" that function structurally *and* manifest in microlevel social interactions in the neighborhood. Using the method of ethnography, Pattillo immersed herself in the history and present of NKO to understand the everyday practices and institutional dynamics (e.g., housing policy, historic preservation, urban planning, etc.) of "Black gentrification" in this community. Pattillo aptly directs our attention to the concept of "lifestyle" and "status" toward the end of this piece, suggesting that these constructs more adequately tap what it is people mean when they talk *around* class in the NKO and American society more broadly. While the intersections of race, space, and class may be the most obvious foci of Pattillo's work, it is equally important to consider how she rethinks these dimensions of difference in terms of her participants' lived experiences and how these axes of difference shape one another. In this case, African American culture is anything but monolithic, and the analytic power of "lifestyle" reveals the subtle dynamics of class and culture that influence diverse performances of Blackness and the spatial politics of the city.

17. Black on the Block*

Along Chicago's south lakefront, a mile from the campus of the University of Chicago, and a ten-minute drive from downtown, North Kenwood-Oakland (NKO) has been rediscovered as ripe for new investment, as have many inner-city neighborhoods across the United States, and in many European cities as well. The City of Chicago is actively facilitating this process, having designated the neighborhood in 1990 as a "conservation area." That status, legally supported in both state and federal law, enabled community residents to work with city planners to develop a conservation plan. Ongoing advising and monitoring of the conservation area and its plan is done by the Conservation Community Council (CCC), a body of residents approved by the alderman—the community's elected representative to city government—and the mayor. Meetings of the CCC are central sites of negotiation and contestation over visions of NKO's future.

Given its literal divisiveness and its association with dispossession and exclusion, present-day urbanists have disavowed "urban renewal" as a planning strategy. The move, however, seems more semantic than substantive. The contemporary lexicon favors words such as "renovation" and "rehab," when referring to specific buildings, or "revitalization," "conservation," and "gentrification," when speaking of entire neighborhoods. But the ghost of urban renewal is always present. "After all," anthropologist Arlene Dávila notes, "gentrification—whether called renewal, revitalization, upgrading, or uplifting—always involves the expansion and transformation of neighborhoods through rapid economic investment and population shifts, and yet it is equally implicated with social inequalities." The line between revitalization and gentrification is a thin one. For some, gentrification is heralded as exactly what cities need, an infusion of tax dollars and disposable incomes. For others, gentrification suggests the kind of robbery of poor people's neighborhoods by elites that urban renewal came to symbolize. "Revitalization," on the other hand, often connotes a more bottom-up process, but in some respects it is just a more polite term since revitalization without the intervention or introduction of the gentry is rare. The common thread in all of these approaches is the desire to attract

---

* Excerpted from M. Pattillo, *Black on the Block: The Politics of Race and Class in the City* (Chicago: University of Chicago Press, 2007).

middle- and upper-income families to working-class or poor urban neighbor-hoods. In North Kenwood-Oakland this has entailed both the mass construc-tion of new, high-end homes and condominiums by developers alongside the more piecemeal rehabilitation of existing old homes by individual investors. The result is a general upward trend in land, housing, and rental prices and the influx of people who can afford them. This sounds a lot like gentrification, so I use the term, along with words like revitalization, throughout this book.

Gentrification, however, is only half the story. Coincident with the plan-ning and ongoing implementation of its conservation plan, NKO is making decisions about public and other subsidized housing in the neighborhood. In the 1980s and early 1990s, nonprofit groups like the Kenwood Oakland Community Organization rehabbed hundreds of dilapidated and abandoned apartment buildings as affordable housing using an array of federal housing programs. This happened relatively quietly. The more contentious fight was over the future of six public housing high-rises referred to generically as the Lakefront Properties. The buildings, built in the 1950s and 1960s, were closed for renovation in 1986. The families that lived there were dispersed across the city with the promise that they would be able to return after the renovations. Two buildings were remodeled and reopened in 1991, but it soon became ap-parent that the other four high-rises would instead be demolished. Following protests from activist public housing residents, and after acrimonious negotia-tions and court proceedings, the Chicago Housing Authority was authorized to build 241 public housing apartments in North Kenwood-Oakland to par-tially replace the demolished high-rises. The process of getting the new public housing built in the neighborhood, placing families in it, and managing it has since been consistently on the agenda of the Conservation Community Coun-cil. Such agenda items almost always reopen the debate over the optimal socio-economic mix for the neighborhood, and over the integration of poor families with their new neighbors, who have paid a pretty penny for their homes.

Extensive new construction is possible in NKO because of past depop-ulation and demolition. Between 1960 and 1990, Kenwood lost over half of its population, and Oakland lost two-thirds, following a pattern of decline and concentrated poverty experienced by many inner-city black neighbor-hoods across the country. In 1990, Oakland was the poorest of Chicago's sev-enty-seven official communities in terms of both median family income and the proportion of families who were poor: 70 percent of Oakland's families had incomes below the federal poverty line. North Kenwood was only slightly better off, with 51 percent of its families living in poverty. Between 1990, when the city recognized the neighborhood as a conservation area, and 2000, the overall demographic story shows considerable upward socioeconomic change. By 2000, 20 percent of the families in the neighborhood earned more than

$50,000 per year, up from 6 percent a decade earlier. During the same period, the neighborhood's poverty rate declined precipitously, median family income more than doubled, the home ownership rate nearly doubled, and the cost of housing skyrocketed.

Despite these changes, Oakland was still the second poorest of Chicago's communities in terms of income and had the third highest neighborhood poverty rate in 2000. North Kenwood had the twelfth lowest median family income and the eighth highest poverty rate. Part of the reason for this is that in 2000 nearly 40 percent of North Kenwood-Oakland's housing stock—more than two thousand units—was publicly subsidized, either as public housing for families, the elderly, or the disabled or through other federal and state programs. Eligibility for these units is based on household income, with cut-offs that include some moderate-income workers and people receiving various forms of public assistance, many of whom also work. The presence of subsidized housing thus ensures the presence of poor and working-class families in NKO at least until the government contracts, which can range from fifteen to ninety-nine years, expire. When that time comes, landlords can either renew the contracts, thereby keeping their apartments affordable for the tenants who live there, or opt out of whatever subsidy program was used to finance the building. Those who opt out can then charge higher rents or convert the buildings to cooperatives or condominiums. During the course of this research, two subsidized buildings, with six apartments each, converted to for-sale condominiums.

Amid significant income flux, North Kenwood-Oakland remains predominantly black. It has been so since the 1950s, and it is for the most part experiencing "black gentrification." Black professionals are moving in from other Chicago neighborhoods, from other cities, and back to the city from the suburbs. For some African Americans, the move is motivated by what legal scholar Sheryll Cashin calls "integration exhaustion," the sociopsychological fatigue experienced especially by blacks who work in integrated environments or have been pioneers in white neighborhoods. Respondents in North Kenwood-Oakland, though, talked more about factors that pulled them toward a black neighborhood than factors that pushed them away from whites.

This process is also fueled by the growing affluence of African Americans in Chicago. The proportion of black households in Chicago with incomes over $50,000 doubled between 1990 and 2000, from 14 percent to 28 percent. The share of black households earning $100,000 or more rose even more dramatically, albeit from a smaller base, from 1 percent to 6 percent over the same time period. The expansion of the black middle and upper classes outpaced the expansion of high-income earners in any other racial or ethnic group. These households (especially at the highest end) are the likely newcomers to North

Kenwood-Oakland, where in 2006 a two-bedroom, two-bathroom condominium could cost as much as $300,000.

Some whites have moved into the neighborhood, but the discourse among black residents concerning the imminence of whites' arrival is more extensive and more telling than their actual presence. North Kenwood-Oakland was less than 1 percent white in 1990, and 1.2 percent white in 2000. Still, residents are convinced of an impending white offensive; I choose the word "offensive" precisely because it suggests an organized purpose. "Quite frankly," one resident asserted, "we were never supposed to be here. Black people were never supposed to be here." Another concurred: "There's no way in the world they're gonna leave between McCormick Place [the Chicago convention center] and the Museum [of Science and Industry] to us. I mean, let's face it, you know, they're not going to leave it with us. If we don't make the money and build up our own community within ourselves, they gon' take it."

Low-income black residents are doubly threatened, first by the price of the new housing and second by the prospect of racial exclusion. Tying these two issues together, one public housing resident in Oakland said, "Well, the changes I see now, they tearing down all the buildings and they getting ready to build homes. You know how they say the white people moved all the way to the suburbs because they don't want to be around us? So now they building all these homes knowing damn well most of us cannot afford them. So they trying to get the white people back in. And that's the system. And they want this lakefront back." Another public housing resident had a simple but bleak forecast for the neighborhood: "No more blacks." "No more blacks?" I asked. "Couple. Coupla blacks. They got money." From this resident's perspective, the neighborhood's future owners were white, or black people with money. She was not included in either scenario.

The fact of racial homogeneity does not preclude the importance of difference, divisions, and distinctions. There are many ways to categorize people in North Kenwood-Oakland: men and women, Baptists and African Methodist Episcopalians, native Chicagoans and out-of-towners, people who went to different Chicago high schools. The categories that this book is most preoccupied with, however, are those that relate to *class*. Technical definitions of class, as framed by academics, government officials, and other definition makers, include some combination of how much money a person has, what kind of work he does, and how far she went in school. Common, everyday practices of determining if someone is in the lower, working, middle, or upper class are likely to be based on similar criteria. But people do not wear their diplomas on their sleeves or have their net worth written on their foreheads. Because we often cannot know the "hard facts" of class position, we usually settle for observing and making sense of "soft facts" instead. We express our own class standing and read others' class positions through signs of language, dress, demeanor, performance, and other objects and behaviors that have social meaning and that can be mapped onto the class hierarchy. This kind of stratification in the social order is what Max Weber called "status," where status groups are stratified according to the principles of their *consumption* of goods. The habits and manners with which people use the things they buy (or use their free time or deploy their bodies) constitute "styles of life," or lifestyles. Weber argues that the two spheres of *class* and *status* are closely connected. "The social order is of course conditioned by the economic order to a high degree," Weber writes, "and in its turn reacts upon it."

The intertwined economic and social orders are both important in North Kenwood-Oakland. But as in American society more generally, discussions about lifestyles and status are more salient, whereas there is relative silence on the topics of class and the materiality of economic circumstances. Americans talk *around* class by using the vocabulary of status and lifestyles. Instead of referring to how much money someone makes, we describe their overseas vacations or their fancy cars. Instead of looking at a person's résumé to see if he or she attended college, we dismiss him because he has cornrows or her because she wears long press-on nails.

Many people also call this the realm of culture. Unfortunately, the word "culture" has been overly biologized. Ever since anthropologist Oscar Lewis proclaimed, dreadfully, that "by the time slum children are age six or seven they have usually absorbed the basic values and attitudes of their subculture and are not psychologically geared to take full advantage of changing conditions or increased opportunities which may occur in their life-time" there have been academic wars over just how much a pathological culture is to blame for poverty, and black poverty in particular. As a result of those debates, and despite many attempts to rescue the term, "culture" now conjures up notions of a way of life to which people are so attached that they cannot part with it or change it. Poor people's (and black people's) culture has been cast as a defective body part that causes debilitating stress on the entire collective organism. Because people are so stuck in a dysfunctional culture, one outside the "mainstream," they must be, goes the argument, *morally* deficient. From biology to morals, the word has taken on too much baggage. So while "culture" may be the more common rubric for the facets of life that I describe in this book, "lifestyle" is more *analytically* powerful because it avoids the preachy muck in which culture often gets stuck. The lifestyle markers that take center stage in the debates about who should be included in and excluded from North Kenwood-Oakland can always be traced back to and mapped forward onto the hard facts of economic inequality, or the silent salience of class in American society.

CULTURE AND THE
POLITICS OF REPRESENTATION

Media as Sites/Sights of Justice

Patrick R. Grzanka

"Culture" is always at risk of disappearing into nothingness. By this I do not mean that popular culture is monotonous trash, as the founding theorists of the Frankfurt School of Critical Theory basically concluded when they took a hard, close look at American culture in the mid-twentieth century (Horkheimer and Adorno 1947). Nor do I mean that multiculturalism in the United States is mixing cultures to the extent that "pure," traditional cultures are being lost to cultural hybridity and bastardization, though this is certainly a common refrain from cultural conservatives on the Right and the Left (Gray 2005). Rather, I am referring to the precarious use of the term "culture" in sociology, women's studies, American studies, anthropology, and related fields in which culture can mean everything and nothing at the same time. Indeed, critical inquiry into culture often gets bottlenecked at the get-go, because developing sufficiently specific but adequately flexible definitions of culture is a battle in and of itself. On the other hand, there's the flippant and sloppy use of "culture" which assumes everyone shares a definition of the concept. To sociologists of culture, this is the academic equivalent of nails on a chalkboard, and could be likened to overuse and misuse of the term "society," which by no coincidence is often conflated with "culture"! Nonetheless, we need to get a sense of what culture means and what kind of culture we are talking about in order to consider what intersectional cultural studies does or might look like.

Sociologist and cultural studies founder Stuart Hall (1997) defined culture as "shared meanings." Drawing on the work of theorist Paul du Gay, Hall offered the "circuit of culture" as a way to think of the complex interchanges between consumers, producers, regulation, identities, and representation, none of which is fully separate from the other processes in the circuit. For example, it is impossible to imagine a producer of culture (e.g., a visual artist, journalism, filmmaker) who is not also a consumer. To Hall, and to practitioners of his brand of cultural studies, language is the medium through which culture moves, because "meanings can only be shared through our common access to language" (1). Language means more than spoken or written words; language, according to Hall, refers to any kind of system through which meaning can travel between social actors, including digital images, music, food, signs, and symbols. Accordingly, cultural studies is concerned with language because it is where meaning is made and exchanged; therefore, language is the social landscape in which representation occurs. All of this matters to Hall, because language is where ideas, feelings, and thoughts are represented, and representation is always political.

To assert that representation is political is to say that no representation ever occurs in a social vacuum, and because all social interaction happens in a field of power relations, representation is like any other social process that may involve the exercise or exchange of power. We come to know and create meanings of race, gender, class, sexuality, and other dimensions of difference through representations, so intersectionality is both a structural *and* a representational phenomenon. In this unit, the readings explore the *politics of representation:* where, when, and how representations produce, reflect, and potentially subvert inequalities. In the interest of developing a coherent dialogue about how these intersectional analyses of representations work, I have chosen to focus on scholarship that explores media as a site of social inequality. Media, particularly mass media such as film, television, journalism, popular fiction, and all Internet-based media (e.g., blogs, YouTube, Tumblr, Twitter, etc.), are an important domain of intersectional critique especially because of how they communicate and produce powerful ideas about social groups and social problems.

Thinking critically about culture is not a new or recent development in sociology, nor is thinking about culture in relationship to social structures. Indeed, the development of Frankfurt School Critical Theory (e.g., Horkheimer & Adorno 1947), British cultural studies (Hall 1981, 1997), and the sociology of culture itself (e.g., Williams 1981; Bourdieu 1993) are all deeply indebted to Marxist approaches that connect culture to the inner workings of systemic oppression. A society's "superstructure," in traditional Marxist framings, is the realm of culture and ideas, and the superstructure reflects the "base," which is where economic activity (i.e., labor and the production of capital) happens. In capitalism, the exploitation of the masses is legitimated in the realm of culture, and so the superstructure reflects the ruling classes' interests. Like all

Marxisms, this perspective—as variously articulated by Horkheimer, Adorno, Hall, Williams, and Bourdieu—emphasizes class dynamics and sometimes insists that structures and identities such as race, gender, and sexuality are the products of capitalism—though Hall and Bourdieu's work are notable exceptions. Racism, sexism, and ableism, for example, are figured in the traditional Marxist frame as various forms of capitalist technologies of social control. Marxism continues to exert tremendous influence on how scholars think about culture across the disciplines, but intersectional approaches to culture, which do not foreground class at the expense of other forms of social inequality, are likely to reject the idea that all dimensions of difference are derived from and serve the interests of class domination.

bell hooks (1992), for example, is invested in class critique, but her work interlocks race, class, and gender in what she terms "White supremacist capitalist patriarchy" (reading 18). hooks echoes Collins's (1990/2000) notion of the matrix of domination, in which intersections of oppression are organized within a highly complex and contextually dynamic framework of inequality. Though still thoroughly historical like Marxism, this approach examines how race and class reinforce one another and collaborate in the production of inequality, rather than posit one as prior to the other historically or conceptually. hooks views popular media culture as a site of discourse about race, gender, class, and sexuality that works through multiple languages, especially visual images. To her, the film *Paris Is Burning,* about drag balls in New York City organized largely by gay men and transgender women of color, is a "sight" of intersectional oppression, because the film shores up ideas about Black femininity's inferiority to all other forms of feminine expression and beauty. She views director Jennie Livingston's construction of film to be acutely racist, sexist, and classist, and she uses experiential evidence of watching the film with affluent Whites to explore how the images in *Paris Is Burning* are easily co-opted by and through a hegemonic lens.

Philosopher Judith Butler (1993, reading 19), on the other hand, offers a different reading of the film, and through her theory of "performativity" elaborates on the cultural politics of so-called "subversive" images. Rather than decide that *Paris Is Burning* is fundamentally a progressive or conservative text, Butler plays with the possibilities of a) Livingston's film, b) the real people in it, and c) its viewers to reify or undermine dominant cultural ideology of sexuality, race, and gender. She takes up a more ambivalent reading of the film than hooks and foregrounds the polysemy (i.e., multiple meanings) of *Paris Is Burning* and drag performances in general. In this sense, Butler's critique is consonant with sociologist Darnell Hunt's (2005) position that analyses of race and identity in media move beyond binary frameworks that suggest media can be reduced to "positive" or "negative" images. Hunt explains that such texts:

cannot be understood without also considering the social context in which the texts are embedded, as well as audience needs, interests, and proclivities. "Positive" or "negative" means very little in isolation. Meaning is indeed relational, and representational consequences are often a double-edged sword. Coming to terms with the *text/context/audience* triad is essential to making sense of the ideological work performed by Blackness on television. (15–16)

Hunt's perspective above, which lacks explicit attention to intersectionality, is nonetheless a useful way of thinking about the potential of intersectional cultural studies, because moving beyond a positive/negative binary facilitates the discovery of unexpected and unpredictable meanings that emerge when intersectional images are produced, disseminated, and consumed in intersectional contexts. For example, a single-axis analysis concerned only with evaluating gender representations might prematurely conclude that a film or television series supports feminist or gender-progressive ideas while incidentally eliding racist or classist images in the text (Grzanka 2010; Grzanka and Mann, forthcoming). These kinds of analyses leave little room for representational complexity and obfuscate how gender is never isolated from race, sexuality, and other dimensions of difference. Imagine the trouble with concluding "'Series X' presents complex and progressive representations of women" without considering how those women, as is the case in *Sex and the City* or *Girls,* are almost exclusively wealthy and White. And when a positive/negative evaluation is the goal of such a project, this logic quickly unravels even when attempting to think intersectionally: "The gender elements of the show are 'good,' but the racial elements of the show are 'bad.'" This mode of thinking erases how identities and representations are constructed along several dimensions and allows no space for thinking about groups whose experiences are defined by multiple axes of inequality, such as working-class women and queers of color. This also ignores how images can be understood and interpreted in widely variable ways by different social groups in different social contexts (i.e., audiences).

Intersectional analyses that wrestle with what Hunt (2005) calls the "text/context/audience" triad ask different questions and seek different answers so as to promote critical thinking on the relations between multiple dimensions of difference, cultural production, and meaning-making practices in media. For example, Rosalind Gill (2009, reading 21) explores the representation of men's bodies in advertising and focuses on the constitution of the "sixpack" as the epitome of aesthetically desirable masculinity. She pushes back against the notion that the objectification of (racially diverse) men in magazine and television advertising signals gender, sexual, or racial equality. By foregrounding intersectionality in her analyses, she finds that:

advertising images of the last two decades have been designed to offset or diffuse some of the anxieties and threats generated by presenting men as objects of an "undifferentiated" sexual gaze. Neither hegemonic masculinity nor the institution of heterosexuality have been destroyed—though we are seeing more fractured hegemonies perhaps—and "sexualized" representation of the male body has not proved incommensurable with male dominance. Rather it appears that a highly specific set of modes of representing the male body have emerged—which are quite different from sexualized representations of women's bodies. (2009, 147–148).

Kara Keeling (2009, reading 20) likewise studies the film *The Aggressives* to explore counterhegemonic constructions of Black queer female masculinities, and she connects her insights to social theoretical conceptualizations of time and affect. Keeling's and Gill's work are not geared toward deciding whether or not the texts they are studying are good or bad. Rather, they connect them to larger cultural constructs and social forces that may simultaneously reflect or subvert structural inequalities.

In his influential book *Cultural Moves,* sociologist Herman Gray explains that, "In many areas of cultural production, both marginal and mainstream, representations and discourses cannot be read clearly and coherently, predictably and correctly in the direction and interest of only one kind of politics of political vision" (2005, 116). Diverting attention away from simplistic renderings of cultural politics, Gray introduces the idea of "palace discourse": "those systems of thought and habit of mind emanating from the crystal palaces of Western power/knowledge (of which aesthetics is merely one)" (114). Gray argues that culture in the contemporary United States is dominated by palace discourse that actively co-opts theoretical categories such as "difference," "multiculturalism," and "diversity" (c.f., Grzanka and Maher 2012). Gray's work is important because it challenges media scholars to attend to the dangers of calls for representational inclusion (e.g., more people of color on network television) that merely incorporate difference into stereotypical, hegemonic frameworks. The palace of US corporate media, Gray asserts, has a complicated relationship to difference: it simultaneously and contradictorily ignores and represses difference; hierarchically orders difference; celebrates difference while eliding the history of difference as a tool of oppression; and marks difference as an impediment to "grander narratives of global twenty-first-century homogeneity" (Gray 2005, 115). Because intersectionality rejects the palace discourse of single-axis frameworks, it possesses the *potential* to challenge palace discourse in other sites, including the media. But Gray cautiously reminds us to think otherwise about media and cultural criticism, so as to not fall into the traps of hegemonic logic that would have us embrace multicultural, utopian metanarratives; fetishize difference; or forget about how "difference operates as the basis for cultural and social domination, terror and repression" (119). Accordingly, the readings in this unit are a call to think about difference and injustice in the cultural sphere, and to cultivate intersectional discourses that might displace and replace palace discourse—not so much in the interest of "multiculturalism" or "diversity," but for futures occupied by complex images that do more than reflect inequalities. Then, media and culture might become sites/sights of counterhegemonic imagination, radical creativity, and new politics of representation.

References and Further Reading

Anderson, E., and M. McCormack. 2010. "Intersectionality, Critical Race Theory, and American Sporting Oppression: Examining Black and Gay Male Athletes." *Journal of Homosexuality* 57: 949–967.

Bourdieu, P. 1993. *The Field of Cultural Production: Essays on Art and Literature*. New York: Columbia University Press.

Butler, J. 1993. *Bodies That Matter: On the Discursive Limits of "Sex."* New York: Routledge.

Carroll, H. 2011. *Affirmative Reaction: New Formations of White Masculinity*. Durham, NC: Duke University Press.

Collins, P. H. (1990) 2000. *Black Feminist Thought: Knowledge, Consciousness, and the Politics of Empowerment*. Second edition. New York: Routledge.

Collins, P. H. 2005. *Black Sexual Politics: African Americans, Gender and the New Racism*. New York: Routledge.

Davis, A. Y. 1990. *Women, Culture, and Politics*. New York: Vintage.

Davis, K. C. 2004. "Oprah's Book Club and the Politics of Cross-Racial Empathy." *International Journal of Cultural Studies* 7: 399–419.

Dubrofsky, R. E. 2006. "*The Bachelor*: Whiteness in the Harem." *Critical Studies in Media Communication* 23: 39–56.

Gamson, J. 1999. *Freaks Talk Back: Tabloid Talk Shows and Sexual Nonconformity*. Chicago, IL: University of Chicago Press.

Gill, R. 2009. "Beyond the 'Sexualization of Culture' Thesis: An Intersectional Analysis of 'Sixpacks,' 'Midriffs' and Hot Lesbians' in Advertising." *Sexualities* 12: 137–160.

Gray, H. S. 2005. *Cultural Moves: African Americans and the Politics of Representation*. Berkeley: University of California Press.

Grzanka, P. R. 2010. "Buffy the Black Feminist? Intersectionality and Pedagogy." In *Buffy in the Classroom: Essays on Teaching with the Vampire Slayer*, edited by J. A. Kreider and M. K. Winchell, 186–201.

Grzanka, P. R., and J. T. Maher. 2012. "Different, Like Everyone Else: *Stuff White People Like* and the Marketplace of Diversity." *Symbolic Interaction* 35: 368–393.

Grzanka, P. R., and E. S. Mann (forthcoming). "Queer Youth Suicide and the Psychopolitics of 'It Gets Better.'" *Sexualities*.

Hall, S. (1981) 2011. "Notes on Deconstructing 'the Popular.'" In *Cultural Theory: An Anthology*, edited by I. Szeman and T. Kaposy. Oxford, UK: Wiley-Blackwell.

Hall, S. 1997. "Introduction." In *Representation: Cultural Representations and Signifying Practices,* edited by S. Hall, 1–12. London: Sage Publications & Open University.

hooks, b. 1992. *Black Looks: Race and Representation.* Cambridge, MA: South End Press.

Horkheimer, M., and T. W. Adorno. (1947) 2002. *Dialectic of Enlightenment: Philosophical Fragments.* Palo Alto, CA: Stanford University Press.

Hunt, D. M., ed. 2005. *Channeling Blackness: Studies on Television and Race in America.* New York: Oxford University Press.

Keeling, K. 2009. "Looking for M—: Queer Temporality, Black Political Possibility, and Poetry from the Future." *GLQ: A Journal of Lesbian and Gay Studies* 15: 565–582.

Lee, R. C. 2004. "'Where's My Parade?': Margaret Cho and the Asian American Body in Space." *The Drama Review* 48: 108–132.

Muñoz, J. E. 1999. *Disidentifications: Queers of Color and the Politics of Performance.* Minneapolis: University of Minnesota Press.

Parks, S. L. 2010. *Fierce Angels: The Strong Black Women in American Life and Culture.* New York: One World/Ballantine.

Perry, I. 2004. *Prophets of the Hood: Politics and Poetics in Hip-Hop.* Durham, NC: Duke University Press.

Rose, T. 1994. *Black Noise: Rap Music and Black Culture in Contemporary America.* Middletown, CT: Wesleyan University Press.

Williams, R. 1981. *The Sociology of Culture.* Chicago: University of Chicago Press.

Williams-Forson, P. 2006. *Building Houses out of Chicken Legs: Black Women, Food, and Power.* Chapel Hill: University of North Carolina Press.

Zarkov, D. 2011. "Exposures and Invisibilities: Media, Masculinities and the Narratives of Wars in an Intersectional Perspective." In *Framing Intersectionality: Debates on a Multi-faceted Concept in Gender Studies,* edited by H. Lutz, M. T. H. Vivar, and L. Supik, 105–120. Burlington, VT: Ashgate Publishing Company.

bell hooks

bell hooks is one of the most prolific and well-known authors in African American studies and women's studies. Her writing is both accessible and radical, and her ideas have made her the equivalent of a household name in many academic circles, including the sociology of race, gender, ethnicity, and class. She is Distinguished Professor in Residence in Appalachian Studies at Berea College in her home state of Kentucky. Born Gloria Jean Watkins in Hopkinsville, Kentucky, she chose the lowercase pen name "bell hooks" as a combination of her mother and grandmother's names and to emphasize the substance of her writing as opposed to who she is: at this point, a renowned public intellectual. She holds a PhD from the University of California, Santa Cruz, and she is the author of over twenty books, including *Ain't I a Woman?: Black Women and*

Feminism (1981), *Killing Rage: Ending Racism* (1995), and *Black Looks: Race and Representation* (1992), a collection of twelve essays that explores the politics of race and representation in the context of White supremacist American culture at the end of the twentieth century.

In the following essay from *Black Looks,* hooks explains her critique of the film *Paris Is Burning,* a controversial documentary by the White lesbian filmmaker Jennie Livingston that chronicles the lives of gay men and transgender women of color in the now legendary drag balls of New York City in the 1980s and early 1990s. hooks questions Livingston's subject position as documentarian in ways that the film itself does not, exploring how Livingston's unmarked gaze—that of a White middle-class woman documenting and, therefore, constructing the lives of working class gay men of color—may reinforce, rather than subvert, interlocking dominant racist, White supremacist ideologies of race, gender, class, and sexuality. The camera's supposed position of neutrality is, to hooks, an impossible, imaginary position, because Livingston *and* her viewers bring their intersectionally informed perspectives to the production and consumption of *Paris Is Burning.* In this sense, hooks figures the film as a kind of dialogic mediascape in which Whiteness and Blackness, as well as masculinity and femininity, are in a process of making and remaking each other. In characteristic hooks style, the author insists that Livingston's film warrants serious examination for what it does (e.g., presents a spectacle of otherness) and does not do (e.g., explore the roles that Whiteness, capitalism, misogyny, and heterosexism play in informing the reception and uptake of the drag queens of the balls). Note that Judith Butler's response to hooks appears in the next section (reading 19); together, they represent an indispensable exemplar of intersectional cultural analyses.

18. Why Are You Laughing?*

Within white supremacist, capitalist patriarchy the experience of men dressing as women, appearing in drag, has always been regarded by the dominant heterosexist cultural gaze as a sign that one is symbolically crossing over from a realm of power into a realm of powerlessness.

For black males to take appearing in drag seriously, be they gay or straight, is to oppose a heterosexist representation of black manhood. Gender bending and blending on the part of black males has always been a critique of phallocentric masculinity in traditional black experience. Yet the subversive power of those images is radically altered when informed by a racialized fictional

---

* Excerpted from b. hooks, *Black Looks: Race and Representation* (Cambridge, MA: South End Press, 1992).

construction of the "feminine" that suddenly makes the representation of whiteness as crucial to the experience of female impersonation as gender, that is to say when the idealized notion of the female/feminine is really a sexist idealization of white womanhood. This is brutally evident in Jennie Livingston's new film *Paris Is Burning*. Within the world of the black gay drag ball culture she depicts, the idea of womanness and femininity is totally personified by whiteness. What viewers witness is not black men longing to impersonate or even to become like "real" black women but their obsession with an idealized fetishized vision of femininity that is white. Called out in the film by Dorian Carey, who names it by saying no black drag queen of his day wanted to be Lena Horne, he makes it clear that the femininity most sought after, most adored, was that perceived to be the exclusive property of white womanhood. When we see visual representations of womanhood in the film (images torn from magazines and posted on walls in living space) they are, with rare exceptions, of white women. Significantly, the fixation on becoming as much like a white female as possible implicitly evokes a connection to a figure never visible in this film: that of the white male patriarch. And yet if the class, race, and gender aspirations expressed by the drag queens who share their deepest dreams is always the longing to be in the position of the ruling-class woman then that means there is also the desire to act in partnership with the ruling-class white male.

Any viewer of *Paris Is Burning* can neither deny the way in which its contemporary drag balls have the aura of sports events, aggressive competitions, one team (in this case "house") competing against another etc., nor ignore the way in which the male "gaze" in the audience is directed at participants in a manner akin to the objectifying phallic stare straight men direct at "feminine" women daily in public spaces. *Paris Is Burning* is a film that many audiences assume is inherently oppositional because of its subject matter and the identity of the filmmaker. Yet the film's politics of race, gender, and class are played out in ways that are both progressive and reactionary.

When I first heard that there was this new documentary film about black gay men, drag queens, and drag balls I was fascinated by the title. It evoked images of the real Paris on fire, of the death and destruction of a dominating white western civilization and culture, an end to oppressive Eurocentrism and white supremacy. This fantasy not only gave me a sustained sense of pleasure, it stood between me and the unlikely reality that a young white filmmaker, offering a progressive vision of "blackness" from the standpoint of "whiteness," would receive the positive press accorded Livingston and her film. Watching *Paris Is Burning*, I began to think that the many yuppie-looking, straight-acting, pushy, predominantly white folks in the audience were there because the film in no way interrogates "whiteness." These folks left the film saying it was "amazing," "marvelous," "incredibly funny," worthy of statements like, "Didn't you just love it?" And no, I didn't just love it. For in many ways the film was a graphic documentary portrait of the way in which colonized black people (in this case black gay brothers, some of whom were drag queens) worship at the throne of whiteness, even when such worship demands that we live in perpetual self-hate, steal, lie, go hungry, and even die in its pursuit. The "we" evoked here is all of us, black people/people of color, who are daily bombarded by a powerful colonizing whiteness that seduces us away from ourselves, that negates that there is beauty to be found in any form of blackness that is not imitation whiteness.

The whiteness celebrated in *Paris Is Burning* is not just any old brand of whiteness but rather that brutal imperial ruling-class capitalist patriarchal whiteness that presents itself—its way of life—as the only meaningful life there is. What could be more reassuring to a white public fearful that marginalized disenfranchised black folks might rise any day now and make revolutionary black liberation struggle a reality than a documentary affirming that colonized, victimized, exploited, black folks are all too willing to be complicit in perpetuating the fantasy that ruling-class white culture is the quintessential site of unrestricted joy, freedom, power, and pleasure. Indeed it is the very "pleasure" that so many white viewers with class privilege experience when watching this film that has acted to censor dissenting voices who find the film and its reception critically problematic.

Livingston's film is presented as though it is a politically neutral documentary providing a candid, even celebratory, look at black drag balls. And it is precisely the mood of celebration that masks the extent to which the balls are not necessarily radical expressions of subversive imagination at work undermining and challenging the *status quo.* Much of the film's focus on pageantry takes the ritual of the black drag ball and makes it spectacle. Ritual is that ceremonial act that carries with it meaning and significance beyond what appears, while spectacle functions primarily as entertaining dramatic display. Those of us who have grown up in a segregated black setting where we participated in diverse pageants and rituals know that those elements of a given ritual that are empowering and subversive may not be readily visible to an outsider looking in. Hence it is easy for white observers to depict black rituals as spectacle.

Jennie Livingston approaches her subject matter as an outsider looking in. Since her presence as white woman/lesbian filmmaker is "absent" from *Paris Is Burning* it is easy for viewers to imagine that they are watching an ethnographic film documenting the life of black gay "natives" and not recognize that they are watching a work shaped and formed by a perspective and standpoint specific to Livingston. By cinematically masking this reality (we hear her ask questions but never see her), Livingston does not oppose the way hegemonic whiteness "represents" blackness, but rather assumes an imperial overseeing position that is in no way progressive or counter-hegemonic. By shooting the film using a conventional approach to documentary and not making clear how her standpoint breaks with this tradition, Livingston assumes a privileged location of "innocence." She is represented both in interviews and reviews as the tender-hearted, mild-mannered, virtuous white woman daring to venture into a contemporary "heart of darkness" to bring back knowledge of the natives.

A review in the *New Yorker* declares (with no argument to substantiate the assertion) that "the movie is a sympathetic observation of a specialized, private world." An interview with Livingston in *Outweek* is titled "Pose, She Said" and we are told in the preface that she "discovered the Ball world by chance." Livingston does not discuss her interest and fascination with black gay subculture. She is not asked to speak about what knowledge, information, or lived understanding of black culture and history she possessed that provided a background for her work or to explain what vision of black life she hoped to convey and to whom. Can anyone imagine that a black woman lesbian would make a film about white gay subculture and not be asked these questions? Livingston is asked in the *Outweek* interview, "How did you build up the kind of trust where people are so open to talking about their personal experiences?" She never answers this question. Instead she suggests that she gains her "credibility" by the intensity of her spectatorship, adding, "I also targeted people who were articulate, who had stuff they wanted to say and were very happy that anyone wanted to listen." Avoiding the difficult questions underlying what it means to be a white person in a white supremacist society creating a film about any aspect of black life, Livingston responds to the question, "Didn't the fact that you're a white lesbian going into a world of Black queens and street kids make that [the interview process] difficult?" by implicitly evoking a shallow sense of universal connection. She responds, "If you know someone over a period of two years, and they still retain their sex and their race, you've got to be a pretty sexist, racist person." Yet it is precisely the race, sex, and sexual practices of black men who are filmed that is the exploited subject matter.

So far I have read no interviews where Livingston discusses the issue of appropriation. And even though she is openly critical of Madonna, she does not convey how her work differs from Madonna's appropriation of black experience. To some extent it is precisely the recognition by mass culture that aspects of black life, like "voguing," fascinate white audiences that creates a market for both Madonna's product and Livingston's. Unfortunately, Livingston's comments about *Paris Is Burning* do not convey serious thought about either the political and aesthetic implications of her choice as a white woman focusing on an aspect of black life and culture or the way racism might shape and inform how she would interpret black experience on the screen. Reviewers like Georgia Brown in the *Village Voice* who suggest that Livingston's whiteness is "a fact of nature that didn't hinder her research" collude in the denial of the way whiteness informs her perspective and standpoint. To say, as Livingston does, "I certainly don't have the final word on the gay black experience. I'd love for a black director to have made this film" is to oversimplify the issue and to absolve her of responsibility and accountability for progressive critical reflection and it implicitly suggests that there would be no difference between her work and that of a black director. Underlying this apparently self-effacing comment is cultural arrogance, for she implies not only that she has cornered the market on the subject matter but that being able to make films is a question of personal choice, like she just "discovered" the "raw material" before a black director did. Her comments are disturbing because they reveal so little awareness of the politics that undergird any commodification of "blackness" in this society.

Had Livingston approached her subject with greater awareness of the way white supremacy shapes cultural production—determining not only what representations of blackness are deemed acceptable, marketable, as well worthy of seeing—perhaps the film would not so easily have turned the black drag ball into a spectacle for the entertainment of those presumed to be on the outside of this experience looking in. So much of what is expressed in the film has to do with questions of power and privilege and the way racism impedes black progress (and certainly the class aspirations of the black gay subculture depicted do not differ from those of other poor and underclass black communities). Here, the supposedly "outsider" position is primarily located in the experience of whiteness. Livingston appears unwilling to interrogate the way assuming the position of outsider looking in, as well as interpreter, can, and often does, pervert and distort one's perspective. Her ability to assume such a position without rigorous interrogation of intent is rooted in the politics of race and racism. Patricia Williams critiques the white assumption of a "neutral" gaze in her essay "Teleology on the Rocks" included in her new book *The Alchemy of Race and Rights*. Describing taking a walking tour of Harlem with a group of white folks, she recalls the guide telling them they might "get to see some services" since "Easter Sunday in Harlem is quite a show." William's critical observations are relevant to any discussion of *Paris Is Burning*:

> What astonished me was that no one had asked the churches if they wanted to be stared at like living museums. I wondered what would happen if a group of blue-jeaned blacks were to walk uninvited into a synagogue on Passover or St. Anthony's of Padua during high mass—just to peer, not pray. My feeling is that such activity would be seen as disrespectful, at the very least. Yet the aspect of disrespect, intrusion, seemed

irrelevant to this well-educated, affable group of people. They deflected my observation with comments like "We just want to look," "No one will mind," and "There's no harm intended." As well-intentioned as they were, I was left with the impression that no one existed for them who could not be governed by their intentions.

This insightful critique came to mind as I reflected on why whites could so outspokenly make their pleasure in this film heard and the many black viewers who express discontent, raising critical questions about how the film was made, is seen, and is talked about, who have not named their displeasure publicly. Too many reviewers and interviewers assume not only that there is no need to raise pressing critical questions about Livingston's film, but act as though she somehow did this marginalized black gay subculture a favor by bringing their experience to a wider public. Such a stance obscures the substantial rewards she has received for this work. Since so many of the black gay men in the film express the desire to be big stars, it is easy to place Livingston in the role of benefactor, offering these "poor black souls" a way to realize their dreams. But it is this current trend in producing colorful ethnicity for the white consumer appetite that makes it possible for blackness to be commodified in unprecedented ways, and for whites to appropriate black culture without interrogating whiteness or showing concern for the displeasure of blacks. Just as white cultural imperialism informed and affirmed the adventurous journeys of colonizing whites into the countries and cultures of "dark others," it allows white audiences to applaud representations of black culture, if they are satisfied with the images and habits of being represented.

Watching the film with a black woman friend, we were disturbed by the extent to which white folks around us were "entertained" and "pleasured" by scenes we viewed as sad and at times tragic. Often individuals laughed at personal testimony about hardship, pain, loneliness. Several times I yelled out in the dark: "What is so funny about this scene? Why are you laughing?" The laughter was never innocent. Instead it undermined the seriousness of the film, keeping it always on the level of spectacle. And much of the film helped make this possible. Moments of pain and sadness were quickly covered up by dramatic scenes from drag balls, as though there were two competing cinematic narratives, one displaying the pageantry of the drag ball and the other reflecting on the lives of participants and value of the fantasy. This second narrative was literally hard to hear because the laughter often drowned it out, just as the sustained focus on elaborate displays at balls diffused the power of the more serious critical narrative. Any audience hoping to be entertained would not be as interested in the true life stories and testimonies narrated. Much of the individual testimony makes it appear that the characters are estranged from any community beyond themselves. Families, friends, etc., are not shown, which adds to the representation of these black gay men as cut off, living on the edge.

Certainly the degree to which black men in this gay subculture are portrayed as cut off from a "real" world heightens the emphasis on fantasy, and indeed gives *Paris Is Burning* its tragic edge. That tragedy is made explicit when we are told that the fair-skinned Venus has been murdered, and yet there is no mourning of him/her in the film, no intense focus on the sadness of this murder. Having served the purpose of "spectacle" the film abandons him/her. The audience does not see Venus after the murder. There are no scenes of grief. To put it crassly, her dying is upstaged by spectacle. Death is not entertaining.

For those of us who did not come to this film as voyeurs of black gay subculture, it is Dorian Carey's moving testimony throughout the film that makes *Paris Is Burning* a memorable experience. Carey is both historian and cultural critic in the film. He explains how the balls enabled marginalized black gay queens to empower both participants and audience. It is Carey who talks about the significance of the "star" in the life of gay black men who are queens. In a manner similar to critic Richard Dyer in his work *Heavenly Bodies,* Carey tells viewers that the desire for stardom is an expression of the longing to realize the dream of autonomous stellar individualism. Reminding readers that the idea of the individual continues to be a major image of what it means to live in a democratic world, Dyer writes:

> Capitalism justifies itself on the basis of the freedom (separateness) of anyone to make money, sell their labor how they will, to be able to express opinions and get them heard (regardless of wealth or social position). The openness of society is assumed by the way that we are addressed as individuals—as consumers (each freely choosing to buy, or watch, what we want), as legal subjects (equally responsible before the law), as political subjects (able to make up our minds who is to run society). Thus even while the notion of the individual is assailed on all sides, it is a necessary fiction for the reproduction of the kind of society we live in . . . Stars articulate these ideas of personhood.

This is precisely the notion of stardom Carey articulates. He emphasizes the way consumer capitalism undermines the subversive power of the drag balls, subordinating ritual to spectacle, removing the will to display unique imaginative costumes and the purchased image. Carey speaks profoundly about the redemptive power of the imagination in black life, that drag balls were traditionally a place where the aesthetics of the image in relation to black gay life could be explored with complexity and grace. Without being sentimental about suffering, Dorian Carey urges all of us to break through denial, through the longing for an illusory star identity, so that we can confront and accept ourselves as we really are—only then can fantasy, ritual, be a site of seduction, passion, and play where the self is truly recognized, loved, and never abandoned or betrayed.

Judith Butler

In this excerpt from *Bodies that Matter: On the Discursive Limits of "Sex"* (1993), Judith Butler revisits her theory of performativity to explore *Paris Is Burning* and to respond to bell hooks's critique of the documentary (see reading 18). Butler, a leading feminist philosopher who currently holds professorships at both the University of California, Berkeley, and the European Graduate School, uses the concept of performativity to explore how gender is a reiterative, repetitive *process* whereby gender is best characterized as a citational practice in which subjects "do" or "perform" gender in relation to previously established norms. Performativity comes to calcify what counts as normal, acceptable gender performance, and Butler argues in *Bodies that Matter* that so-called "subversive" gender performances must also be understood in relation to norms. Butler's writing is notoriously difficult to comprehend, particularly on a first read, but it is important not to misinterpret her use of the term *performativity* as implying that gender is defined by the agency of the subject, like an identity or a practice that is freely chosen by individuals and performed without regard to social structures. Performativity, to Butler, captures how gender becomes a violent, material, oppressive system driven by what she terms the "heterosexual imperative."

Butler's entry point here is Venus Extravaganza, arguably the "star" of *Paris Is Burning*, who is murdered—presumably by a john, perhaps in response to the discovery of Venus's anatomy—before Livingston completed the film. Butler investigates the "realness" that Venus and the other queens pursue, and the ways in which they use realness to judge each other's literal and figurative performances of gender, race, and class. Drawing on the work of the Marxist theorist of hegemony (i.e., social domination) Antonio Gramsci, Butler asks whether drag should be evaluated as *either* subversive or conservative, and questions hooks's reading of drag and the film as misogynist and racist. Butler does not disagree with hooks per se; rather, she opts for a greater degree of ambivalence toward the film and the complex representations therein. In one of the most famous passages in all of Butler's writing, in which she pithily claims that all gender is (a) drag, she provocatively suggests that drag is only subversive to the extent that, in reproducing or imitating heterosexual norms, drag reminds us of what a charade heterosexuality really is. And heterosexuality, to both hooks and Butler, is intimately connected to the reiterative practices of White supremacy and capitalism, which also coproduce intertwined standards of what can be identified as "real," "natural," and "original."

19. Ambivalent Drag*

Venus, and *Paris Is Burning* more generally, calls into question whether parodying the dominant norms is enough to displace them; indeed, whether the denaturalization of gender cannot be the very vehicle for a reconsolidation of hegemonic norms. Although many readers understood *Gender Trouble* to be arguing for the proliferation of drag performances as a way of subverting dominant gender norms, I want to underscore that there is no necessary relation between drag and subversion, and that drag may well be used in the service of both the denaturalization and reidealization of hyperbolic heterosexual gender norms. At best, it seems, drag is a site of a certain ambivalence, one which reflects the more general situation of being implicated in the regimes of power by which one is constituted and, hence, of being implicated in the very regimes of power that one opposes.

To claim that all gender is like drag, or is drag, is to suggest that "imitation" is at the heart of the *heterosexual* project and its gender binarisms, that drag is not a secondary imitation that presupposes a prior and original gender, but that hegemonic heterosexuality is itself a constant and repeated effort to imitate its own idealizations. That it must repeat this imitation, that it sets up pathologizing practices and normalizing sciences in order to produce and consecrate its own claim on originality and propriety, suggests that heterosexual performativity is beset by an anxiety that it can never fully overcome, that its effort to become its own idealizations can never be finally or fully achieved, and that it is consistently haunted by that domain of sexual possibility that must be excluded for heterosexualized gender to produce itself. In this sense, then, drag is subversive to the extent that it reflects on the imitative structure by which hegemonic gender is itself produced and disputes heterosexuality's claim on naturalness and originality.

In her provocative review of *Paris Is Burning,* bell hooks criticized some productions of gay male drag as misogynist, and here she allied herself in part with feminist theorists such as Marilyn Frye and Janice Raymond. This tradition within feminist thought has argued that drag is offensive to women and that it is an imitation based in ridicule and degradation. Raymond, in

---

* Excerpted from J. Butler, *Bodies that Matter: On the Discursive Limits of "Sex"* (New York: Routledge, 1993).

particular, places drag on a continuum with cross-dressing and transsexualism, ignoring the important differences between them, maintaining that in each practice women are the object of hatred and appropriation, and that there is nothing in the identification that is respectful or elevating. As a rejoinder, one might consider that identification is always an ambivalent process. Identifying with a gender under contemporary regimes of power involves identifying with a set of norms that are and are not realizable, and whose power and status precede the identifications by which they are insistently approximated. This "being a man" and this "being a woman" are internally unstable affairs. They are always beset by ambivalence precisely because there is a cost in every identification, the loss of some other set of identifications, the forcible approximation of a norm one never chooses, a norm that chooses us, but which we occupy, reverse, resignify to the extent that the norm fails to determine us completely.

The problem with the analysis of drag as only misogyny is, of course, that it figures male-to-female transsexuality, cross-dressing, and drag as male homosexual activities—which they are not always—and it further diagnoses male homosexuality as rooted in misogyny. The feminist analysis thus makes male homosexuality *about* women, and one might argue that at its extreme, this kind of analysis is in fact a colonization in reverse, a way for feminist women to make themselves into the center of male homosexual activity (and thus to reinscribe the heterosexual matrix, paradoxically, at the heart of the radical feminist position). Such an accusation follows the same kind of logic as those homophobic remarks that often follow upon the discovery that one is a lesbian: a lesbian is one who must have had a bad experience with men, or who has not yet found the right one. These diagnoses presume that lesbianism is acquired by virtue of some failure in the heterosexual machinery, thereby continuing to install heterosexuality as the "cause" of lesbian desire; lesbian desire is figured as the fatal effect of a derailed heterosexual causality. In this framework, heterosexual desire is always true, and lesbian desire is always and only a mask and forever false. In the radical feminist argument against drag, the displacement of women is figured as the aim and effect of male-to-female drag; in the homophobic dismissal of lesbian desire, the disappointment with and displacement of men is understood as the cause and final truth of lesbian desire. According to these views, drag is nothing but the displacement and appropriation of "women," and hence fundamentally based in a misogyny, a hatred of women; and lesbianism is nothing but the displacement and appropriation of men, and so fundamentally a matter of hating men—misandry.

And the case of drag is difficult in yet another way, for it seems clear to me that there is both a sense of defeat and a sense of insurrection to be had from the drag pageantry in *Paris Is Burning*, that the drag we see, the drag which is after all framed for us, filmed for us, is one which both appropriates and subverts racist, misogynist, and homophobic norms of oppression. How are we to account for this ambivalence? This is not first an appropriation and then a subversion. Sometimes it is both at once; sometimes it remains caught in an irresolvable tension, and sometimes a fatally unsubversive appropriation takes place.

Paris Is Burning (1991) is a film produced and directed by Jennie Livingston about drag balls in New York City, in Harlem, attended by, performed by "men" who are either African-American or Latino. The balls are contests in which the contestants compete under a variety of categories. The categories include a variety of social norms, many of which are established in white culture as signs of class, like that of the "executive" and the Ivy League student; some of which are marked as feminine, ranging from high drag to butch queen; and some of them, like that of the "bangie," are taken from straight black masculine street culture. Not all of the categories, then, are taken from white culture; some of them are replications of a straightness which is not white, and some of them are focused on class, especially those which almost require that expensive women's clothing be "mopped" or stolen for the occasion. The competition in military garb shifts to yet another register of legitimacy, which enacts the performative and gestural conformity to a masculinity which parallels the performative or reiterative production of femininity in other categories. "Realness" is not exactly a category in which one competes; it is a standard that is used to judge any given performance within the established categories. And yet what determines the effect of realness is the ability to compel belief, to produce the naturalized effect. This effect is itself the result of an embodiment of norms, a reiteration of norms, an impersonation of a racial and class norm, a norm which is at once a figure, a figure of a body, which is no particular body, but a morphological ideal that remains the standard which regulates the performance, but which no performance fully approximates.

Significantly, this is a performance that works, that effects realness, to the extent that it *cannot* be read. For "reading" means taking someone down, exposing what fails to work at the level of appearance, insulting or deriding someone. For a performance to work, then, means that a reading is no longer possible, or that a reading, an interpretation, appears to be a kind of transparent seeing, where what appears and what it means coincide. On the contrary, when what appears and how it is "read" diverge, the artifice of the performance can be read as artifice; the ideal splits off from its appropriation. But the impossibility of reading means that the artifice works, the approximation of realness appears to be achieved, the body performing and the ideal performed appear indistinguishable.

But what is the status of this ideal? Of what is it composed? What reading does the film encourage, and what does the film conceal? Does the denaturalization of the norm succeed in subverting the norm, or is this a denaturalization in the service of a perpetual reidealization, one that can only oppress, even as, or precisely when, it is embodied most effectively? Consider the different fates of Venus Xtravaganza. She "passes" as a lightskinned woman, but is—by virtue of a certain failure to pass completely—clearly vulnerable to homophobic violence; ultimately, her life is taken presumably by a client who, upon the discovery of what she calls her "little secret," mutilates her for having seduced him. On the other hand, Willi Ninja can pass as straight; his voguing becomes foregrounded in het video productions with Madonna et al., and he achieves post-legendary status on an international scale. There is passing and then there is passing, and it is—as we used to say—"no accident" that Willi Ninja ascends and Venus Xtravaganza dies.

Now Venus, Venus Xtravaganza, she seeks a certain transubstantiation of gender in order to find an imaginary man who will designate a class and race privilege that promises a permanent shelter from racism, homophobia, and poverty. And it would not be enough to claim that for Venus gender is *marked by* race and class, for gender is not the substance or primary substrate and race and class the qualifying attributes. In this instance, gender is the vehicle for the phantasmatic transformation of that nexus of race and class, the site of its articulation. Indeed, in *Paris Is Burning,* becoming real, becoming a real woman, although not everyone's desire (some children want merely to "do" realness, and that, only within the confines of the ball), constitutes the site of the phantasmatic promise of a rescue from poverty, homophobia, and racist delegitimation.

The contest (which we might read as a "contesting of realness") involves the phantasmatic attempt to approximate realness, but it also exposes the norms that regulate realness as *themselves* phantasmatically instituted and sustained. The rules that regulate and legitimate realness (shall we call them symbolic?) constitute the mechanism by which certain sanctioned fantasies, sanctioned imaginaries, are insidiously elevated as the parameters of realness. We could, within conventional Lacanian parlance, call this the ruling of the symbolic, except that the symbolic assumes the primacy of sexual difference in the constitution of the subject. What *Paris Is Burning suggests,* however, is that the order of sexual difference is not prior to that of race or class in the constitution of the subject; indeed, that the symbolic is also and at once a racializing set of norms, and that norms of realness by which the subject is produced are racially informed conceptions of "sex" (this underscores the importance of subjecting the entire psychoanalytic paradigm to this insight).

This double movement of approximating and exposing the phantasmatic status of the realness norm, the symbolic norm, is reinforced by the diagetic movement of the film in which clips of so-called "real" people moving in and out of expensive stores are juxtaposed against the ballroom drag scenes.

In the drag ball productions of realness, we witness and produce the phantasmatic constitution of a subject, a subject who repeats and mimes the legitimating norms by which it itself has been degraded, a subject founded in the project of mastery that compels and disrupts its own repetitions. This is not a subject who stands back from its identifications and decides instrumentally how or whether to work each of them today; on the contrary, the subject is the incoherent and mobilized imbrication of identifications; it is constituted in and through the iterability of its performance, a repetition which works at once to legitimate and delegitimate the realness norms by which it is produced.

In the pursuit of realness this subject is produced, a phantasmatic pursuit that mobilizes identifications, underscoring the phantasmatic promise that constitutes any identificatory move—a promise which, taken too seriously, can culminate only in disappointment and disidentification. A fantasy that for Venus, because she dies—killed apparently by one of her clients, perhaps after the discovery of those remaining organs—cannot be translated into the symbolic. This is a killing that is performed by a symbolic that would eradicate those phenomena that require an opening up of the possibilities for the resignification of sex. If Venus wants to become a woman, and cannot overcome being a Latina, then Venus is treated by the symbolic in precisely the ways in which women of color are treated. Her death thus testifies to a tragic misreading of the social map of power, a misreading orchestrated by that very map according to which the sites for a phantasmatic self-overcoming are constantly resolved into disappointment. If the signifiers of whiteness and femaleness—as well as some forms of hegemonic maleness constructed through class privilege—are sites of phantasmatic promise, then it is clear that women of color and lesbians are not only everywhere excluded from this scene, but constitute a site of identification that is consistently refused and abjected in the collective phantasmatic pursuit of a transubstantiation into various forms of drag, transsexualism, and uncritical miming of the hegemonic. That this fantasy involves becoming in part like women and, for some of the children, becoming like black women, falsely constitutes black women as a site of privilege; they can catch a man and be protected by him, an impossible idealization which of course works to deny the situation of the great numbers of poor black women who are single mothers without the support of men. In this sense, the "identification" is composed of a denial, an envy, which is the envy of a phantasm of black women, an idealization that produces a denial. On the other hand, insofar as black men who are queer can become feminized by hegemonic straight culture, there is in the performative dimension of the ball a significant *reworking of* that feminization, an occupation of the identification that is, as it were, *already* made between faggots and women, the feminization of the faggot, the feminization of the black faggot, which is the black feminization of the faggot.

These hegemonies operate, as Gramsci insisted, through *rearticulation*, but here is where the accumulated force of a historically entrenched and entrenching rearticulation overwhelms the more fragile effort to build an alternative cultural configuration from or against that more powerful regime. Importantly, however, that prior hegemony also works through and as its "resistance" so that the relation between the marginalized community and the dominative is not, strictly speaking, oppositional. The citing of the dominant norm does not, in this instance, displace that norm; rather, it becomes the means by which that dominant norm is most painfully reiterated as the very desire and the performance of those it subjects.

In these senses, then, *Paris Is Burning* documents neither an efficacious insurrection nor a painful resubordination, but an unstable coexistence of both. The film attests to the painful pleasures of eroticizing and miming the very norms that wield their power by foreclosing the very reverse-occupations that the children nevertheless perform.

This is not an appropriation of dominant culture in order to remain subordinated by its terms, but an appropriation that seeks to make over the terms of domination, a making over which is itself a kind of agency, a power in and as discourse, in and as performance, which repeats in order to remake—and sometimes succeeds. But this is a film that cannot achieve this effect without implicating its spectators in the act; to watch this film means to enter into a logic of fetishization which installs the ambivalence of that "performance" as related to our own. If the ethnographic conceit allows the performance to become an exotic fetish, one from which the audience absents itself, the commodification of heterosexual gender ideals will be, in that instance, complete. But if the film establishes the ambivalence of embodying—and failing to embody—that which one sees, then a distance will be opened up *between* that hegemonic call to normativizing gender and its critical appropriation.

Kara Keeling

Kara Keeling is an associate professor in the School of Cinematic Arts at the University of Southern California and an emerging leader in queer theory and critical race studies whose work explores representations of race, gender, and sexuality in cinema. Her first book, *The Witch's Flight: The Cinematic, the Black Femme, and the Image of Common Sense,* explores the role of cinematic images in the production and maintenance of hegemony while interrogating the connections between cinematic visibility, minority politics, and the possibilities for creating alternative organizations of social and cultural life.

Keeling links macrolevel and microlevel social dynamics by investigating the reciprocal relations between media images and social structures. In this sense, Keeling's scholarship exemplifies social justice work in the humanities that targets systemic social problems by way of cultural analysis and media critique, which—methodologically speaking—has not been central to the discourse on intersectionality long dominated by legal studies and social science. Like hooks and Butler earlier in this unit (and historically), Keeling uses cinematic spaces to a) trouble matters of difference, b) elaborate how and why difference matters, and c) promote different ways of engaging with film and media. In this piece from *GLQ* published in 2009, Keeling reads director Daniel Peddle's documentary *The Aggressives* as a counterhegemonic text that depicts a social world in which traditional markers of sexual and gender identity—lesbian, gay woman, genderqueer—do not apply. At the intersection of sexuality, race, gender, and class, the subjects represented in *The Aggressives* certainly challenge heteronormative logics of identity and culture, but also dominant framings of affect and time. What Keeling does here with identity and difference is important, but equally compelling is how she links her intersectional critique to other normative social theoretical concepts, pointing to how the insights offered by the documentary and its subjects may be of value and application beyond the relatively marginalized cultural spaces of *The Aggressives*. In this sense, she provides not just an account of an instance or site of intersectional oppression (i.e., a theory *about* difference), but an intersectional analysis of social life with broad, critical implications (i.e., a *different* kind of theory).

20. **Unconventional Subjects***

Peddle's documentary follows several "aggressives," who identify as female and/or as women and present themselves as masculine or male. The complexity of this mode of self-identification is highlighted by M—'s claim at the beginning of the film that s/he lives life as a man, but that doesn't change the fact that s/he is a woman. *The Aggressives* is, in my view, an important intervention in contemporary discourse about the politics and lives of lesbian, gay, bisexual, and transgender people precisely because it refuses to be located easily within the terms that currently animate that discourse and its manifold movements. Instead of *lesbian* or *gay woman, ftm* or *genderqueer,* the film offers us *aggressives,* a term used to negotiate complex senses of belonging, self-creation, and self-expression that are related to lesbian, dyke, butch, and transgender but

---

* Excerpted from K. Keeling, "Looking for M—: Queer Temporality, Black Political Possibility, and Poetry from the Future." *GLQ: A Journal of Lesbian and Gay Studies* 15 (2009): 565–582. Copyright, 2009, Duke University Press. All rights reserved. Republished by permission of the copyright holder, Duke University Press, www.dukeupress.edu.

excessive to each of those categories. In their adoption of a language of sex and gender expression forged, at least in part, within the sociocultural spaces carved out by people of color, the aggressives participate in making queer gender discourse more responsive to the particularities of their present experiences of gender and sexuality, experiences marked by their race and class.

To the extent that, as Octavia explains in the film, "aggressive" is a formation with currency both inside and outside prison, the designation of oneself as "aggressive" or "AG" is part of a broader convergence of black popular culture with prison culture and therefore cannot be divorced from other discourses of contemporary black existence in the United States and of class and black masculinity as it is informed and deformed by the prison industry. Because of this, *The Aggressives* also paves avenues of common interest between maturing queer movements and dynamic, urgent prison abolitionist movements. Peddle's film is part of a larger fascination with and fear of black sexual deviance, black poverty, and black gender expressions at the same time as it contributes to and complicates an energetic emergent U.S.-based genderqueer movement whose current interests antagonistically enmesh it with regulatory state regimes of identification, recognition, and valorization.

As a conventional documentary framing unconventional subjects, *The Aggressives* mediates its subjects' expressions of what it means to be an aggressive female and its viewers' access to the social and cultural milieu the aggressives themselves create. The aggressives' organizations of social life are enabled by creative engagements with common sense. These engagements are part of what circumscribes *The Aggressives* as belonging indelibly to our time. What the aggressives articulate in the film (sometimes despite the film's formal constraints) as the common sense that conditions their belonging to the category aggressives is a set of possibilities for articulating a range of existing expressions and politics currently perceptible as genderqueer. Via their articulation of aggressive common sense, the aggressives challenge existing genderqueer discourses to become more responsible to aggressive common senses and their attendant forms of social life, which describe and navigate racialized and nonbourgeois experiences of gender expression.

The Aggressives challenges us to make sense of the world of the aggressives, a world to which it seems to provide unlimited access while nevertheless giving few of the usual markers documentaries employ to assist their viewers in doing so. For instance, *The Aggressives* requires its viewers to work to locate the subjects in time and space, often giving only what the subjects themselves say about their time, location, and the passage of time captured in the film. Apparently, the film was shot between 1999 and 2004, but Peddle does not give us specific dates, times, or locations. He gives the first names of the people he is interviewing and occasionally their surnames, and his presence during the interviews is indicated by his subjects' reactions to his prompts. But the viewer's anchoring in space and time remains tenuous and dependent on the information gleaned from Peddle's subjects. There are some establishing shots (of the jail in which Octavia is incarcerated, for instance, or of street signs), but in general *The Aggressives* does little to enforce a "natural" spatiotemporal structure that anchors the action in space, in specific neighborhoods, for example, or in exact years, months, or days. While it is worth noting that this aspect of the film elicits an anthropological gaze at the film's subjects by generalizing them as exotic others whose natural habitat is any urban jungle, the unintended consequence of this aesthetic choice is of interest here: it provides a highly subjective and culturally dependent sense of the subjects' time by relying on their own references as markers of their location in space and the passage of time.

Aggressive subcultural time is organized in part by patterns of consumption and other social and communicative practices that require that participants in that subculture spend time on them. By the end of the documentary, a couple of the aggressives have become distant from the subcultural activities in which they participated so enthusiastically when they were younger. Octavia, for instance, the aggressive who also does time in jail, does not have the time at the end of the film to participate in the aggressive subcultural life, a fact that reveals that the construction of aggressives as a category, like any identity category, indexes a dynamic investment of time and labor rather than a stable identity. Foregrounding aggressive as an index of an organization of time, rather than of a discrete and identifiable group, helps explain the difficulties its subjects pose for the film's conventional, linear narrative form. Prison time, the market time of popular cultural commodities, subcultural time and queer life cycles, and the temporalities of radical alterity as described, albeit differently, by Fanon and Edelman cannot be made to conform to the linear time the film seeks to impose on them. Under irreconcilable pressure from the forced imposition of conventional documentary time, many things escape, becoming invisible and/or unrecognizable within the film's stylistic and narrative framework. One of them is M—.

The storyline for M— involves hir joining the military to earn money for college. The film provides images and interviews of hir while s/he is in the military. In the film's postscript, designed to provide narrative closure on the stories of the aggressives it features, the viewer learns that "during the US Invasion of Iraq." M— "abruptly left the Army. Her current whereabouts are unknown."

Given that M—'s disappearance from the film's mise-en-scène is a form of resistance and survival, what are the ethical implications of looking for hir and to what extent are they imbricated in a thinking through of black queer temporality and political possibility? M—'s disappearance from the film's mise-en-scène is hir refusal to remain bound to its visual economy. It is a political act that both undoes the film's pretense toward omniscient linear narration, narrative closure, and spatiotemporal continuity and opens a space of black queer desire that arises simultaneously from M—'s resistance to hir working-class immobility (a resistance that rationalized hir enlistment in the army) and from hir efforts toward self-valorization via mechanisms outside the nation-state and its military, which, as s/he puts it. does not "care" about hir anyway. While the military and its police might look for hir, attempting to recognize hir in a specific space, they will not look after hir in either senses of that phrase discussed above. Though each deploys different logics of visibility vis-à-vis sexuality, the primary axis that animates their looking for M— subsequent to hir disappearance is spatial; they might seek to recognize hir according to their hegemonic common senses to locate where s/he physically is now.

The collective histories that have enabled hir appearance to date and the future beings desiring hir into existence today are what must be excised from the social body with hir captivity and conscription (in whatever form of service to the state) in order for the current hegemony to be maintained. This is accomplished through a variety of wars, in the United States and beyond its borders. In M—'s case, by "abruptly disappearing" and thereby refusing to become a conscript of war, M—might live. Yet doing so also makes hir legible within the juridical logics of the state. To resist the terms of hir reinscription within the state's logics, s/he disappears, becoming invisible and, therefore, utterly unprotected and vulnerable.

If disappearing enables M— to live, dragging M— into sight here implicates my own work in the very processes and situations I seek to illuminate and challenge. To disappear, M— also becomes invisible within the regime of the image that renders "the aggressives" visible throughout the film. The fact that s/he must disappear from the film's narrative highlights the ways that a critical apparatus predicated on making visible hidden images, sociocultural formations, ideas, concepts, and other things always drags what interests it onto the terrain of power and the struggle for hegemony. On this terrain, the benefits of visibility are unevenly distributed.

In the colonial world of which Fanon writes, for example, the hypervisibility of blacks and the organizations of space that rationalize their hypervisibility are crucial techniques through which colonial power and white supremacy were maintained. Insofar as colonial logics can be said to undergird present socioeconomic relations, black people can become visible only through those logics, so danger, if not death, attends every black's appearance. Yet precisely because what is visible is caught in the struggle for hegemony and its processes of valorization, one cannot not want the relative security promised by visibility.

In relation to this discussion, an earlier documentary film to which *The Aggressives* is often compared, Jennie Livingston's *Paris Is Burning* (1990) should provide an important caution. As Judith Halberstam observes, five of the queens who were the subjects of that documentary were dead within five years of the film's release, whereas Livingston became a filmmaker and the pop star Madonna made a fortune by appropriating voguing, the dance style the queens innovated and displayed in Livingston's film.

My point in bringing *Paris Is Burning* into this conversation is not to place blame on Livingston for the disappearance, death, or continuing poverty of her documentary subjects. Instead, I issue this caution because it underscores the complicity of our critical endeavors with this unequal calculus of visibility distribution. At the same time, it calls forth the insistent need to attend to the ghosts, specters, and absences within what appears and to interrogate what is achieved through those appearances. If my own critical work in this article might contribute to fashioning a politics capable of redressing the very inequalities and injustices it illuminates rather than simply furthering my career by feeding the academy's contradictory need for knowledge about and sometimes by queers of color, the first question that must be asked of M— is not where is s/he but when might s/he be.

At the end of the film, it might be said that M— is out of time (and unlocatable). After the transition that the official narrative of the U.S. nation, adopted here by the film, marks with "September 11, 2001 and the subsequent invasion of Iraq," M— abruptly disappears. Hir disappearance must prompt us to ask not the policing question attuned to the temporal and spatial logics of surveillance and control (where is M— today), but, rather, in this case, the political question of when M—'s visibility will enable hir survival by providing the protection the realm of the visible affords those whose existence is valued, those we want to look for so we can look out for and look after them.

A "looking" for M— that begins by asking *where* s/he is now inevitably operates by harnessing the capacity of those temporal structures and epistemological enterprises of policing and surveillance inherent in any framing of questions of representation and visibility. Because of this, asking where s/he is now is complicit with the needs of the prison- and military-industrial complexes, the industries that proliferate in the very spaces (prisons and barracks) that already violently and antagonistically structure the time of *The Aggressives* and, indeed, are central to constituting the category and some of the logics of aggressives itself. Rather, a "looking" for M— that asks when s/he might be, even as s/he haunts us now, invests in an interpretive project that, while circumscribed by the exigencies of the present, is nonetheless creative. It seeks to think in a moment of crisis while remaining open and vulnerable to the (im)possibility of a rupture now. It is predicated on recognizing the ways the film seeks to enforce a straight time but fails to do so because its own subjects disturb that time by repeatedly pointing to the violences that guarantee it.

In the temporality the film seeks to impose on the aggressives, there is no known future for M—, yet she persists in it, haunting the film's attempt at narrative closure and pointing toward another organization of time implicit and yet antagonistic to it. As Hong reminds us through her suggestion that "perhaps that is all that we are now and will ever be: the fragments and figments of someone's imagination, of someone's desire for us to exist," a queer futurity is animated by a future desire only perceptible ("perhaps")—not recognizable—now. The temporal structures M— haunts are those characterized not only by a reproductive futurity wherein what is reproduced is what already exists but also by the related but distinct orders of colonial temporality. That the straight time of reproductive futurity and (post)colonial reality is achieved at the expense of M—, several years of Octavia's life, and the drag queens of *Paris Is Burning,* among others, should alert us to the ways that present institutions and logics dissemble a fear of a black future. From within the logics of reproductive futurity and colonial reality, a black future looks like no future at all.

Understood in this way, then, looking for M— entails reading the historical index of *The Aggressives* while acknowledging that something always exceeds such a reading and that it is precisely this excess, which we cannot name or know, that divorces our looking from all efforts to redeem it, whether in the name of a morality or law that would send M— to prison or to war or in the form of a political project that asserts its authority as an urgent imperative in which we must participate. Here, without redemption and indifferent to its call, undisciplined and vulnerable, firmly rooted in our time, looking for M— might touch the erotic as power within us and, in touch with that power, insist that we not look away.

Sakia Gunn, the person to whom *The Aggressives* is dedicated, was murdered on a street corner in Newark, New Jersey, in May 2003. She was a black lesbian; some accounts of her describe her as transgender, signaling that she was masculine in appearance. The night of her murder, as she was returning home from a night out in Greenwich Village, Gunn and three of her friends were approached by two men who began flirting with those in the group with more feminine appearances. When Gunn intervened, asserting that they were lesbians, one of the men stabbed her in the chest. At age fifteen, she was out of time. But we still look for her in order to look after her. Out of time, she has become a figure of our time, one we invoke as a way to make palpably present the objectionable distance between, for instance, the contemporary focus on gay marriage by national lesbian and gay political organizations and an innovative, radical politics that looks after and therefore looks out for the lives of queer youth of color. As a figure, Gunn has been used by José Esteban Muñoz, for instance, to point to the present complexity of "the sensuous intersection-alities that mark our experience." For Munoz, Gunn serves as an example of the modes of existence that misogynist, transgenderphobic, and homophobic violences today cut off at the root. By inciting academics and activists to "call on a utopian political imagination that will enable us to glimpse another time and place: a 'not-yet' where queer youths of color actually get to grow up," Munoz also prompts us to ask the spatiotemporal question I am formulating here—when might Sakia Gunn be?

That *The Aggressives* is offered "in memory of Sakia Gunn" reminds us that its subjects live, strive, labor, and love within the terms of a world whose regulatory regimes are guaranteed through a generalized, dispersed violence and reinforced via the persistent threat of physical violence directed at those such regulatory regimes do not work to valorize. A quotidian violence is the ground on which the spatiotemporal structures of the film rest—the violence that maintains the disjointed urban spaces in which the aggressives live, that secures the fact and characterizes the culture of Octavia's jail and M—'s bar-racks. Violence also underpins the labor required of aggressive female mas-culinity and the political economy that secures such phenomena as black masculine unemployment, rising rates of incarceration, and feminicide. An intolerable yet quotidian violence to which many of us have learned to numb ourselves out of habit is the historical index *The Aggressives* carries of its belong-ing to our time. This violence is an index of the imposition of straight times and of the constraints they place on black possibility and on queer existence coterminously. Such violence is all we can find today when we look for M—.

Undisciplined and vulnerable, firmly rooted in our time, might we never-theless feel, even without recognition, the rhythms of the poetry from a future in which M— might be? Might we allow those rhythms to move us to repel the quotidian violence through which we currently are defined without de-manding of the future from which they come that it redeem our movements now or then? Might we look after M— now without waiting for the future in which M— might be to issue our present cries?

Rosalind Gill

Originally trained as a social psychologist, Rosalind Gill is a professor of social and cultural analysis at King's College London whose research has focused on a variety of topics in gender studies, sociology, media, and technology studies. In addition to publishing numerous articles and several books, Gill has served on the United Nations Commission on the Status of Women and produced two BBC documentaries. Most recently, her research has contributed to debates on the "sexualization of culture," which she approaches with an expressly intersectional lens. Gill's cultural analyses highlight how social groups are differentially situated (by age, class, gender, race, sexuality, and other dimensions) in relation to sexualization, which we might think of as an ongoing argument about if, how, and when Western cultures have become increasingly sexualized. In the excerpt below, initially published in the journal *Sexualities,* Gill directs our attention to a persistently unmarked and often neglected site of critical social inquiry: heterosexual masculinity. In the last two decades, the emerging area of masculinity studies has helped to illuminate not only how hegemonic forms of masculinity shape women's lives—in the form of rape culture, "enlightened" sexism, and persistent wage inequality—but also how hegemonic masculinity disciplines and restricts men's lives, albeit in extremely heterogeneous ways. In this piece, Gill's focus is on the symbolic contours of the "sixpack" and its deployment in advertising. The point here is not a sexist apology that might sound something like: "Look, men have it just as bad as women!" On the contrary, Gill's thesis pertains to the meaningful differences between men's and women's objectification in popular media cultures, and the ways in which the political economy of advertising is choreographed by and within multiple axes of difference—not just gender.

21. The Sixpack as "High Art"*

One of the most profound shifts in visual culture in the last two decades has been the proliferation of representations of the male body. Where once women's bodies dominated advertising landscapes now men's have taken their place alongside women's on billboards, cinema screens and in magazines. However, it is not simply that there are more images of men circulating, but that a specific kind of representational practice has emerged for depicting the male body: namely an idealized and eroticized aesthetic showing a toned, young body. What is significant about this type of representation is that it codes men's bodies in ways that give permission for them to be looked at and desired.

This transformation has prompted much discussion, with claims that "we are all objectified now" and that idealized-sexualized representational strategies are no longer limited to women's bodies. Indeed, many concerns have been raised about the impact of this representational shift on men's wellbeing—their self-esteem, mental health, and the possibility that they will become

---

* Excerpted from R. Gill, "Beyond the 'Sexualization of Culture' Thesis: An Intersectional Analysis of 'Sixpacks,' 'Midriffs' and 'Hot Lesbians' in Advertising," *Sexualities* 12 (2009): 137–160. Reprinted by Permission of SAGE. Some in-text citations have been excised for length.

increasingly susceptible to eating disorders and other body-image-related conditions. There is a growing sense in much writing that visual culture has become *equalized,* and that we are *all* today subject to relentless sexualization.

I want to contest this and to argue that there are good reasons for going beyond general claims about "sexualization" to look at the specific ways in which men's bodies materialize in visual culture. I want to suggest that, despite the apparent similarities, there are in fact profound differences in the ways in which men's and women's bodies are represented sexually. Moreover, these patterns of "sexualization" have different determinants, employ different modes of representation, and are likely to be read in radically different ways because of long, distinct histories of gender representations and the politics of looking.

The catalysts for this shift in visual culture have been considered by a number of writers (Beynon, 2002; Chapman and Rutherford, 1988; Edwards, 1997; Mort, 1996; Nixon, 1996; Wernick, 1991). At a general level the representations can be understood as part of the shift away from the "male as norm" in which masculinity lost its unmarked status and became visible as gendered. Sally Robinson (2000) argues that white masculinity was rendered visible through pressure from black and women's liberation movements, which were highly critical of its hegemony. A variety of new social movements galvanized the creation of the "new man", the reinvention of masculinity along more gentle, emotional and communicative lines. More specifically, the growing confidence of the gay liberation movement in western countries, and the increasing significance of the "pink economy" helped to produce a greater range of representations of the male body in gay magazines and popular culture. Part of the shift can be understood in terms of these images "going mainstream" and, as they did so, opening up space for an active gaze among heterosexual women (Moore, 1988). Moreover, the shift had significant economic determinants: retailers, marketers and magazine publishers were keen to develop new markets and had affluent men in their sights as the biggest untapped source of high spending consumers (Edwards, 1997). Style magazines like *The Face* helped this enterprise by producing a new visual vocabulary for the representation of men's bodies, and this too opened up space for eroticized practices of representation (Mort, 1996; Nixon, 1996). As Rowena Chapman (1988) argues, "new man" was a contradictory formation, representing both a response to critique from progressive social movements, and a gleam in the eyes of advertisers, marketers and companies aspiring to target young and affluent men. Perhaps the figure of the metrosexual that has come to prominence more recently symbolizes the extent to which marketing-driven constructions won out over more explicitly political articulations of "new" masculinity.

The radical transformation in the portrayal of men in mainstream visual culture began more than 20 years ago. By the early 1990s the eroticized representation of male bodies was well established, particularly in fashion and fragrance advertising and the emerging market for male grooming products. But rather than a diversity of different representations of the male body, most adverts belong to a very specific type. The models are generally white, they are young, they are muscular and slim, they are usually clean-shaven (with perhaps the exception of a little designer stubble), and they have particular facial features which connote a combination of softness and strength—strong jaw, large lips and eyes, and soft looking, clear skin (Edwards, 1997). As Tim Edwards (1997) has argued, this combination of muscularity/hardness and softness in the particular "look" of the models allows them to manage contradictory expectations of men and masculinity as strong and powerful but also gentle and tender—they embody, in a sense, a cultural contradiction about what a man is "meant to be".

Older bodies are strikingly absent and there are strong and persistent patterns of racialization to be found in the corpus of eroticized images. White bodies are over-represented, but they are frequently not Anglo-American or northern European bodies, but bodies that are coded as "Latin", with dark hair and olive skin, referencing long histories of sexual Othering and exoticism (Nixon, 1996). Black, African American and African Caribbean bodies are also regularly represented in a highly eroticized manner, but these bodies are usually reserved for products associated with sport, drawing on cultural myths about black male sexuality and physical prowess. It is also worth noting that adverts depicting black men frequently use black male *celebrities* (e.g. Tiger Woods, Thierry Henri), in contrast to the unknown models who are used when the sexy body is white. Peter Jackson (1994) has argued that this does nothing to challenge the underlying racial logic of representation, but in fact reinforces it by presenting the "acceptable" face of black masculinity shorn of the more "threatening associations" of a stereotypically anonymous black manhood.

For many commentators, the representation of men as objects of the gaze rather than as the ones doing the looking constituted a major shift. Frank Mort (1996) argued that it was nothing short of the "visual reassembly of masculinity" and claimed that the cropping of male bodies to focus on selected, eroticized areas e.g. the upper arms, the chest and the "sixpack" represented a metaphorical fragmenting or fracturing of male power. Mark Simpson argued that, quite simply, male dominance and heterosexuality would not survive this transformation in visual culture:

Men's bodies are on display everywhere; but the grounds of men's anxiety is not just that they are being exposed and commodified but that their bodies are placed in such a way as to passively invite a gaze that is undifferentiated: it might be female or male, hetero or homo. Traditional male heterosexuality, which insists that it is always active, sadistic and desiring, is now inundated with images of men's bodies as passive, masochistic and desired. Narcissism, the desire to be desired, once regarded as a feminine quality par excellence, is, it seems, in popular culture at least, now more often associated with men than with women. Sexual difference no longer calls the shots, active no longer maps onto masculine, nor passive onto feminine. Traditional heterosexuality cannot survive this reversal: it brings masculinity into perilously close contact with that which must always be disavowed: homosexuality. (Simpson, 1994: 4)

In advertising, a number of strategies were developed to deal with the anxieties and threats produced by this shift. On the one hand, many adverts used models with an almost "phallic muscularity" the size and hardness of the muscles "standing in for" male power. Indeed, writing about an earlier generation of male pinups, Richard Dyer (1982) talked about representations of the male body having a "hysterical" feel. Likewise, Susan Bordo (1997) argued that many male striptease routines tend to eroticize the teasing display of *male power* rather than the sexiness of the bodies themselves (but see her later argument in *Male Bodies,* 1999, and see also Smith, 2007). The use of photographic conventions and mise-en-scène from "high art" also served as a distancing device to diffuse some of the potential threats engendered by "sexualizing" the male body. Giving the representations an "arthouse" look and feel through the use of black and white photography or "sculpted" models that made reference to classical iconography, offered the safety of distance, as well as connoting affluence, sophistication and "class".

The organization of gazes within adverts also works to diminish the transgressive threat discussed by Simpson. Men tend not to smile or pout, nor to deploy any of the bodily gestures or postures discussed by Goffman (1979) as indices of the "ritualised subordination" of women in advertising, and nor are they depicted in mirror shots so long a favoured mode for conveying women's narcissism. In contrast, in what we might call "sixpack advertising" men are generally portrayed standing or involved in some physical activity, and they look back at the viewer in ways reminiscent of street gazes to assert dominance or look up or off, indicating that their interest is elsewhere (Dyer, 1982). They are mostly pictured alone in ways that reference the significance of independence as a value marking hegemonic masculinity (Connell, 1995), or they are pictured with a beautiful woman to "reassure" viewers of their heterosexuality.

However it is not simply the case that these representations must disavow homoerotic desire. On the contrary, gay men are a key target audience for such advertising representations, being acknowledged as fashion leaders and early adopters in clothing, grooming and the purchase of fragrances. Indeed, through the figure of the "metrosexual" marketing professionals sought to rearticulate these interests in "looking good" to a heterosexual agenda. The representations advertisers construct have to appeal simultaneously to (at least) three different constituencies: gay men, heterosexual women and heterosexual men in such a way as not to antagonize, alienate or frighten straight men. Discussing the way advertisers managed this, Tim Edwards (1997) highlights the paradoxical nature of men's magazines as a site for such images, pointing to the "fundamentalist" assertion of heterosexuality in written texts juxtaposed with page after page of homoerotic images of the male body as one example of how this contradiction was managed, through a splitting that operated between the visual and written texts.

In addition to the threats posed by homoeroticism, there are also anxieties related specifically to gender hierarchy—namely to the presentation of male bodies as objects of a heterosexual female gaze. The anxieties threatened here are often dealt with through humour. This can be seen in a long-running advert for Diet Coke on British television (and elsewhere). In this advert a number of attractive women (in their mid-30s) turn up in an unspecified office environment claiming to be there for their "11 o'clock appointment". The camera cuts between their arrival in reception and their seat in the waiting room in which each of them is depicted in a state of obvious sexual anticipation (licking lips, breathing heavily, rearranging hair and so on). Only then does the camera reveal the cause of their arousal—an attractive labourer, *sans* T-shirt, pausing to drink his Diet Coke on a scaffold outside the window. The choice of labourer is an interesting one since men in the building trade have become iconic signifiers of a particular kind of "in your face" sexism. This is profoundly racialized and classed, located as white, working class and distinguished from the more "seemly" or "respectable" sexism of other groups. Where once building workers ogled women, the advert playfully suggests, now women ogle them! However, the camp and exaggerated desire of the women and the comic nature of the 11 o'clock appointment serve to place the advert in humorous, ironic quotation marks. The exchange of looks between the females and the male are not equivalent, and are not straightforward reversals of patterns of power involved in men's looks at women. This is partly because each individual gaze operates in the context of our collective knowledge about the politics of looking—"men look at women and women watched themselves being looked at" as John Berger famously put it—and is also weighted by a long cultural history of the beauty myth (Wolf, 1990) in which women are subject to constant scrutiny and assessment of their appearance. No single instance of women looking at men could reverse that, nor, without this history, does it have the authentic, referential quality of examples of men looking at women though this is changing in the context of cultural shifts in which women do "look back" in certain sites and—as McRobbie has argued—in which among young women in particular, feisty girl power discourses can include "ogling" men, catcalling and giving them marks out of 10 for "fitness" or "buffness".

In multiple ways, then, advertising images of the last two decades have been designed to offset or diffuse some of the anxieties and threats generated by presenting men as objects of an "undifferentiated" sexual gaze. Neither hegemonic masculinity nor the institution of heterosexuality have been destroyed—though we are seeing more fractured hegemonies perhaps—and "sexualized" representation of the male body has not proved incommensurable with male dominance. Rather it appears that a highly specific set of modes of representing the male body have emerged—which are quite different from sexualized representations of women's bodies.

Gender and sexuality have been central to the analysis produced here, but this intersectional reading has also paid attention to other axes of difference. In particular, age, class and race have been identified as central to the way in which "sexualization" operates. To a large extent, older people—particularly older women—have been "excluded" from what many referred to as the "sexualization of culture".

I have also documented some features of the strong patterns of racialization operating in the "sexualized" visual economy of advertising. The midriff in advertising appears as an almost exclusively white phenomenon, a racialized postfeminist icon. Black women are not constructed in advertising as feisty sexually desiring subjects (despite the fact that popular music is a site where such constructions are found). The sexualization of black men, too, is highly specific. Black men's bodies are rarely rendered objects of the gaze—except when celebrity status allows a figure to signify a particularized set of meanings, distinct from black masculinity more generally. Dark haired, olive skinned Latin-looking men dominate the advertising corpus of eroticized images of the male body, and it is notable how rarely Asian male bodies are constructed as sexy (Nixon, 1996).

I have argued, then, that the term "sexualization" needs to be used with greater care, specificity and attention to *difference*. I have pointed to the differences *between* the ways in which the three figures examined here are "sexualized", and have also highlighted some of the patterns and exclusions *within* these bodies of representation—organized around class, race, gender, sexuality, age and appearance.

VIOLENCE, RESISTANCE, AND ACTIVISM

On Pragmatism
Patrick R. Grzanka

Theorist of hegemony Antonio Gramsci (1971) explains that hegemonies are such powerful and effective forms of domination because they manifest in social reality as "natural" and legitimate forms of social order. Accordingly, to Gramsci, the first step in challenging hegemony is the development of "critical consciousness," which begins with recognizing that one exists within a hegemonic context; next, he says, one must seek to unify this critical consciousness (i.e., "theory") with "praxis." Praxis, to Gramsci, explains how we act or behave practically in the social world, which can reinforce or undermine hegemonic social relations. Black feminist thought shares much in common with the philosophy of this neo-Marxist philosopher, as intersectionality insists upon, "no essential divide between theory and practice" (James 2009, 92). This unit takes up the unity of theory and practice in the response to personal and institutional violence. Some of the scholar-activists in this unit tell stories of their relationships with personal and institutional discrimination, prejudice and hate; others describe their experiences bearing witness to intersectional oppressions that have devastated communities; all elaborate on the multifarious ways in which intersectionality has informed pragmatic strategies of counterhegemonic resistance.

The term "pragmatism" has many associations, but in sociology it is most closely linked to the American pragmatist school of philosophy—comprised of such legendary figures as Williams James, John Dewey, George Herbert Mead, and Charles Sanders Pierce—from which American sociology emerged in the late nineteenth and early twentieth centuries. Pragmatism was preoccupied, as Patricia Hill Collins (2012) describes, with "democracy, science, enlightenment, fairness, and societal good" in ways that other forms of continental philosophy were not (444). As it developed during the Progressive Era, Collins explains, "American pragmatism gained legitimacy primarily as a methodology or set of tools that one might use in studying particular social phenomena. As a result, social inequality, power, and politics were defined out of the *center* of American pragmatism" (445). But where pragmatism lacked a self-reflexivity and an explicit attention to race, gender, class, sexuality, ethnicity, or nationality, as Collins elaborates, intersectionality emerged in the latter half of the twentieth century as a theory holistically committed to "analysis of the interconnectedness of race, class, gender, and sexuality as systems of power that was clearly tied to social justice projects and social movement politics" (450). There has been a renewed scholarly interest in exploring the latent connections between American pragmatism and intersectionality as forms of critical social theory because, as Collins stipulates:

> Pragmatism presents a provocative analysis of *community* that provides a useful framework for understanding the processes by which social structures are constructed, yet its neglect of power relations limits its own arguments. Intersectionality provides a distinctive analysis of social inequality, power, and politics, yet the relative newness of this field in the academy has produced provisional analyses of these themes. In all, in both discourses, using the pragmatist construct of community and infusing it with intersectionality's ideas about social inequality, power, and politics might animate new avenues of investigation. (2012, 444)

The readings in this unit are not philosophical per se, but they represent an opportunity to consider Collins's ideas about a coalition between pragmatism and intersectionality that could "animate new avenues of investigation" around the concept of community. The works showcased herein elucidate how critical social theory works *in action* as mechanisms and avenues for the cultivation of social justice.

We start with Audre Lorde (1984, reading 22), whose writing on the uses of anger foregrounds the role emotions can play in informing resistance and serving as a form of resistance in and of themselves. Emotions are often used by oppressors to invalidate the experiences of the oppressed: "you're being too emotional," "control your feelings," "calm down," "be rational," and "why are you so angry?" are common refrains people in positions of power use to trivialize, minimize, and dismiss those who protest their experiences of unfair and unjustified treatment. "Anger" is the most taboo of these emotions, but Lorde's essay embraces anger—not as an "apology" for anger or an attempt to "validate" such feelings, but to insist upon the realities of anger and the potency of rage to liberate, strengthen, and transform:

> Every woman has a well-stoked arsenal of anger potentially useful against those oppressions, person and institutional, which brought that anger into being. Focused with precision it can become a powerful source of energy serving progress and change. And when I speak of change, I do not mean a simple switch of positions or a temporary lessening of tensions, nor the ability to smile or feel good. I am speaking of a basic and radical alteration in those assumptions underlining our lives. (1984, 127)

Lorde's essay traverses multiple registers of feeling as she asks her audience to consider their own relationships with anger, guilt, fury, and hopelessness. Her writing highlights the similarities among women's experiences of misogyny and the ways that racism differentiates White women's and women of color's relationships to men and institutions. She writes:

> Anger is an appropriate reaction to racist attitudes, as is fury when the actions arising from those attitudes do not change. To those women here who fear the anger of women of Color more than their own unscrutinized racist attitudes, I ask: Is the anger of women of Color more threatening than the women-hatred that tinges all aspects of our lives? (129).

From their positions of privilege as professional academics, Patricia Clough and Michelle Fine (2007, reading 24) reflect upon their own activism as antiracist feminist professors to explore the personal and political complexities of doing social justice work from within the confines of institutions, including higher education and the prison industrial complex. Their stories are both distinct and intertwined, because they face similar experiences of being politically committed to activist work but deeply concerned about institutional restrains that inhibit meaningful social transformation. Clough, in particular, describes the tremendous ambivalence she felt and feels toward "reform" strategies that work from within the system. "I had learned," she explains, "that program, policy, and legislative reform often better serve those who design, and administer and regulate these reforms than they do those for whom the reform policy and programming were supposedly intended" (267). After years of education and community organizing experience, Clough embarked upon an activist project with persons in the process of "reentry" into society after a period of incarceration. Though she initially thought her academic knowledge—Gramsci might call this "theory"—would be useless or even prohibitive of developing

pragmatic policy recommendations and reform (i.e., practice), Clough ultimately was convinced otherwise: her academic knowledge provides her a critique of policy and reform that would otherwise be missing from the discourse.
She writes:

> I wanted to retreat, so as to engage in critical self-reflective scholarship. I
> now believe that scholars and critics should not retreat, if in fact they can
> retreat; rather, they should more fully invest their intellectual energies. It
> is on the plane of policy, program, and legislative reform that study, learn-
> ing, and teaching should be occurring. It is here that there should be in-
> sistent criticism, while keeping in mind that reform itself is rarely critical
> enough or aimed at radical change. But radical change is necessary. (272)

Clough and Fine describe the process of linking activism and pedagogy as
deeply challenging and complex, but their journeys offer a template for how to
go about dismantling the binary of "researcher and researched, service provider
and client, teacher and student" (273).

Marla Kohlman (2004, reading 23) turns our attention to the workplace
to explore the demographic landscape of sexual harassment, a pervasive social
phenomena in which individuals experience "behavior that is unwelcome or
unsolicited, sexual in nature, and is deliberate or repeated" (143). Her intersectional quantitative analyses reveal differences in men's and women's experiences that are crosscut by race and class, particularly with regard to whether or
not individuals report being targeted for sexual harassment in the workplace.
Social identity *and* position in workplace hierarchy both affect experiences of
sexual harassment, according to Kohlman. She explains that racial and ethnic minorities in her study were less likely to report being targeted for sexual
harassment, but that, "On the other hand, a pattern clearly emerged which
provides evidence for the contention that women and men experience being
targeted for sexual harassment in the workplace very differently. For men, it
is a function of occupational position and for women it is a function of personal demographics" (158). She concludes with a call for further intersectional
research to examine how differences in when or how individuals report sexual
harassment may further explain the role of race and ethnicity in the demography of harassment.

Finally, Rachel Luft (2009, reading 25) focuses on community responses
to catastrophe in her work on the afterlife of Hurricane Katrina. She explicates
how post-Katrina social movements in New Orleans drew upon long-standing
knowledge of institutionalized racism, poverty, and community disinvestment
in the months and years following Hurricane Katrina to develop programs
that addressed the effects of the storm *and* the social problems that made it
so devastating to the New Orleans and the Gulf Coast region. To community

organizers, the storm's effects were inextricable from the social forces that ex-
acerbated Katrina's impact and that had left so much of New Orleans's population acutely vulnerable:

> They insisted that "the storm began a long time before Katrina." When
> they asked visitors if they were "preparing for the Katrina in your own
> backyard," they were not referring to the threat of natural disaster else-
> where (though they reminded them of such a threat when nonlocals
> wondered whether New Orleans should be rebuilt), but rather to every
> community's structures of disenfranchisement. (508)

Luft explains that, from the perspective of the community members who lived
in New Orleans and understood the nuances of local infrastructure disinvestment and the political ineptitude that characterized federal Katrina relief efforts,
"the attending conditions of natural disaster, such as evacuation and reentry, are
decentered; they are then reinterpreted as *opportunities*, either for social control *or* for resistance" (509). Luft found that certain Katrina movement groups
"de-exceptionalized disaster" to address opportunities for social transformation
in New Orleans, including criminal justice system reform, day laborer rights,
affordable health care, safe public housing, and reproductive freedom.

The writings in this unit speak to the various ways in which people experience, manage, and resist social forces of violence and discrimination that
almost always feel too big, too unwieldy, and too powerful to do anything
about. In many instances, these authors attend to the dynamics of community
organizing and critical consciousness-raising as a strategy to protect one another and cultivate tactics of defiance in the face of profound hardship. Patricia
Hill Collins (2012, 448) reminds us of the place of community in a pragmatic
social justice project, and ponders what intersectionality's future could look
like in such projects:

> A more dynamic, future-oriented understanding of community creates
> space for imagining something different than the present and a world-
> view that critically analyzes existing social arrangements. In this sense,
> participating in building a community is simultaneously political, for ne-
> gotiating differences of power within a group; dynamic, for negotiating
> practices that balance individual and collective goals; and aspirational.
> The challenge, however, of sustaining this dynamic conception of com-
> munity lies in finding ways to negotiate contradictions.

References and Further Reading

Buss, D. 2009. "Sexual Violence, Ethnicity, and Intersectionality in International
Criminal Law." In *Law, Power and the Politics of Subjectivity: Intersectionality and*

Beyond, edited by E. Grabham, D. Cooper, J. Krishnadas, and D. Herman, 105–124. London: Routledge.

Chun, J. J., G. Lipsitz, and Y. Shin. 2013. "Intersectionality as a Social Movement Strategy: Asian Immigrant Women Advocates." *Signs: The Journal of Women in Culture and Society* 38: 917–940.

Clough, P. T., and M. Fine. 2007. "Activism and Pedagogies: Feminist Reflections." *Women's Studies Quarterly* 35: 255–275.

Collins, P. H. 2012. "Social Inequality, Power, and Politics: Intersectionality and American Pragmatism in Dialogue." *Journal of Speculative Philosophy* 26: 442–457.

Crenshaw, K. W. 1991. "Mapping the Margins: Intersectionality, Identity Politics, and Violence Against Women of Color." *Stanford Law Review* 46: 1241–1299.

Doetsch-Kidder, S. 2012. *Social Change and Intersectional Activism: The Spirit of Social Movement.* New York: Palgrave Macmillan.

Ferree, M. M., and S. Roth. 1998. "Gender, Class, and the Interaction Between Social Movements: A Strike of West Berlin Day Care Workers." *Gender & Society* 12: 626–648.

Goldberg, S. B. 2009. "Intersectionality in Theory and Practice." In *Law, Power and the Politics of Subjectivity: Intersectionality and Beyond,* edited by E. Grabham, D. Cooper, J. Krishnadas, and D. Herman, 124–158. London: Routledge.

Gramsci, A. 1971. *Selections from the Prison Notebooks of Antonio Gramsci (1929–1935),* translated and edited by Q. Hoare and G. N. Smith. New York: International Publishers.

Griffin, S., and C. Woods. 2009. "The Politics of Reproductive Violence: An Interview with Shanna Griffin by Clyde Woods." *American Quarterly* 61: 583–591.

James, V. D. 2009. "Theorizing Black Feminist Pragmatism: Forethoughts on the Practice and Purpose of Philosophy as Envisioned by Black Feminists and John Dewey." *The Journal of Speculative Philosophy* 23: 92–99.

Jenkins, E. 2002. "Black Women and Community Violence: Trauma, Grief, and Coping." *Women & Therapy* 25: 29–44.

Kohlman, M. H. 2004. "Person or Position: The Demographics of Sexual Harassment in the Workplace." *Equal Opportunities International* 23: 143–161.

Lockhart, L. L., and F. S. Danis, eds. 2010. *Domestic Violence: Intersectionality and Culturally Competent Practice.* New York: Columbia University Press.

Lorde, A. 1984. *Sister Outsider: Essays and Speeches.* Berkeley, CA: The Crossing Press.

Luft, R. 2009. "Beyond Disaster Exceptionalism: Social Movement Developments in New Orleans After Hurricane Katrina." *American Quarterly* 61: 499–527.

Naples, N. A., ed. 1998. *Community Activism and Feminist Politics: Organizing Across Race, Class, and Gender.* New York: Routledge.

Paschel, T. S., and M. Q. Sawyer. 2008. "Contesting Politics as Usual: Black Social Movements, Globalization, and Race Policy in Latin America." *Souls* 10: 197–214.

Pulido, L. 2006. *Black, Brown, Yellow, and Left: Radical Activism in Los Angeles.* Berkeley, CA: University of California Press.

Spivak, G. C. 1988. "Can the Subaltern Speak?" In *Marxism and the Interpretation of Culture,* edited by C. Nelson and L. Grossberg, 271–313. Urbana: University of Illinois Press.

Audre Lorde

Audre Lorde's illustrious career and incalculable influence stretches across the disciplines, but she holds a special place in the genealogy of intersectionality. With *Sister Outsider*, a collection of speeches and essay initially published in 1984, Lorde's declaration that "the master's tools will never dismantle the master's house" became a rallying cry for Black feminist politics and an ideological framework for the burgeoning discourse of intersectionality in women's studies, in particular. In that speech, which Lorde delivered at a women's studies conference to which she had been invited at the last minute as one of the two Black women presenters, Lorde indicted her fellow feminists and alleged allies for their elision of racism, heterosexism, and classism in the feminist movement and their articulation of its political aims. Lorde (1984) asked all in attendance to "reach down into that deep place of knowledge inside herself and touch that terror and loathing of any difference that lives there. See whose face it wears. Then the personal as the political can begin to illuminate *all* our choices" (113). The master's tools are in many ways the metaphorical exigency for Black feminist and multiracial feminist theory and praxis, because they signify the hegemonic power of *anti-intersectional* thinking that pervades even social theory and movements that explicitly claim a politics of social justice, such as first- and second-wave feminism in the United States. To Lorde and her collaborators, including Barbara Smith, the obfuscation of intersecting dynamics of race, gender, class, and sexuality was a quintessential tool of the master (i.e., White supremacist, capitalist heteropatriarchy) to divide, distract, and disinvest marginalized communities and social groups. *Difference* must be recognized, according to Lorde, because it is real and complicated; through an honest reconciliation with the violence and inequalities that have been carried out in the name of difference, human cultural diversity can be reclaimed and remade as a tool for alliances and empowerment.

The essay below, on anger and racism, is an example of the kind of unpretentious and forthright exposition on difference for which Lorde is so celebrated. She unapologetically weaves her lived experiences as a Black lesbian into a structural critique of racist heteropartriarchy. In doing so, she explicates a theory of anger: anger is often dismissed as irrational, useless, unproductive, and immature, but anger is a completely rational and powerful response to the persistence of racism in the contemporary United States and in the women's movement of the late 1970s and 1980s, specifically. "It is not the anger of other women that will destroy us," she writes, "but our refusals to stand still, to listen to its rhythms, to learn within it, to move beyond the manner of presentation to the substance, to tap that anger as an important source of empowerment" (1984, 130). Lorde died after a battle with cancer in 1992, which she chronicled in her acclaimed *Cancer Journals*; her words remain startlingly relevant today, and are particularly important as we consider how to figure both emotion and the material consequences of violence into intersectionality as *critical* social theory—that is, social theory for social justice. She helps us to explore the question: what does intersectionality *feel* like?

22. Anger as a Response to Racism*

If women in the academy truly want a dialogue about racism, it will require recognizing the needs and the living contexts of other women. When an academic woman says, "I can't afford it," she may mean she is making a choice about how to spend her available money. But when a woman on welfare says, "I can't afford it," she means she is surviving on an amount of money that was barely subsistence in 1972, and she often does not have enough to eat. Yet the National Women's Studies Association here in 1981 holds a conference in which it commits itself to responding to racism, yet refuses to waive the registration fee for poor women and women of Color who wished to present and conduct workshops. This has made it impossible for many women of Color—for instance, Wilmette Brown, of Black Women for Wages for Housework—to participate in this conference. Is this to be merely another case of the academy discussing life within the closed circuits of the academy?

To the white women present who recognize these attitudes as familiar, but most of all, to all my sisters of Color who live and survive thousands of such encounters—to my sisters of Color who like me still tremble their rage under harness, or who sometimes question the expression of our rage as useless and disruptive (the two most popular accusations)—I want to speak about anger, my anger, and what I have learned from my travels through its dominions.

Every woman has a well-stocked arsenal of anger potentially useful against those oppressions, personal and institutional, which brought that anger into being. Focused with precision it can become a powerful source of energy serving progress and change. And when I speak of change, I do not mean a simple switch of positions or a temporary lessening of tensions, nor the ability to smile or feel good. I am speaking of a basic and radical alteration in those assumptions underlining our lives.

---

* Excerpt from A. Lorde, "The Uses of Anger: Women Responding to Racism." In *Sister Outsider: Essays and Speeches* (Berkeley, CA: The Crossing Press, 1984/2007). Reprinted by permission of the Charlotte Sheedy Literary Agency.

I have seen situations where white women hear a racist remark, resent what has been said, become filled with fury, and remain silent because they are afraid. That unexpressed anger lies within them like an undetonated device, usually to be hurled at the first woman of Color who talks about racism.

But anger expressed and translated into action in the service of our vision and our future is a liberating and strengthening act of clarification, for it is in the painful process of this translation that we identify who are our allies with whom we have grave differences, and who are our genuine enemies.

Anger is loaded with information and energy. When I speak of women of Color, I do not only mean Black women. The woman of Color who is not Black and who charges me with rendering her invisible by assuming that her struggles with racism are identical with my own has something to tell me that I had better learn from, lest we both waste ourselves fighting the truths between us. If I participate, knowingly or otherwise, in my sister's oppression and she calls me on it, to answer her anger with my own only blankets the substance of our exchange with reaction. It wastes energy. And yes, it is very difficult to stand still and to listen to another woman's voice delineate an agony I do not share, or one to which I myself have contributed.

In this place we speak removed from the more blatant reminders of our embattlement as women. This need not blind us to the size and complexities of the forces mounting against us and all that is most human within our environment. We are not here as women examining racism in a political and social vacuum. We operate in the teeth of a system for which racism and sexism are primary, established, and necessary props of profit. Women responding to racism is a topic so dangerous that when the local media attempt to discredit this conference they choose to focus upon the provision of lesbian housing as a diversionary device—as if the Hartford *Courant* dare not mention the topic chosen for discussion here, racism, lest it become apparent that women are in fact attempting to examine and to alter all the repressive conditions of our lives.

Mainstream communication does not want women, particularly white women, responding to racism. It wants racism to be accepted as an immutable given in the fabric of your existence, like eveningtime or the common cold.

So we are working in a context of opposition and threat, the cause of which is certainly not the angers which lie between us, but rather that virulent hatred leveled against all women, people of Color, lesbians and gay men, poor people—against all of us who are seeking to examine the particulars of our lives as we resist our oppressions, moving toward coalition and effective action.

Any discussion among women about racism must include the recognition and the use of anger. This discussion must be direct and creative because it is crucial. We cannot allow our fear of anger to deflect us nor seduce us into settling for anything less than the hard work of excavating honesty; we must be quite serious about the choice of this topic and the angers entwined within it because, rest assured, our opponents are quite serious about their hatred of us and of what we are trying to do here.

And while we scrutinize the often painful face of each other's anger, please remember that it is not our anger which makes me caution you to lock your doors at night and not to wander the streets of Hartford alone. It is the hatred which lurks in those streets, that urge to destroy us all if we truly work for change rather than merely indulge in academic rhetoric.

This hatred and our anger are very different. Hatred is the fury of those who do not share our goals, and its object is death and destruction. Anger is a grief of distortions between peers, and its object is change. But our time is getting shorter. We have been raised to view any difference other than sex as a reason for destruction, and for Black women and white women to face each other's angers without denial or immobility or silence or guilt is in itself a heretical and generative idea. It implies peers meeting upon a common basis to examine difference, and to alter those distortions which history has created around our difference. For it is those distortions which separate us. And we must ask ourselves: Who profits from all this?

Women of Color in america have grown up within a symphony of anger, at being silenced, at being unchosen, at knowing that when we survive, it is in spite of a world that takes for granted our lack of humanness, and which hates our very existence outside of its service. And I say *symphony* rather than *cacophony* because we have had to learn to orchestrate those furies so that they do not tear us apart. We have had to learn to move through them and use them for strength and force and insight within our daily lives. Those of us who did not learn this difficult lesson did not survive. And part of my anger is always libation for my fallen sisters.

Anger is an appropriate reaction to racist attitudes, as is fury when the actions arising from those attitudes do not change. To those women here who fear the anger of women of Color more than their own unscrutinized racist attitudes, I ask: Is the anger of women of Color more threatening than the woman-hatred that tinges all aspects of our lives?

It is not the anger of other women that will destroy us but our refusals to stand still, to listen to its rhythms, to learn within it, to move beyond the manner of presentation to the substance, to tap that anger as an important source of empowerment.

I cannot hide my anger to spare you guilt, nor hurt feelings, nor answering anger; for to do so insults and trivializes all our efforts. Guilt is not a response to anger; it is a response to one's own actions or lack of action. If it leads to change then it can be useful, since it is then no longer guilt but the beginning of knowledge. Yet all too often, guilt is just another name for impotence, for defensiveness destructive of communication; it becomes a device to protect ignorance and the continuation of things the way they are, the ultimate protection for changelessness.

But the strength of women lies in recognizing differences between us as creative, and in standing to those distortions which we inherited without blame, but which are now ours to alter. The angers of women can transform difference through insight into power. For anger between peers births change, not destruction, and the discomfort and sense of loss it often causes is not fatal, but a sign of growth.

My response to racism is anger. That anger has eaten clefts into my living only when it remained unspoken, useless to anyone. It has also served me in classrooms without light or learning, where the work and history of Black women was less than a vapor. It has served me as fire in the ice zone of uncomprehending eyes of white women who see in my experience and the experience of my people only new reasons for fear or guilt. And my anger is no excuse for not dealing with your blindness, no reason to withdraw from the results of your own actions.

When women of Color speak out of the anger that laces so many of our contacts with white women, we are often told that we are "creating a mood of hopelessness," "preventing white women from getting past guilt," or "standing in the way of trusting communication and action." All these quotes come directly from letters to me from members of this organization within the last two years. One woman wrote, "Because you are Black and Lesbian, you seem to speak with the moral authority of suffering." Yes, I am Black and Lesbian, and what you hear in my voice is fury, not suffering. Anger, not moral authority. There is a difference.

Marla H. Kohlman

Marla Kohlman, professor of sociology at Kenyon College, has been a vocal and consistent contributor to the literature on intersectionality for the past fifteen years. Her core area of expertise is the study of sexual harassment, but her scholarship has also contributed to the study of military personnel issues, gender dynamics in colleges, and quantitative methods. Most recently, she and Bonnie Thornton Dill coauthored an essay on intersectionality for the *Handbook of Feminist Research: Theory and Praxis* (2012, 2nd edition, edited by Sharlene Nagy Hesse-Biber) in which they posit two forms of intersectional research: "strong intersectionality," which refers to analyses of systems of inequality and identities in relationship to one another, and "weak intersectionality," which denotes explorations of "difference" without any attention to critical analyses or the interrogation of power structures. In particular, Kohlman's work advances understanding of how to conduct quantitative intersectional analyses, which can seem antithetical to much of the theory undergirding intersectional paradigms (see Shields 2008, Unit III, reading 13). If dimensions of difference (e.g., race, class, gender) are co-constitutive phenomena as opposed to discreet, nonoverlapping variables, how can we analyze them statistically without obscuring the realities of these social dynamics and/or reinforcing the idea that race, class, and gender (among others) are merely identity variables that can be parsed out, disentangled, or controlled for? In the excerpt below, Kohlman's work in sociology points to some answers by explaining how individual experiences of harassment and exploitation "cannot be properly understood through the limited lenses of class position, race, or gender alone or as additive processes." I have highlighted Kohlman's conclusions below, so that we can see how relatively simple quantitative analyses can yield robust and nuanced claims about social trends and "demographics."

23. **The Demography of Sexual Harassment**[*]

Most of the current literature on sexual harassment, both academic and legal, shares the common theme that sexual harassment is behavior that is unwelcome or unsolicited, sexual in nature, and is deliberate or repeated. Agreement has not been reached, nonetheless, on the types of behavior that constitute sexual harassment. The elements of gender, class, age, marital status, and occupation (i.e., demographics) emerge as particularly relevant to any serious study of sexual harassment in the labor market, regardless of discipline, although the dynamics of race are rarely, if ever, explicitly mentioned in this literature.

The current study contributes to the literature on sexual harassment by explicitly modeling race as a significant predictor of sexual harassment in combination with gender and occupation, rather than regarding each demographic characteristic as though experienced separately from others.

The predictions tested in this analysis seek to provide support for the contention that we cannot, as many have argued, treat individuals as members of any monolithic racial or gender grouping (Collins 1998; Collins 1990; Amott and Matthaei 1996; Zinn and Dill 1996; Spelman 1988) in current analyses of labor market processes. We must proceed with the understanding that

---

[*] Excerpted from M. H. Kohlman, "Person or Position: The Demographics of Sexual Harassment in the Workplace," *Equal Opportunities International* 23 (2004): 143–161. © Emerald Group Publishing Limited, all rights reserved. Some in-text citations have been excised for length.

individual men and women are subject to many intersecting forces of oppression which shape their individual experiences of exploitative, or harassing, behavior in ways which cannot be properly understood through the limited lenses of class position, race, or gender alone or as additive processes.

The Vulnerability Hypothesis

The primary research question posed by this study is whether some members of the U.S. labor market are more vulnerable to sexual harassment than others for some identifiable reason such as age, gender, marital status, race, or occupational position. Because it is understood that sexual harassment is not the result of misunderstandings based simply upon gender differences and issues of attraction, the vulnerability hypothesis posited by this study is that those groups in society imbued with less power should be more readily targeted for sexual harassment in the workplace. We should expect to see this because they are either perceived as more vulnerable by those who target others for harassment or because they occupy a position in society or the workplace which is deemed to be less powerful.

This study also predicts that women, in particular, are perceived as vulnerable in the labor market and are, therefore, targeted for sexual harassment based upon the gender dominance and sex role spillover explanations for sexual harassment.

The Dominance Perspective

According to this perspective, sexual harassment is about power—gaining power or retaining power over subordinates by those in positions of authority. In fact, according to the gender dominance perspective, sexual harassment is a means by which men in privileged positions have reinforced their privilege and "maintained dominance over women at work and in society more generally" (Padavic and Orcutt 1997:683). Moreover, "[m]ost harassment has little to do with erotic concerns and is not designed to elicit cooperation but to insult, deride, and degrade women" (Fitzgerald 1993:5).

The Sex-Role Spillover Explanation

The sex-role spillover explanation is distinct from the dominance theoretical perspective, then, because it illuminates the resentment some men may feel when women are perceived as violating the public sphere dominated by men, having wrongfully left their proper role in the domestic sphere. One way to combat that is to place women in occupations that accentuate their ascribed status as caretakers in society. It is not surprising, then, that we find women concentrated in occupations such as teachers, day-care workers, secretaries, and the like.

The sex-role spillover theory of sexual harassment posits that women, in general, are vulnerable to being targeted for sexual harassment simply because they have "opted" to be part of the labor market, but those women who are employed in occupations which have been traditionally gendered male, are especially vulnerable to being targeted.

Statement of Hypotheses

The question which serves as the dependent variable for this analysis provides a rich source of data to answer the question "Who is most likely to report having been targeted for sexual harassment?" This means that respondents are self-reporting incidents and behaviors in the workplace that have occurred to them which they perceived to have been sexual harassment, thereafter reporting them as such to an [National Occupational Research Center] NORC interviewer.

A principal element of these hypotheses is the contention that sexual harassment is most likely to occur in occupations where power dynamics are most apparent. These include occupations in which employers typically grant an appreciable amount of autonomy to managerial employees, where men are more numerous than women, white employees more numerous than minorities, etc. It is also expected that more sexual harassment is reported in those occupations where women have been traditionally excluded until recently, for example, professional occupations such as medical surgery or corporate law and in traditional blue collar positions.

In addition, we must be wary of any explanation which would fail to account for "the dynamics of a world in which multiple hierarchies can make people simultaneously powerful and powerless relative to others" (Miller 1997:50). The hypotheses which follow address this concern by seeking to locate the *intersections* of experience to be found within the occupational structures represented in the analysis. This includes tests that seek to ascertain how the effects of race and gender condition class and occupation based upon the likelihood of respondents' reporting sexual harassment.

H_1 Women are more likely to report incidents of sexual harassment than men regardless of race, class, or occupation.

H_2 Women are less likely to report experiences of sexual harassment in those occupations in which the percentage of women is the highest.

H_3 Men and women of color are more likely to report incidents of sexual harassment than white men and women.

There are some reservations about the direction of this last prediction. Although the prevailing theory of dominance would seem to suggest that the more vulnerable members of our labor market (i.e., those who have suffered discrimination because of race, gender, national origin, etc.) are more likely to experience incidents of sexual harassment, it is also plausible that men and women of color are more apt to ignore such incidents than white women because of the concern as to whether the behavior is motivated by some other factor, e.g. racial prejudice or concerns about the fairness of the system overall where they are concerned. This could also render them less likely to report such incidents under any circumstance.

This is expected because we know that the less powerful individuals in our society are more vulnerable. Thus, one should expect that these vulnerable individuals are even less powerful in situations where there are fewer of them (Eson 1992; Kanter 1977) as is the case in many work settings where men and women of color have more to lose, in terms of overall life chances, than white men and women who have greater access to the more affluent sectors of the labor market.

On the other hand, one could argue that men and women of color may have less confidence in reporting instances of harassment because of uncertainty as to whether the behavior in question constitutes harassment based upon race, occupational status, gender, or some interaction of all these factors (Murrell 1996). Another explanation for this may be that minority men and women may have less confidence in the workplace overall and, therefore, would not bother to report perceived instances of sexual harassment having dismissed such an incident as altogether irrelevant or inappropriate to be isolated, labeled as sexual harassment, and reported to a disinterested interviewer.

All of these dynamics contribute to one another, culminating in the inability to define one situation as race, class, or gender discrimination, as an instance of sexual harassment, or some amalgam of any of these various dynamics. The main point here is that all of these factors construct one another which, in turn, could result in sexual harassment not being recognized, perceived, or reported as such although it may be reasonable to expect that those who feel relatively powerless are more likely to report an incident of sexual harassment in an interview situation outside of his/her place of business.

Data and Methods

The data that form the basis for this study are derived from the *General Social Survey* (GSS), a broad, national survey of the United States population. This data set was chosen as the sample population for this analysis because it contains a pointed, though imperfect, question about experiences of sexual harassment as well as a wealth of information about race, gender, educational status, and occupational position of the respondents.

The GSS has been conducted by the NORC every year or two years during February, March, and April since 1972. The sample is composed of respondents who are English speaking, 18 years of age or older, and living in non-institutional arrangements within the United States. The respondents are interviewed in their homes by interviewers hired and trained by NORC. The survey years 1994 and 1996 will be the only ones included in this analysis because the sexual harassment question which serves as the dependent variable for this study was only included in the GSS during these years.

The Variables: Dependent Measure

The phrasing of the sexual harassment question is as follows: "Sometimes at work people find themselves the object of sexual advances, propositions, or unwanted sexual discussions from co-workers or supervisors. The advances sometimes involve physical contact and sometimes just involve sexual conversations. Has this ever happened to you?"

Independent Measures

The independent variables are designed to predict the levels of harassment experienced by different types of respondents. These independent variables include measures of sex, age, years of education, marital status, race, labor force participation status, occupational prestige, and percent female and sex of each occupation.

Discussion of Results

The findings reported in this study contribute support to each of the theoretical paradigms tested because they strongly suggest that those respondents employed in jobs not traditionally ascribed to their gender are perceived as threats in these occupations and are, therefore, specifically targeted for sexual harassment.

The [logistic regression] models presented below were designed to ascertain whether the effects of sexual harassment reported by respondents evince any discernible patterns by gender, race, occupation, or any combination of these factors.

Are Women More Likely To Report?

The first prediction of this study is that women are more likely to report being targeted for sexual harassment than men, regardless of race, class, or occupation. What the results reveal is that this statement derives only partial support from this data. In fact, it is reported that women are not reporting more sexual harassment based upon any one overriding factor integrally related to their gender. What does emerge as most significant for the female respondents in this analysis is their demographic status; i.e., age, education, race or marital status rather than any indications of being targeted for sexual harassment based upon occupational position. Indeed, there is no occupational position reported as significant for the women in this analysis in their reports of sexual harassment. Likewise, the demographic characteristics of the male respondents are reported as significant in some respects, but not with the same strength of statistical significance, if any at all, as the female respondents.

For men, all occupational niches except skilled blue-collar workers report more sexual harassment than laborers and operatives (the occupational grouping omitted for purposes of comparison). The odds ratios reported indicate that men employed as professionals are 46% more likely to report sexual harassment than laborers and operatives, while technicians are 99% more likely to report being targeted for sexual harassment in comparison to laborers and operatives. These results suggest, then, that occupational position is irrelevant for female respondents but of considerable significance for male respondents.

Marital status, in particular, emerges as a significant predictor of sexual harassment in this model but with the caveat that being single makes a difference in reporting for women but not for men. According to the odds ratios, the women in this sample who are divorced or separated are 75% *more* likely to report being targeted for sexual harassment than married female respondents, while divorced and separated men also report more sexual harassment than married men, but the distinction of being single is not as stark as it is for women.

These findings provide support for the gender dominance explanation for sexual harassment in that female respondents appear to be targeted based upon perceived vulnerability as individuals in the workplace, while men appear to be targeted based upon perceived power differentials within the occupational structure of the workplace.

Does the Percentage of Women in the Occupation Matter?

The second prediction of this analysis was tested most directly with the variables "percent female" and "job gender context" of the respondent's occupation. Here, it was predicted that women in occupations where the percentage of women is highest are less likely to report being targeted for sexual harassment. The odds ratios reported for this measure indicate that in occupations where women are more numerous, women report 51% less sexual harassment; i.e., those women in jobs gendered male are *more* likely to be targeted for sexual harassment.

Moreover, this is only true for men employed in positions that have high percentages of female workers. These findings suggest, then, that the gendered composition of the occupation is only important relative to the respondent's own gender. Thus, it is not whether or not a particular occupation is gendered female that is important, it is whether or not the respondent is employed in a job-gender context that corresponds to his/her own gender.

Prestige of occupation is also shown to be a marginally significant predictor of men being targeted for sexual harassment. Men in occupations with more prestige are slightly more likely to report sexual harassment than men with less prestige. This is not a strong effect but it is noteworthy, nonetheless, in light of the fact that prestige of occupation has no marked effect on women's likelihood of reporting sexual harassment.

This set of results provide support for the sex-role spillover explanation for sexual harassment in that the job-gender context of respondent's occupation is most determinative of being targeted for sexual harassment; most specifically, the significant positive effect for men means that men in predominantly female jobs report more sexual harassment and the significant negative result for women means women report more in male jobs.

Does Race Make a Difference?

The final prediction tested in this study is whether men and women of color are more likely to predict being targeted for sexual harassment than the white men and women represented in the sample.

The results for race are striking in that they differ markedly according to the intersection of gender and occupation. As with the findings reported above for women, we again find the opposite of my cautious prediction that women of color would report more sexual harassment than white women. For the men, however, the result is quite different. Instead, it is reported that Black men are significantly *more* likely to report sexual harassment than white men. Thus, the hypothesis for minority respondents receives some support in this analysis, but only for Black men, and not for minority women. In fact, this set of findings specifically address one reservation stated earlier in this analysis; that is, that race could be a complicating factor which might render some respondents *less* likely to report being targeted for sexual harassment.

The effects reported for Blacks and Hispanics are also quite revealing of differing gender dynamics within the workplace. Both analyses report that Black women are significantly less likely to report sexual harassment than white women, while Black men are significantly more likely to report sexual harassment than white men. On the other hand, it is also reported that Hispanic men are no more likely to report being targeted for sexual harassment than white men, but Hispanic women are 26% less likely to report sexual harassment in comparison to white women.

This would tend to support my hypothesis that those in vulnerable social roles, racial ethnic minorities and women, are more likely to report than white men in some instances but that we must also be ever cognizant of the fact that men are not a monolithic group possessing uniform levels of power in the labor market any more than we should believe that women all suffer the same types of victimization as targets of sexual harassment.

Concluding Remarks

The predictions of this study which seek to measure the dynamic of power manifest in race dynamics and gender composition of respondent's workplace provided ambiguous support for the prediction that those in more vulnerable positions in the workplace, and in society overall, are more likely to be targeted for sexual harassment. It was hypothesized, for example, that members of minority racial-ethnic groups would be more likely to report having been targeted and my findings were that some of these respondents were *less* likely to report having been targeted for sexual harassment.

On the other hand, a pattern clearly emerged which provides evidence for the contention that women and men experience being targeted for sexual harassment in the workplace very differently. For men, it is a function of occupational position and for women it is a function of personal demographics.

In general, the power theory that dictated these analyses was not revealed to be as strong nor as pervasive as initially expected. More specifically, it was not shown to explain the dynamics of race, occupation, or marital status to the same extent that it clearly illustrated underlying gender dynamics. This means that further research in this area must investigate other ways of conceptualizing power manifest in sexual harassment in order to explain how the dynamics of gender, race and class may, or may not, be a fundamental part of the understanding of how or when an individual reports an experience of sexual harassment.

Patricia Ticineto Clough and Michelle Fine

Patricia Ticineto Clough and Michelle Fine come from different disciplinary backgrounds, but their work meets at the interdisciplinary crossroads of women's studies. Clough is a professor of sociology and women's studies at Queens College and the Graduate Center of the City University of New York (CUNY), and her work has been particularly influential in the area of affect studies and theory. Fine is a Distinguished Professor of Women's Studies, Social Personality, and Urban Education, also at the Graduate Center of CUNY. This coauthored essay from *Women's Studies Quarterly* weaves between their two experiences with large-scale, scholar-activist projects: Fine's participatory action research in a women's prison, and Clough's work with women and men "postrelease" from incarceration. The parts in italics represent Fine's field notes, in which she reflects upon her own position of privilege as a researcher working with an extremely vulnerable population (i.e., women in prison, some of whom were incarcerated on life sentences). Clough's writing is a reflection—several years after being exposed to Fine's work inside prisons—on her own experiences founding Community, Leadership, and Education After Reentry, or CLEAR, a "research-based working group of women and men who have been incarcerated and whose research is focused on shaping critical debate on reentry reform of the criminal justice system." In their writing, both authors refuse the lip service of "scholar-activism" in the academy, which is a label all-too-easily applied and yet exceedingly difficult to cultivate meaningfully and fairly. In the academy, it is common to hear scholars lament on how undervalued activist and applied work is to promotion and tenure committees, not to mention the greater scientific community. Clough and Fine do not necessarily deny that here, but they offer another perspective: much of what gets called "scholar-activism" serves the scholar doing the activism much more than the people and communities who are supposedly the target of productive interventions. Neither takes the label of "activist" as an *a priori* role, instead questioning the intersectional dynamics that make activist research such a proverbial minefield, to borrow Sengupta's metaphor from Unit III. Accordingly, Clough and Fine embrace the political complexities of their identities as researchers and community members, and their work here symbolizes how hard *and* important applying intersectional insights toward systemic social change really is.

24. **Academia and Activism**[*]

Together our two essays move between scenes of teaching and researching with women and men who are or have been in prison. Having written on ethnography, autoethnography, and participatory research, we both have sought a method that would allow us to abandon superficial identifications, mistaken for deep connection, with those who are or have been incarcerated. While we are conscious of the failures and successes of our attempts, we nonetheless write because what we have learned about the state's support *for* mass incarceration and the state's retreat *from* public higher education—particularly for persons of color—more than warrants it. With this essay, we invite readers to take seriously, as we do, the relation of mass incarceration and what today is called "prisoner reentry" to all that is implied by the terms "the personal," "the political," "the economic," and "the social."

We begin with Michelle Fine's story, with italicized field notes and a narrative about participatory research in a women's prison, and then we turn to Patricia Ticineto Clough's work with women and men postrelease. What is "activist" about the work we do is our commitment to change policy, legislation,

---

[*] Excerpted from P. T. Clough and M. Fine, "Activism and Pedagogies: Feminist Reflections," *WSQ: Women's Studies Quarterly* 35 (Fall–Winter 2007). Copyright © 2007 by the Feminist Press at the City University of New York. Used by permission of the publishers, www.feminist press.org. All rights reserved.

and programming. To do this, we have found it necessary to insert analyses of racism and classism into theories of security, crime, and punishment.

Documenting Possibility in Hell: A Participatory Research Project by Women In and Out of Prison

Michelle Fine

We had just completed the interviews and focus groups, all conducted by a prisoner researcher and an (outside) graduate student researcher. The transcripts were complete, and our analyses emerging. Researchers from the Graduate Center brought the analytic frameworks into the prison to see what the women thought about the analysis, interpretations, coding scheme. As an unfamiliar tension circled the table, I asked, "So we get to collect the data, but you do the analysis? What kind of division of labor is that?" A delicate question, bathed in political insight. In the name of ethics and confidentiality, we had (unwittingly?) separated data collection from the political and theoretical work of analysis. And so a[nother] long talk about power, process, and politics ensued. We struggled to figure out a way to bring the transcribed interviews into the prison and leave them there (prisoners have no access to locked cabinets, and confidentiality would be violated if these interviews were allowed to lie around for public viewing). With prisoner and outside collaborative wit, and a bit of subversion, we figured it out.

A year later we had completed the tasks of gathering material—interviews, focus groups, Department of Correctional Services recidivism study, a cost-benefit analysis, letters from women who were out, interviews with women on the outside, surveys from university faculty and presidents, interviews with children of the women and corrections officers—and we were trying to figure out how to write our text.

Now that we have worked together for years, and we're all writing, do we produce a policy text as single voiced, or multivoiced? Filled with the questions and contradictions of participatory work, or coherent and authoritative? Stuffed with feminist complexity or social science parsimony? How should we determine authorship—Alphabetize? Separate prisoner researchers and Graduate Center researchers? Put Michelle's name first because of "legitimacy"? Don't put some of the high-profile prisoners' names first because of concerns about perceptions? Place the most "wanted" of us all upfront to demonstrate the power of our chutzpa and collaboration? ? ?

We sought to convince the New York State legislature to restore funds for college in prison programs. But we also wanted to produce materials for use on college campuses, in other prisons, by prison advocacy groups, by families of persons in prison, and so on. So we decided to craft multiple products. Our primary document would be a single-voiced, multimethod, rigorous, and

professionally graphic-designed report, available widely on a Web site (www
.changingminds.ws) with quotes and endorsements from people on the political Left and Right. The prisoners wanted Michelle Fine to be the first name,
and "Missy" insisted that that was the name she would use. This report was
distributed to every governor in the United States and to all the New York State
senators and members of the Assembly. We would, as well, construct additional
essays on feminist methodology in which our contradictions would be interrogated. We produced one thousand organizing brochures in English and Spanish that carried a strong voice of advocacy and demands for justice and action.
These brochures were distributed across a series of community-based organizations, national advocacy groups, and colleges and universities. We created (and
have sustained for six years) our Web site, where activists, organizers, students,
faculty, criminal justice administrators, and prisoners and their families can
download a full copy of the report, loaded with photos, letters, charts, graphs,
cost benefit analyses, and the rich words of the women. To date, the Web site
has been "hit" more than five thousand times, the California State Department
of Corrections has ordered fifty copies of the report, feminist and critical education faculty have assigned the report in class, a father whose daughter committed suicide in prison has decided to sponsor a college-in-prison project, and
he has ordered copies for a number of administrators in his home state.

As we struggled with the section on who is the "we" of the research collective,
Michelle naively offered, "What if we write something like, 'We are all women
concerned with violence against women—intimate, structural, economic, racial,
and state violence. Some of us have experienced such violence, most of us have wit-
nessed it, and all are outraged.'" To which Donna said, "Michelle, please don't
romanticize us. Your writing is eloquent, but you seemed to have left out the part
that some of us are here for murder." Another woman extended the point, "and
some of us for murder of our children." The argument was growing clear: "When
we're not here, in the college, and we're alone in our cells, we have to think about
the people affected by our crimes. We take responsibility and we need you to repre-
sent that as well as our common concerns as women, as feminists, as political. . . . "

As powerful as our participatory work has been behind bars, the women
in prison are always extremely vulnerable to systemic abuse, alternately called
discipline, management, security. . . . *Their* poetry, books, journals, favorite
seasonings, letters from home, hair dye, private documents were searched, ran-
sacked, tossed out, when someone in administration decided to exert power or
tried to warn the women, in the sadomasochistic rhythm of prison, about what
they were writing. And the critical consciousness that accompanies participatory research comes with the anger, outrage, and a recognition of injustice that
boils in prison. Participatory action research speaks to an outside world, but
often, inside, little changes.

Other prisons have been developing college programs, and a number of other states have relied on the original model to craft their own. And back at the original site, where the research took place, the program survives. Participation, however, has been squeezed out. There is still college, but the radical passion and politics that infused its birth have been stripped away.

The question of "for whom" we have crafted the research hovers. We decided to write for policy makers, activists, women in prison and their families, the general public, women's studies classes, and courses on higher education and participatory methods. But beneath the generative list we were/are haunted by the question, Is anyone listening? Have we been so co-opted as to think the mass incarceration of women of color is a "cognitive problem"?

At one state legislative hearing, the two of us (Michelle and Maria) presented the findings and concluded, "College in prison is morally important to individuals, families, and communities; financially wise for the state; and builds civic engagement and leadership in urban communities. In fact, college in prison even saves taxpayers money. A conservative Republican, as well as your more progressive colleagues, should support these programs . . . unless, of course, the point is simply to lock up Black and Brown bodies at the Canadian border." To which one of the more progressive state legislators responded, "Doctor, I'm afraid that is the point. You know that in New York, downstate's crime is upstate's industry." That is, the social fabric of New York State is divided by a relatively white and rural "upstate" and then substantial poverty and communities of color "downstate" in New York City (with pockets of urban poverty distributed throughout the state). One analysis of prisoners suggested that 80 percent of New York State prisoners come from eight communities in New York City. Thus, the crime in the city produces the industry and jobs—hotels, bus service, movies, restaurants, correctional personnel, etc.—for the upstate population.

The concept of prisons as *banal social control* has infected our national consciousness and our national as well as the global economy. In modest response, in the midst of a global struggle against the mass incarceration of people of color, and women in particular, the Changing Minds project offered an electric current of research and activism through which critique and possibility could travel over the walls. Together, women inside and out could bear witness to the atrocity and testify to the possibility.

Theoretical Heights, Clear Thinking: Research in the Postprison
Patricia Ticineto Clough

I first read the study about which Michelle Fine writes in 2000, when I was becoming involved in working with women who, immediately upon release from prison or shortly thereafter, were seeking support for returning to college, obtaining a master's degree or a Ph.D. As the new director of the Center for the Study of Women and Society (CSWS) at the Graduate Center of the City University of New York, I had accepted a generous offer of funding to house a program to support women in the pursuit of higher education as part of their process of "reentry"—the term, I learned, being used by program reformers, policy makers, and legislators to capture the time of readjustment to society after incarceration.

The reentry program that came to be located at CSWS was named College and Community Fellowship (CCF) and just as Michelle Fine's research showed the importance of higher education to women and men in prison, CCF would impressively demonstrate the importance of higher education for those living with criminal convictions outside prison, women and men who are suffering the "collateral consequences" of conviction, including the denial of civil rights and the restriction of social, political, and economic opportunities. While the experience of reentry therefore often is an experience of ongoing punishment, "an invisible punishment" without end, CCF would show that higher education can make a real difference.

Yet most existing reentry initiatives have not been funded to address the need or desire for higher education among those living with criminal convictions. Higher education has not been a primary policy, legislative, or program aim. Why this is so seemed like a good research question, one that might best be pursued in a research project that involved as researchers those most affected—people living with criminal convictions after incarceration, those who have been called ex-convicts, ex-felons, ex-inmates, the formerly incarcerated, and most recently "prisoners-in-reentry."

It would not be until late 2003 that I would invite some of the members of CCF to do research and develop a critical perspective on the reentry reform of mass incarceration. Before that time, however, I would explore a critical perspective with mostly faculty and graduate students in the Conviction Project seminar, which was begun in 2000, funded in part by CSWS and in part by the funder of CCF. Limiting the development of a critical perspective on reentry to the Conviction Project seminar resulted in part from my need to find a certain kind of relief from the narrow focus of reentry reform and the everyday activities of reentry programming, including the everyday effort to raise funds for CCF, one of the activities required of me as director of CSWS. But it also resulted from my understanding that a critical perspective on reentry would most likely involve engaging in a deeply theoretical and a wide-ranging rethinking of governance, culture, and economy in order to address issues of race, class, gender, ethnicity, and sexuality in relation to imprisonment, surveillance, and control. I supposed that such rethinking would not be appealing to policy makers, legislators, and program reformers, from whom we were seeking financial support and institutional recognition of CCF.

I had been a student activist, a community organizer, and a welfare-rights worker, and when I stopped organizing in order to return to school, I did so because I thought education would assist me in figuring out how to "do politics" successfully. I had become convinced that reforming policy, programming, and legislation was not politically radical enough, as did many others then, in the late 1960s and early 1970s. I had learned that program, policy, and legislative reform often better serve those who design, and administer and regulate these reforms than they do those for whom the reform policy and programming were supposedly intended. At least it might be said that whether reform succeeds or fails to meet its own aims, it usually succeeds in constituting a subject, the subject of reform, what might be called a "client-subject." I was concerned not to participate in the making of a "client-subject of reentry" in my efforts to support CCF. I was, however, drawn to analyze what kind of client-subject was being shaped for those living with convictions after incarceration.

As I already have remarked, when I first became involved in CCF, I believed the highly theoretical and critical orientation of my scholarship and research would be useless in seeking resources from funders of policy, program, and legislative reform. I was sure that reform is not a radical critique; it is not even able to be self-reflective of its own effects. About this, I have not changed my mind. Indeed, in learning about mass incarceration and reentry with those most affected and those who are engaged in reform, I am more convinced than ever that social, political, and cultural politics have been shaped, if not misshaped, by the overlay of policy, programming, and legislative reform on society. It was this plane of policy, programming, and legislative reform from which I wanted to retreat, so as to engage in critical self-reflective scholarship. I now believe that scholars and critics should not retreat, if in fact they can retreat; rather, they should more fully invest their intellectual energies. It is on the plane of policy, program, and legislative reform that studying, learning, and teaching should be occurring. It is here that there should be insistent criticism, while keeping in mind that reform itself is rarely critical enough or aimed at radical change. But radical change is necessary.

So perhaps more important to reflect upon is the time it took before I convened CLEAR as well as the time it would take before I would share with CLEAR members my own research and scholarship, to share with them what had become my views about identity, voice, speaking for oneself, and racism in its current transformations, about political economy and governance—all subjects developed in the Conviction Project seminar. My hesitancy came in part out of a deep understanding that CLEAR research and analysis could not just be mine, if mine at all. However, while it is right to respect the issues around authorization to speak, I was wrong not to offer what I had come to think about matters of importance to CLEAR research. By no means was I suffering from a false sense of humility. No, the point is that I really had come to believe that theory and criticism had become irrelevant outside the academy, if not in it.

In part, this insecurity is a result of my own family, a matter of a class, race, gender, and ethnic background that has always made me insecure about doing scholarship. No matter how much I do, I still find myself seeking ways to deal with the insecurity. But what I learned from being part of CLEAR is that my theoretically and critically oriented scholarship is not merely a psychological defense against insecurity, if that at all. Rather, what insecurity caused was that it led me to believe that communicating from theoretical and critical heights would be, if not incomprehensible, useless to the members of CLEAR. My insecurity had made me prey to an intellectual environment shared by academics and policy, program, and legislative reformers alike, an environment that itself is marked by a defensive and opportunistic opposition of scholarship and activism, useful research and theoretical abstraction, understandable language and elaborated linguistic form. I have learned that these opposites rest on a fundamental opposition, which is very much in the way of those seeking to get beyond reentry—that is, the opposition between researcher and researched, service provider and client, teacher and student. Of course there are important differences represented by each of these pairs of opposites, but what must happen and happen often is the overcoming of the oppositions on behalf of the process of scholarship, research, and criticism of policy, program, and legislative reform. In the spectacular moments of overcoming, everyone learns and learns to learn together.

Rachel Luft

Rachel Luft is an associate professor in the Department of Anthropology, Sociology, and Social Work at Seattle University. She earned her PhD from the University of California, Santa Barbara, and previously taught at the University of New Orleans in sociology and women's and gender studies. Luft's forthcoming book, *Disaster Patriarchy: An Intersectional Analysis of Post-Katrina Social Movements,* explores the intersectional dynamics of race, class, and gender politics in the activist work that emerged in New Orleans in the wake of Hurricane Katrina. Luft's scholarship is in many ways an extension of earlier intersectional social movement research by Joshua Gamson, and can be placed in conversation with the contemporary work of Amin Ghaziani. In this excerpt from an essay in *American Quarterly,* Luft explains what it means to think beyond "disaster exceptionalism," a theoretical (and indeed highly political) framework that conceptualizes disasters as unique, sudden, and explosively different from other harmful events. Based on her fieldwork in New Orleans in the years after that devastating 2005 hurricane, Luft explores how the social positions of populations in and around New Orleans left victims of Katrina "socially vulnerable." She explains how grassroots leaders—who possessed sophisticated, expert knowledges derived from their lived experiences before, during, and after the storm—challenged mass-mediated and "official" narratives (i.e., produced and disseminated by the state and nongovernmental aid organizations) about Katrina's so-called exceptional nature and instead focused on the *social construction* of the disaster. This, of course, does not mean that these grassroots organizers claimed that Katrina was fictional or imaginary, but that the dynamics and structures that made Katrina so especially devastating are rooted in social forces, not wind and rain. As Luft learned, activists used this social constructionist framework to link Katrina recovery efforts and hurricane readiness initiatives to the amelioration of ongoing social problems, including poverty, racial discrimination, labor exploitation, and reproductive injustice in New Orleans and the Gulf Coast region.

25. Social Movements in the Wake of Katrina*

In the three and a half years since Katrina, scholarship on the hurricane events has exploded. Eighteen academic journals from various disciplines have produced special Katrina volumes. The Social Science Research Council's "Hurricane Katrina Research Bibliography," updated monthly, is nearly seventy pages, and grouped by area of study, such as culture and tradition, evacuation, and housing. Eminent disaster scholar Kai Erikson predicts Katrina will be the most studied disaster in history.

Traditionally, scholars have distinguished disasters from other kinds of harmful events by characterizing them as "sudden" or "explosive," discrete or "unique," and "acute." These designations have sought to render exceptional both the disasters themselves and the experience of the people who encounter them. In the 1980s, a new, constructionist school of disaster scholarship began to emphasize the preexisting social conditions that contribute to and exacerbate disaster, pointing to the social origins of disaster and calling into question the notion of their suddenness and discreteness. It emphasized the ongoing conditions of "social vulnerability"—poverty, racism, sexism—that construct

* Excerpted from R. E. Luft, "Beyond Disaster Exceptionalism: Social Movement Developments in New Orleans after Hurricane Katrina," *American Quarterly* 61:3 (2009): 501–502, 506–509. © 2009 The American Studies Association. Reprinted with permission of the Johns Hopkins University Press.

and interact with disaster. Understanding these enduring social problems as disastrous in their own right has further challenged the narrow assessment of natural disasters and other emergencies as exceptionally acute. From this perspective, "the line separating the chronic from the acute becomes even more blurred."

Social vulnerability scholarship has helped to identify how "the challenges of life are a 'permanent disaster'" for people already oppressed by class, race, gender, sexuality, disability, age, and other forces of systemic oppression. It moves to displace "natural" disasters as the greatest risk to human well-being and to replace them with an understanding of the social and ongoing conditions that produce daily risk, suffering, and trauma. It also helps to explain the behavior of people who already experience daily hazards because they live at the intersection of poverty, racism, and/or sexism when they face what appears to be a discrete disaster.

Within weeks of Hurricane Katrina's landfall, social scientists were publishing analyses of the disaster from social constructionist and social vulnerability perspectives. They noted that years of human and infrastructural neglect—the racialized poverty that had 27 percent of New Orleans's inhabitants living below the poverty line; the poorly designed and maintained levees; and the federal government's inadequately managed and funded emergency management operations agency, to cite only the most obvious examples—had produced the devastating outcomes of the storm. At the same time, grassroots movement leaders were also pointing to the social construction of the disaster. In addition to identifying the particular race, class, and gender determinants of Katrina's outcomes, they also contextualized them in the long history of U.S. imperialism, the "national oppression" of Blacks, and the disenfranchisement of women and children. Instead of emphasizing the exceptional elements of Hurricane Katrina, these grassroots leaders saw in the policy decisions that helped produce its outcomes, the standard operating procedure of the U.S. government; they likened the displacement, impoverishment, and service deprivation of hurricane survivors to the chronic conditions of racialized poverty. Additionally they predicted that the reconstruction would turn the Gulf Coast, and in particular New Orleans, into a laboratory for privatization as part of what Naomi Klein calls "disaster capitalism." They further anticipated that the reconstruction of New Orleans would become a bellwether for incursions into domestic infrastructure in other parts of the country, calling it the canary in the mines of U.S. homeland policy. As movement lawyer Bill Quigley put it more recently, responding to the federal bailout of financial institutions in late 2008, "Welcome to Katrina world."

Social constructionist and social vulnerability perspectives were apparent at the grassroots in the narrative devices first-generation movement organizers used to link pre- and postdisaster New Orleans to sites around the country. As they spoke to a steady stream of volunteers, movement leaders urged visitors to "make the connections" between their own communities and New Orleans. They insisted that "the storm began a long time before Katrina." When they asked visitors if they were "preparing for the Katrina in your own backyard," they were not referring to the threat of natural disaster elsewhere (though they reminded them of such a threat when nonlocals wondered whether New Orleans should be rebuilt), but rather to every community's structures of disenfranchisement. These refrains were picked up by solidarity activists nationwide, who helped to make the linkages. In an early article, San Francisco-based Catalyst Project organizer Molly McClure tied disaster exceptionalism to a charitable—as opposed to political and systemic—response to the storm: "With charity, I don't have to connect the dots between sudden catastrophes like Katrina, and the perhaps slower but very similar economic devastation happening in poor communities and communities of color, every day, right here, in my city."

First-generation Katrina movement groups de-exceptionalized disaster in order to reframe the recovery and reconstruction process in the broader context of ongoing U.S. social problems. Second-generation groups did so in order to move beyond Katrina to the ongoing social problems themselves. Although Safe Streets began with Katrina triage, for example, it proceeded to tackle the New Orleans criminal justice system. "The criminal justice and public safety system in New Orleans was in crisis long before Katrina devastated our city," explained an SSSC brochure in 2007.

> From the tragic waters of Katrina, we have been given an opportunity for a fresh start. As we rebuild our homes, schools, parks and levees, let us rebuild a criminal justice system that provides safety from all forms of violence and crime, and is democratic, fair and accountable.

Similarly, The New Orleans Workers' Center first targeted day laborer rights abuses, and then sought to reform the H2B (temporary guest worker) visa itself. Second-generation SMOs produced an anti-exceptionalist discourse of the disaster by targeting the systemic conditions that helped to create it.

Like Safe Streets and the New Orleans Workers' Center for Racial Justice, the New Orleans Women's Health Clinic was birthed by a poststorm crisis, specifically in affordable health care. Organizers on the ground perceived the federal, state, and local governments to be using Katrina as an opportunity to remake both public policy and New Orleans itself, especially through the drastic curtailment of public infrastructure such as public housing, public education, and public health care. In the wake of the impending health-care disaster due more to post-Katrina policy than to the hurricane itself, the women of

INCITE! founded the clinic to meet women's reproductive and sexual health needs. After observing the interlocking effects of the State's response to Katrina on low-income women of color, cofounder and interim director Shana Griffin began to understand the way in which disaster was being used as a vehicle for limiting reproductive freedom in a larger program of population control. From this perspective, the attending conditions of natural disaster, such as evacuation and reentry, are decentered; they are then reinterpreted as *opportunities,* either for social control *or* for resistance, where in this case resistance means reproductive justice. Griffin explained, "I'm less interested in talking now about hurricanes, and more about disasters. The disaster is the government response. It has to do with government policy and population control; with disenfranchisement, forced assimilation, reproduction."

Griffin's comments came seven days after Hurricane Gustav and five days before Hurricane Ike. Her recontextualization was striking in an environment in which the social and physical impact of the latest round of major storms was literally all around us. Despite the upheaval, Griffin was already moving from hurricanes to reproductive justice, and then back again, as she sought to apply her developing model to emergency preparedness:

> We've thought deeply about this for the last few days. Okay [the clinic] raised some money [for Gustav efforts]. What would a more proactive response be? . . . What is justice in the context of sexual health and reproduction? What does preparing a disaster kit look like in the context of reproductive justice? Having safer sex supplies, having resources in the cities where women are likely to go, information on WIC, free formula, diapers, battered women's shelter information in the cities, because the shelters are not safe.

Since Katrina, movement organizers who live at ground zero for hurricane threats understand that a narrow approach to disaster will ensure neither well-being nor justice.

NATIONS, BORDERS, AND MIGRATIONS

Transnational Interventions

Patrick R. Grzanka

To speak of transnational or postcolonial feminisms as possessed of a singular voice or universal message is to flatten differences between the women (and men) from around the world who have challenged Western feminism on the grounds of its implicit ethnocentrism, persistent disregard for issues that are perceived to be non-Western, and the simultaneous fetishization of the "third world woman." There are key themes, nonetheless, that echo throughout this diverse body of scholar-activism, including the centralization of "nation" as an axis on which oppression is organized.

Gayatri Chakravorty Spivak (1988), a founding postcolonial philosopher and critic, is perhaps most responsible for popularizing the term "subaltern," or at least introducing the term to Western audiences who were largely ignorant to theoretical import of postcolonial feminisms. Spivak launches her critique with the assertion that Western intellectuals' constitution of the colonial subject as "Other" is a form of "epistemic violence" that reinscribes colonial ideologies onto postcolonial subjects while excusing Western intellectuals from their complacency and collusion with colonial hegemony. Spivak and her colleagues in the Subaltern Studies Group theorized from the position of the subaltern— the postcolonial subject situated outside of the hegemonic power elite—and elaborated a critique of Western continental philosophy *and* Western feminism. In the postcolonial era, the subaltern has become a category of personhood or subjectivity *projected onto* the postcolonial Other to represent his or her subordination. She posits the sentence "White men saving brown women from brown men" to explore the epistemology of the Western intellectual who remains invested in imperialism even as he claims the role of patriarchal savior. As Spivak argues, "Imperialism's image as the establishment of a *good* society is marked by the espousal of the woman as *object* of protection from her own kind" (1988, 299). Or, put another way, "the protection of woman (today the 'third-world woman') becomes a signifier for the establishment of a good society" (298). In Western feminism, study of the "third world woman" replicated and reinforced this logic; rather than learning to speak with and listen to subaltern women, Western feminism was caught up with representing "her" (i.e., the subaltern) as a victim of colonialism and nativist forms of patriarchy. Accordingly, the alleged social justice of Western feminism was predicated upon a thoroughly colonial version of liberation that denied subaltern women agency and vocality. Spivak's question then, "Can the subaltern speak?" gets at the core of postcolonial criticism: Western intellectuals' persistent silencing of non-Western subjects and perspectives (i.e., epistemic violence).

This unit begins with an excerpt from Chandra Talpade Mohanty's classic essay "On Western Eyes" (1984, reading 26) to begin to wrestle with the internal politics of feminist discourse: "Thus, feminist scholarly practices (whether reading, writing, critical or textual) are inscribed in relations of power—relations which they counter, resist, or even perhaps implicitly support" (334). If conducted un-reflexively or in isolation, feminist analyses are just as capable of reinforcing hegemonic knowledge/power relations as any other social movement—even hegemonic ideas about gender. Mohanty writes:

> An analysis of "sexual difference" in the form of a cross-culturally singular, monolithic notion of patriarchy or male dominance leads to the construction of a similarly reductive and homogenous notion of what I call the "Third World Difference"—that stable, ahistorical something that apparently oppresses most if not all the women in these countries. And it is in the production of this "Third World Difference" that Western feminisms appropriate and "colonize" the fundamental complexities and conflicts which characterize the lives of women of different classes, religions, cultures, races and castes in these countries. (334–335)

Mohanty's writing is a sobering reminder of the differences between claiming radical politics and doing radical politics. But it is an active critique and a call—very much ongoing—to invigorate antiracist feminisms in the United States and Europe (i.e., the global North) with a transnational knowledge-politics that refuses to sideline multinational, postcolonial, and neocolonial dynamics in intersectional analyses.

Mohanty's and much of the writing in this unit advances a critique of Western feminisms, including a critique of intersectional scholarship that is complicit in the elision of nation as an organizing dimension of difference and inequality. But nation itself is a category in need of much unpacking, as Kandice Chuh (2003, reading 27) argues in *Imagine Otherwise*. As Chuh explains, "Vital to generative deployment of postcolonial critique in the U.S. frame is a reworking of the internal/external, center/periphery metaphor that organizes the 'postcolonial' of postcolonial studies" (122). Chuh's intervention suggests that the capacity of postcolonial feminist criticism to interrogate the US's role in postcolonial geopolitics is fundamentally inhibited if "colonialism and decolonization cannot be understood primarily in terms of 'here' and 'there,' metropole and distant colony" (122). Vrushali Patil (2013) likewise reiterates that intersectionality must reorient itself toward more complex understandings of nations, borders, and migrations: "If we continue to neglect cross-border dynamics and fail to problematize the nation and its emergence via transnational processes, our analyses will remain tethered to the spatialities and temporalities of colonial modernity" (863). If nation remains a tacit, taken-for-granted construct, then we will inevitably reproduce colonial logic even while attempting and claiming to do something different, according to Patil and Chuh. Their work underscores a methodological cornerstone of intersectionality: dimensions of difference co-construct one another. To incorporate any category (e.g., nation) as an axis of difference without examining how it is cocreated by and coproductive of other dimensions of inequality (e.g., gender, sexuality) is likely to reinforce hegemonic knowledge about that category. This represents "weak intersectionality" as delineated by Dill and Kohlman (2011), because it fails to treat dimensions of inequality *in relation to one another*. In such "weak" frameworks, "nation" is transmogrified into an independent variable, rather than a historical process that is produced within and by local and global gender, sexual, economic, and racial politics (which it also affects).

As a corrective to neocolonial logic, Patil (2013) suggests, "We need to recenter the notion that there are no locals and globals, only locals in relation to various global processes" (863). There are seemingly multiple ways to recenter Patil's notion of local-global relations, though this seems to beg some questions about methods (i.e., how exactly do we do that?). Elsewhere, Floya Anthias (2002) articulates one possible solution as "translocational positionality," which is a way of sensitizing feminisms to spatial *and* affective politics. Anthias says we need to think beyond static locations, borders, nations, and identities toward an amalgamation of *locations* and *belongings*. Because subjects and groups are often not located in the place to which they feel most connected and social groups exhibit tremendous within-group heterogeneity, we need to do more than "locate" or "identify" social groups. In order to better account for the experiences of diasporic groups and to address the realities of movement, migration, and dislocation as central practices of contemporary social life, we need to think beyond narrow parameters of here and there. Likewise, Anthias explains, translocational positionality:

> avoids assumptions about subjective processes on the one hand and culturalist forms of determinism on the other. Moreover, it acknowledges that identification is an enactment that does not entail fixity or permanence, as well as the role of the local and the contextual in the processes involved. It becomes possible to pay attention to spatial and contextual dimensions, treating the issues involved in terms of processes rather than possessive properties of individuals. (277)

An emphasis on *processes* as opposed to *properties* further destabilizes sedentary constructions of identity and difference that might assume "nation" to be a social category simply derived from and determined by a document, birthplace, nationality, or temporary location.

Exemplifying how transnational criticism is not merely for the critique of "elsewhere," Siobhan Somerville (2005, reading 28) takes up a critical postcolonial lens in the interest of bringing the intersections of nation and sexuality to the fore in American and queer studies. In "Notes Toward a Queer History of Naturalization," she provokes a queer reading of naturalization doctrine in the United States to *transnationalize* queer studies and to *queer* transnational studies. Such moves, according to Somerville, extend:

> the possibilities of queer scholarship by placing race, migration, and nation at the center of analysis, but also offer a bracing corrective to the fields of migration studies and citizenship studies, which have tended to assume that immigrants are heterosexual or/and that queer subjects are already legal citizens. (659)

She examines the legal production of the naturalized citizen for the ways in which the state itself, in contrast to the more abstract concept of "nation," produces citizens. She finds that even though naturalization has been conceptualized as fully distinct from birthright citizenship, naturalization "has historically been encumbered with assumptions about a heterosexual, reproductive subject, and so tends to reinforce the model of an organic, sexually reproduced citizenry" (663). Similarly, in the realm of cinematic representation, Heather Hewett (2009, reading 29) examines the film *La Misma Luna* for its depiction of a mother fighting to maintain a relationship with her son across the US-Mexico border. While she concludes that the film presents sympathetic depictions of the hardships facing immigrant Latina women like the film's heroine Rosario, the film reinforces both Euro-American and Latino cultural framings of desirable femininity imbued with tropes of desexualized, virginal motherhood. Hewett's and Somerville's work, in conversation with that of Jasbir Puar (2007, Unit X, reading 42), Chandan Reddy (2005, Unit I, reading 4) and Carlos Decena (2011), represents a robust area of inquiry within intersectional research that facilitates the disentangling of American, White, middle-class framings of heterosexual, lesbian, gay, bisexual, and transgender identities from analyses of nonnormative sexualities and gender identities both within US borders and in other cultural contexts. Moreover, this emergent discourse on sexual citizenship and migration can illuminate how categories of citizenship are ordered and consolidated by transnational sexual and gender politics—as opposed to parallel analyses that would conceptualize citizenship, sexuality, and gender as discreet phenomena.

References and Further Reading

Alvarez, S. 2000. "Translating the Global: Effects of Transnational Organizing on Local Feminist Discourses and Practices in Latin America." *Meridians* 1: 29–67.

Anthias, F. 2002. "Beyond Feminism and Multiculturalism: Locating Difference and the Politics of Location." *Women's Studies International Forum* 25: 275–286.

Anthias, F., and N. Yuval-Davis. 1992. *Racialised Boundaries: Race, Nation, Gender, Colour and Class and the Anti-racist Struggle.* London: Routledge.

Briggs, L. 2002. *Reproducing Empire: Race, Sex, Science, and U.S. Imperialism in Puerto Rico.* Berkeley, CA: University of California Press.

Caldwell, K. L. 2007. *Negras in Brazil: Re-envisioning Black Women, Citizenship, and the Politics of Identity.* New Brunswick, NJ: Rutgers University Press.

Caldwell, K. L. 2009. "Black Women and the Development of Intersectional Health Policy in Brazil." In *The Intersectional Approach: Transforming the Academy Through Race, Class, and Gender,* edited by M. T. Berger and K. Guidroz, 118–135. Chapel Hill, NC: University of North Carolina Press.

Chuh, K. 2003. *Imagine Otherwise: On Asian Americanist Critique.* Durham, NC: Duke University Press.

Collins, P. H. 1998. "It's All in the Family: Intersections of Gender, Race, and Nation." *Hypatia* 13: 62–82.

Decena, C. U. 2011. *Tacit Subjects: Belonging and Same-Sex Desire Among Dominican Immigrant Men.* Durham, NC: Duke University Press.

Dill, B. T., and M. H. Kohlman. 2011. "Intersectionality: A Transformative Paradigm in Feminist Theory and Social Justice." In *The Handbook of Feminist Research: Theory and Praxis,* second edition, edited by S. N. Hesse-Biber, 154–174. Thousand Oaks, CA: SAGE Publications.

Eng, D. 2010. *The Feeling of Kinship: Queer Liberalism and the Racialization of Intimacy.* Durham, NC: Duke University Press.

Hewett, H. 2009. "Mothering Across Borders: Narratives of Immigrant Mothers in the United States." *Women's Studies Quarterly* 37: 121–139.

Jónasdóttir, A. G., V. Bryson, and K. B. Jones, eds. 2011. *Sexuality, Gender and Power: Intersectional and Transnational Perspectives.* New York: Routledge.

Lewis, G. 2009. "Celebrating Intersectionality? Debates on a Multi-faceted Concept in Gender Studies: Themes from a Conference." *European Journal of Women's Studies* 16: 203–210.

Lewis, G. 2013. "Unsafe Travel: Experiencing Intersectionality and Feminist Displacements." *Signs: The Journal of Women in Culture and Society* 38: 869–892.

Mohanty, C. 1984. "Under Western Eyes: Feminist Scholarship and Colonial Discourses." *boundary 2* 12: 333–358.

Mohanty, C. 2013. "Transnational Feminist Crossings: On Neoliberalism and Radical Critique." *Signs: The Journal of Women in Culture and Society* 38: 967–991.

Mullally, S. 2009. "Migrant Women Destabilizing Borders: Citizenship Debates in Ireland." In *Law, Power and the Politics of Subjectivity: Intersectionality and Beyond,* edited by E. Grabham, D. Cooper, J. Krishnadas, and D. Herman, 251–270. London: Routledge.

Patil, V. 2013. "From Patriarchy to Intersectionality: A Transnational Feminist Assessment of How Far We've Really Come." *Signs: The Journal of Women in Culture and Society* 38: 847–867.

Puri, J. 1999. *Woman, Body, Desire in Post-colonial India: Narratives of Gender and Sexuality.* New York: Routledge.

Sandoval, C. 2000. *Methodology of the Oppressed.* Minneapolis: University of Minnesota Press.

Somerville, S. 2005. "Notes Toward a Queer History of Naturalization." *American Quarterly* 57: 659–675.

Spivak, G. C. 1988. "Can the Subaltern Speak?" In *Marxism and the Interpretation of Culture,* edited by C. Nelson and L. Grossberg, 271–313. Urbana: University of Illinois Press.

Yuval-Davis, N. 2012. *The Politics of Belonging: Intersectional Contestations.* London: SAGE Publications.

Chandra Talpade Mohanty

We return to Chandra Mohanty's work (she was also featured in Unit III, reading 11) with the 1984 piece that launched her into the spotlight of conversations and debate about the place of the "Third World Woman" in feminist studies. In this foundational essay of transnational feminist criticism, she takes several taken-for-granted concepts to task, not the least of which are "the West," "colonization," "Western feminism," "culture," and "woman" itself. Mohanty—like Edward Said, Franz Fanon, Paolo Friere, Chela Sandoval, Gloria Anzaldúa (Unit IV, reading 14), Gayatri Spivak, and other postcolonial critics—is interested in the hegemonic elements of colonization, and how the logic and ideology of colonialism infuses itself into even allegedly leftist or progressive intellectual and social movements, such as feminism and critical race studies in the United States. In the portion of the essay excerpted below, Mohanty lays out the terms of her argument and enumerates three tropes of Western feminist criticism on the "third world" that reinforce narratives of Western superiority, silence women of color feminists, and measure all women's experiences against those of women in the West. Contesting the categories, methods, and theories of power invoked in Western feminist studies of women in the third world, Mohanty interrupts the repetitious invocation of "Other" women's oppression that characterized mainstream US feminism in the second half of the twentieth century and opens up spaces for a new form of transnational feminist criticism that denies Western cultural imperialism.

26. Feminism and Colonialism*

It ought to be of some political significance at least that the term "colonization" has come to denote a variety of phenomena in recent feminist and left writings in general. However sophisticated or problematical its use as an explanatory construct, colonization almost invariably implies a relation of structural domination, and a supression—often violent—of the heterogeneity of the subject(s) in question. What I wish to analyze is specifically the production of the "Third World Woman" as a singular monolithic subject in some recent (Western) feminist texts. The definition of colonization I wish to invoke here is a predominantly *discursive* one, focusing on a certain mode of appropriation and codification of "scholarship" and "knowledge" about women in the third world by particular analytic categories employed in specific writings on the subject which take as their referent feminist interests as they have been articulated in the U.S. and Western Europe.

My concern about such writings derives from my own implication and investment in contemporary debates in feminist theory, and the urgent political necessity (especially in the age of Reagan) of forming strategic coalitions across class, race, and national boundaries. Clearly Western feminist discourse and political practice is neither singular nor homogeneous in its goals, interests or analyses. However, it is possible to trace a coherence of *effects* resulting from the implicit assumption of "the West" (in all its complexities and contradictions) as the primary referent in theory and praxis. My reference to "Western feminism" is by no means intended to imply that it is a monolith. Rather, I am attempting to draw attention to the similar effects of various textual strategies used by

---

* Excerpted from C. Mohanty, "Under Western Eyes: Feminist Scholarship and Colonial Discourses," *boundary 2* 12 (1984): 333–358. Copyright, 1984, Duke University Press. All rights reserved. Republished by permission of the copyright holder, Duke University Press, www .dukeupress.edu.

particular writers that codify Others as non-Western and hence themselves as (implicitly) Western. It is in this sense that I use the term "Western feminist." The analytic principles discussed below serve to distort Western feminist political practices, and limit the possibility of coalitions among (usually White) Western feminists and working class and feminists of color around the world. These limitations are evident in the construction of the (implicitly consensual) priority of issues around which apparently *all* women are expected to organize. The necessary and integral connection between feminist scholarship and feminist political practice and organizing determines the significance and status of Western feminist writings on women in the third world, for feminist scholarship, like most other kinds of scholarship, is not the mere production of knowledge about a certain subject. It is a directly political and discursive *practice* in that it is purposeful and ideological. It is best seen as a mode of intervention into particular hegemonic discourses (for example, traditional anthropology, sociology, literary criticism, etc.); it is a political praxis which counters and resists the totalizing imperative of age-old "legitimate" and "scientific" bodies of knowledge. Thus, feminist scholarly practices (whether reading, writing, critical or textual) are inscribed in relations of power—relations which they counter, resist, or even perhaps implicitly support. There can, of course, be no apolitical scholarship.

The relationship between "Woman"—a cultural and ideological composite Other constructed through diverse representational discourses (scientific, literary, juridical, linguistic, cinematic, etc.)—and "women"—real, material subjects of their collective histories—is one of the central questions the practice of feminist scholarship seeks to address. This connection between women as historical subjects and the re-presentation of Woman produced by hegemonic discourses is not a relation of direct identity, or a relation of correspondence or simple implication. It is an arbitrary relation set up by particular cultures. I would like to suggest that the feminist writings I analyze here discursively colonize the material and historical heterogeneities of the lives of women in the third world, thereby producing/re-presenting a composite, singular "Third World Woman"—an image which appears arbitrarily constructed, but nevertheless carries with it the authorizing signature of Western humanist discourse. I argue that assumptions of privilege and ethnocentric universality on the one hand, and inadequate self-consciousness about the effect of Western scholarship on the "third world" in the context of a world system dominated by the West on the other, characterize a sizable extent of Western feminist work on women in the third world. An analysis of "sexual difference" in the form of a cross-culturally singular, monolithic notion of patriarchy or male dominance leads to the construction of a similarly reductive and homogeneous notion of what I call the "Third World Difference"—that stable, ahistorical something that apparently oppresses most if not all the women in these countries. And it is in the production of this "Third World Difference" that Western feminisms appropriate and "colonize" the fundamental complexities and conflicts which characterize the lives of women of different classes, religions, cultures, races and castes in these countries. It is in this process of homogenization and systemitization of the oppression of women in the third world that power is exercised in much of recent Western feminist discourse, and this power needs to be defined and named.

In the context of the West's hegemonic position today, of what Anouar Abdel-Malek calls a struggle for "control over the orientation, regulation and decision of the process of world development on the basis of the advanced sector's monopoly of scientific knowledge and ideal creativity," Western feminist scholarship on the third world must be seen and examined precisely in terms of its inscription in these particular relations of power and struggle. There is, I shall argue, no universal patriarchal framework which this scholarship attempts to counter and resist—unless one posits an international male conspiracy or a monolithic, ahistorical power hierarchy. There is, however, a particular world balance of power within which any analysis of culture, ideology, and socio-economic conditions has to be necessarily situated. Abdel-Malek is useful here, again, in reminding us about the inherence of politics in the discourses of "culture":

> Contemporary imperialism is, in a real sense, a hegemonic imperialism, exercising to a maximum degree a rationalized violence taken to a higher level than ever before—through fire and sword, but also through the attempt to control hearts and minds. For its content is defined by the combined action of the military-industrial complex and the hegemonic cultural centers of the West, all of them founded on the advanced levels of development attained by monopoly and finance capital, and supported by the benefits of both the scientific and technological revolution and the second industrial revolution itself.

Western feminist scholarship cannot avoid the challenge of situating itself and examining its role in such a global economic and political framework. To do any less would be to ignore the complex interconnections between first and third world economies and the profound effect of this on the lives of women in these countries. I do not question the descriptive and informative value of most Western feminist writings on women in the third world. I also do not question the existence of excellent work which does not fall into the analytic traps I am concerned with. In fact I deal with an example of such work later on. In the context of an overwhelming silence about the experiences of women in these countries, as well as the need to forge international links between women's political struggles, such work is both pathbreaking and absolutely essential. However, it is both to the *explanatory potential* of particular analytic strategies employed by such writing, and to their *political effect* in the context of the hegemony of Western scholarship, that I want to draw attention here. While feminist writing in the U.S. is still marginalized (except from the point of view of women of color addressing privileged White women), Western feminist writing on women in the third world must be considered in the context of the global hegemony of Western scholarship—i.e., the production, publication, distribution and consumption of information and ideas. Marginal or not, this writing has political effects and implications beyond the immediate feminist or disciplinary audience. One such significant effect of the dominant "representations" of Western feminism is its conflation with imperialism in the eyes of particular third world women. Hence the urgent need to examine the *political* implications of *analytic* strategies and principles.

The first principle I focus on concerns the strategic location or situation of the category "women" vis-a-vis the context of analysis. The assumption of women as an already constituted, coherent group with identical interests and desires, regardless of class, ethnic or racial location or contradictions, implies a notion of gender or sexual difference or even patriarchy (as male dominance—men as a correspondingly coherent group) which can be applied universally and cross-culturally. The context of analysis can be anything from kinship structures and the organization of labor to media representations. The second principle consists in the uncritical use of particular methodologies in providing "proof" of universality and cross-cultural validity. The third is a more specifically political principle underlying the methodologies and the analytic strategies, i.e., the model of power and struggle they imply and suggest. I argue that as a result of the two modes—or, rather, frames—of analysis described above, a homogeneous notion of the oppression of women as a group is assumed, which, in turn, produces the image of an "average third world woman." This average third world woman leads an essentially truncated life based on her feminine gender (read: sexually constrained) and being "third world" (read: ignorant, poor, uneducated, tradition-bound, domestic, family-oriented, victimized, etc.). This, I suggest, is in contrast to the (implicit) self-representation of Western women as educated, modern, as having control over their own bodies and sexualities, and the freedom to make their own decisions. The distinction between Western feminist re-presentation of women in the third world, and Western feminist *self*-presentation is a distinction of the same order as that made by some marxists between the "maintenance" function of the housewife and the real "productive" role of wage labor, or the characterization by developmentalists of the third world as being engaged in the lesser production of "raw materials" in contrast to the "real" productive activity of the First World. These distinctions are made on the basis of the privileging of a particular group as the norm or referent. Men involved in wage labor, first world producers, and, I suggest, Western feminists who sometimes cast Third World women in terms of "ourselves undressed" (Michelle Rosaldo's term), all construct themselves as the referent in such a binary analytic.

By women as a category of analysis, I am referring to the critical assumption that all of us of the same gender, across classes and cultures, are somehow socially constituted as a homogeneous group identified prior to the process of analysis. This is an assumption which characterizes much feminist discourse. The homogeneity of women as a group is produced not on the basis of biological essentials, but rather on the basis of secondary sociological and anthropological universals. Thus, for instance, in any given piece of feminist analysis, women are characterized as a singular group on the basis of a shared oppression. What binds women together is a sociological notion of the "sameness" of their oppression. It is at this point that an elision takes place between "women" as a discursively constructed group and "women" as material subjects of their own history. Thus, the discursively consensual homogeneity of "women" as a group is mistaken for the historically specific material reality of groups of women. This results in an assumption of women as an always-already constituted group, one which has been labelled "powerless," "exploited," "sexually harrassed," etc., by feminist scientific, economic, legal and sociological discourses. (Notice that this is quite similar to sexist discourse labeling women weak, emotional, having math anxiety, etc.) The focus is not on uncovering the material and ideological specificities that constitute a particular group of women as "powerless" in a particular context. It is rather on finding a variety of cases of "powerless" groups of women to prove the general point that women as a group are powerless.

What is problematical, then, about this kind of use of "women" as a group, as a stable category of analysis, is that it assumes an ahistorical, universal unity between women based on a generalized notion of their subordination. As suggested above, such simplistic formulations are both reductive and ineffectual in designing strategies to combat oppressions. All they do is reinforce binary divisions between men and women.

It is only by understanding the *contradictions* inherent in women's location within various structures that effective political action and challenges can be devised.

What happens when this assumption of "women as an oppressed group" is situated in the context of Western feminist writing about third world women? It is here that I locate the colonialist move. In other words, Western feminist discourse, by assuming women as a coherent, already constituted group which is placed in kinship, legal and other structures, defines third world women as subjects *outside* of social relations, instead of looking at the way women are constituted as women *through* these very structures. Legal, economic, religious, and familial structures are treated as phenomena to be judged by Western standards. It is here that ethnocentric universality comes into play. When these structures are defined as "underdeveloped" or "developing" and women are placed within these structures, an implicit image of the "average third world woman" is produced. This is the transformation of the (implicitly Western) "oppressed woman" into the "oppressed third world woman." While the category of "oppressed woman" is generated through an exclusive focus on gender difference, "the oppressed third world woman" category has an additional attribute—the "third world difference!" The "third world difference" includes a paternalistic attitude towards women in the third world. Since discussions of the various themes I identified earlier (e.g., kinship, education, religion, etc.) are conducted in the context of the relative "underdevelopment" of the third world (which is nothing less than unjustifiably confusing development with the separate path taken by the West in its development, as well as ignoring the directionality of the first-third world power relationship), third world women as a group or category are automatically and necessarily defined as: religious (read "not progressive"), family-oriented (read "traditional"), legal minors (read "they-are-still-not-conscious-of-their-rights"), illiterate (read "ignorant"), domestic (read "backward") and sometimes revolutionary (read "their-country-is-in-a-state-of-war-they-must-fight!"). This is how the "third world difference" is produced. When the category of "sexually oppressed women" is located within particular systems in the third world which are defined on a scale which is normed through Eurocentric assumptions, not only are third world women defined in a particular way prior to their entry into social relations, but since no connections are made between first and third world power shifts, it reinforces the assumption that people in the third world just have not evolved to the extent that the West has. This mode of feminist analysis, by homogenizing and systematizing the experiences of different groups of women in these countries, erases all marginal and resistant modes of experiences.

Resistance can thus only be defined as cumulatively reactive, not as something inherent in the operation of power. If power, as Michel Foucault has argued recently, can really be understood only in the context of resistance, this misconceptualization of power is both analytically as well as strategically problematical. It limits theoretical analysis as well as reinforcing Western cultural imperialism. For in the context of a first/third world balance of power, feminist analyses which perpetrate and sustain the hegemony of the idea of the superiority of the West produce a corresponding set of universal images of the "third world woman," images like *the veiled woman, the powerful mother, the chaste virgin, the obedient wife,* etc. These images exist in universal, ahistorical splendor, setting in motion a colonialist discourse which exercises a very specific power in defining, coding and maintaining existing first/third world connections.

Kandice Chuh

Kandice Chuh is a professor of English at the Graduate Center of the City University of New York (CUNY); she earned a PhD from the University of Washington and taught at the University of Maryland for many years before moving to CUNY. Her research expertise is in twentieth-century US literature, Asian American studies, and comparative ethnic studies, though the impact of her work has been far-reaching across the humanities, particularly in American studies. Her book *Imagine Otherwise: On Asian Americanist Critique* (2003) is part literary criticism and part sociology of knowledge insomuch as Chuh uses literature, history, and cultural theory to consider the development and travels of the concept "Asian American" and the configuration of Asian American studies around the modern subject of the "Asian American." Destabilizing this construct—she argues for a "subjectless discourse"—manufactures a new field of inquiry and imagines new possibilities for Asian Americanist criticism where the intersectionality of nation is paramount to the ongoing project of social justice.

This excerpt takes us from the introduction to the analytic crescendo of her book, in which Chuh pivots from an argument about the complexities of Asian America to a call for deconstruction of the US nation as an epistemological framework and taken-for-granted category of historical and cultural inquiry. Imagining *otherwise,* Chuh suggests that a "'friendly' alliance" between Asian American studies and postcolonial studies will provoke a renewed critique of "America" that moves beyond considering *instances* of US neocolonialism and toward the inherent contradictions of the "modern, sovereign, liberal nation-state itself." Her writing can be read as a template for scholars in myriad disciplines wrestling with how to revitalize critical inquiry and to embrace intersectional frameworks that implicate academic disciplines themselves in the perpetuation of hegemony and injustice.

27. **Imagine Otherwise***

Imagine Otherwise argues that current conditions call for conceiving Asian American studies as a *subjectless discourse*. I mean subjectlessness to create

---

* Excerpted from K. Chuh, *Imagine Otherwise: On Asian Americanist Critique* (Durham, NC: Duke University Press, 2003). Copyright, 2003, Duke University Press. All rights reserved. Republished by permission of the copyright holder, www.dukeupress.edu.

the conceptual space to prioritize difference by foregrounding the discursive constructedness of subjectivity. In other words, it points attention to the constraints on the liberatory potential of the achievement of subjectivity, by reminding us that a "subject" only becomes recognizable and can act as such by conforming to certain regulatory matrices. In that sense, a subject is always also an epistemological object. If Asian Americanists have mounted sophisticated interrogations of representational objectifications of Asian-raced peoples in the United States, of dehumanizing images that affiliate certain objective meanings to certain bodies, we have not, I think, always paid such critical attention to "Asian Americans" and to "Asian American studies" as "subjects" that emerge through epistemological objectification. Part of the difficulty in doing so results from the powerful demands of the U.S. nation-state's celebration of citizenship, or national subjectivity, held out as "natural" and tantamount to achieved equality and so long denied to Asian-raced peoples. In spite of claims about the death of the Subject heralded by postmodernism, the idea and importance of a consummate subjectivity remains unabashedly vital in the state apparatuses of the law. As the uniquely authorized discourse of the nation, and in contrast to the postulation of the modern era that subjects (to monarchal power) have transformed into consensual citizens (of a nation-state), law requires subjection/subjectification. The centrality of citizenship and subjectivity to the politics of modernity both motivates and explains Asian American studies' central concerns with representation and representational politics in similar terms. The importance of political/legal subject status telescopes into the importance of discursive subject status; the metaphor of marginalization manifests the distance between these—between, that is, the "American" and the "Asian American." And clearly, as long as the state demands subjectivity and wields its particular kinds of power, Asian Americanists cannot simply dismiss those terms altogether.

At the same time, and despite how enormously enabling citizenship continues to be in the garnering of access to certain material resources, subjectivity itself, alone, cannot remedy injustice. Recognition of the subject as epistemological object cautions against failing endlessly to put into question both "Asian American" as the subject/object of Asian Americanist discourse and of U.S. nationalist ideology, and Asian American studies as the subject/object of dominant paradigms of the U.S. university. Otherwise, Asian American studies can too easily fall into working within a framework, with attendant problematic assumptions of essential identities, homologous to that through which U.S. nationalism has created and excluded "others." Subjectlessness, as a conceptual tool, points to the need to manufacture "Asian American" situationally. It serves as the ethical grounds for the political practice of what I would describe as a strategic anti-essentialism—as, in other words, the common ethos underwriting the coherency of the field. If we accept a priori that Asian American studies is subjectless, then rather than looking to complete the category "Asian American," to actualize it by such methods as enumerating various components of differences (gender, class, sexuality, religion, and so on), we are positioned to critique the effects of the various configurations of power and knowledge through which the term comes to have meaning. Thinking in terms of subjectlessness does not occlude the possibility of political action. Rather, it augurs a redefinition of the political, an investigation into what "justice" might mean and what (whose) "justice" is being pursued.

Reconstituting Asian American studies in difference helps us to recognize that Asian Americanist critique must be consistently and insistently critical of both U.S. nationalism and its apparatuses of power, and of analytic frameworks that, however unintentionally, homologously reproduce U.S. nationalism's promotion of identity over difference. Part of the exigency underwriting this argument lays in the institutionalized settings of Asian American studies. The remainder of this introduction maps the term "Asian American" and examines its functions as a marker of "otherness" and as a sign of an academic discourse. That consideration underscores the importance of recognizing Asian American studies as unfolding within the spaces of the U.S. university, an institution, in David Lloyd's words, that "continues to organize crucial social functions" (1998, 15). Within this particular setting, I suggest, emphasizing the literary, discursive nature of the term "Asian American" helps make clear the necessity of revising what counts as "political" in Asian Americanist practices by revising understanding of the status of the subject(s) / object(s) of Asian American studies.

In a 1995 essay, Jenny Sharpe posed the question, "Is the United States postcolonial?" The answer she offered was that it is not, or rather, that it is not postcolonial in an immediately critically meaningful way. Extending in some ways Ruth Frankenburg and Lata Mani's (1993) delineation of the differing meanings and periodizations accruing to "postcolonial," Sharpe rightly points out that applied to the United States, the term can lose its analytical edge and serve as yet another racialized identity in the catalogue of liberal multicultural enumerations of difference. Descriptively, the "postcolonial" of "postcolonial studies" in the U.S. academy generally denotes the post–World War II proliferation of national independence (independence as nation-states) by the "Third World" through liberation movements and various projects of "decolonization." Rather than taking for granted a state of postcoloniality, however, postcolonial studies has put into question the aftermath of colonialism and liberation. Postcolonial in this regard bears a silent but insistent question mark, serving as an inquiry rather than a description, an evaluative entry point rather than a conclusion. It recognizes the difficulties of decolonization given the impossibility of simply dissolving the effects of colonialism. Postcolonial studies confirms in this manner that colonized societies did not remain untransformed by colonialism to emerge after political liberation in some essential, "pure" form. Rather, the ways that the values and institutions accompanying colonial rule were grafted onto already dynamic and complex societies as part of the process of effectively instituting colonial domination condition the lack of "a clear focus and target of decolonization" (Pieterse and Parekh 1995). Under the rubric of postcolonial studies have accordingly emerged critiques of the various possibilities for and constraints on liberation and what follows thereafter, and the articulation and imagination of possibilities for forms of political and cultural life based on neither wholesale assimilation nor rejection of colonial life ways. This "postcolonial" invokes in the same breath colonization *and* decolonization. As Frankenburg and Mani have suggested, defining decolonization as referring to "a political, economic and discursive shift, one that is decisive without being definitive" positions the term as "enabl[ing] us to concede the shift effected by decolonization without claiming . . . a complete rupture in social, economic and political relations and forms of knowledge" (1993, 300).

At the same time, the frame of the postcolonial extends critical focus to imperial metropolitan spaces as well, to interrogate what cultural and political shifts the loss of empire might have set into motion in the "center" rather than "periphery." In this regard, the postcolonial as a term of criticism signals shifting locations, from nations-*nee*-colonies (from the Third World, from empire) to imperial metropoles-*nee*-nations (to the First World, to the heart of empire). These physical movements between "there" and "here" have found counterparts in theorizations of the mutual hybridization that also serve to blur distinctions between center and periphery. While such theories have importantly undermined essentialist notions of the purity of either metropolitan or colonial subjectivities, societies, and cultures, critical debates in postcolonial studies have made clear that the variegatedness of the historical foundations underwriting these "postcolonial" identities must be addressed. "Postcolonial," even as it refers generally to Third World decolonization, cannot and does not have the same meaning across the differentiated histories that constitute India and Britain, for example (Frankenburg and Mani 1993; Sharpe 1995).

Already, the difficulties of applying this "postcolonial" meaningfully to the United States begin to become evident. For the histories of U.S. empire-building have unfolded in a manner and time scale different from those of its European analogs, resulting as a general rule not in the sovereignty of its colonies but in their absorption into the U.S. nation. Thus Hawai'i "became" the nation's fiftieth state, and Guam and Puerto Rico seemingly permanent protectorates, overseas extensions of the United States. Peoples indigenous to the continent continue to face the extinguishing of life ways in spite of having an official pseudo-sovereign status. The Philippines is a notable exception, though the continuing and insistent presence of U.S. military forces on the islands suggests that formal independence has not meant a total disconnection from U.S. power. I cite these examples to emphasize that U.S. colonialism and "postcoloniality" have been both *intra*territorial and extraterritorial, a condition that resists description by the Europe-based postcolonial. As Eva Cherniavsky has argued, "U.S. history is marked by a *convergence* of nationalism and colonialism, so that independence transfers power from imperialist interests abroad to imperialist interests on American soil—from white men to white men" (1996, 86; emphasis original). The celebrated liberation from England that genetically grounds U.S. national identity formation also marks the beginning of the story of colonization of the continent. But struggles for liberation in relation to the United States have largely been articulated as struggles for political and economic power by groups minoritized along racialized, gendered, and sexualized lines. While at times those struggles have been mounted in solidarity with and by using frameworks analogous to liberation movements in the Third World, they have been forwarded for the most part for the sake of gaming equality (civil rights) rather than sovereignty.

To be sure, as noted above, Third World decolonization has had an impact on the United States as global migratory and economic patterns conditioned by colonialism and postcoloniality have resulted in changing gendered and sexualized race and class relations within the United States. The United States may not be postcolonial in the ways that Britain or India may be, but it does nonetheless negotiate postcoloniality as a global condition. Along these lines, Sharpe has suggested with regard to the United States that "the 'postcolonial' be theorized as the point at which internal social relations intersect with global capitalism and the international division of labor" (1995, 184). She explains, "In other words, I want us to define the 'after' to colonialism as the neocolonial relations the United States entered into with decolonized nations" (1995, 184). This redefinition forms an axis of investigation for which the United States as a neocolonial power serves as target of inquiry. It emphasizes colonialism's imposition of capitalism on noncapitalist societies and underscores the United States' contemporary role in advancing and sustaining global capitalism.

What does all of this mean for the various resistance discourses (antiracism, antisexism, antiheterosexism) in the United States? The danger here in emphasizing analysis of U.S. *neo*colonialism lies in its potential to hinder engagement with the particularities marking U.S. intraterritorial histories of racialized, patriarchal heteronormativity. Vital to generative deployment of postcolonial critique in the U.S. frame is a reworking of the internal/external, center/periphery metaphor that organizes the "postcolonial" of postcolonial studies. That is, in the U.S. context, colonialism and decolonization cannot be understood primarily in terms of "here" and "there," metropole and distant colony. U.S. history is marked by an "internalization of 'extraterritorial' spaces and extroversion of colonized peoples" from the "space of an 'American' national politics and culture" (Cherniavsky 1996, 87). I am not arguing here for reintroduction of the model of "internal colonization" deployed in the 1960s and 1970s to "harness the language of decolonization" for politically strategic purposes (Sharpe 1995, 183). Rather, I am emphasizing the need to pay equal attention to recognizing the United States as a historic as well as a "new" colonial power. In other words, for the postcolonial to be useful in articulation to the United States, it must contend with the nation's past in addition to present practices of empire. As Cherniavsky summarizes, "If postcolonial critical practice emerges in, and in response to, the failures of decolonization (to the impossibility of simply unraveling colonial power . . .), a postcolonial approach to U.S. history and culture would speak to the contradictions of a *naturalized/ nationalized colonial domination*" (1996, 88; emphasis added). Accordingly, *denaturalization/denationalization* in this inseparably coupled form articulates the critical frame of empire in a way attentive to the specificities and generative for studies of U.S. culture and politics.

I would suggest that denaturalization/denationalization maps onto Asian American studies as a tactical orientation, one that urges Asian Americanist practice toward deconstruction. Postcolonial studies scholarship "about" postcoloniality helps Asian American studies understand the intranational social formations and relations consequent to the demographic impact of Third World decolonization and global capitalism. Decolonization initiated migratory patterns that include immigration from formerly colonized Asian countries, which in turn contributes to disassembling "Asian American" as a category of identity on the descriptive level alone. Moreover, postcolonial studies' demonstrations of the contingency of local socio-political/cultural identities on structures and relations of power both proximate and global underscore the constructedness of "Asian American" identities. "Indigenous" to "precolonial" to "colonial" to "national" to "immigrant" to "American" outlines the profound instability of and inscription by multiple kinds and registers of relations of power of such identities, narrativized through the developmental *telos* marking modernity. In this way, the limits of a politics of identity are firmly established. Postcolonial studies also, by marking the U.S. nation as simultaneously nation and empire, encourages the deconstruction of U.S. nation-ness itself, its seemingly inevitable status as nation, an insight crucial for Asian American studies, as I explain below.

Gayatri Spivak initiates a parallel if differently focused argument in asking "Can the Subaltern Speak?"; she demonstrates in the well-known essay by that name that what counts as knowledge in the "First World" academy is produced by epistemological categories foundationally incapable of representing (re-presenting) the "poor, black female" as exemplary subaltern. Collectively, these and other similarly oriented arguments map onto Asian American studies in such a way as to insist that Asian Americanist discourse interrogate its epistemological assumptions. In other words, I am suggesting that the particular kinds of questions being raised in postcolonial studies about nation as an *epistemological* category provide a model through which Asian American studies might reflect upon its own work. Conceiving of nation in this manner means understanding the modern nation-state as inherently contradictory. The fundamental contradiction, in other words, is not between "America" the ideal and "America" the lived form, but rather is *internal* to the idea of the modern, sovereign, liberal nation-state itself. In this regard, America as lived form, with all of its contradictions, is its ideal. It is already the exemplary manifestation of liberalism; it cannot be made any "better" by criticizing its contradictions alone.

Siobhan B. Somerville

Siobhan Somerville is a professor of English, gender and women's studies, and African American studies at the University of Illinois at Urbana-Champaign. Her work in science studies is featured elsewhere in this volume (see Unit IX, reading 34), because of her remarkable influence on the development of intersectionality in the humanities. Somerville's intellectual contributions span feminist theory, queer studies, critical Black studies, and American literature, and her more recent scholarship has turned toward the intersections of sexuality, race, and nation. In this excerpt from "Notes Toward a Queer History of Naturalization" (2005), Somerville demonstrates the purpose and potency of "queer reading," which is often misunderstood and maligned as "reading into things" for homoerotic subtext where none exists. The power of the queer reading, as Somerville shows, lies in its ability to uncover sexual dynamics in sites that are otherwise presumed to be nonsexual, such as the state, business, education, engineering, architecture, etc. Moreover, Somerville never relents in forwarding an *intersectional* queer reading, so the dynamic interplay between sexuality and other dimensions of difference are simultaneously uncovered, illuminating a fuller picture of how oppression actually works.

In this piece, specifically, Somerville poses a series of questions about the nature of naturalization, the process by which individuals become American citizens. She resists making a finite thesis *per se* in the interest of prompting further critical inquiry into the sexual contours of US citizenship as documented in congressional legislation and the historical records of our so-called forefathers. In this excerpt, Somerville undermines any sense we might have of naturalization law as the by-product of cold calculations made solely in the interest of population management. Instead of reciting only the explicit racism of US immigration laws already well documented by historians, legal scholars, and political scientists, Somerville finds the creation of "citizenship" wrapped up in heteronormative expectations of biological reproduction and misogynist framings of unwanted "immoral women." Furthermore, she turns our attention to the *affective* realm in which Jefferson and others' writings betray a sense of "America's desire" for particular kinds of citizens and, likewise, noncitizens' imagined desires for America, which here signifies the "idea" of the United States.

28. Thomas Jefferson's Desires*

It is generally understood that, historically, the United States has reproduced its citizenry in two ways: first, through "birthright citizenship"; and, second, through naturalization. In existing scholarship, the distinction drawn between these two models of producing citizens has centered on the question of consent. Birthright citizenship is a nonconsensual means of granting citizenship, linked to feudal, hierarchical models of allegiance. In contrast, naturalization is understood as a consensual process of conferring citizenship, associated with Lockean and later Enlightenment models of a contractual relationship between citizen and state, principles that have been seen as fundamental to liberal democracies. Peter Schuck and Rogers Smith refer to this tension as "one between the rival principles of ascription and consent." Thus, birthright citizenship as an ascriptive model confers status upon a child based on factors that are not under her/his control, such as place of birth or biological parentage. Naturalization, on the other hand, enacts a contractual relationship, a voluntary allegiance based on mutual consent between the immigrant and the state. In the United States, the individual establishes that contract with the state by taking a public oath, the full text of which currently reads:

> I hereby declare, on oath, that I absolutely and entirely renounce and abjure all allegiance and fidelity to any foreign prince, potentate, state or sovereignty, of whom or which I have heretofore been a subject or citizen; that I will support and defend the Constitution and laws of the United States of America against all enemies, foreign and domestic; that I will bear true faith and allegiance to the same; that I will bear arms on behalf of the United States when required by the law; that I will perform

---

* Excerpted from S. B. Somerville, "Notes Toward a Queer History of Naturalization," *American Quarterly* 57(3) (2005): 662–672. © 2005 The American Studies Association. Reprinted with permission of the Johns Hopkins University Press.

noncombatant service in the armed forces of the United States when required by the law; that I will perform work of national importance under civilian direction when required by the law; and that I take this obligation freely without any mental reservation or purpose of evasion; so help me God.

Unlike birthright citizenship, then, naturalized citizenship is produced through this self-conscious, presumably voluntary declaration of the citizen's agreement to the terms of this contract with the state. Perhaps not coincidentally, in form, language, and effect, the oath of allegiance has similarities to traditional vows of marriage: both are speech acts that transform the speaker's legal status; both use the language of "fidelity" and "obligation"; and both establish an exclusive—one might even say "monogamous"—relationship to the other party.

In fact, the echoes of monogamous marriage vows in the oath of allegiance suggest another way that we might contrast birthright citizenship and naturalization, by focusing on how the sexual is situated in each. As the term suggests, birthright citizenship entails the literal production of citizens through sexual reproduction. In the United States, citizenship is granted at birth to anyone born within the nation's territory (regardless of the citizenship status of the child's parents) or to any child of a U.S. citizen (regardless of the place of birth). Notably, the United States is somewhat anomalous in granting the first kind of birthright citizenship (*jus soli*, being born within the nations territory); most nations, especially in Europe, assign citizenship at birth according to the citizenship status of at least one parent (*jus sanguinis*). Nevertheless, both forms of birthright citizenship are seemingly "natural" or organic forms of the production of citizens through sexual reproduction. In contrast, naturalization presumably entails the nonsexual production of national subjects, so that citizenship is acquired rather than ascribed. In a self-consciously performative process, naturalization takes place through speech acts (oaths and pledges of allegiance) adjudicated by the state. In this way, there appears to be something very queer at the heart of the naturalization process, a performance whose very theatricality exposes the constructed nature of citizenship itself. At least, that is one way to describe the radical potential of naturalization: to enact a purely consensual form of citizenship, without any necessary relationship to sexual reproduction or ancestry.

Yet, even though naturalization is theoretically a performative, nonreproductive model of producing citizens, the very term *naturalization* demonstrates the difficulties that modern states have had in imagining the full potential of that process. Instead of breaking with a model of citizenship based on bloodline, the very language of naturalization has historically been encumbered with assumptions about a heterosexual, reproductive subject, and so tends to reinforce the model of an organic, sexually reproduced citizenry. As I argue, we should be more skeptical of the distinction typically drawn between birthright citizenship and naturalization—ascriptive versus consensual—and attend to the ways that the opposition between the two models actually serves to mask how both have historically been embedded within (hetero) sexualized understandings of production. Despite its potential to make good on the liberal promise of consent, even naturalization cannot escape a logic of belonging that depends on the transmission of citizenship through biological reproduction. This is not simply because legislation has tended to instantiate exclusionary ideologies of identity (race, gender, class, sexual orientation) that have "spoiled" the liberal promise of citizenship in the United States, but also, and perhaps more stubbornly, because this blood logic is embedded within the very metaphors through which such a form of producing citizenship is imagined.

Historians have tended to locate the origins of more repressive (and now more familiar) federal policy on immigration and naturalization in the late nineteenth century, with explicitly exclusionary laws that defined immigration in negative terms. In 1875, with the Page Act, Congress passed the first federal legislation that enumerated specific types of people who were excluded from entry into the United States. Illicit sexuality was at the center of the legislators' attention: the Page Act prohibited women "imported for the purposes of prostitution." Although the legislation was aimed at the traffic in *all* "immoral women," the figure of the prostitute in this law was, in fact, inherently racialized, because the Page Act required U.S. consuls to ensure that any immigrant from China, Japan, or other Asian countries was not under contract for "lewd and immoral purposes." Seven years later, in 1882, Congress passed the first legislation that used race as an explicit criterion for exclusion, the Chinese Exclusion Act, which barred all Chinese immigrants from entry into the United States and thus from citizenship.

When compared with these restrictions of the late nineteenth century, earlier U.S. policy may seem to have encouraged immigration and naturalization, but in fact the first federal law on naturalization was implicitly exclusionary. In 1790, Congress set down "An Act to establish an uniform Rule of Naturalization," which stated:

> *Be it enacted by the Senate and House of Representatives of the United States of America in Congress assembled,* That any alien, being a free white person, who shall have resided within the limits and under the jurisdiction of the United States for the term of two years, may be admitted to become a citizen thereof, on application to any common law court of record, in any one of the states wherein he shall have resided for the term

of one year at least, and making proof to the satisfaction of such court, that he is a person of good character, and taking the oath or affirmation prescribed by law, to support the constitution of the United States, which oath or affirmation such court shall administer; and the clerk of such court shall record such application, and the proceedings thereon; and thereupon such person shall be considered as a citizen of the United States. And the children of such persons so naturalized, dwelling within the United States, being under the age of twenty-one years at the time of such naturalization, shall also be considered as citizens of the United States. And the children of citizens of the United States, that may be born beyond sea, or out of the limits of the United States, shall be considered as natural born citizens; *Provided,* That the right of citizenship shall not descend to persons whose fathers have never been resident in the United States: *Provided* also, That no person heretofore proscribed by any state, shall be admitted a citizen as aforesaid, except by an act of the legislature of the state in which such person was proscribed.

This law clearly and quite self-consciously restricted naturalization to "free white persons," thus racializing naturalized American citizenship at the very moment in which it was codified as a legal status. In fact, the 1790 act was the first federally enacted law that referred to race explicitly. While the precise meaning of "white" has never been stable in the enforcement of this law, historically, the naturalization process has been embedded in an explicit policy of racial exclusion and the logic of white supremacy.

The Naturalization Act of 1790 reinforced the assumption that slaves were not potential citizens—whether by birthright or naturalization: slave status removed an individual from being recognized as a potential participant in a contractual or consensual relationship with the state (except as property). Slaves, along with the larger category of people not considered "white," were thus constructed as "unnaturalizable."

The glaring racialization of naturalized citizenship in the 1790 act and its indirect reference to slavery may blind us temporarily to the other ways that this legislation implicitly constructs prospective citizens. What these passages make clear is that this earliest juridical statement on naturalization presumed that the prospective citizen would be not only white and free but also a (potential) parent.

What I want to call attention to in this passage is the way that ("natural born") citizens and "naturalized persons" are imagined to *have* children. That is, the seemingly abstract citizen invoked here is actually one who is also delineated through his/her (sexually) reproductive capacity, a capacity that, like the racial prerequisite, curiously re-embodies this seemingly abstract national subject. As the first law outlining naturalization as an ostensibly consensual and contractual relationship between the citizen and the state, the 1790 act contains within it assumptions about biological kinship that seem to revert, contradictorily, to an ascriptive process of conferring citizenship through the accident of birth.

The 1790 act thus seems to confuse two different logics of national belonging—blood and contract. This confusion, I want to suggest, indicates an ambivalence about the model of naturalized citizenship articulated in the first part of the law, one that represents, on its own, a more performative model of citizenship. The act's shift in attention toward children suggests that lawmakers were unable to imagine a truly nonascriptive model of citizenship. The reference to *jus sanguinis* seems to derail the act's attempt to narrate a model of contractual citizenship, but this derailment serves an important function, allowing an older model of allegiance based on biological kinship to prevail in the face of the law's earlier narrative of a citizen bound to the state by nothing more than contract. The reference to (white) (sexual) reproduction reanimates a more (literally) familiar model—and perhaps a more familiar affect—of national belonging produced through bloodlines.

Thomas Jefferson approaches the same issue in a more scientific fashion in *Notes on the State of Virginia* (1787), his wide-ranging compendium of statistical information, natural history, and philosophical thought. The most extended discussion of immigration appears in Query VIII, on "Population," in which Jefferson offers numerical data on the historical and existing populations of Virginia and compares different models for increasing its citizenry. In the process, he boldly articulates the assumed desire of the new nation toward immigration, but then takes a skeptical stance toward it: "The present desire of America is to produce rapid population by as great importation of foreigners as possible. But is this founded in good policy?" Jefferson clearly recognizes the state as an affective realm: America "desires" an increase in population (and therefore desires immigrants). Jefferson then ponders the relative costs and benefits of, on the one hand, the "importation of foreigners" and, on the other, "natural propagation." To determine which makes better policy, he presents, in true Enlightenment fashion, a statistical comparison of the two methods, calculating that it would take twenty-seven and a quarter years to double the existing "stock" of Virginia but noting that the population could be doubled in a single year through immigration. If it is true that "the present desire of America is to produce rapid population," then it seems obvious that the best and most efficient option is to encourage immigration. Questioning his own mathematical logic, however, Jefferson argues that there are hidden costs in relying on immigration to increase the population:

[Immigrants] will bring with them the principles of the [monarchical] governments they leave, imbibed in their early youth; or, if able to throw them off, it will be in exchange for an unbounded licentiousness, passing, as is usual, from one extreme to another. It would be a miracle were they to stop precisely at the point of temperate liberty. These principles, with their language, they will transmit to their children. In proportion to their numbers, they will share with us the legislation. They will infuse into it their spirit, warp and bias its direction, and render it a heterogeneous, incoherent, distracted mass. (84–85)

Jefferson denies any existing heterogeneity by projecting the blame for the "warp[ed]" and "bias[ed]" deformation of politics onto immigrants. Echoing the 1790 act, Jefferson takes for granted that these immigrant citizens are reproductive, destined to transmit to their children both the "principles" and "language" or monarchical governments, which they have "imbibed" (like mothers milk) "in their early youth." In this scenario, political ideologies are inevitably transmitted through biological reproduction. Despite the numerical data that seem to favor immigration and despite Jefferson's own espoused commitment to the principles of liberal democracy, he ultimately seems persuaded not by scientific or political argumentation, but rather by emotion, a fear that compels him toward a "safer" (but hardly rational) conclusion.

My goals in this essay have been to begin to construct a history of the state's production of citizens through naturalization in the United States and to explore the ways in which this practice has been fundamentally sexualized. In doing so, I am aware that citizenship, as a relation of belonging, is not reducible to the state; there are differences between citizenship as a formal status in the law and as a substantive category of belonging. Yet it is important to consider how the state functions as a site of affective power that has shaped the conditions of possibility for the production of U.S. citizens.

Given the founders' emphasis on a model of citizenship based on active consent, rather than passive inheritance, it would have been consistent with that principle for acquired citizenship (i.e., naturalization) to have become the default model, rupturing inherited logics of kinship and blood as the primary basis for political belonging. Yet even the most contract-based articulations of citizenship in the early national period—from the Naturalization Act of 1790 to Jefferson's *Notes*—repeatedly revert to the logic of sexual reproduction, perhaps as a way to contain social panic about the potential political disintegration associated with the contractual production of citizens. In the texts that I have analyzed here, we see the limits of social contract ideology as it has actually been enacted and embodied: the liberal project of putting into practice a model of consensual citizenship stumbles when it confronts its own queer potential (and perhaps inherent demand) to detach political belonging from (hetero)sexual reproduction.

Heather Hewett

Heather Hewett is an associate professor of women's studies and English at the State University of New York at New Paltz. In this 2009 essay, Hewett reads the 2007 film *La Misma Luna* as a reductive portrait of the lives of undocumented women struggling to survive in the United States. She finds that the film offers an implicit critique of US immigration policy and dramatic images of the hardships facing single immigrant mothers, but that the film simultaneously reinforces "powerful scripts about what it means to be a 'good' mother in both Euro-American and Latino cultures." Critical film and media studies are not primarily about identifying "good" or "bad" images (i.e., "This film is racist, while this film is not"), but are about exploring the complexities of media at all stages: production, distribution, consumption, etc. In this sense, critical media studies embrace the polysemy (i.e., multiple meanings) of mass-mediated texts and investigate the often contradictory meanings that viewers make when interacting with film, television, and other media (see Unit V). Hewett zooms in on the relationship between representations in *La Misma Luna* and salient, intertwined cultural ideologies about femininity, motherhood, religion, kinship, and citizenship. Her version of textual analysis speaks to the overarching concerns of intersectionality insomuch as Hewett's reading of the film connects media images to broader structures of oppression and resistance. Though media studies has arguably not been a key site in the development of intersectionality or transnational feminist perspectives—largely because of some strands of media studies' lack of attention to structural inequalities—Hewett's essay signals the productive possibilities of intersectional media studies.

29. Rosario's Lament: Mothering Across Borders*

Literary studies reminds us that creative texts do not provide transparent windows onto the world, but rather individually crafted frames that require us to ask questions about issues of representation and interpretation—to think

---

* Excerpted from H. Hewett, "Mothering Across Borders: Narratives of Immigrant Mothers in the United States," *WSQ: Women's Studies Quarterly* 37 (Fall–Winter 2009). Copyright © 2009 by the Feminist Press at the City University of New York. Used by permission of the publishers, www.feministpress.org. All rights reserved.

about *how* we see in addition to *what* we see. Furthermore, literature can help create reality and, as Rita Felski puts it, the "self as a cultural reality" (1989, 78). However, as Susan Stanford Friedman points out, *only* to focus on issues of representation and interpretation is to run the risk of erasing the woman's life in the text; instead, we need to pay attention to the interplay between the process of making meaning and the meaning that is made out of women's lives (2002). Thus a careful and conscientious use of social science research in literary studies can help us think about broader issues of gender and power. Likewise, some social scientists have suggested that incorporating an examination of literature can benefit social science research. Avery Gordon argues that "literary fictions" can play an important role "for the simple reason that they enable other kinds of sociological information to emerge" (2008, 25). In the case of migration, Paul White observes that "creative literature contains some of the most effective explorations of identity issues" and the complex psychological shifts that take place as a result of crossing borders (1995, 2).

In this essay I consider one film that explore[s] the experiences of transnational mothers in the United States. The film, *La Misma Luna* (2007), with the English title *Under the Same Moon,* was written and filmed by a Mexican-born writer (Ligiah Villalobos) and director (Patricia Riggen) and distributed by Fox Searchlight/The Weinstein Brothers to both English and Spanish-speaking audiences (although it was filmed entirely in Spanish, it has English subtitles).

La Misma Luna tells the story of a single mother, Rosario (Kate del Castillo), who works in Los Angeles as a domestic worker and sends remittances back home to Mexico to her nine-year-old son, Carlitos (Adrian Alonso), in the care of his grandmother. (His father, we eventually learn, has separately migrated to the United States, so that caregiving remains squarely in the province of women.) When his grandmother dies, the spirited Carlitos takes the money he has been saving and sets out in search of his mother, encountering a range of slightly menacing, flawed, and helpful characters along the way. Picaresque in flavor, *La Misma Luna* offers an implicit critique of U.S. immigration policies by way of several scenes: an opening sequence depicting Rosario's harrowing border crossing, a scene in which the sound effects are provided by a Latino radio broadcast critiquing the unnamed governor's anti-immigrant policies, and an extended chase scene during an Immigration and Customs Enforcement (ICE) raid. The main conflict of the film stems from the physical separation of mother and son, and the plot is driven by their mutual desire to be reunited.

Rosario is a beautiful and appealing character primarily defined by her identity as a mother. She is always thinking of her son (and he of her), suggested by the film's parallel opening sequence in which mother and son wake up to alarm clocks, apparently only a few feet from each other; quickly, however, the audience realizes that they are separated by thousands of miles.

Although emotionally connected, they live physically apart—they share only the experience of living under the same moon. Rosario's resulting preoccupation with her son extends into every area of her life. All her life decisions emanate from caring for her son and making his life better: she risks the dangers of crossing the border and working without papers in the United States so that she can send Carlitos money for food, clothes, and school; she calls him every week on the same day and time; she leaves LA to search for him as soon as she learns that he has left home. A devoted mother, she hides her own emotional suffering and pain from her son, though the film makes her suffering clear to audiences: she silently cries on the phone when she talks with him; she sadly tucks in a child while babysitting; and she refuses to go out with her roommate Alicia, who is in search of love and a good time.

Rosario's physical distance from her son forces her to perform long-distance emotional care work. Her demonstrations of "emotional intimacy" accord with what Joanna Dreby has found among transnational Mexican mothers (2006, 34). Like Rhacel Salazar Parrenas, Dreby finds "gender expectations in parenting to be durable in the transnational context" (2006, 56). In her study of Mexican parents in New Jersey, Dreby observes that "mothers' relationships with their children in Mexico are highly dependent on demonstrating emotional intimacy from a distance, whereas fathers' relationships lie in their economic success as migrant workers. . . . These differences are tied to Mexican gender ideology in which women's maternal role is sacralized whereas the father's role is tied to financial provision" (34). In keeping with these gendered inflections of parenting, *La Misma Luna* includes a subplot involving Carlitos's father, a migrant in Tucson who has been out of touch with his family and does not accompany Carlitos to find his mother in LA, even after promising to do so. Although the film does not elaborate, the key to understanding his failure as a father may be tied to his inability (or refusal) to send remittances home to his son. As Dreby observes, "Fathers only communicate with children in Mexico as long as they are sending money home to them" (55). At stake is not just their identity as fathers but perhaps also that as men; as Marit Melhuus observes of Mexican gender categories, a "man's first responsibility is to maintain his family" economically, and the "inability to provide" is tantamount to failure of a man's masculinity (1996, 242).

Dreby's analysis further suggests that when Mexican mothers migrate, traditional understandings of gender, motherhood, and caregiving do not necessarily change. Likewise, in her work on transnational Filipino families, Parrenas has found that the care children received from relatives or other caregivers became obscured because it was not performed by their mothers. Parrenas argues that the resulting "gender paradox" harms "children's acceptance of the reconstitution of mothering and consequently hampers their acceptance of growing up in households split apart from their mothers" (2005, 92). *La Misma Luna* suggests that this may be the case for Carlitos. Although he is cared for by his maternal grandmother (a situation common within transnational Mexican and Latin American families [Schmalzbauer 2005; Dreby 2006; Hondagneu-Sotelo and Avila 2007]), Rosario remains the always-desired figure. As Carlitos says to her on the telephone, she has been absent for too many years; the implicit suggestion is that her absence has begun to undermine her capacity to mother. Carlitos's victimization by his mother's absence sends a powerful message to the audience: no mother's sacrifice, no matter how great, can make up for her presence. While emotionally powerful, this message idealizes and naturalizes the biological mother as the only legitimate caregiver. Indeed, Rosario's entire success as a mother hinges upon her ability to fulfill her son's expectations.

Perhaps as a consequence, Rosario's devoted and self-sacrificial mothering extends further, exhibiting itself in the denial of her own sexuality. In contrast to Alicia, who routinely dates, Rosario works and stays at home. She even rebuffs the romantic advances of the honorable and loyal Paco, a security guard at one of the houses she cleans. Although Rosario eventually agrees to marry Paco, who offers her the possibility of a green card, it is a pragmatic decision she subsequently realizes she cannot honor. (Rosario agrees to Paco's proposition only after she is unjustly fired and is unable to find more work.) Romance remains absent, not because Rosario does not feel physically attracted to Paco (in fact, their one slow dance suggests that she might be, if she let herself), but rather because Rosario has room only for Carlitos in her heart.

Rosario's denial of her own sexuality reinforces powerful scripts about what it means to be a "good" mother in both Euro-American and Latino cultures. In Euro-American culture, enduring images of the "good" mother (always defined against the "bad" mother) emphasize qualities of selflessness and self-denial. An ideal with roots in the nineteenth-century "cult of domesticity," the "good" mother has more recently morphed into the practice of "intensive mothering" among middle- and upper-middle-class mothers (Hays 1996, 103). The ultimate good mother, of course, is the Virgin Mary—pure, devoted, nurturing, asexual—frequently posited as the opposite of Mary Magdalene, a prostitute. These two powerful mythic figures provide a simplified and binaristic view of female sexuality. In *La Misma Luna,* Rosario fits into the category of saintly mother; the contrast provided by her foil, Alicia (the "party girl"), emphasizes Rosario's saintliness and works to ensure that audiences will view Rosario as a good mother. After all, the film's success depends upon the audience's sympathetic identification with Rosario's struggle, and several potential pitfalls might ruin this affectual response. One is the possibility that the film might trigger any one of the anti-immigrant stereotypes circulating at the time of the film's release; another is that the film might trigger the stigma associated with maternal absence. As Diana Gustafson argues, "Few mothers are more stigmatized than those living apart from their children" (2005, 1). Indeed, given the narrowly defined prescriptions of ideal maternity presented by the figure of the at-home, solo mother—grounded in race and class privilege, and utterly unavailable to a single, working-class, Mexican-born, undocumented, and noncustodial mother—one can understand why the film carefully and repeatedly demonstrates that Rosario is, without question, a good mother.

Furthermore, idealized notions of the good mother circulate within many Latin American cultures. As Hondagneu-Sotelo and Avila observe,

> Women of color have always worked. Yet, many working women—including Latinas—hold the cultural prescription of solo mothering in the home as an ideal. This ideal is disseminated through cultural institutions of industrialization and urbanization, as well as from pre-industrial, rural peasant arrangements that allow for women to work while tending to their children. It is not only white, middle-class ideology but also strong Latina/o traditions, cultural practices, and ideals—Catholicism, and the Virgin Madonna figure—that cast employment as oppositional to mothering. Cultural symbols that model maternal femininity, such as the Virgen de Guadalupe, and negative femininity, such as La Llorona and La Malinche, serve to control Mexican and Chicana women's conduct by prescribing idealized visions of motherhood. (2007, 391)

In a similar vein, Gloria Anzaldúa observes that "*la Virgen de Guadalupe* is the single most potent religious, political and cultural image of the Chicano/*mexicano*" who, while a powerful "symbol of hope and faith," has also been "used by the Church" to "make us docile and enduring" (1987, 30–31). Anzaldúa further argues that the Virgin of Guadalupe, along with "*La Llorona*" and "*La Malinche*," has "encouraged the *virgen/puta* (whore) dichotomy" (31). The resulting idealization of motherhood, known among Latin American scholars as *marianismo,* is described by Evelyn Stevens as "the cult of feminine spiritual superiority" (1973, 91) that emphasizes women's "semidivinity, moral superiority, and spiritual strength" (94). Central to this construction are the ideas that "spiritual strength engenders abnegation, that is, an infinite capacity for humility and sacrifice" (94) and a sexual ideal of "premarital chastity" and "postnuptial frigidity" (96). Melhuus further elaborates the connections between suffering and female sexuality, inscribed in the Virgin of Guadalupe as Virgin Mother: "It is through the particular suffering evoked by the Virgin that the basis for women's chastity is generated. It is suffering, explicitly expressed in a form of self-sacrifice, which serves to transcend sexuality and becomes the mark of motherhood. Thus suffering becomes a virtue, and women are its victims" (1996, 247). Indeed, Rosario's self-denial and silent suffering provide a transnational twist on the religious iconography of the *mater dolorosa,* the Virgin mother who weeps for her son (Stevens 1973, 96).

These resonances with iconic Euro-American and Latin American figures of motherhood explicitly identify Rosario as the suffering mother. It is also possible, of course, that *La Misma Luna* accurately represents the psychological reality of an undocumented Mexican migrant mother, whose emotional pain would likely be inflected by the ideals of *marianismo.* At the same time, the film does not provide any metanarrative reflections about the presence of these cultural scripts of motherhood. I sense that the film, sympathetic to the plight of undocumented immigrants and reluctant to stir controversy, refuses to explore more complex dimensions of Rosario's identity. Likewise, the film silences the anxiety of truly unsettling scenes (such as Rosario's border crossing) with easily identified and somewhat clichéd characters, light comedy, and a happy ending. The result, a one-dimensional presentation of Rosario, reinscribes gendered ideologies of the self-effacing and martyred mother. We are left with the near-perfect idealization of motherhood that young children seem to possess. The more sobering realities of the emotional turmoil that may surface after mother and child are reunited, not to mention their continuing vulnerability as undocumented immigrants, lie outside the frame of the happy ending (Menjívar and Abrego 2009). The film's previous critique of anti-immigrant policies is abandoned, so that the workings of the state become obscured by the emotional high of their reunion. Unfortunately, while the film achieves a great deal in telling the story of a transnational mother, it ultimately provides a feel-good fairy tale ending that shies away from more disturbing or complex realities.

As Gretchen Hunt observes, "The story of immigration and the policy debates now circling around the topic are strikingly gendered, and ignore the reality of mothers and their children. So too do the writings and public conversations on motherhood [that] often exclude the stories of immigrant mothers" (2008, para. 5). Only with more of their stories can we begin to examine the damage done by the many distorted narratives about mothers and immigrants, circulating among and between nations, cultures, and people; only then can we work toward a world in which all women can author their own narratives, for themselves and future generations.

POLITICS, RIGHTS, AND JUSTICE

Political Diffractions

Patrick R. Grzanka

The readings in this unit foreground the interdisciplinary study of "politics," which refers to both formal institutions of political power and, more often, negotiations of power, which pervade all aspects of social life. For example, political scientist Ange-Marie Hancock (2007) offers a particularly broad elaboration of intersectionality's relevance to the study of politics:

> Within political science, while the embrace of intersectionality has received its widest acceptance in feminist theory, intersectional research has pushed the boundaries in critical legal studies, social movements, public policy, international human rights, and racial/ethnic politics, though it should by no means be limited to these areas of research. (64)

By opening up the domains in which political analyses might offer important contributions to the study of interlocking inequalities, Hancock encourages us to consider the benefits and possibilities of mixed- and multiple-methods approaches to intersectionality, as well as interdisciplinary coalitions between scholars with different backgrounds, training, and expertise. Because the standard analytic mechanisms of political science remain configured around single-axis and multivariable approaches that fail to conceive identities and institutions as co-constitutive, intersectionality "can fundamentally reshape the way in which political science research is conducted," according to Hancock (74).

All of the readings in this unit address the consequences of neoliberalism on politics and society in the United States. Though readings in other units have addressed dimensions of neoliberalism (e.g., Nero 2005, Unit IV, reading 15; Boyd 2008, Unit IV, reading 16; Reddy 2005, Unit I, reading 4), this unit foregrounds theories of neoliberalism and their specific consequences for thinking about and doing research on politics. Lisa Duggan (2003, reading 30), political scientist and cultural critic, describes neoliberalism as developing primarily in the United States and secondarily in Europe as the descendent of "capital 'L' Liberalism," drawing upon "classical liberalism's utopianism of benevolent free markets and minimal governments" (x). The Liberalism of the Enlightenment, so deeply entrenched in US rhetoric on the Right and the Left about "founding fathers," "freedom," "liberty," and "inalienable rights," provided "a set of rationales, moral justifications, and politically inflected descriptions of the institutions of developing capitalism" (x). Though Duggan stresses that neoliberalism, like capitalism, has never been a unified or monolithic system, there are certain structural dimensions of neoliberal hegemony that make it historically and conceptually coherent (I paraphrase):

1. Attacks on the New Deal coalition, on progressive unionism, and on progressive redistributive movements during the 1950s and 1960s;
2. Attacks on downwardly redistributive social movements, for example, Civil Rights and Black Power, feminism, lesbian and gay liberation, etc. during the 1960s and 1970s;
3. Pro-business activism driven by upwardly distributive interests in the 1970s as US-based corporations faced the bottom-line consequences of global competition from emerging markets;
4. Domestic "culture wars," attacks on public institutions and spaces designed to promote democratic public life; the alliance between conservative political forces and religious moralists (e.g., the Christian Coalition) and racial nationalists;
5. Emergent "multicultural," "diversity," and "equality" politics—the superficial, nonredistributive forms of equality designed for consumption and for the promotion of corporate and national interests, which are increasingly one and the same. (xii)

These macrosociological transformations of social and political life in the United States were always, according to Duggan, reliant upon identity and cultural politics. In our current historical moment, best characterized by point five above, an intersectional critique is necessary to see how inclusion, diversity, and equality politics in the political mainstream serve to reinforce upwardly redistributive economic policies, the disinvestment of minority communities, the dismantling of the US welfare state and of governmental international aid programs, and the corporatization (i.e., privatization) of all spheres of social life, including education, health care, and government.

As Duggan and Jodi Melamed (2006, reading 31) explicate, the most successful "ruse of neoliberal dominance in both global and domestic affairs is the definition of *economic* policy as primarily a matter of neutral, technical expertise" (Duggan 2003, xiv). Economics have been discursively positioned as categorically separate and distinct from politics and culture, such that any criticism of economic inequality may be dismissed as socialism, class warfare, or anti-Americanism; similarly, claims of social injustice on the grounds of race, gender, or sexuality are rejected as being merely cultural or private matters, the result of nonstructural forces which are wholly separate from economic or political interests. This logic facilitates an antisociological perspective on social problems, and directs attention to the choices, behaviors, and "cultural backgrounds" of both minoritized and privileged social groups (i.e., meritocracy), while diverting focus away from the structural advantages and disadvantages that predict life chances and that make certain "choices" tenable and others impossible. Accordingly, these processes are exceedingly difficult to see when looking through a dominant framework or paradigm (i.e., hegemony) that is designed to foreground agency and underemphasize structures in the organization of social life. Neoliberalism affects many aspects of social life, including the institutions (i.e., universities, think tanks, and nonprofit advocacy groups) that fund research on intersectionality, so Duggan and Melamed compel a degree of analytic vigilance and sensitivity to the places and spaces in which neoliberalism influences how we interpret and understand social problems.

Melamed (2006), in particular, investigates how multiculturalism and neoliberalism could possibly be so compatible in contemporary discourse on diversity in the United States. In other words, how can institutions manage to perpetuate racism, especially, while rhetorically promoting multicultural social politics? While Melamed focuses on political economy and ideology, Ruth Wilson Gilmore (2007) offers a case study in the ramifications of neoliberal social policy on the criminal justice system and the countless lives it now touches across the United States and especially in California. In the excerpt from *Golden Gulag* (reading 32) featured here, Gilmore tells the story of a family torn apart by a system increasingly choreographed to do just that: unfairly separate families on unjust grounds, incarcerate indefinitely, destroy lives. Gilmore posits her influential theory of racism in *Golden Gulag* to capture the material consequences of a process too often diluted in popular rhetoric to mean "attitudes" or "stereotyping": "Racism is the state-sanctioned and/or extralegal production and exploitation of group-differentiated vulnerability to premature death. Prison expansion is a new iteration of this theme" (247). But Gilmore's is certainly not a single-axis analysis; her focus in the excerpt here is on working-class women of color who formed community-based activist organizations to challenge California's legal system. The social cartography of these women's lives is shaped by contours of gender, race, and class that place them in the isolating position to defend their families' survival. Finally, though Beth Reingold and Adrienne Smith's (2012, reading 33) research is methodologically distinct from the other selections in this unit, an imagined conversation between Reingold and Smith, Gilmore, Melamed, and Duggan can illuminate the diverse factors that produce state-sponsored racist, sexist, and upwardly redistributive social policies. According to Reingold and Smith's analysis of state-by-state variations in welfare policymaking in the 1990s—a key moment of neoliberalism's encroachment into domestic life in the United States—both gender and race representation in legislative bodies influenced what kind of legislation is crafted and approved by state governments. Their work underlines the limits of single-axis perspectives to explore phenomena that are more complicated than can be explained by race or gender alone.

Each of the projects in this unit exemplify scholar-advocacy; indeed, Duggan's academic writing on homonormativity was linked to the development of Beyond Marriage, a coalition of advocates formed in 2006 to provide an alternative and inclusive discourse on contemporary LGBT politics. The coalition's work (www.beyondmarriage.org) provides pathways to think especially about the impact of scholarship and the place of academic research in shaping public policy. Intersectional analyses of politics tend to derive concepts and principles inductively, rather than deductively, which allows for creative theorizations of taken-for-granted concepts such as "rights" and "justice." This is distinct from postmodern approaches that might be primarily invested in the deconstruction of "civil rights," "equality," and other political concepts that trace their origins to classical liberalism. Intersectional scholar-activism remains invested in justice and social transformation, but in creating policy agendas from the ground up—based in the experiences of multiply marginalized social groups—rather than simply adjusting neoliberal or otherwise hegemonic policies to accommodate or include social minorities (see also Queers for Economic Justice: www .q4ej.org). Philosopher Donna Haraway (2004) writes about critical social theory's radical potentials with the term "diffraction," a metaphor she uses to suggest "mapping of interference, not of replication, reflection or reproduction. A diffraction pattern does not map where differences appear, but rather maps where the effects of difference appear" (217). Diffractions like the ones in this unit can provoke the rejection of politics-as-usual, and potentially intervene in neoliberalism's organization of intersecting oppressions. Diffractions do not promise political utopia, but they can mark elusive, evasive logics of neoliberal systems of inequality, and *sometimes* they function as loud interruptions in the monotonously upward flows of power.

References and Further Reading

Alexander, M. 2010. *The New Jim Crow: Mass Incarceration in the Age of Colorblindness.* New York: The New Press.

Barak, G., P. Leighton, and J. Flavin. 2007. *Class, Race, Gender, and Crime: The Social Reality of Criminal Justice.* Second edition. Lanham, MD: Rowman & Littlefield.

Berlant, L., and L. Duggan, eds. 2001. *Our Monica, Ourselves: The Clinton Affair and the National Interest.* New York: New York University Press.

Bosworth, M., and J. Flavin, eds. 2007. *Race, Gender, and Punishment: From Colonialism to the War on Terror.* New Brunswick, NJ: Rutgers University Press.

Cole, E. R., L. R. Avery, C. Dodson, and K. D. Goodman. 2012. "Against Nature: How Arguments about the Naturalness of Marriage Privilege Heterosexuality." *Journal of Social Issues* 68: 46–62.

Davis, A. Y. 1990. *Women, Culture & Politics.* New York: Vintage.

Dhamoon, R. K. 2011. "Considerations on Mainstreaming Intersectionality." *Political Research Quarterly* 64: 230–243.

Duggan, L. 2003. *The Twilight of Equality?: Neoliberalism, Cultural Politics, and the Attack on Democracy.* Boston: Beacon Press.

Duggan, L. 2008. "Beyond Same-Sex Marriage." *Studies in Gender and Sexuality* 9: 161–171.

Flavin, J. 2009. *Our Bodies, Our Crimes: The Policing of Women's Reproduction in America.* New York: New York University Press.

Gilmore, R. W. 2007. *Golden Gulag: Prisons, Surplus, Crisis, and Opposition in Globalizing California.* Berkeley: University of California Press.

Hancock, A.-M. 2008. "Intersectionality as a Normative and Empirical Paradigm." *Politics & Gender* 3: 248–254.

Hancock, A.-M. 2007. "When Multiplication Doesn't Equal Quick Addition: Examining Intersectionality as a Research Paradigm." *Perspectives on Politics* 5: 63–79.

Haraway, D. 2004. "The Promises of Monsters: A Regenerative Politics for Inappropriate/d Others." In *The Haraway Reader,* edited by D. Haraway, 63–124. New York: Routledge.

Melamed, J. 2006. "The Spirit of Neoliberalism: From Racial Liberalism to Neoliberal Multiculturalism." *Social Text* 89: 1–24.

Powell, J. A. 2007. "The Race and Class Nexus: An Intersectional Perspective." *Law & Inequality* 25: 355–428.

Reingold, B., and A. R. Smith. 2012. "Welfare Policymaking and Intersections of Race, Ethnicity, and Gender in U.S. State Legislatures." *American Journal of Political Science* 56: 131–147.

Richie, B. E. 2012. *Arrested Justice: Black Women, Violence, and America's Prison Nation.* New York: New York University Press.

Rios, V. 2009. "The Consequences of the Criminal Justice Pipeline on Black and Latino Masculinity." *The ANNALS of the American Academic of Political and Social Science* 623: 150–162.

Sawyer, M. Q. 2001. "Unlocking the Official Story: Comparing the Cuban Revolution's Approach to Race and Gender." *UCLA Journal of International Law & Foreign Affairs*, 403–417.

Verloo, M. 2013. "Intersectional and Cross-Movement Politics and Policies: Reflections on Current Practices and Debates." *Signs: The Journal of Women in Culture and Society* 38: 893–915.

Wadsworth, N. D. 2011. "Intersectionality in California's Same-Sex Marriage Battles: A Complex Proposition." *Political Research Quarterly* 64: 200–216.

Wilson, A. R. 2013. *Situating Intersectionality: Politics, Policy, and Power.* New York: Palgrave Macmillan.

Lisa Duggan

Lisa Duggan is a political theorist, social critic, and public intellectual currently appointed as a professor of social and cultural analysis at New York University; in 2013, she was elected president of the American Studies Association. She is a leading theorist of neoliberalism, which scholars have used to describe and critique social and political economy since the Reagan era. The guiding principle of advocates of neoliberalism is that market forces and logic can solve all problems—political (i.e., international relations), economic (i.e., income inequality), social (i.e., health care), and so forth. Critics of neoliberalism, such as Duggan and many of the scholars featured in this book, have documented the heterogeneous ways in which neoliberal policies—deregulation, privatization, corporatization of everything—have consolidated wealth and resources while exacerbating inequalities in the United States and worldwide. Whereas critics of neoliberalism such as David Harvey began theorizing the concept in the realm of political economy and macrolevel social processes, Duggan is recognized for bringing the neoliberal critique to the cultural level. Her scholarship explores how neoliberalism has played out in domestic policies, popular culture, and debates about civil rights in the United States. Her book *The Twilight of Equality?* (2003), excerpted below, is a treatise on and against neoliberalism and an elaboration of her concept of "homonormativity," which she coined to describe the ethos of mainstream LGBT social movements today. One might be inclined to ask: What does sexuality have to do with political economy? Homonormativity, as Duggan theorizes it, denotes how White, middle-class, heteronormative ideals have been repackaged and embraced by mainstream gay and lesbian activists in the interest of achieving "progress" for some segments of the LGBT community, namely marriage equality. As Duggan explains, homonormativity "is a politics that does not contest dominant heteronormative assumptions and institutions," but rather seeks a place at the table of privilege while positioning leftist activists as "extremists"; homonormative politics advance a "remapping of public/private boundaries designed to shrink gay public spheres, and redefine gay equality against the 'civil rights agenda' and 'liberationism,' as access to the institutions of domestic privacy, the 'free' market, and patriotism." The intersectional dynamics here are potent, and unlike many traditional scholars in political science, Duggan makes clear how race, gender, sexuality, and other dimensions of difference are not secondary but central to neoliberalism. Finally, Duggan complicates neoliberalism to the extent that she helps us to understand it not as a monolithic phenomenon but as a multifarious set of dynamic social forces that affect populations in diverse ways.

30. **The New Homonormativity**[*]

What happened? How did the forces of upward redistribution so forcefully trump the broad-based, expansive "revolution" toward downward redistributions that seemed so vital still in 1972? In the United States, the uneasy and uneven New Deal consensus among business, government, and big unions, built during the 1930s and more or less in place through the Great Society era of the 1960s, was dismantled. But this did not occur in order to remedy the undemocratic and antiegalitarian features of that consensus, or in order to generate greater democratic participation, material equality, cultural diversity, and good global citizenship, as many "revolutionaries" had hoped. Rather, the New Deal consensus was dismantled in the creation of a new vision of national and world order, a vision of competition, inequality, market "discipline," public austerity, and "law and order" known as *neoliberalism*.

Within the U.S. specifically, one might divide the construction of neoliberal hegemony up into five phases: (1) attacks on the New Deal coalition, on progressive unionism, and on popular front political culture and progressive redistributive internationalism during the 1950s and 1960s; (2) attacks on downwardly redistributive social movements, especially the Civil Rights and Black Power movements, but including feminism, lesbian and gay liberation, and countercultural mobilizations during the 1960s and 1970s; (3) pro-business activism during the 1970s, as U.S.-based corporations faced global competition and falling profit rates, previously conflicting big and small business interests increasingly converged, and business groups organized to redistribute resources *upward;* (4) domestically focused "culture wars" attacks on public institutions and spaces for democratic public life, in alliances with religious moralists and racial nationalists, during the 1980s and 1990s; and (5) emergent "multicultural," neoliberal "equality" politics—a stripped-down, nonredistributive form

---

[*] Excerpt from L. Duggan, *The Twilight of Equality?: Neoliberalism, Cultural Politics, and the Attack on Democracy* (Boston: Beacon Press, 2003), x, xi, 45–48, 49–50. Copyright © 2003 by Elizabeth Duggan. Reprinted by permission of Beacon Press, Boston.

234 | UNIT VIII: POLITICS, RIGHTS, AND JUSTICE

of "equality" designed for global consumption during the twenty-first century, and compatible with continued upward redistribution of resources.

During every phase, the construction of neoliberal politics and policy in the U.S. has relied on identity and cultural politics. The politics of race, both overt and covert, have been particularly central to the entire project. But the politics of gender and sexuality have intersected with race and class politics at each stage as well.

No longer representative of a broad-based progressive movement, many of the dominant national lesbian and gay civil rights organizations have become the lobbying, legal, and public relations firms for an increasingly narrow gay, moneyed elite. Consequently, the push for gay marriage and military service has replaced the array of political, cultural, and economic issues that galvanized the national groups as they first emerged from a progressive social movement context several decades earlier.

The Human Rights Campaign (HRC), for instance—the richest national gay and lesbian civil rights lobby in Washington, D.C.—inaugurated the new millennium with a march on Washington. Promoted as the successor to many previous such national mobilizations, the Millennium March actually broke decisively with the history of gay movement organizing in the United States. Brought to you by corporate sponsors corralled by a corporate-style board of directors with little outside input, the Millennium March was more of a public relations media campaign than a grassroots action. Community organizers nationwide protested the top-down corporate planning process and the Benetton-ad style of "diversity" politics that the march deployed. The protestors built on the outrage generated by HRC just two years earlier when its board endorsed antiabortion Republican Al D'Amato over liberal-centrist Democrat Charles Schumer for a New York Senate seat.

Since September 11, 2001, this rightward drift toward neoliberal politics has intensified, with an added emphasis on the Americanism of model gay "heroes" and "victims" as a rhetorical boost for demands for inclusion in marriage and the military. The potential for jingoistic blindness in this moment was starkly illustrated when the National Coalition of Anti-Violence Programs responded to an instance of homophobia that occurred early in the U.S. bombing of Afghanistan during fall 2001. An Associated Press photograph of a bomb being loaded onto the USS *Enterprise* showed a warhead emblazoned with the dare, "Hijack this Fags." The antiviolence projects protested in a press release,

> The message equates gays with the "enemy," it places gay, lesbian and bisexual servicemembers, who are serving as honorably as anyone else at this time at risk and dishonors them. . . .The warhead on the USS

Enterprise is as contemptible and a far more serious instance of gay-bashing because it comes from those charged with our protection and defense.

New York activist Bill Dobbs commented in reply,

Yes, the graffiti in question is deplorable. But then there is the slight matter of the bomb itself. And what happens when it is armed, dropped from the air and explodes. Does the National Coalition of Anti-Violence Programs (a coalition of gay groups) speak to such matters? Surely "violence" is implicated in this setting. While many Americans raise questions about the current military campaign—amidst reports of civilian casualties—NCVAP avoids any messy policy issues and sends the message that the bombs and the dropping of same is fine. As long as there is no bad graffiti on them. Given this sort of Gay Tunnel Vision, I wonder if NCVAP would put out a laudatory statement if the missions had gay/lesbian/bisexual/ transgender bombardier(s).

The Human Rights Campaign and the National Coalition of Anti-Violence Programs have not been alone in developing versions of such blinkered political vision. Often misunderstood and criticized by progressive activists as single issue politics—thus the tag "gay tunnel vision"—national gay civil rights politics in the new millennium is actually developing as the "gay equality" branch of multi-issue neoliberalism.

Another example: At the 1999 "Liberty for All" Log Cabin National Leadership Conference in New York, assembled gay Republicans from across the U.S. heard a keynote address from then New York City mayor Rudolph Giuliani, and a series of plenary lectures from Winnie Stachelberg of the Human Rights Campaign, Brian Bond of the Gay and Lesbian Victory Fund, Jonathan Rauch of the *National Journal,* and Urvashi Vaid, director of the National Gay and Lesbian Task Force Policy Institute. From her plenary platform, Vaid called for real dialogue, mutual respect, and even affinity between gay groups and gay leaders at serious political odds, against a backdrop of community unity.

But the conference sponsors were only superficially receptive to Vaid's call for respectful, inclusive dialogue. Rich Tafel, executive director of the Log Cabin Republicans, expressed a different notion of the basis for gay political unity—a transformed movement with a new center and definite exclusions:

The conference was the most important we've ever held, and its success solidified a clear shift that is taking place in the gay movement. There is a transformation going on across the country. . . . And [as] with any such transformation, those who had the most invested in the polarized status quo, notably extremists on the far left and far right, are beginning to resort to increasingly desperate tactics to stop it.

At the conference, Jonathan Rauch named that new center as "libertarian radical independent" and pointed to the online writers' group, the Independent Gay Forum (IGF), as the "cutting edge" of a new gay movement.

Under the banner "Forging a Gay Mainstream," the IGF Web site proclaims the organization's principles:

- We support the full inclusion of gays and lesbians in civil society with legal equality and equal social respect. We argue that gays and lesbians, in turn, contribute to the creativity, robustness, and decency of our national life.
- We share a belief in the fundamental virtues of the American system and its traditions of individual liberty, personal moral autonomy and responsibility, and equality before the law. We believe those traditions depend on the institutions of a market economy, free discussion, and limited government.
- We deny "conservative" claims that gays and lesbians pose any threat to social morality or the political order.
- We equally oppose "progressive" claims that gays should support radical social change or restructuring of society.
- We share an approach, but we disagree on many particulars. We include libertarians, moderates, and classical liberals. We hold differing views on the role of government, personal morality, religious faith, and personal relationships. We share these disagreements openly: we hope that readers will find them interesting and thought provoking.

On the surface the IGF Web site's collection of downloadable articles is targeted at conservative moralists, antigay church doctrine, and ex-gay propaganda on the one hand (Paul Varnell's "Changing Churches" and "The Ex-Gay Pop-Gun"), and at queer cultural and intellectual radicalism on the other (Stephen O. Murray's "Why I Don't Take Queer Theory Seriously" and Jennifer Vanasco's "Queer Dominance Syndrome"). But surrounding and shaping the familiar political triangulation, and the repeated assimilationist tirades against more flamboyant in-your-face gay activists, is a broader agenda for the future of democracy. This highly visible and influential center-libertarian-conservative-classical liberal formation in gay politics aims to contest and displace the expansively democratic vision represented by progressive activists such as Urvashi Vaid, replacing it with a model of a narrowly constrained public life cordoned off from the "private" control and vast inequalities of economic life. This new formation is not merely a position on the spectrum of gay movement politics, but is a crucial new part of the cultural front of neoliberalism in the United States.

By producing gay equality rhetoric and lobbying for specific policies that work within the framework of neoliberal politics generally, the IGF and its affiliated writers hope to (1) shore up the strength of neoliberalism in relation to its critics on the right and left, but especially in relation to the gay left, becoming what journalist Richard Goldstein has called antiprogressive-left "attack queers," and (2) push the neoliberal consensus in the direction of their brand of libertarian/moderate/conservative gay politics and away from politically attractive antigay alternatives.

The beachhead established by the writers now posted on the IGF site has been remarkably effective in creating what Michael Warner has called "a virtual gay movement" in the mainstream and gay press since the mid-1990s. By invoking a phantom mainstream public of "conventional" gays who represent the responsible center, these writers have worked to position "liberationists" and leftists as irresponsible "extremists" or as simply anachronistic (in this way, they echo the efforts of right-wing talk-radio hosts, conservative television news commentators, and many mainstream neoliberal politicians to smear all opinion to the left of them as "extreme" or "old-fashioned"). But this group has been much less successful in influencing national policy; they have failed to persuade many mainstream politicians to support their core issues of full gay access to marriage and military service. But they are certainly not yet defeated on these issues or in their overall project of providing a new sexual politics for neoliberalism in the new millennium.

The new neoliberal sexual politics of the IGF might be termed *the new homonormativity*—it is a politics that does not contest dominant heteronormative assumptions and institutions, but upholds and sustains them, while promising the possibility of a demobilized gay constituency and a privatized, depoliticized gay culture anchored in domesticity and consumption. IGF writers produce this politics through a double-voiced address to an imagined gay public, on the one hand, and to the national mainstream constructed by neoliberalism on the other.

Jodi Melamed

Jodi Melamed is an associate professor of English and African studies at Marquette University and the author of the book *Represent and Destroy: Rationalizing Violence in the New Racial Capitalism* (2011). Her work in literary studies is deeply sociological to the extent that she situates literary production within global political and social currents and examines literature as a fundamentally social object. In this piece, which might otherwise be called "Against Multiculturalism," Melamed invites a reconsideration of the diversity rhetoric so pervasive in contemporary life. She begins with a simply stated question: How have multiculturalism and neoliberalism become harmonious? The answer, she explains, lies in the reformulation of "racial liberalism" in the context and interests of transnational capitalism. The language here is lofty, but the point is relatively simple: though multiculturalism has many forms, a dominant strand of multiculturalism in business, government, civil society, and education has merely become a kind of diversionary tactic. As neoliberalism and its effects march on—upward redistribution of wealth, privatization, neocolonialism, corporate-sponsored war—these policies disguise themselves in the rhetoric of multicultural social progress. Multiculturalism has come to signify a nefarious form of American superiority over and against other countries and civilizations. As Melamed details, the consequences of this shift are profound.

31. The Spirit of Neoliberalism[*]

Multicultural reference masks the centrality of race and racism to neoliberalism. Race continues to permeate capitalism's economic and social processes, organizing the hyperextraction of surplus value from racialized bodies and naturalizing a system of capital accumulation that grossly favors the global North over the global South. Yet multiculturalism portrays neoliberal policy as the key to a postracist world of freedom and opportunity.

How can neoliberalism appear to be in harmony with some version of antiracist goals? What configures and restricts racial politics and meanings to make this possible? More specifically, what allows neoliberalism to incorporate U.S. multiculturalism in a manner that makes neoliberalism appear just, while obscuring the racial antagonisms and inequalities on which the neoliberal project depends?

How do race and capitalism relate in the current moment of U.S. global power? In what follows, I describe the contemporary relation between race and capitalism as a historical development of the liberal race thinking and politics that emerged after World War II with the victory of racial liberalism over white supremacy. I term this new, still-consolidating development "neoliberal multiculturalism." As racial liberalism did for U.S. global ascendancy in the early Cold War, neoliberal multiculturalism seeks to manage racial contradictions on a national and international scale for U.S.-led neoliberalism.

---

* Excerpted from J. Melamed, "The Spirit of Neoliberalism: From Racial Liberalism to Neoliberal Multiculturalism," *Social Text* 89 (2006): 1–24. Copyright, 2006, Duke University Press. All rights reserved. Republished by permission of the copyright holder, www.dukeupress.edu.

"What can Brown do for you?"—the slogan for the United Parcel Service (UPS)—nicely sums up racial reference in the era of neoliberal multiculturalism. In the 1970s, "brown" emerged as an antiracist coalition-building term among people of color, a shorthand for racial pride and solidarity, short-circuiting restrictive "black or white" notions of race relations. UPS's Brown keeps the color but blots out the people and the movement. Even as it erases manifest antiracist reference, Brown appropriates earlier, positive associations of *brown* with pride, warmth, solidarity, and functioning community networks. More insidiously, it also plays on racist associations of people of color with service. "What can Brown do for you?" thus takes a watchword of progressive 1970s antiracism and turns it into a slogan of happy subservience promising efficient access to the networks of the global economy. By appropriating and abstracting earlier racial reference, what Brown does for UPS is sell its services. What U.S. multiculturalism does for neoliberalism, as we shall see, is analogous: it legitimates as it obfuscates.

In this section, I consider how neoliberal multiculturalism repeats some of the core procedures of racial liberalism. It sutures official antiracism to state policy in a manner that hinders the calling into question of global capitalism, it produces new privileged and stigmatized forms of humanity, and it deploys a normative cultural model of race (which now sometimes displaces conventional racial reference altogether) as a discourse to justify inequality for some as fair or natural. The racial contradictions that such procedures disavow or manage for global capitalism today manifest both within and beyond color lines. On the one hand, the racial divisions engendered by white supremacy, colonialism, and slavery continue in the hyperextraction of surplus value from racialized bodies, as we find in free trade zones, sometimes called "new slave zones" for their killing conditions of labor and their legal impunity to exploit workers of color. Similarly, a racial-economic schema continues to associate white bodies and national populations with wealth and nonwhite bodies and national populations with want, naturalizing a system of capital accumulation that grossly favors the global North over the global South. On the other hand, neoliberal multiculturalism breaks with an older racism's reliance on phenotype to innovate new ways of fixing human capacities to naturalize inequality. The new racism deploys economic, ideological, cultural, and religious distinctions to produce lesser personhoods, laying these new categories of privilege and stigma across conventional racial categories, fracturing them into differential status groups.

Both components of the term *neoliberal multiculturalism* have important conventional usage histories. *Neoliberalism* was first used by Thatcherites to describe a return to nineteenth-century free trade. Because liberalism in England (as in most of the world) was associated with business conservatism, in the United States British neoliberals were originally aligned with U.S.

neoconservatives. The political history of U.S. neoliberalism begins with the Democratic Leadership Council under Clinton's first administration, which also advocated free trade, while promoting it as a means to reinvigorate the antisexism and antiracism of Cold War liberalism. Current political neoliberalism under the George W. Bush administration combines Clinton's superficial multiculturalism with the aggressive neoconservatism and imperialism of the Reagan and George H. W. Bush administrations. *Neoliberalism*, however, now most commonly refers to a set of economic regulatory policies including the privatization of public resources, financial liberalization (deregulation of interest rates), market liberalization (opening of domestic markets), and global economic management.

In defining neoliberal multiculturalism, I work with a more expansive understanding of *neoliberalism* as a term for a world historic organization of economy, governance, and biological and social life. We can think of neoliberalism as an organization of political governance by recognizing the paradigm shift in its demand that nation-states act in the first place as subsidiary managers of the global economy. We can recognize neoliberalism as a rationalization of biological and social life on the basis of the violence that individuals and communities have had to absorb with social and economic restructuring for neoliberalism.

The conventional usage history of the term *multiculturalism* begins in the 1970s, when it denoted grassroots movements in primary and secondary education for community-based racial reconstruction. By the late 1980s, the valence of the term had expanded, taken a cultural turn, and become controversial. For some, *multiculturalism* meant resistance to Euro-American norms and a renewal of protest against white racism. For its centrist and neoconservative detractors, it represented an attack on America's common culture. For its progressive detractors, *multiculturalism* became a byword for a kind of accommodation that replaced a focus on substantive political and economic goals with an emphasis on cultural diversity. Since the 1990s, *multiculturalism* has become a policy rubric for business, government, civil society, and education. Those who continue to use it to describe movements for justice on the part of historically marginalized groups often lean on modifiers to emphasize an idea of "strong" or "transformative multiculturalism."

While some of my insights overlap with those of the term's progressive detractors, my usage of the term *multiculturalism* in *neoliberal multiculturalism* comes out of my attempt to discern the characteristic logics of liberal race formations after World War II in relation to the development of transnational capitalism. Specifically, I refer to the contemporary incorporation of U.S. multiculturalism into the legitimating and operating procedures of neoliberalism, conceived as a world-historic organization of economy, governance, and social and biological life.

Although the formation began to take shape under the first Clinton administration, the current Bush administration is an advanced purveyor of neoliberal multiculturalism. The defense of indefinite detention at Guantanamo Bay prison camp is a stunning example. Multicultural codes do not generally oppose or contradict the holding and interrogation of Arab and Muslim "detainees" at the Guantanamo prison camp. To the contrary, the Bush administration consistently deploys multicultural language and signifying practices to make the detention appear just, despite the abrogation of the Geneva conventions. Providing prisoners with copies of the Koran, granting them time to pray, and other markers of cultural sensitivity represent Guantanamo not as a betrayal of U.S. multicultural ideals, but as the logical extension of them for the so-called war on terror. Furthermore, a multiculturalist U.S. exceptionalism justifies the flaunting of international law that Guantanamo represents. According to its logic, multiculturalism in the United States is so singular and successful that the nation embodies the universal, so that U.S. government and military actions are to be understood as being for a supranational good. As U.S. multiculturalism becomes a marker of legitimate privilege and universality, monoculturalism becomes a category of stigma that justifies torture. We might say that in Guantanamo, Arab and Muslim detainees are given copies of the Koran and nothing but, so that they may be tortured, while in Abu Ghraib prison, specific acts of torture (forced alcohol drinking and masturbation) produce the tortured as a caricature of "Islam violated." This new racism successfully obscures the continuation of older racial antagonisms (that is, Arab vs. white) in the present. At the same time, it extends racializing practices and discipline beyond the color line, recreating "multicultural" and "monocultural" as new privileged and stigmatized racial formations semidetached from conventional racial categories.

Neoliberal multiculturalism revises racial liberal reference and logic. Like racial liberalism, contemporary neoliberal multiculturalism sutures official antiracism to state policy in a manner that prevents the calling into question of global capitalism. However, it deracializes official antiracism to an unprecedented degree, turning (deracialized) racial reference into a series of rhetorical gestures of ethical right and certainty. Concepts previously associated with 1980s and 1990s liberal multiculturalism—"openness," "diversity," and "freedom"—are recycled such that "open societies" and "economic freedoms" (shibboleths for neoliberal measures) come to signify human rights that the United States has a duty to secure for the world.

We see this in the Bush administration's 2002 *National Security Strategy*, in which "opening" markets signifies as a multicultural imperative. According to the document's logic, opening societies to the diversity of the world (meaning its investment capital and products) fulfills the spirit of multicultural inclusiveness that would "include all the world's poor in the expanding circle of development." Similarly, the document's rhetoric of "freedom" collapses freedoms of commerce ("economic freedom . . . a moral right . . . freedom to pick and to choose") with social freedoms (of religion, association, etc.), transforming economic freedoms into multicultural imperatives by rhetorical transference. According to this "official" race-erased and militarized antiracism, "America's experience as a great multi-ethnic democracy" obligates the United States to secure "political and economic liberty" for "every person, in every society."

The 2006 version of the Bush administration's *National Security Strategy* ups its claims for "economic freedom" and the divine responsibility of the United States to secure these for all people as "principles true and right for people everywhere." It relies specifically on a neoliberal multicultural discourse of "economic rights" that incorporates the rhetoric of civil rights to portray "economic rights" as the most fundamental civil right and to advocate in an absolutist manner for deregulation, privatization, regulated "free markets," and other neoliberal measures as the only way to guarantee economic rights.

The Patriot Act is another example of neoliberal multiculturalism's revision of racialized privilege and stigma. It rhetorically privileges Arab Americans in order to discriminate against—and to obscure discrimination of—Arabs, Muslims, or South Asians in the United States who cannot or do not claim to be American in a nationalist or idealist sense. The act begins with a lengthy section titled "Sense of Congress Condemning Discrimination against Arab and Muslim Americans." This multiculturalist gesture of protection for patriotic "Arab Americans," "Muslim Americans," and "Americans from South Asia" rhetorically excuses the racializing violence that the act enables—namely, the stripping of civil and human rights from nonpatriotic or non-American Arabs, Muslims, and South Asians. In all the examples above, neoliberal multiculturalism arranges racial meaning to mitigate the charge of racism (according to conventional race categories), while innovating a new racism that rewards or punishes people for being or not being "multicultural Americans," an ideological figure that arises out of neoliberal frameworks.

Ruth Wilson Gilmore

Ruth Wilson Gilmore is a professor of geography in the doctoral program in earth and environmental sciences at the Graduate Center of the City University of New York. She is an activist—particularly in the area of prison abolition—and a past president of the American Studies Association. She is a founding member of California Prison Moratorium Project, Critical Resistance, and the Central California Environmental Justice Network, and she has received numerous awards and honors from community justice organizations, the California State Center, and the Los Angeles Board of Supervisors, among others. Her first book, *Golden Gulag: Prisons, Surplus, Crisis and Opposition in Globalizing California* (2007), has become an indispensible text in the field of critical prison, or "carceral," studies, specifically, and critical studies of race and racism more broadly. Gilmore's definition of racism, "the state-sponsored and/or extralegal production of group-differentiated vulnerabilities to premature death," has become especially influential for its pointed identification of the deep-rooted structural processes that produce inequality and violence.

In this excerpt from *Golden Gulag,* Gilmore recounts the harrowing story of Bernice Hatfield, who fought against her son's "legal kidnapping" by police in Southern California. Her story is one of an individual's resilience and a community's resistance of state-sponsored oppression, but it is also a case study in the race, gender, and class dynamics of pervasive prisonization in the United States. Mothers Reclaiming Our Children (ROC) is one organization that Bernice Hatfield worked within to uncover the systemic injustices her son faced in the California's criminal justice system in a direct response to her personal family crisis. But the "ROCers" exist as a response to the intersecting forces of racism, sexism, and classism that put low-income women of color in a position to financially sustain their families while also fighting massive institutions that have been designed to destroy those families. One among many strengths of Gilmore's scholarship is illustrated by the articulation of intersectionality that concludes this piece, which warrants both our critical attention and sustained outrage: "poor people of color have the most loved ones in prison. . . . and to free their loved ones encounter one another as laborers with similar triple workdays—job, home, justice."

32. **A Mother's Plea for Help**[*]

Early on a Thursday morning in 1992, just before that year's long Independence Day weekend, a dozen officers from the San Bernardino and Los Angeles County Sheriff's Departments and the West Covina Police kicked in Bernice Hatfield's front door. Hearing what sounded like an explosion, followed by footsteps, falling furniture, and shouting, Bernice rushed to the top of the stairs in her modest suburban condominium, and looked down on a vision of

---

[*] Excerpted from R. W. Gilmore, *Golden Gulag: Prisons, Surplus, Crisis, and Opposition in Globalizing California* (Berkeley: University of California Press, 2007), 212–215, 217–221, 236–237.

terror. Guns drawn, the police stood in the knees-bent, two-hands-on-the-pistol crouch that tells every television viewer that bullets are sure to fly. The officers were calling for the surrender of her seventeen year-old son, "Stick," and they hollered at her to put her hands where they could see them. Bernice raised her hands over her head and edged down the stairs, trembling as she asked over and over again, "What are you doing here? What do you want?" As it turned out, they wanted to charge Stick with six counts of attempted murder. The officers took the teenager away that morning; and for the next decade, Bernice fought against what in her periodic newsletter, *A Mother's Plea for Help*, she called "the legal kidnapping of my child."

Never a naive woman, Bernice grew up Black and working class in a postwar southern New England city, living inequality and racism in generally unremarkable ways. Determined not to be poor all her life, she studied hard in school, became a nurse, and worked for twenty years to care for and reassure the sick and suffering. Bernice thought she knew about how the justice system worked. While she did not expect it to be truly unbiased, she did expect that when someone is charged with a crime, there is probably some evidence, whether genuine or bogus. The "people's" case against her son consisted of contradictory testimony and there were no injuries, no gun, no motive, and no clear reason for him to have been brought up on charges in the first place. Yet he was charged, and as a gang member.

The powers of and pressures on the principal players in the criminal justice system were augmented by the California Street Terrorism Enhancement and Prevention Act (STEP Act) of 1988, and a host of related laws. California declared war on gangs during the first phase of the prison expansion program in the mid 1980s, and specifically targeted Los Angeles County, where Bernice and her family lived, as the region where new programs would be developed. Sacramento directed local law enforcement agencies to identify all gang members in their jurisdictions so that the state could develop a comprehensive, centralized gang database.

Stick had never before been in custody, but about a year earlier, after he was pulled over for a motor vehicle infraction, his name had been entered into the state's gang database. In early 1993, after he and his mother rejected a plea bargain offering him six years in the Youth Authority, the prosecutors decided to try him on the six counts. With sentence enhancements, or extra time per charge, due to his gangster status, the state assured him that he faced ninety-one years in prison. Stick, who by then had turned eighteen, decided to accept the bargain, which required him to confess guilt and to waive any rights to an appeal; in the interim, the prosecutor increased the minimum term from six to nineteen years, even though nothing in the case had changed except Stick's age. Bernice could not legally intervene, because the child had reached majority. In her view, he had been coerced into the confession by those who promised him a lifetime behind bars if he went to trial and lost. Young and scared, he tried to act hard and worldly. Although Stick was a minor at the time of his arrest, the sentencing judge bound him over to the custody of the California Department of Corrections (CDC) Adult Authority.

Bernice found that while she was struggling to free her child, because his arrest was simply a mistake, the state was working systematically to hold onto him, because his arrest was part of a program to take people "like him" off the streets. For Bernice, the crucial given was that her son had never been in trouble with the law before; for the state, the crucial given was his prior identification as a gang member. For a long time, she refused to engage the state on its own terms, because she thought things should work out fairly: "I believed I had constitutional rights. I mean, I *really* thought I had constitutional rights. But I found out . . . in the courtroom . . . that I am a second-class citizen. The Constitution does not apply to me."

For African Americans there is nothing new in realizing, once again, second-class citizen status. But while repetition is part of the deadly drama of living in a racial state, the particular challenge is to work out the specific realignments of the social structure in a period of rapid change.

Toward the end of one of her long, lonely days, before the confession and plea-bargain deal was struck, Bernice drove toward home from a visit with Stick, frightened that they were losing and unable to understand why. She happened to tune in a radio program about the trial of the LA Four and heard a defendant's mother talking about ROC. While Bernice had thrown herself into her child's case because she was his mother, she had never thought about forming alliances with parents in similar circumstances. Keenly aware that being able to claim her maternal relation to Stick made some difference— court officers and bureaucrats might return a mother's call or respond to one who spends hours waiting on molded plastic seats in anterooms or standing in corridors—Bernice decided to attend a Mothers ROC meeting to see if they could help her.

The ROCers encouraged her to get her story out, to start a chapter over in her part of the county, and to reach out to other mothers like herself in the places where she spent so much time on Stick's behalf. Bernice promptly wrote the first edition of *A Mother's Plea for Help*. She visited a number of copy shops looking for affordable rates and found an establishment run by a man who became sympathetic with her cause after she explained her plight. He agreed to let her use his machines at a discounted rate; and she began to produce her news on brightly colored paper (usually orange, sometimes startling blue) to catch the prospective reader's eye. Combining narrative, scripture, and cartoons, Bernice's two-to-six-page broadsides attracted the attention of mothers and others engaged in the unwaged reproductive labor of reclaiming the future by saving their children.

The STEP Act, and the events leading up to its implementation, made abundantly clear what the mothers feared: the "system" had for years been designating a profile of young persons whose rights and prospects were statutorily different from those of others in their cohort. The Task Force on Youth Gang Violence had stipulated that the region most in need of surveillance and control was in the Southland, and that Black and Brown youths were most likely to be gang members. While it had stretched the analysis of gang violence to encompass suicidal propensities among white middle-class "Heavy Metal" and "Satanic" gangs, the task force absolutely ignored, for instance, the growing skinhead and neo-Nazi gangs concentrated in the Southland.

The act's directive compelling local enforcement to identify all gang members in their jurisdictions seemed to the mothers likely to produce indiscriminate listings that would include people based on race and space, and that this, in turn, would transform any kind of youthful stepping out of line into major confrontations with the system. Acting on their new knowledge about the STEP Act, the ROCers decided to expand their stage of activism in order to prepare audiences and future actors for what the drama was really all about. They produced a flyer titled *MOTHERS WARN YOUR CHILDREN,* alerting principal caregivers to forbid their dependents to sign papers or allow their pictures to be taken by police on the street. Minors should insist that their parents be called. Adults should politely but firmly demur. The flyers were extremely effective ways to start conversations at bus stops, in the blistering sun at the county jail parking lot, and outside schools, courthouses, and police stations. Both men and women took the flyers—often promising to duplicate and distribute them at church or work. New people arrived at the Inland Empire meeting, flyer in hand, to learn more about the act.

In the short run, neither new knowledge nor new comrades made Bernice's struggle easier; on the contrary, she realized that she would have to work longer and harder hours as the mother of a kidnapped child. Since Stick's accomplices were never charged with anything, since people not enrolled in gang databases charged with similar offenses receive far lighter sentences, and since young people from different racial, class, or regional positions are often diverted to rehabilitation programs, Bernice set out to make the case of discriminatory prosecution, augmented by other claims, such as ineffective counsel. Indeed, Bernice perceived what had once been a state-identified chink in its own armor a generation earlier, when the first set of postwar federal antigang street crime acts was enacted between 1968 and 1970. At that time, law enforcement hesitated to exercise the statutes because of civil rights concerns—especially in the area of discriminatory prosecution. However, more than two decades of political-economic crisis, coupled with intensive and extensive crime sensationalism in the media (political campaigns, news programming, reality-based shows, movies, and television series), had produced the notion that some people's rights should be restricted based on prior patterns of behavior, which was now perceived as common sense.

The intensification of Bernice's anxieties and labors on behalf of her son, coupled with her new occupation helping out and reassuring other mothers in similar predicaments, impeded her nursing. She had always derived great satisfaction from caring for sick people. However, not long before Stick's troubles began, a racist patient in the regional hospital where she had worked for several years had informed a floor supervisor that he did not want the Black nurse to touch him. Bernice decided to find a new job serving a predominantly African American clientele, and she loved looking after "my Black patients," most of whom suffered from chronic, and often terminal, ailments. As is the case with so much "women's" work, nursing requires physical, intellectual, and emotional labor. This, on top of Stick's plight, wore Bernice out—especially emotionally. Ironically, she gave up "women's" paid work in order to do "women's" unpaid work, her inability to nurse enabling her to become a full-time mother. But full-time mothering meant being a "co-mother" with the ROCers, an advocate for her son and all the others—adults and children—caught up in the system.

California's expanding criminal justice system overlaid the state's restructuring landscape with new prisons, new laws targeting people in specific areas, new mandates for law enforcement, prosecutors, and judges; these territorial and discursive regions constituted the system's political geography that the mothers were trying to find their way through. Their techniques of mothering, in and as Mothers ROC, extended past the limits of household, kinship, and neighborhood, to embrace the political project to reclaim children of all ages whose mothers were losing them, at a net rate of fifty-five statewide per business day, into the prison system.

By enlivening African American practices of social mothering, the ROCers engaged a broadening community in their concern for the circumstances and fate of prisoners. That social opening provided avenues for all kinds of mothers (and others) to join in the work, because the enormous labor confronting each mother tended to encourage all of them both to accept and extend help. I make no claim for "social mothering" as an exclusively or universally African American cultural practice; it is neither. However, Barbara Meredith's commonsense invocation of mothering as collective action made possible the group's integration of mothers with similar or quite different maternalist assumptions. In other words, techniques developed over generations on behalf of Black children and families within terror-demarcated, racially defined enclaves provided contemporary means to choreograph interracial political solidarity among all kinds of caregivers losing their loved ones into the prison system. These mothers and others identified one another in the tight public spaces between their socially segregated residential living places and the unitized carceral quarters in which their loved ones are caged. Some were shy about jumping into the process, while others came to the ROC for help on their individual cases only; but all who persisted practiced the "each one teach one" approach.

The process of integrating different kinds of mothers and others into the ROC involved extensive outreach designed to permeate the social organization of space. These projects also caught people in the "betweens" of segregated lives: at work, for example, or on the bus. Like the Justice for Janitors Los Angeles crusade, however, this approach raised a more general problem of identification. The ROCers easily recognized one another in the spaces of the criminal justice system. Outside those areas, how do people resemble each other? If we are not all Black, and if all activists are not mothers, and if all prisoners are not (minor) children, then who are we? Poor people who work. As a community of purpose, Mothers ROC acted on the basis of a simple inversion: we are not poor because our loved ones are in prison; rather, our loved ones are in prison because we are poor. It followed that outreach should target working poor people and their youth. Class, then, while the context for this analysis and action, cannot displace or subsume the changing role and definitions of race: poor people of color have the most loved ones in prison.

As a matter of fact, the primacy of class is thoroughly gendered: women who work to support their families and to free their loved ones encounter one another as laborers with similar triple workdays—job, home, justice.

Beth Reingold and Adrienne R. Smith

Beth Reingold is a professor of political science and women's, gender, and sexuality studies at Emory University; her former doctoral student and coauthor Adrienne Smith is now assistant professor at the University of Tennessee, Knoxville. Their scholarship focuses on women, gender, and feminism in American politics, particularly questions about what factors (e.g., party affiliation, representation) influence policymaking that affects women and racial minorities. Their work here—a case study in the social politics of welfare legislation—begins from a well-documented historical phenomenon: "race and racial politics have had a profound impact on state implementation of welfare policy." Research has increasingly shown that the presence of African Americans and

Latinos on state legislatures may offset or buffer racial backlash against welfare recipients. Their work, however, seeks to complicate this finding by investigating the gendered nature of American welfare policy and the role of women legislators in crafting welfare policy. They take an intersectional approach to investigating legislatures' demographics and the policies they produce; though their findings are too extensive to include in full here, I have focused on their theoretical framework and how they interpreted their findings. Reingold and Smith demonstrate the value of intersectionality to political science and, accordingly, the weaknesses of single-axis frameworks for understanding race and gender in contemporary American politics.

33. Legislative Representation and Welfare Policymaking*

In many ways, the Personal Responsibility and Work Opportunity Reconciliation Act (PRWORA) of 1996 marked a new era in American welfare policy. Gone was the federal entitlement to means-tested benefits in the form of Aid to Families with Dependent Children (AFDC). Taking its place, Temporary Assistance to Needy Families (TANF) is restricted to a lifetime maximum of five years, contingent upon work-related activity outside the home, and subject to numerous sanctions for uncooperative or unproductive behavior. Its primary goals are to reduce welfare caseloads by instilling or otherwise requiring more "responsible" behavior on the part of recipients. And while the PRWORA imposes a number of goals, limits, and minimal requirements, it grants the states a lot more discretion over welfare policy than they had before.

Yet, despite all these changes in the law, one thing has remained constant: race and racial politics have had a profound impact on state implementation of welfare policy. As was the case with AFDC, the more racially diverse the state welfare rolls (or population), the less generous the TANF benefits and the more rigid the rules and regulations governing eligibility and work requirements. State policymakers, it appears, have responded to or internalized the racial stereotypes, resentments, and fears that shape judgments of welfare recipients and drive the call for less generous, get-tough welfare policy among whites.

There is growing evidence, however, that the presence and power of African Americans and Latinos in state legislatures can offset this sort of racial backlash. In effect, states with relatively large proportions of black and Latino

---

* Excerpted from B. Reingold and A. R. Smith, "Welfare Policymaking and Intersections of Race, Ethnicity, and Gender in U.S. State Legislatures," *American Journal of Political Science* 56 (2012): 131–147. Copyright © 2011, Midwest Political Science Association.

citizens and welfare recipients would have even less generous welfare benefits and rules if they had not managed to elect black and Latino representatives—and if those black and Latino representatives had not managed to accumulate some modicum of legislative power. The research thus far contributes greatly to our understanding of the racialization of American welfare policy and politics, as well as the significance of the election and political incorporation of racial and ethnic minorities in the states. Notably missing, however, is sustained attention to the *gendered* nature of American welfare policy and politics, and the role of female policymakers in the states. Our inquiry begins, therefore, with the question of whether the election and incorporation of women into state legislatures has any effect on state welfare policy.

Yet the politics of welfare may not be properly understood in terms of *either* race *or* gender. More likely, welfare policymaking in the states is "raced-gendered"—shaped simultaneously by both racial and gender politics. For that reason, we take an *intersectional* approach to the study of welfare policy, recognizing race and gender as intersecting and/or interdependent political forces. To illustrate and test the analytic critique of intersectionality, we undertake and compare an "additive" and an "intersectional" approach to incorporating gender into the study of race, representation, and state welfare policy. For the contrast between the two most powerfully demonstrates what intersectionality as a research paradigm (Hancock 2007) or analytic tool (Simien 2007) is and offers. Our additive approach treats gender as a separate, "single-axis" category of analysis, independent of race and ethnicity; highlights the gendered nature of American welfare politics; and gauges the impact of all state legislative women (undifferentiated by race/ethnicity) on welfare policy, controlling for the impact of their African American and Latino colleagues. Our intersectional approach, in contrast, treats gender and race/ethnicity as overlapping, interlocking categories of analysis, highlights the "raced-gendered" nature of welfare politics, and compares the impact of legislative women of color to that of other women and men of color.

An Additive Approach, as suggested above, examines welfare policy and politics through a gender (-only) lens, adding women (undifferentiated by race or ethnicity) to the theoretical and empirical story. It begins with the observation that the history and politics of welfare in the United States are gendered in many of the same ways they are raced. One can see gender in the demographic composition of welfare recipients and the poor more generally; in the history of social welfare policymaking and implementation; in public opinion; and in the behavior of elected officials. In all of these arenas, gender biases and differences suggest that welfare is very much a "women's issue" and that those who advocate for and actively represent women on this issue will fight to make welfare policy more generous and accessible—in effect, more women-friendly.

Researchers have long noted the "feminization of poverty" (McLanahan and Kelly 1999; Pearce 1978). In 2008, for example, the poverty rate for women and girls (14.4%) was approximately 2% higher than that for men and boys (12.0%), which translates into almost 4.5 million more females living in poverty. Because poverty assistance is targeted almost exclusively to poor families with dependent children and most of those families are headed by single women, adult welfare recipients are almost always female. In FY1996, 87% of all adult AFDC recipients were female. Under TANF, little has changed. In FY2006, a full 90% of all adult recipients were female.

These figures only begin to capture the myriad ways in which social welfare policy, from colonial times to the present, has been gendered. In its design and implementation, the American welfare state has been quite selective, extending its most generous assistance to those "deserving" women whose morals, marital status, sexuality, and reproductive lives comport with dominant gender and family norms (e.g., widows with small children). For those deemed undeserving (e.g., unmarried mothers), assistance has been either denied altogether, or meted out in the most miserly, intrusive, and punitive fashion. Women receiving welfare benefits often have been subject to state surveillance and regulation of their personal lives, not simply to prevent waste, fraud, and abuse, but also to ensure morally "suitable" homes and proper parenting. PRWORA is certainly not the first attempt to regulate women's lives, police women's sexuality, restrict poor women's fertility, and instill more "personal responsibility" among low-income, single mothers. But it may be the most emphatic and explicit.

Researchers have not examined policymakers' attitudes toward welfare recipients directly, but there is evidence to suggest that gender gaps in the welfare policy preferences and priorities of the electorate are reflected in those of elected officials. Research spanning multiple decades and levels of office shows that, compared to their male counterparts, female officials are more liberal and more likely to take the lead on a variety of women's rights and social welfare issues, including poverty alleviation (Reingold 2008). Other studies have found that women are more likely than men to introduce welfare or antipoverty legislation, even after controlling for party, district demographics, and committee assignments (Bratton and Haynie 1999; Bratton, Haynie, and Reingold 2006; but see Reingold 2000; Thomas 1994). In these ways, shared gender identity is thought to motivate female legislators to pursue more liberal welfare policies.

Yet, while evidence suggests female legislators are more likely to act for poor women on or in need of welfare, it is still unclear whether they could, as a group, exert enough influence to impact state policy. When the PRWORA was signed into law in 1996, women had never claimed a majority of the seats in any state legislative chamber. In most states (38, to be exact), women held no more than a quarter of the seats in the legislature (CAWP 1996). Perhaps for this reason, studies that have examined the impact of legislative women on state policy outcomes report mixed results, at best. In the most comprehensive study to date, Cowell-Meyer and Langbein (2009) find that the percentage of women in state legislatures is associated with the adoption of only eight of the 34 women-friendly policies examined; and in three instances, the relationship is in the opposite direction. Likewise, on the seven dimensions of TANF policy examined, the greater presence of female legislators is just as likely to increase the odds of adoption as it is to decrease the odds, as it is to have no effect at all (Cowell-Meyer and Langbein 2009; see also Keiser 1997).

Some studies of welfare policymaking are more optimistic about the liberal influence of women in power. In-depth analyses of legislative efforts leading up to the passage of the PRWORA in the Republican-dominated 104th Congress show that some of the more senior, moderate Republican women were able "to temper or moderate some of the harsher effects of the proposed legislation and to expand the legislation to include provisions for child care, child support, and child protection" (Hawkesworth et al. 2001, 46; Dodson 2006). Poggione (2004b) also finds that state legislative women can have an impact on TANF policy, under certain conditions. When the percentage of women in the majority party is high and the majority party holds a slim margin, and when the percentage of women on welfare-related committees is high and the committees are relatively autonomous, TANF policies are significantly more liberal.

As these studies suggest, "sheer numbers" of legislative women may not be enough. The impact of women on state policy outputs may also depend on their incorporation into dominant coalitions and leadership structures. We therefore anticipate that it is the *combination* of women's descriptive representation and legislative incorporation—their presence and positions of power in the legislature—that enables them to move welfare policy in a more liberal, generous, accommodating, and women-friendly direction.

H1 (Single-Axis Hypothesis): The greater the incorporation of women in the state legislature, the more generous, accessible, flexible, and lenient the state welfare policy.

An Intersectional Approach posits that welfare politics in the United States is not simply gendered or raced, or even gendered and raced; it is raced-gendered (Hawkesworth 2003; Neubeck and Cazenave 2001). The raced-gendered nature of welfare is perhaps best understood where it is most powerfully manifested: in the distinctive position—real or imagined—of poor women of color. It is, after all, not simply women, African Americans, or Latinos who are overrepresented among welfare recipients; it is women of color. As the histories of social welfare policy make clear, determinations of which women are more or less deserving of assistance, privacy, and dignity have always been tainted by racial and ethnic biases. As a result, poor women of color have been subject to the most stringent eligibility requirements, the most intense moral scrutiny, and the harshest penalties welfare policy has to offer.

Evidence also suggests that it is not simply racial or gender stereotypes of lazy or overly fecund welfare recipients that have fueled successive waves of disciplinary welfare reform. Rather, it is the "controlling image" of the raced-gendered welfare queen who promiscuously gives birth to multiple children in order to receive more benefits and avoid working that has come to symbolize the typical recipient and all that is wrong with American welfare policy (Collins 2000). In Foster's (2008) analysis, for example, public support for government welfare spending is contingent upon the predicted reproductive behavior of (hypothetical) *black* welfare mothers, not that of white welfare mothers. O'Brien (2004) finds that, as the number of black women on welfare rose and the welfare queen emerged in popular discourse, women no longer spoke in one voice about the need to alleviate poverty. Starting in the late 1970s, African American women became much more likely than other women to consider poverty a major national priority. Perhaps as a result, gender gaps in public support for "welfare" spending in particular were noticeably absent in the 1990s and early 2000s; national samples of (mostly white) women and men were equally opposed (Clark and Clark 2006; Gilens 1999; but see Dyck and Hussey 2008).

The raced-gendered images and assumptions associated with the welfare queen, which featured prominently in congressional debates on welfare reform in the 1990s may have had similar effects on the behavior of legislators. According to Hawkesworth, "Congresswomen of color were among the most outspoken opponents" of the PRWORA precisely because they saw "the Republican focus on out-of-wedlock births, unwed mothers, and single-women heads of households . . . [as] a thinly veiled attack upon poor women of color" (2003, 542–43). But while congresswomen of color were united in their opposition to welfare reform, their white female colleagues were deeply divided; some, in fact, were on the forefront of efforts to frame poverty and welfare reform in terms of deviant behavior and the lack of "personal responsibility" associated with the welfare queen. Here again, scholars point to collective identities and experiences as motivating factors; only this time, those identities and experiences are intersectional. Hawkesworth argues that it was the "anger and resistance engendered by . . . experiences of racing-gendering in the halls of Congress" (2003, 532) that compelled congresswomen of color to "devote such time and energy to the representation of an unorganized majority-white underclass" (539). Mink (1998, 1–27) and Neubeck and Cazenave (2001, 170–76), on the other hand, attribute the relative indifference of white feminists in Congress and elsewhere to their own positions and experiences of race and class privilege.

For all these reasons, one might expect that, at the state legislative level, it is women of color who are the most vocal and active advocates for more generous and less punitive approaches to welfare and who, in the end, have the greatest countervailing influence on welfare policy. It might even be the case that what previous studies (e.g., Preuhs 2006, 2007) have characterized as the ability of (all) black and Latino legislators to "mitigate [welfare] policy backlash" is really the doing of black female and Latina legislators. And, given how racially polarized the experience and politics of welfare have been, white female legislators may be more ambivalent about welfare reform, and more reluctant to become involved. As a result, they may make little or no distinct impression upon state welfare policy.

H2 (Intersectional Hypothesis): The (liberal) impact of legislative women of color on state welfare policy will be greater than that of other women or of men of color.

But while legislative women of color may be the most committed and active advocates for poor women, they also may be the least influential. The women of color who fought so hard against welfare reform in Congress met with little success. Even when they had a seat at the table (during the Democratically controlled 103rd Congress), their efforts were rebuffed or ignored altogether and their credibility was repeatedly impugned. Hawkesworth, in fact, uses welfare reform as a "particularly appropriate case" for examining "racing-gendering" within Congress and the mechanisms by which elected women of color are themselves marginalized and disempowered (2003, 539). As in Congress, state legislative women of color often lacked the "sheer numbers" and positions of power with which to influence the development of TANF policies. In 1997, they were entirely absent from 12 state legislatures, constituted less than 10% of the remaining legislatures, and held positions of leadership (top party positions or committee chairs) in only 19. Furthermore, Smooth's (2008) study of African American women serving in the Georgia, Maryland, and Mississippi legislatures illustrates how women of color can be effectively denied power and influence even when they possess (relatively) large numbers, seniority, majority party status, and positions of leadership.

Nonetheless, other studies suggest that state legislative women of color can and do have influence, under some circumstances at least. Orey et al. (2006) find that, contrary to their expectations, bills sponsored by African American women in the Mississippi state house in the late 1980s and 1990s were no less likely to pass than those introduced by others. By empirically gauging the distinct impact of state legislative women of color on welfare policy, this study sheds additional light on these debates about the power of intersectionality in legislative settings.

For reasons explained below, we focus on the states' initial (pre-1999) reactions to the PRWORA mandate. To gauge the impact of legislative women on state welfare policy with attention to the intersecting dynamics of race and ethnicity, we compare two models of policy adoption. The first, *additive* model tests the single-axis hypothesis (H1) by gauging the relationship between state welfare policy and the presence and power of all women in the legislature, controlling for the presence and power of (all) black and Latino legislators. The second, *intersectional* model tests the intersectional hypothesis (H2) by gauging the impact of the size and power of three potential legislative coalitions, each identified in terms of gender *and* race/ethnicity: women of color, other "white" women, and men of color. Our empirical analysis relies on data we collected for all 50 states, starting (when possible) with 1996, the last year AFDC was in effect, and ending (when possible) with 2007. For reasons explained below, we focus on the states' initial (pre-1999) reactions to the PRWORA mandate.

Results

We first assess whether the legislative incorporation of all women, regardless of race and ethnicity, affects states' initial decisions regarding TANF benefits and rules. The key independent variables in these additive models are our factor scores of the political incorporation of all women, all black, and all Latino legislators. Overall, the models provide lackluster and contradictory findings regarding the single-axis hypothesis. In only one instance—eligibility requirements—does the presence and power of (all) women legislators even come close to having a significant, liberal effect on TANF policy. In other areas, namely cash benefit levels, female legislative incorporation may have the reverse effect. For the remaining TANF policies, however, legislative women seem to have no significant impact at all.

In contrast to the additive models, the intersectional models distinguish the potential impact of women of color from that of other women and from that of men of color, on the same set of state TANF policies. The key independent variables for the intersectional models are factor scores of the legislative incorporation of women of color, other "white" women, and men of color.

In sum, our intersectional analyses indicate that in the formative years of TANF policymaking, legislative women of color did play a distinct role. Our results also demonstrate that the additive model may sometimes obscure the impact of race, ethnicity, and gender as they interact to affect state politics and policymaking. Intersectional models such as ours appear more adept at capturing such complex and contingent relationships (McCall 2005).

Conclusions

At first glance, looking through a single-axis lens, it may seem as if state legislative women failed to move welfare policy in a more liberal, women-friendly direction, even in a period of policy disequilibrium. At best, they may have managed to relax the eligibility criteria a bit; at worst, they may have had a hand in reducing cash benefit levels. But on most policy dimensions examined here, the presence and power of (all) women in state legislatures seem to have made very little difference.

The picture looks quite different, however, when viewed through an intersectional lens. Taking into account the intersecting gender and racial/ethnic identities of state legislators highlights both the contingent effects of gender and the pivotal role of women of color. In some instances, our analysis suggests that legislative women of all racial/ethnic backgrounds made a difference in state TANF policy. Eligibility restrictions were eased somewhat in states where legislative women of color and white women were more numerous and powerful. In other instances, legislative women of color seem to have acted without their white female counterparts. It was the incorporation of women of color, along with that of men of color, that pushed some states to adopt more flexible work requirements, not that of other women. At the same time, the presence and power of women of color (alone) made some states more reluctant to grant time limit waivers to victims of domestic violence. Given the initial uncertainties surrounding state implementation of the Family Violence Option, legislative women of color may have been most wary of the unintended but potentially harmful consequences of this seemingly women-friendly policy. In yet another instance, legislative women of color and other women appear to have worked at cross-purposes. While the presence and power of white women in the legislature are associated with a decrease in cash benefits, the incorporation of women of color is associated with an increase in cash benefits. Across all these divergent patterns, however, one trend is clear: the legislative incorporation of women of color mattered, suggesting they were indeed the most effective advocates for poor women in the era of welfare reform (Fraga et al. 2008).

As our results imply, the impact of women on welfare policy depends on which women and which policies one examines. Nonetheless, it is quite remarkable that women—especially women of color—had any effect whatsoever. Women as a whole were a minority of legislators and legislative leaders in every state, a small minority in most. Women of color enjoyed fewer resources still. During the transition from AFDC to TANF, black women and Latinas never claimed more than 10% of the votes; they held top leadership positions and chaired social service committees in few states. State welfare policy itself proved resistant to nonincremental change, even in a period of disequilibrium. Overcoming inertia and pushing against the popular mandate of get-tough welfare reform was a tall order, indeed. Yet, women of color, when they were able to gain a foothold within their legislative institutions, managed to make a difference.

The implications of our findings are equally notable. They demonstrate, first and foremost, the utility of intersectionality as a concept and an analytic tool, as well as the limitations of more "parsimonious" single-axis or additive approaches to studying the politics of gender, race, and class. The politics of welfare and other cross-cutting issues may *not* be properly understood in terms of either race or gender or class. Nor can we be content with simply adding women (or racial/ethnic minorities or poor people) to the equation, literally or figuratively. Doing so may very well obscure more than it reveals.

SCIENCE, TECHNOLOGY, AND BODIES

Science and Technology Studies as Tools for Social Justice

Patrick R. Grzanka

Because science is such a pervasive and consequential element of contemporary global society, it seems obvious that scholars of intersectionality would be particularly interested in studying scientific knowledge production and practices. Likewise, one would expect that intersectionality's insights would be of special value to sociologists, anthropologists, historians, and others who do science and technology studies (STS)*, because—of all people—those are the scholars who know how deeply *social* science really is. However, despite recent innovations in the field, STS remains very much a frontier when it comes to intersectionality: it is essentially uncharted territory. There is some uptake of intersectional considerations by STS scholars and some integration of STS issues into traditional centers of intersectional inquiry in women's studies and sociology, but STS and intersectionality remain largely parallel, nonoverlapping discourses. The pieces in this unit are exceptional to the extent that they engage in explicit and implicit conversations about the productive value of intersectionality to the critical study of science, technology, medicine, health, and society, and they represent the cutting edges of theoretical and methodological work on difference, power, and science.

---

* I use the acronym "STS" broadly and inclusively to denote diverse work in social studies of science, technology, and medicine, including the history, philosophy, anthropology, and sociology of science.

Just like intersectionality, STS is an interdisciplinary, loosely organized domain that traverses across disciplines and is articulated in vastly different ways even within disciplines such as sociology or history. STS is in many ways a shorthand, umbrella term to denote the various sites across the humanities, social sciences, and natural science where critical work on scientific knowledge production, technological applications, and the dissemination and institutionalization of science happens. Science itself is an enormous, heterogeneous domain, and encompasses fields as varied as epidemiology, engineering, geology, computer science, nursing, and physics. Historians and philosophers of science may use different methods (e.g., historiography and dialectal reasoning) than sociologists or anthropologists of science (e.g., ethnography, survey research, and participant observation), but they generally share an assumption that science is a social and cultural process like any other form of human interaction, including human interaction with the nonhuman elements of the universe. Furthermore, in critical strands of STS, especially feminist STS, social studies of science are conducted not simply in the interest of learning how science happens, but in identifying how scientific practices manage and order bodies, influence the distribution of life-saving and life-enhancing resources, control and manipulate natural resources, determine public policy, and reflect broader social norms. In feminist STS, "science" is figured as diverse sites of possibilities for innovation, discrimination, progress, and oppression.

Feminist and antiracist inquiry in STS has become increasingly complex and nuanced in the past several decades and has moved beyond reductive narratives in which science and technology are always oppressive and/or the key to social utopia. As Helen Kennedy (2005) explains:

> Rejections of technology as masculine and oppressive or celebrations of its liberating potential for women have, on the whole, been superseded by less polarized approaches that seek to understand both technology and gender as mutually constitutive social process. Consequently, the proposals within feminist STS that we perceive of both gender identities and technology as cultural constructions and that gender is embodied in technology, while technologies shape our understandings of gender, are now widely accepted. (472)

In her influential ethnography of lesbian reproductive practices at the turn of the twentieth century, for example, medical sociologist Laura Mamo (2007) found that her participants' relationship to heteronormative ideologies of parenting and kinship were neither wholly regressive nor progressive. Instead, she found that women were complexly negotiating their relationships to reproductive health, and that these processes were deeply embedded in the advanced biotechnologies at their disposal in the fertility industry. The meanings of kinship, gender, and pregnancy were transformed and re-created in these women's interactions with biomedical knowledge and reproductive "technoscience," which refers to the impossible-to-disentangle nexus of science and technology in the late twentieth and early twenty-first century.

If Mamo's work is pointing toward intersectionality with an interrogation of gender and sexual dynamics in pregnancy, Khiara Bridges's (2011) work turns the volume up on the intersectional dynamics of reproductive medicine. In her book *Reproducing Race* (reading 37), Bridges confronts how race itself is reiterated and re-created in a New York City hospital that serves many working-class women of color seeking reproductive health care. In the selection included here, Bridges details how the hospital staff's interactions with these women come to produce the figure of the "wily patient," whose identity is closely aligned with the trope of the "welfare queen." In terms of race, class, and sexuality, Bridges's participants sit in stark contrast to the affluent, mostly White parents in Mamo's ethnography who pursue expensive fertility services at for-profit clinics. Collectively, their work reinforces the importance of intersectional thinking to recognize how the very same biomedical phenomenon—pregnancy—can materialize in radically different ways along the dimensions of race, class, and sexuality.

Kennedy (2005) credits Donna Haraway (see Unit II, reading 6), in particular, with theorizing a feminist STS project that was always as much about race as it was about gender. She recalls how the cyborg metaphor (Haraway 1985), arguably Haraway's most lasting contribution to the field, was a racially and sexually hybrid figure, and yet single-axis thinking in feminist STS took up the cyborg as just about gender (and not about race, or anything else, for that matter). Recently, critical STS scholarship has more deeply attended to the intersections of race, gender, and class, while also considering other configurations and manifestations of difference. Jessie Daniels's (2009) research on cyberfeminism, for example, extends research on the multiple and diverse meanings that emerge from online community building (see reading 36). While cyberspace has been thought to offer the promise of disembodiment—and a consequent escape from race, gender, and other body-markers that calcify differences and inequalities—Daniels paints a more complicated picture in which race and gender dynamics reiterate themselves online as persistent inequalities. Janet Shim (2005, reading 35) underscores this point in her work on cardiovascular disease, a contested terrain of epidemiological research and clinical treatment in which race is differentially defined and deployed by physicians and patients to explain how and why different groups are at different risk for the disease. In her now-classic research on the development of sex hormones as technoscientific objects, Nelly Oudshoorn (1994) uncovered the salience of race, ethnicity, and nation in a story that might have otherwise be understood as solely about gender. Oudshoorn traced how Puerto Rican women's bodies were the sites of astonishing violence at the hands of medical researchers seeking to harness the power of hormone treatments to quickly develop and market fertility drugs and oral contraception in the United States; Puerto Rico offered a haven away from traditional regulations and oversight in the continental United States, as well as a "supply" of poor women of color who could be exploited and coerced to participate in medically dangerous and unethical research. Takeshita (2012) has continued the conversation about race, nation, gender, and contraception technologies in her recent multisite ethnography of intrauterine devices (IUDs), which investigates the differential use, marketing, and state-sponsored deployments of IUDs in the global North and South to manage women's reproductive capacities. Takeshita found that shifting assumptions about race, class, and women's sexuality profoundly influenced research, development, and policies about IUDs, whereby the IUD can be conceptualized as a site on which the global political economy of women's bodies has played out.

The body has long been a key site for theoretical and empirical inquiry in feminist studies of science, technology, and medicine, and intersectional research in STS reflects this commitment accordingly. Early work by Siobhan Somerville (1994) and Rosemarie Garland Thomson (1997) took up the making of bodies as their foci of critical inquiry in queer studies and disability studies, respectively. Somerville, in particular, investigates how White European and American cultural ideas about race, sexuality, and gender shaped the emergent sexology of the late nineteenth and early twentieth centuries, producing interdependent knowledge about the new implicitly White "homosexual" individual and Black women's sexuality. Somerville explains how thoroughly unscientific ideas about Black people's bodies—and Black women's, especially—shaped the scientific constitution of the homosexual, and vice versa. Hirschmann (2012, reading 38) has recently made an impassioned argument for a focus on disability in intersectionality studies, because "disability is so very variant as to strike at the core of human identity" (402). Drawing on Thomson (1997) and Siebers (2008), Hirschmann identifies disability as an encompassing axis of difference from which new imaginings of intersectionality can be theorized. For example, Robert McRuer (2006) has posited "crip theory" as a tool to rethink the relations between bodies, sexuality, and inequality. In a patently intersectional move drawing on the well-known rhetoric of Adrienne Rich's "compulsory heterosexuality" (1980), McRuer elaborates:

> I put forward here a theory of what I call "compulsory able-bodiedness"
> and argue that the system of compulsory able-bodiedness, which in a

sense produces disability, is thoroughly interwoven with the system of compulsory heterosexuality that produces queerness: that, in fact, compulsory heterosexuality is contingent on compulsory able-bodiedness, and vice versa. (2006, 2)

Crip theory becomes, therefore, an analytic lens through which to dissect the mutually beneficial relationship between heterosexism and ableism.

Finally, critical studies of health and illness, including health disparities, public health, and theoretical work on the constitution of "health" as cultural value and resource, have offered increasingly robust inquiry into intersectionality (Shim 2010). Steven Epstein's (2007) important book *Inclusion: The Politics of Difference in Medical Research* pushes back against the notion that the incorporation of racial, ethnic, and sexual minorities as study participants in scientific research has or will automatically produce better, equitable science. His research resonates with the critiques of superficial versions of multiculturalism lodged elsewhere in this volume (e.g., Melamed 2006, Unit VIII, reading 31), highlighting how diversity alone is no guarantee of more emancipatory or counterhegemonic knowledge production. To the contrary, according to Epstein "inclusion" is perhaps better understood as "incorporation," whereby differences are absorbed and managed by scientific disciplines, institutions, and normative research practices that are designed to highlight or minimize them in the interest of reproducing the status quo. Alondra Nelson's (2011) celebrated work on the Black Panther Party's health activism provides a rich example of creative forms of resistance against medical discrimination and health inequities. Nelson foregrounds an intersectional understanding of health and discrimination in order to accentuate how race was but one among many intersecting forces that shaped activism among the Black Panthers; a single-axis approach to understanding the Black Panthers' goals misses the complexity of that community's experiences of systemic discrimination and their responses to it. In public health, Lynn Weber (Weber 2005; Weber and Parra-Medina 2003), Ruth Zambrana (Zambrana and Dill 2005), and Lisa Bowleg (2012) have been leaders of the articulation of methods with which to explore health disparities between communities that are vulnerable to health discrimination and inequity along multiple dimensions, including US Latinas. And Sonja Mackenzie's (2013) book on the AIDS crisis among the Black population in the United States charts an intersectional critique to expose how structural inequalities (poverty, racism, heterosexism) do more than *reflect* health disparities; to the contrary, Mackenzie asserts, health disparities (e.g., the disproportionate spread of HIV among Blacks in the United States), social identities, and structural oppressions are caught up in an interwoven process of making and remaking each other.

In domains as varied as reproductive health; psychotherapy; environmental justice; women and racial minorities' participation in science, technology, engineering, and mathematics (STEM) professions; pharmaceuticals; science journalism; sexual dysfunction; clinical trials; and countless others, an STS lens sensitized to intersectional processes is a crucial tool with which to understand and challenge how science is conducted and what is done with it. STS and intersectionality are well suited to a strategic alliance for the reasons outlined above and elaborated by the scholars featured in this unit, but also because critical forms of STS share intersectionality's commitment to activism. STS scholars make important contributions to how science and technology are developed and implemented, and STS scholars frequently serve as consultants for major scientific research projects, government agencies, and even corporations. The knowledge derived from STS research has the capacity to advance science itself, as well as the field of STS. STS's investment in doing better science and fostering better scientific knowledge, practice, and policy speaks to intersectionality's fundamental goal of interventionist politics. Accordingly, the chance to resist harmful science makes intersectional STS a site of great potential to design and implement "laboratories for innovation," as opposed to "gatekeepers for established norms and practices" that maintain and exacerbate systems of inequality (Zambrana and Dill 2009, 276–277).

References and Further Reading

Bowleg, L. 2012. "The Problem with the Phrase 'Women and Minorities': Intersectionality, an Important Theoretical Framework for Public Health." *American Journal of Public Health* 102: 1267–1273.

Bridges, K. M. 2011. *Reproducing Race: An Ethnography of Pregnancy as a Site of Racialization.* Berkeley: University of California Press.

Daniels, J. 2009. "Rethinking Cyberfeminism(s): Race, Gender and Embodiment." *Women's Studies Quarterly* 37: 101–124.

Epstein, S. 2007. *Inclusion: The Politics of Difference in Medical Research.* Chicago: University of Chicago Press.

Haraway, D. 1985. "A Manifesto for Cyborgs: Science, Technology and Socialist-Feminism in the 1980s." *Socialist Review* 80: 65–107.

Haraway, D. 1997. *Modest_Witness@Second_Millenium: FemaleMan_Meets_OncoMouse.* New York: Routledge.

Hatch, A. R. 2014. "Technoscience, Racism, and the Metabolic Syndrome." In *The Routledge Handbook of Science, Technology, and Society,* edited by D. L. Kleinman and K. Moore. New York: Routledge.

Hirschmann, N. J. 2012. "Disability as a New Frontier in Feminist Intersectionality Research." *Politics & Gender* 8: 396–405.

Kennedy, H. 2005. "Subjective Intersections in the Face of the Machine." *European Journal of Women's Studies* 12: 471–487.

Mackenzie, S. 2013. *Structural Intimacies: Sexual Stories in the Black AIDS Epidemic.* New Brunswick, NJ: Rutgers University Press.

Mamo, L. 2007. *Queering Reproduction: Achieving Pregnancy in the Age of Technoscience.* Durham, NC: Duke University Press.

Mamo, L., and J. R. Fishman. 2013. "Why Justice?: Introduction to the Special Issue on Entanglements of Science, Ethics, and Justice." *Science, Technology & Human Values* 38: 159–175.

Mann, E. S. 2013. "Regulating Latina Youth Sexualities." *Gender & Society* 27: 681–703.

McRuer, R. 2006. *Crip Theory: Cultural Signs of Queerness and Disability.* New York: New York University Press.

Mellström, U. 2009. "The Intersection of Gender, Race and Cultural Boundaries, or Why is Computer Science in Malaysia Dominated by Women?" *Social Studies of Science* 39: 885–907.

Minister, M. 2012. "Female, Black, and Able: Representation of Sojourner Truth and Theories of Embodiment." *Disability Studies Quarterly* 32(1).

Nelson, A. 2011. *Body and Soul: The Black Panther Party and the Fight Against Medical Discrimination.* Minneapolis: University of Minnesota Press.

Oudshoorn, N. 1994. *Beyond the Natural Body: An Archaeology of Sex Hormones.* New York: Routledge.

Rich, A. 1980. "Compulsory Heterosexuality and Lesbian Existence." *Signs: The Journal of Women in Culture and Society* 5: 631–660.

Roberts, D. 2011. *Fatal Invention: How Science, Politics, and Big Business Re-create Race in the Twenty-first Century.* New York: New Press.

Roy, D. 2004. "Feminist Theory in Science: Working Toward a Practical Transformation." *Hypatia* 19: 255–279.

Shim, J. K. 2005. "Constructing 'Race' Across the Science-Lay Divide: Racial Formation in the Epidemiology and Experience of Cardiovascular Disease." *Social Studies of Science* 35: 405–436.

Shim, J. K. 2010. "Cultural Health Capital: A Theoretical Approach to Understanding Health Care Interactions and the Dynamics of Unequal Treatment." *Journal of Health and Social Behavior* 51: 1–15.

Shim, J. K. 2014. *Heart-Sick: The Politics of Risk, Inequality, and Heart Disease.* New York: New York University Press.

Siebers, T. 2008. *Disability Theory.* Ann Arbor, MI: University of Michigan Press.

Somerville, S. 1994. "Scientific Racism and the Emergence of the Homosexual Body." *Journal of the History of Sexuality* 5: 243–266.

Takeshita, C. 2012. *The Global Biopolitics of the IUD: How Science Constructs Contraceptive Users and Women's Bodies.* Cambridge, MA: MIT Press.

Thomson, R. G. 1997. *Extraordinary Bodies: Figuring Physical Disability in American Culture and Literature.* New York: Columbia University Press.

Weasel, L. H. 2004. "Feminist Intersections in Science: Race, Gender and Sexuality Through the Microscope." *Hypatia* 19: 183–193.

Weber, L. 2005. "Reconstructing the Landscape of Health Disparities Research: Promoting Dialogue and Collaboration Between Feminist Intersectional and Biomedical Paradigms." In *Gender, Race, Class, and Health: Intersectional Approaches,* edited by A. J. Schulz and L. Mullings, 21–59. San Francisco, CA: Jossey-Bass.

Weber, L., and D. Parra-Medina. 2003. "Intersectionality and Women's Health: Charting a Path to Eliminating Health Disparities." In *Advances in Gender Research: Gender Perspectives on Health and Medicine,* edited by V. Demos and M. T. Segal, 181–230. Emerald Publishing Group.

Zambrana, R. E., and B. T. Dill. 2005. "Disparities in Latina Health: An Intersectional Analysis." In *Gender, Race, Class, and Health: Intersectional Approaches,* edited by A. J. Schulz and L. Mullings, 192–227. San Francisco, CA: Jossey-Bass.

Zambrana, R. E., and B. T. Dill. 2009. "Conclusion: Future Directions in Knowledge Building and Sustaining Institutional Change." In *Emerging Intersections: Race, Class, and Gender in Theory, Policy, and Practice,* edited by B. T. Dill and R. E. Zambrana, 274–290. New Brunswick, NJ: Rutgers University Press.

Siobhan B. Somerville

Siobhan Somerville, whose work was also featured in Unit VII (reading 28), brings her literary criticism lens to the history of science in this landmark essay from the *Journal of the History of Sexuality,* which also served as the foundation for her first book, *Queering the Color-Line* (2000). If the dominant strands of intersectionality research spent the 1990s articulating the methodologies by which the race-class-gender nexus would be unpacked, it was at the periphery of intersectional scholarship where the co-constitution of race, gender, and sexuality was traced and theorized. Somerville's work represents such a watershed moment in the development of the paradigm, because she was ahead of the "mainstream" of both intersectionality and queer theory/LGBT studies, which has been criticized for its unacknowledged-but-persistent fixation on the White gay bourgeois subject.

If the disciplines on which Somerville draws were represented in a Venn diagram, we might imagine history, African American Studies, and English representing three intersecting circles. The content matter of the piece (i.e., object of study), on the other hand, might be the intersecting domains of scientific knowledge, racial formation, and the history of sexuality. Science is the discourse through which the intertwined processes of modern racial formation and sexual orientation become articulated, according to Somerville. Her archival work into the annals of nineteenth- and twentieth-century sexology reveal, however, that the genealogy of scientific racism and the "invention" of the modern category of the homosexual are not a matter of simple filial lineage by which science gives birth to racial categories and deviant sexualities or vice versa. Instead, Somerville finds in the historical record a complex dialogue between culture, history, and science through which contemporary racial prejudices and beliefs about heteropatriarchy and colonialism inflect themselves into scientific knowledge production and amalgamate into new forms: the biogenetically inferior "Negro" body and the clinically pathological (but curable?) homosexual. The brilliance of Somerville's insight, moreover, is that these two new "objects" of science were not created by ways of parsimonious, parallel research programs (i.e., one exploring racial difference, the other investigating differences in sexual behavior), but by way of the nefarious crossroads of racism and heterosexism.

34. Science, Race, and Sexuality*

One of the most important insights developed in the fields of lesbian and gay history and the history of sexuality has been the notion that homosexuality and, by extension, heterosexuality are relatively recent inventions in Western culture, rather than transhistorical or "natural" categories of human beings. As Michel Foucault and other historians of sexuality have argued, although sexual acts between two people of the same sex had been punishable through legal and religious sanctions well before the late nineteenth century, they did not necessarily define individuals as homosexual per se. Only recently, in the late nineteenth century, did a new understanding of sexuality emerge, in which sexual acts and desires became constitutive of identity. Homosexuality as the condition, and therefore identity, of particular bodies is thus a production of that historical moment.

Medical literature, broadly defined to include the writings of physicians, sexologists, and psychiatrists, has been integral to this historical argument. Although medical discourse was by no means the only—nor necessarily the most powerful—site of the emergence of new sexual identities, it does nevertheless offer rich sources for at least partially understanding the complex development of these categories in the late nineteenth and early twentieth centuries. Medical and sexological literature not only became one of the few sites of explicit engagement with questions of sexuality during this period but also held substantial definitional power within a culture that sanctioned science to discover and tell the truth about bodies.

As historians and theorists of sexuality have refined a notion of the late nineteenth-century "invention" of the homosexual, their discussions have drawn primarily upon theories and histories of gender. George Chauncey, in particular, has provided an invaluable discussion of the ways in which paradigms of sexuality shifted according to changing ideologies of gender during this period. He notes a gradual change in medical models of sexual deviance, from a notion of sexual inversion, understood as a reversal of one's sex role, to a model of homosexuality, defined as deviant sexual object choice. These categories and their transformations, argues Chauncey, reflected concurrent shifts

---

* Excerpted from S. Somerville, "Scientific Racism and the Emergence of the Homosexual Body," *Journal of the History of Sexuality* 5(1994): 243–266. Copyright ©1994 by the University of Texas Press. All rights reserved.

in the cultural organization of sex/gender roles and participated in prescribing acceptable behavior, especially within a context of white middle-class gender ideologies.

While gender insubordination offers a powerful explanatory model for the "invention" of homosexuality, ideologies of gender also, of course, shaped and were shaped by dominant constructions of race. Indeed, although it has received little acknowledgment, it is striking that the "invention" of the homosexual occurred at roughly the same time that racial questions were being reformulated, particularly in the United States. This was the moment, for instance, of *Plessy v. Ferguson,* the 1896 U.S. Supreme Court ruling that insisted that "black" and "white" races were "separate but equal." Both a product of and a stimulus to a nationwide and brutal era of racial segregation, this ruling had profound and lasting effects in legitimating an apartheid structure that remained legally sanctioned for over half of the twentieth century. The *Plessy* case distilled in legal form many widespread contemporary fears about race and racial difference at the time. A deluge of "Jim Crow" and antimiscegenation laws, combined with unprecedented levels of racial violence, most visibly manifested in widespread lynching, reflected an aggressive attempt to classify and separate bodies as either "black" or "white."

Is it merely a historical coincidence that the classification of bodies as either "homosexual" or "heterosexual" emerged at the same time that the United States was aggressively policing the imaginary boundary between "black" and "white" bodies? Although some historians of sexuality have included brief acknowledgment of nineteenth-century discourses of racial difference, the particular relationship and potentially mutual effects of discourses of homosexuality and race remain unexplored. This silence around race may be due in part to the relative lack of explicit attention to race in medical and sexological literature of the period. These writers did not self-consciously interrogate race, nor were those whose gender insubordination and sexual transgression brought them under the medical gaze generally identified by race in these accounts. Yet the lack of explicit attention to race in these texts does not mean that it was irrelevant to sexologists' endeavors. Given the upheavals surrounding racial definition during this period, it is reasonable to imagine that these texts were as embedded within contemporary racial ideologies as they were within ideologies of gender.

Take, for instance, the words of Havelock Ellis, whose massive *Studies in the Psychology of Sex* was one of the most important texts of the late nineteenth-century medical and scientific discourse on sexuality. "I regard sex as the central problem of life," began the general preface to the first volume. Justifying such unprecedented boldness toward the study of sex, Ellis explained, "And now that the problem of religion has practically been settled, and that the problem of labour has at least been placed on a practical foundation, the question of sex—*with the racial questions that rest on it*—stands before the coming generations as the chief problem for solution." Despite Ellis's oddly breezy dismissal of the problems of labor and religion, which were far from settled at the time, this passage points suggestively to a link between sexual and racial anxieties. Yet what exactly did Ellis mean by "racial questions"? More significantly, what was his sense of the relationship between racial questions and the question of "sex"? Although Ellis himself left these issues unresolved, his elliptical declaration nevertheless suggested that a discourse of race—however elusively—somehow hovered around or within the study of sexuality.

I suggest that the structures and methodologies that drove dominant ideologies of race also fueled the pursuit of scientific knowledge about the homosexual body: both sympathetic and hostile accounts of homosexuality were steeped in assumptions that had driven previous scientific studies of race. My aim is not to replace a focus on gender and sexuality with that of race but, rather, to understand how discourses of race and gender buttressed one another, often competing, often overlapping, in shaping emerging models of homosexuality.

Ellis's *Sexual Inversion,* the first volume of *Studies in the Psychology of Sex* to be published, became a definitive text in late nineteenth-century investigations of homosexuality. Despite the series' titular focus on the psychology of sex, *Sexual Inversion* was a hybrid text, poised in methodology between the earlier field of comparative anatomy, with its procedures of bodily measurement, and the nascent techniques of psychology, with its focus on mental development. In *Sexual Inversion* Ellis hoped to provide scientific authority for the position that homosexuality should be considered not a crime but, rather, a congenital (and thus involuntary) physiological abnormality.

Like other sexologists, Ellis assumed that the "invert" might be visually distinguishable from the "normal" body through anatomical markers, just as the differences between the sexes had traditionally been mapped upon the body. Yet the study of sexual difference was not the only methodological precedent for the study of the homosexual body. In its assumptions about somatic differences, I suggest, *Sexual Inversion* also drew upon and participated in a history of the scientific investigation of race.

Ideologies of race, of course, shaped and reflected both popular and scientific understandings of gender. As Gilman has argued, "Any attempt to establish that the races were inherently different rested to no little extent on the sexual difference of the black." Although popular racist mythology in the nineteenth-century United States focused on the supposed difference between the size of African-American and white men's genitalia, the male body was not necessarily the primary site of medical inquiry into racial difference. Instead, as a number of medical journals from this period demonstrate, comparative anatomists repeatedly located racial difference through the sexual characteristics of the female body.

In exploring the influence of scientific studies of race on the emerging discourse of sexuality, it is useful to look closely at a study from the genre of comparative anatomy. In 1867, W. H. Flower and James Murie published an "Account of the Dissection of a Bushwoman," which carefully cataloged the various "more perishable soft structures of the body" of a young Bushwoman. They placed their study in a line of inquiry concerning the African woman's body that had begun at least a half-century earlier with French naturalist Georges Cuvier's description of the woman popularly known as the "Hottentot Venus," or Saartje Baartman, who was displayed to European audiences fascinated by her "steatopygia" (protruding buttocks). Significantly, starting with Cuvier, this tradition of comparative anatomy located the boundaries of race through the sexual and reproductive anatomy of the African female body, ignoring altogether the problematic absence of male bodies from their study.

Flower and Murie's account lingered on two specific sites of difference: the "protuberance of the buttocks, so peculiar to the Bushman race" and "the remarkable development of the labia minora," which were "sufficiently well marked to distinguish these parts from those of any ordinary varieties of the human species" (p. 208). The racial difference of the African body, implied Flower and Murie, was located in its literal excess, a specifically sexual excess that placed her body outside the boundaries of the "normal" female. To support their conclusion, Flower and Murie included corroborating "evidence" in the final part of their account. They quoted a secondhand report, "received from a scientific friend residing at the Cape of Good Hope," describing the anatomy of "two pure bred Hottentots, mother and daughter." This account also focused on the women's genitalia, which they referred to as "appendages." Although their account ostensibly foregrounded boundaries of race, their portrayal of the sexual characteristics of the Bushwoman betrayed Flower and Murie's anxieties about gender boundaries. The characteristics singled out as "peculiar" to this race, the (double) "appendages," fluttered between genders, at one moment masculine, at the next moment exaggeratedly feminine. Flower and Murie constructed the site of *racial* difference by marking the sexual and reproductive anatomy of the African woman as "peculiar"; in their characterization, sexual ambiguity delineated the boundaries of race.

The techniques and logic of late nineteenth-century sexologists, who also routinely included physical examinations in their accounts, reproduce the methodologies employed by comparative anatomists like Flower and Murie. Many of the case histories included in Krafft-Ebing's *Psychopathia Sexualis,* for instance, included a paragraph detailing any anatomical peculiarities of the body in question. Although Krafft-Ebing could not draw any conclusions about somatic indicators of "abnormal" sexuality, physical examinations remained a staple of the genre. In Ellis's *Sexual Inversion,* case studies often focused more intensely on the bodies of female "inverts" than those of their male counterparts. Although the specific sites of anatomical inspection (hymen, clitoris, labia, vagina) differed, the underlying theory remained constant: women's genitalia and reproductive anatomy held a valuable and presumably visual key to ranking bodies according to norms of sexuality.

Sexologists reproduced not only the methodologies of the comparative anatomy of races, but also its iconography. One of the most consistent medical characterizations of the anatomy of both African-American women and lesbians was the myth of an unusually large clitoris. The case histories in Ellis's *Sexual Inversion* differed markedly according to gender in the amount and degree of attention given to the examination of anatomical details. "As regards the sexual organs it seems possible," Ellis wrote, "so far as my observations go, to speak more definitely of inverted women than of inverted men" (p. 256). Ellis justified his greater scrutiny of women's bodies in part by invoking the ambiguity surrounding women's sexuality in general: "we are accustomed to a much greater familiarity and intimacy between women than between men, and we are less apt to suspect the existence of any abnormal passion" (p. 204). To Ellis, the seemingly imperceptible differences between normal and abnormal intimacies between women called for greater scrutiny into the subtleties of their anatomy. He included the following detailed account as potential evidence for understanding the fine line between the lesbian and the "normal" woman:

> *Sexual Organs.*—(a) Internal: Uterus and ovaries appear normal. (b) External: Small clitoris, with this irregularity, that the lower folds of the labia minora, instead of uniting one with the other and forming the frenum, are extended upward along the sides of the clitoris, while the upper folds are poorly developed, furnishing the clitoris with a scant hood. The labia majora depart from normal conformation in being fuller in their posterior half than in their anterior part, so that when the subject is in the supine position they sag, as it were, presenting a slight resemblance to fleshy sacs, but in substance and structure they feel normal. [P. 136]

This extraordinary taxonomy, performed for Ellis by an unnamed "obstetric physician of high standing," echoed earlier anatomical catalogs of African women. The exacting eye (and hand) of the investigating physician highlighted every possible detail as meaningful evidence. Through the triple repetition of "normal" and the use of evaluative language like "irregularity" and "poorly developed," the physician reinforced his position of judgment. Without providing criteria for what constituted "normal" anatomy, the physician simply knew irregularity by sight and touch. Moreover, his characterization of what he perceived as abnormal echoed the anxious account by Flower and Murie. Although the description of the clitoris in this account is a notable exception to the tendency to exaggerate its size, the account nevertheless scrutinized another site of genital excess. The "fleshy sacs" of this woman, like the "appendages" fetishized in the earlier account, invoked the anatomy of a phantom male body inhabiting the lesbian's anatomical features.

Clearly, anxieties about gender shaped both Ellis's and Flower and Murie's taxonomies of the lesbian and the African woman. Yet their preoccupation with gender cannot be understood as separate from the larger context of scientific assumptions during this period, which one historian has characterized as "the full triumph of Darwinism in American thought." Gender, in fact, was crucial to Darwinist ideas. One of the basic assumptions within the Darwinian model was the belief that, as organisms evolved through a process of natural selection, they also showed greater signs of differentiation between the (two) sexes. Following this logic, various writers used sexual characteristics as indicators of evolutionary progress toward civilization. In characterizing either lesbians' or African-American women's bodies as less sexually differentiated than the norm (always posited as white heterosexual women's bodies), anatomists and sexologists drew upon notions of natural selection to dismiss these bodies as anomalous "throwbacks" within a scheme of cultural and anatomical progress.

Although scientific and medical models of both race and sexuality held enormous definitional power at the turn of the century, they were variously and complexly incorporated, revised, resisted, or ignored both by the individuals they sought to categorize and within the larger cultural imagination. My speculations are intended to raise questions and to point toward possibilities for further historical and theoretical work. How, for instance, were analogies between race and sexual orientation deployed or not within popular cultural discourses? In religious discourses? In legal discourses? What were the material effects of their convergence or divergence? How have these analogies been used to organize bodies in other historical moments, and, most urgently, in our own?

In the last few years alone, for example, there has been a proliferation of "speaking perverts"—in political demonstrations, television, magazines, courts, newspapers, and classrooms. Despite the unprecedented opportunities for lesbian, gay, bisexual, and queer speech, however, recent scientific research into sexuality has reflected a determination to discover a biological key to the origins of homosexuality. Highly publicized new studies have purported to locate indicators of sexual orientation in discrete niches of the human body, ranging from a particular gene on the X chromosome to the hypothalamus, a segment of the brain. In an updated and more technologically sophisticated form, comparative anatomy is being granted a peculiar cultural authority in the study of sexuality.

These studies, of course, have not gone uncontested, arriving as they have within a moment characterized not only by the development of social constructionist theories of sexuality but also, in the face of AIDS, by a profound and aching skepticism toward prevailing scientific methods and institutions. At the same time, some see political efficacy in these new scientific studies, arguing that gay men and lesbians might gain access to greater rights if sexual orientation could be proven an immutable biological difference. Such arguments make an analogy, whether explicit or unspoken, to precedents of understanding race as immutable difference. Reverberating through these arguments are echoes of late nineteenth- and early twentieth-century medical models of sexuality and race, whose earlier interdependence suggests a need to understand the complex relationships between constructions of race and sexuality during our own very different historical moment. How does the current effort to rebiologize sexual orientation and to invoke the vocabulary of immutable difference reflect or influence existing cultural anxieties and desires about racialized bodies? To what extent does the political deployment of these new scientific "facts" about sexuality depend upon reinscribing biologized racial categories? These questions, as I have tried to show for an earlier period, require a shift in the attention and practices of queer reading and lesbian and gay studies, one that locates questions of race as inextricable from the study of sexuality, rather than a part of our peripheral vision.

Janet K. Shim

Janet K. Shim is an associate professor at University of California, San Francisco's School of Nursing, where she also earned her PhD in the sociology of medicine. Shim is a leading theorist of "biomedicalization," the socio-historical processes that describe how biomedical science and clinical practice have been transformed since the late 1980s by advanced technologies, globalization, and unregulated capitalism. Her book, *Heart-Sick: The Politics of Risk, Inequality, and Heart Disease* (2014), expands upon her findings in this essay, which explains some key discoveries of an expansive ethnography in which she studied the experiences of both patients who have cardiovascular disease (CVD) and the physicians who treat—and study—them. She uncovered meaningful differences between how patients who have CVD conceptualize their risk factors and the "expert" knowledge produced and disseminated by epidemiologists who research and calculate that same risk. The intersectionality she explains here is organized by the dimensions of race, ethnicity, class, and gender; her nonexpert informants—the actual people living with CVD—understand their risk in terms of life history and structural oppressions, which epidemiologists routinely attribute to "cultural" differences. Race and risk are contested terrains, Shim explains, and while patients and physicians consistently agree that race and ethnicity are mostly inadequate categories by which to capture the complex dynamics of race and health, the patients in her study are the ones who actively promote alternative understandings of risk even as epidemiology ritualistically reifies racial categories.

Those readers interested in methods should pay careful attention to Shim's approach here, which synthesizes symbolic interactionism and intersectionality. Symbolic interactionists use rich, narrative description and in-depth qualitative inquiry (as opposed to quantitative analysis) to observe where meaning-making is happening in a given research situation, which in this case is CVD. The critical advantage of a symbolic interactionist approach in terms of intersectionality is that symbolic interactionism allows the categories under investigation (e.g., race, class, gender) to "emerge" or be defined by the participants—not by the researcher's assumptions or the existing research. Ideally, this means that the theory or explanation derived from a research study comes from the ground up, rather than from the top down. When trying to revisit what we *think we know* about an under-explored population or a social problem that social scientists believe to be a closed and shut case, symbolic interactionism is a useful frame by which to catalyze new conversations and novel understandings. Shim provides an efficacious model here for how to embark upon a symbolic interactionist study while foregrounding intersectional concerns.

35. Race and Risk Across the Science-Lay Divide*

The persistence of racial inequalities in cardiovascular disease (CVD) has increasingly engaged the concern of the public health and biomedical communities, compelling debates about the nature of "race" and its role in cardiovascular health. In this context, cardiovascular epidemiology has emerged as an essential tool for understanding the determinants, risk factors, and distribution of CVD across populations.

Because of the authority accorded to epidemiology as a scientific discipline,

---

* Excerpted from J. K. Shim, "Constructing 'Race' Across the Science-Lay Divide: Racial Formation in the Epidemiology and Experience of Cardiovascular Disease," *Social Studies of Science* 35(2005): 405–436. Copyright © 2005 by SAGE Publications. Reprinted by permission of SAGE.

epidemiological conceptualizations of race and its health effects have the capacity to shape what we believe to be true about individuals bearing such differences. Through its increasing relevance in health policies and disease prevention, and their subsequent effects on institutions, behaviors, and awareness, epidemiological interpretations of race carry the potential to influence individuals' experience of racial difference. As such, it is argued that epidemiology functions as a racial project (Omi & Winant, 1994), a key contemporary site of racial formation, and an active participant in the construction of biomedical "difference" and its social organization (Shim, 2000). But at the same time, alongside epidemiological classifications exist people's own understandings of the ways their race (as well as their class and gender) does or does not influence their health. Therefore, all individuals—experts and otherwise—participate in the construction of categories of difference, and can potentially bring about significant changes in scientific frameworks and practices. As ideologies of biomedicine and health increasingly implicate practices of everyday life, it is critical to examine how epidemiological and lay knowledges both participate in shaping how we understand the connections between race and health.

In this paper, I offer a detailed analysis of the complex ways in which "race" is mobilized and invested with multiple meanings in epidemiologists' scientific accounts and people of color's lay accounts of CVD. My analysis portrays a contested terrain, marked by some accord but, more often, by deep divides between epidemiologists and lay people regarding the credible measurement and meaningful consequences of race for health, risk, and disease. Cardiovascular epidemiologists and people living with CVD agree that the conventional racial and ethnic categories used in epidemiology and in everyday life are mostly inadequate to capture the complex meanings of race and in particular, its implications for cardiovascular health. Yet despite this inadequacy, my research indicates that such racial categories are almost ritualistically included in epidemiological research. I find that there are wide disagreements over how race affects cardiovascular risk between these two participant groups: scientists tend to attribute racial disparities to cultural differences, while those living with CVD forefront the structural and relational dynamics of race in making sense of their risks.

By far the construction of race most routinely invoked by epidemiologists is that of cultural difference: researchers repeatedly refer to differences of a "cultural" or "ethnic" nature, ones they perceive to be related to the customary beliefs, norms, and practices of a racially or ethnically defined social group. In cultural explanations and interpretations of race, there are multiple nuances to the kinds of claims being made. There is an understanding that race can be equated or linked to culture, and that the primary reason for the significance of race in cardiovascular health is differential cultural behaviors and beliefs. For example, one epidemiologist notes: "Race/ethnicity . . . means their culture, their background, their thinking process, how they make decisions. And it's not just diet, not just genetic. It's environmental." Another researcher concurs: "You have the genetics, but far more important is the shared environmental factors that boil down to cultural habits of how they eat, whether they exercise, those kinds of things."

In these ways, racial differences in cardiovascular risk and disease are viewed and constructed through the prism of culture, and imbued with causal reasoning that refers to "ethnic" customs and ways of life. As a result, race is seen to be a methodologically legitimate, though imperfect, proxy for cultural differences that are hypothesized to be significant for heart disease, through their shaping of health-related behaviors and beliefs. In so doing, epidemiologists often assume that such practices can be simply "read off" an individual's or group's racial identification that is, that culture is based *in* race. Even those epidemiologists who acknowledge the possibility of such erroneous extrapolation still work from the assumption that race and ethnicity at the moment are significant because they correspond in some systematic way to "cultural" behaviors. In marked contrast to the prevalence of the cultural prism in epidemiology, epidemiologists very infrequently invoke structural dynamics, such as discrimination and segregation, as possible sources of racial inequalities in CVD.

In contrast, structural constructions of race abound in the narratives of those living with CVD. That is, lay participants in this study are far more likely to attribute the cardiovascular effects of race to numerous interactional experiences and structural dynamics that can be understood as racial formation processes. Omi & Winant (1994: 55) define racial formation as "the sociohistorical process by which racial categories are created, inhabited, transformed, and destroyed". Racial formation occurs through linkages "between the discursive and representational means in which race is identified and signified on the one hand, and the institutional and organizational forms in which it is routinized and standardized on the other" (1994: 60). A vast web of "racial projects" do the work of making these connections between structure and representation. Racial formation, as the outcome or synthesis of the interaction of racial projects, is thus a matter of both cultural representation and social structure, both macro-level social processes and micro-level interactions, occurring in the constant mediation between what race means and the consequences of such meanings for everyday experience and social structures.

Most of the lay participants in this study frequently articulate how, in multiple sites and facets of their lives, their racialization as members of particular racial groups structures and orders their everyday experiences and conditions of life, which, in turn, have consequences for their health. While their constructions of race are highly variable, expansive, and even contradictory and paradoxical, participants with CVD tend to invoke social forces and experiences as members of racially differentiated groups when talking about their cardiovascular risks.

First, lay participants describe a pervasive, oppressive sense of double consciousness (DuBois, 1989 [1903]) as contributing to their cardiovascular risk. For example, as noted earlier, Rudolfo describes an inescapable sense of otherness where he feels forced to see himself as others see him, as black, as defined by his skin color, even though this is not the way that he sees himself. He relates how this double-consciousness "limit[s] and proscribe[s]" his interactions with others. When I ask him later in the interview whether his life experiences contribute in any way to his cardiovascular health, he returns to this sense of racialized otherness and replies, "Yes, I think it has, because it's conditioned everything that I am, unfortunately . . . I can certainly say it has affected [me] because these things stress me out. . . . It's really difficult. . . . It's affected everything. . . . You can't relax. . . . You always have to have a mask." He adds,

> If you know the role that your emotions play on your physical being, then you know that your emotions have been negatively affected. . . . Your emotions are negatively affected *day in and day out* by the fact that you are black, and not a single day goes by that you're not reminded of this . . . So, yes, everything is affected. My health is generally affected by the fact that I'm black.

Thus, Rudolfo draws causal connections between the burden of this racialization, which he experiences as unavoidable and pervasive, and his heart disease.

Many other lay participants describe similar, deep conflicts between their desire to fight back and resist such treatment, their need to survive, and the difficult compromises they had to make. Carmen, for example, identifies as a Latina and was diagnosed with high blood pressure 15 years ago, at the age of 44 years. When I ask her about her understanding of why she developed hypertension, she relates that her physicians have told her it is directly associated with her weight and sedentary lifestyle. But in her mind, she attributes her condition to "the stress that I feel in my life", triggered by her health conditions, her problematic relationship with her doctors, her job, and significantly, from a lifetime of living as a racialized woman. She relates how contemporary racism, particularly in its more covert and slippery forms, affects her:

> You always get that at certain times when people say, "Well, you know, you're Latina. That's how you would think". . . . I usually try to take comments like that or attitudes like that with a grain of salt and say, "Well, you know, I'm not going to let that bother me. Why should I?" . . .

Other times, you want to say something, and sometimes you're able to and other times you're not. . . . But my sense is that if I let it bother me too much, it's going to be harmful to me, and it's not going to change the attitude of the person who's doing it. . . . And it's very subtle. It's not a blatant thing . . . But it's going to happen. It happens every day and it's going to continue to happen.

When I ask her again whether she sees a connection between such experiences and her hypertension, Carmen reiterates,

Yes I do . . . I think just the ways that it's made me think, to a certain extent, about myself, and even though I'm okay with who I am—you know, a Latina of mixed descent or mixed blood—when you're to a certain extent bombarded with a lot of negative attitudes and perceptions, it's going to tend to weigh on you to a certain extent. . . . I get to a point where I get very depressed and very frustrated.

Another set of factors to which many lay participants attribute their heart disease include the health impacts of racial formation processes that shape an array of economic and environmental conditions of life.

In particular, working-class women of color describe interlocking dynamics of race, class, and gender that stratified their educational opportunities, and that structure a racially and sex-segregated labor market. Those employment opportunities most readily available to them were restricted to low-paying jobs, with little potential for advancement, minimal job stability, and little power over the conditions of their hours, pace of work, or the nature of the work process. For instance: Juanita was a data-entry worker; Bonnie had been a seamstress; Mercedes had worked as a seamstress and had cleaned offices; Carmen is an office assistant providing secretarial services for six others; Yolanda just started working part-time as a hotel desk clerk; and Mabel had worked as a housekeeper, home health aide, a cannery worker, and in food service.

Four of these six women draw causal connections between their heart disease and their economic conditions of life as shaped by racial dynamics. Mabel, for example, is a Mexican American woman with severe hypertension, and she describes how hiring practices produced an occupational hierarchy that reflected racial hierarchy.

Mabel speculates that if she had not been Mexican American, she would have had "different kinds of jobs and easier jobs, and a more calm life than I was having. In those days there, you couldn't even work in an office if you were Latin or Black." The consequence of these social structural dynamics for Mabel was a life of working long hours in unskilled, low-paying, and physically taxing jobs. This, combined with single parenthood, is what she believes developed me for having high blood pressure . . . It was hard to take [the kids to the] babysitter, and then going to work, and then everything was rush, rush to me . . . I started getting sick, you know. All this running around, all this worrying about money, money, money. . . . All that I guess brought it up on me . . . If you have a hard life, it stays on you. . . . That's also a lot of anxiety, too . . . working in those factories . . . Make sure that you get up in the morning, take your kids to the babysitter, wait for the bus to get there in time to work. . . . You had to punch in for work, and if you're not there in time, two or three times, they fire you. So, all of this is too much tension for one person that's raising her kids.

The personal narratives of lay participants such as Mabel highlight how social processes and forces of racism and racialization, classism, and sexism intersect to define and structure the terms under which people of different classes, races, and sexes are made to do different kinds of work. These respondents argue that their limited employment options, shaped by stratified access to educational and economic opportunities, served to determine the conditions under which they worked and developed heart disease.

Second, in responding to my queries about the connections between their personal circumstances and their developing heart disease, many lay participants articulate how race structures their environmental contexts in ways that not only impose cardiovascular health risks, but also limit avenues for responding to and modifying such risks. For example, some speak about the impracticality of regular exercise in neighborhoods they deem unsafe, and amidst lives with far more pressing and immediate problems than the risks of a sedentary lifestyle. David offers a picture of some other environmentally mediated effects of race on health:

Early in life, when I started knowing myself, I had to accept an oppressive type of environment, and that strengthens you. But it also weakens you.

And I don't think it's speculative. I think it's actually a fact . . . if you're a product of an oppressed environment, quite naturally you're going to have some health problems that another group of people would not necessarily have in an environment that was entirely different. When I say the environment, that takes it in as a whole. You have to take in the school system, you have to take in the housing, the availability of health facilities . . . you have to take all of these and put them into that pot. You just can't extract one. You have to put them all in there, and then you would see that if that environment is oppressed, the people in that environment are going to come out with some problems, not only emotionally, mentally, social problems, but they're going to come out with a multiplicity of health problems.

Here, David makes an emphatic claim to authority, using his biographical and embodied knowledge as the basis for his expertise in the health effects of racism. He also articulates an understanding of the interlocking effects of race: it deeply affects multiple aspects of one's lived experience, and any one dynamic cannot be separated or dissected from others. Racial meanings and racialized discourses and practices have constructed in contemporary life social, economic, political, and cultural infrastructures that synergistically sustain and reproduce one another.

Finally, many of the lay participants, including some of those quoted earlier, allude to the social-psychological toll imposed by the racialization of economic outcomes and opportunities. Diane, for example, talks about the connections between the chronic exposure to racism and cardiovascular risk behaviors:

> I think that what happens is that when those things happen to you on a daily basis, you naturally do things that are comfortable and reaffirming to you. So, you go home and you eat food that you know is bad, but it tastes good. It makes you feel good. You go home and you may drink because it makes you feel good. . . . You may need to relax and so you're smoking. I think that because of those things, you resort to things that make you feel comfortable; even if they had bad outcomes associated, you still do it. . . . My husband used to smoke. When he would get really upset, the first thing he would do was smoke. My mom when she's upset, she comes home and cooks a huge dinner. . . . A lot of people do that. They do things that are comfortable. . . . When you have a lot of things in your life that hurt you, you have a tendency to do it more often. . . . And I think that's where the direct correlation is.

Here, Diane, like several others I interviewed, attributes heart disease to the psychic and emotional experience of a racialized economic hierarchy and the subsequent promotion of unhealthy behaviors such as smoking, drinking, and comfort-eating as coping strategies.

The varied means through which race is signified and made meaningful, and their interactional and institutional consequences for the social worlds of these respondents with CVD, in turn exact costs to their health. It is these linkages that lay participants draw between their experiences as racial "others" and their heart disease that I contend illustrate how multiple processes and experiences of racial formation can be conceptualized as structural causes of CVD.

In this light, the relative silence on structural causes and the popularity of cultural constructions of racial inequalities on the part of epidemiologists appear very problematic indeed, standing in such sharp contrast to the experiences of those who live with CVD. At the least, the ritualized inclusion of race as a taken-for-granted and unexamined variable, and the continued study of cultural differences in CVD risk, neglect the role of race in organizing social relations of power and defer work on the effects of racial formation and structural racism on health. At the worst, such practices operate to displace and replace structural understandings of race with individualistic ones that ignore the ways in which relations of power are embedded within the social organization of race.

Jessie Daniels

Sociologist Jessie Daniels turns our attention here to the emergent realm of "cyberfeminisms," which the following essay attempts to define while exploring debates and discrepancies in the field. Daniels is an associate professor of urban public health at Hunter College and the Graduate Center of the City University of New York (CUNY) whose publications include *White Lies* (1997) and *Cyber Racism* (2009), both of which explore the intersectional dynamics of White supremacist movements; she is also a prolific blogger and public intellectual whose website *Racism Review* (with sociologist Joe Feagin) is a key resource for antiracist dialogue and debate. In her work on cyberfeminism, Daniels explores the somewhat opposing impulses in cyberfeminist literatures. First, on the one hand, online communities may offer a space to "experience the absence of the body" and therefore the oppressive restrictions of race, gender, and other embodied forms of difference. On the other hand, online social interactions do not occur in an alternate reality per se; cyberspace is a mediated reality in which real people—with races, gender, and experiences living in highly racialized and gendered societies—interact with one another. Her discussion of pro-ana (shorthand for "pro-anorexia") and community-based transgender websites highlights the contradictions inherent to cyberfeminist discourses. Daniels does not suggest, however, that we throw our hands up and abandon cyberspace as a site for innovative, emancipatory feminist theorizing and new social movements. She does, though, encourage more substantive engagement with the ways in which race, gender, and sexuality are inescapable dimensions of social life. Inescapable does not equal "oppressive" or "inflexible," but she does insist that, "The fact that race matters online, as it does offline, counters the oft-repeated assertion that cyberspace is a disembodied realm where gendered and racialized bodies can be left behind." The Internet, by Daniels's account, is not sociologically exceptional: it is a site of subversion and reinforcement, just like everyday life.

36. Cyberfeminisms: Race, Gender, and Embodiment*

Cyberfeminism is neither a single theory nor a feminist movement with a clearly articulated political agenda. Rather, "cyberfeminism" refers to a range of theories, debates, and practices about the relationship between gender and digital culture, so it is perhaps more accurate to refer to the plural, "cyberfeminism(s)." Within and among cyberfeminism(s) there are a number of distinct theoretical and political stances in relation to Internet technology and gender as well as a noticeable ambivalence about a unified feminist political project. Further, some distinguish between the "old" cyberfeminism, characterized by a utopian vision of a postcorporeal woman corrupting patriarchy, and a "new" cyberfeminism, which is more about "confronting the top-down from the bottom-up" (Fernandez, Wilding, and Wright, 2003, 22–23). Thus, any attempt to write about cyberfeminism as if it were a monolith inevitably results in a narrative that is inaccurately totalizing. However, what provides common ground among these variants of cyberfeminism(s) is the sustained focus on gender and digital technologies and on cyberfeminist practices.

The putative invisibility online and the "decoupling identity from any analogical relation to the visible body" (Hansen 2006, 145) to escape race and gender visibility rests on an assumption of an exclusively text-based online world that belies the reality of digital video and photographic technologies, such as webcams (and image-sharing sites, among them Flickr and YouTube), which make images of bodies a quotidian part of the gendered, and racialized, online world. Rather than a libertarian utopia of disembodiment, cyberspace must be considered an environment in which "definitions of situation, body, and identity are both contested and are influenced by power relations" (Pitts 2004, 53–54). The allure of disembodiment for many cyberfeminists alongside the valorization of self-identified women and girls' engagement with Internet technologies suggests an inherent contradiction within cyberfeminism.

The emergence of pro-ana, a shortened term for "pro-anorexia," sites suggests that some (mostly young, predominantly white) women form online communities in order to offer each other nonjudgmental support in finding strategies and tactics for disordered eating behaviors, most often diagnosed as anorexia nervosa or bulimia. These young women both resist and embrace such diagnoses for their behavior. As a young woman quoted in research by

---

* Excerpted from J. Daniels, "Rethinking Cyberfeminism(s): Race, Gender, and Embodiment," *WSQ: Women's Studies Quarterly* 37 (Spring–Summer 2009). Copyright © 2009 by the Feminist Press at the City University of New York. Used by permission of the publishers, www .feministpress.org. All rights reserved.

Fox, Ward, and O'Rourke put it, "Personally, I feel that if a person is starving themselves or throwing up *solely* because of the desire to look like kate moss, devon aoki (hehe . . . my favorite model), gisele, etc . . . they don't have all the criteria to be considered anorexic. Anorexia is defined as a mental disease . . . the ability to play mind-games with yourself relating to anything food or exercise" (2005, 955).

This redefinition of anorexia as "the ability to play mind-games" around food or exercise refigures the usually disabling rhetoric of eating disorders into one of strength and "ability" that does not include everyone who is "starving themselves." The mention of this young woman's "favorite model" is revealing here because famous models and celebrities are part of the cultural products that young women engaged in pro-ana seek out for "thinspiration" (954). The young girls of the pro-ana communities turn to the Internet to support their bodily rituals of diet, exercise, and purging in the relative "safety" of being with their pro-ana peers and away from the judgments of others (mostly parents). Young women who identify as pro-ana report that the bodily rituals associated with this community provide participants with a sense of "control over" their bodies. And increasingly, these images of "thinspiration" appear on YouTube, the video-sharing site, as well as on personal websites. Whatever one thinks of these practices, the young girls involved with pro-ana sites are engaging with Internet technologies in ways that are both motivated by and confirm (extremely thin) embodiment. While those participating in pro-ana sites may appear to be ambivalent about their own embodiment, the fact is that they are not going online to avoid corporeality but rather to engage with others *about* their bodies via text and image in ways that make them feel in control of those bodies.

A second illustration of the way the Internet can be a site for bodily transformation is that of community-based transgendered websites, such as Gender Sanity (http://www.gendersanity.com), and personal webpages, such as Christine Beatty's WebHome (http://www.glamazon.net). These sites, along with Listservs and websites established by trans or trans-friendly physicians, such as TransGender Care (http://www.transgendercare.com), provide information about how to transform the body in specifically gendered ways. The experience of transgendered women, such as Anita, whose pastiche of Internet technologies enables her gender transition, is noteworthy in this context. Many nonheteronormative or queer women, whether they identify as lesbian, bisexual, or transgender, also regard global information technology as an important medium for resisting repressive regimes of gender and sexuality. Combining the metaphors of "tool" and "place," Mary Bryson, in her study of Australian QLBT women's experiences of the Internet, writes: "Internet tools and communities serve a variety of functions that are relevant to, and scaffold, the lives of QLBT women, including . . . interaction with other queer women in a space that is relatively safe" (2004, 249). Like Nouraie-Simone, the women in Bryson's study experience life online as a safe space, an observation that serves to set up an oppositional relationship to life offline ("real" life) as space that is not safe. The Internet provides QLBT women with opportunities to experiment with gender identity and practices, as well as a cultural context within which to learn how to be queer through participation in a subculture. Indeed, the experience of Anita, included in Bryson's research, illustrates this point:

> Anita: I've gotten a lot of information from the tranny hormone list. It was mainly an information sharing thing, and a few other lists along those lines. With the web, I've used transgendered sites for looking up reports of surgeons, photos of surgery, information from the surgeons where they'd posted that stuff up on the Net. Gaining information about hormones is important. I have a fair bit of experience in biochemistry and can read the scientific literature.
>
> Mary: How do you access that information?
>
> Anita: I can get into the MedLine database and that kind of thing. If I want information about any of that stuff, the Net is the first place I go. It's not always easy to find good information though, especially if you are looking for knowledge that is community-based. And if you are going to read the medical articles, you really need to know the jargon and be able to read between the lines. (2004, 246)

Here, Anita describes her use of the Internet to navigate the biomedical sex/gender establishment. She reports getting information from an e-mail Listserv, pursuing further information on particular surgeons, looking for digital photographic evidence of their work, and reading the peer-reviewed medical literature culled from the database MedLine. Both her technique for finding information and her assessment of what she finds demonstrate an example of sophisticated digital fluency. Anita's bricolage strategy combines a number of Internet technologies, including search engines; web-based databases; websites dealing with transgender issues; community-based Listservs; and digital photography of surgical outcomes. Anita's goal in using a patchwork of digital technologies is not to pretend to be another gender online; instead, her aim is to find help in transforming her body *offline* in ways that align with her own sense of gender identity. Anita's piecing together of diverse Internet sources to navigate gender transition suggests that we need a much more nuanced and complex understanding of digital technologies, gender, and feminist politics.

Anita's experience indicates that rather than using the technology to escape embodiment or temporarily "switch" identities online, she and other self-identified women (and men) are actively engaging with digital technologies to more permanently transform their bodies offline. Anita goes online not to experience "the absence of the body" (as Nouraie-Simone does) but to access the information, resources, and technologies that allow her to transform her body into a (differently) gendered body that aligns with her identity. And in ways that are analogous to the pro-ana girls' use of the technology, transgendered women, and men, use digital images as a crucial part of the strategy in gathering reliable information about gender transition.

The allure of disembodiment pointed to by cyberfeminists is understandable, given the significance of racialized embodiment for understanding the lived experience of racism. Yet racialized embodiment and the ways this offline reality is embedded in online worlds is not often remarked upon in the literature about gender online.

In the study of pro-ana online communities by Fox, Ward, and O'Rourke (2005), the authors curiously do not take up racial identity as a point of analysis even when one of the participants explicitly references it: "It started in 8th grade. I had never been really overweight, but I was average—about 115 at 5'3. [T]here was just too much going on in my life . . . mostly, I didn't know who I was maybe I was having a really early mid-life crisis. I'm adopted, and my whole family is white, while I'm Asian. I had/have a lot of issues circling around feelings of abandonment which I partially translated into 'no one loves me . . . not even my real parents' type stuff" (957).

The young girl quoted here indicates that her racial identity and the discordant racial identity of her (adopted) family is a contributing factor in her desire to be involved with pro-ana practices. Yet the authors do not address the issue of racial identity. This is a lost opportunity for an analysis that would further illuminate the connection between gender, race, and online identity by speaking to the compelling research that exists involving gender, "race," and disordered eating.

In contrast, Bryson acknowledges the racial dynamics at work even though in her research her sample of QLBT women includes only one woman of color. The white participants in her study rarely identified racism as a problem of online communities, whereas "the discursive construction of racial identity online was a persistent problem for the Aboriginal participant whose Net experiences were frequently characterized by marginalization, silencing and enforced segregation" (2004, 246). The marginalization, silencing, and enforced segregation that the Aboriginal woman in Bryson's study faces in online spaces is characteristic of what many experience in online communities across lines of difference. Kendall's ethnography on the online community BlueSky is informative on this point. While BlueSky is relatively inclusive, and certainly not "racist" (or "sexist") in any overt way, the inclusiveness is predicated on social structure in which "white middle-class men continue to have the power to include or not to include people whose gender, sexuality or race marks them as other" (Kendall 2000, 272). BlueSky's text-only nature facilitates greater inclusiveness across differences of gender, sexual orientation, and race, yet the predominance of white men simultaneously "limits the inclusiveness to 'others' who can fit themselves into a culture by and for those white men" (272). BlueSky, like the queer online spaces that the QLBT women in Bryson's study seek out and the pro-ana spaces that many young girls find empowering, are predicated on an assumption of whiteness. Unlike either the cyberracism of white supremacists online (Daniels 2009) or the white, masculine desire for community expressed by neoconfederates on Dixie-Net (McPherson 2000), the whiteness that Kendall describes in BlueSky is very much like whiteness in the offline world: an unmarked category that is taken for granted in daily life. Race matters in cyberspace precisely because "computer networks are social networks" (Wellman 2001) and those who spend time online bring their own knowledge, experiences, and values with them when they log on. The fact that race matters online, as it does offline, counters the oft-repeated assertion that cyberspace is a disembodied realm where gendered and racialized bodies can be left behind.

These two examples, the pro-ana and transgendered online communities, shed light on gender, race, and the subversive potential of the Internet. In both instances, self-identified girls and women engage in practices with Internet technologies to manage, transform, and control their physical bodies in ways that both resist and reinforce hierarchies of gender and race. Instead of seeing cyberspace as a place in which to experience the absence of the body, or even a text-only place with no visible representation of the body, these girls and self-identified women use digital technologies in ways that simultaneously bring the body "online" (through digital photos uploaded to the web) and take the digital "offline" (through information gleaned online to transform their embodied selves). Here, digital technologies embedded in everyday life allow for the transformation of corporeal and material lives in ways that both resist and reinforce structures of gender and race. While some cyberfeminists are wildly enthusiastic about the subversive potential of a cyborg future, identity tourism, and disembodiment that is offered by digital technologies, evidence from cyberfeminist practices and empirical research on what people are actually doing online points to a more complicated reality.

Khiara M. Bridges

Khiara Bridges's first book, *Reproducing Race: An Ethnography of Pregnancy as a Site of Racialization* (2011), represents the vanguard of research in social studies of health and medicine. Bridges is an associate professor of law and anthropology at Boston University and holds both a PhD and a JD from Co-lumbia University. Accordingly, she brings the perspective of critical race the-ory from legal studies to her anthropological work on reproductive health and rights. In this excerpt from her book, Bridges introduces us to "Alpha," a hos-pital in New York City with a reputation for serving the city's poorest and most vulnerable populations. The dual figures of the "wily patient" and the "welfare queen" emerge in her ethnography of Alpha, where patients and hospital staff engage in choreographed dance of skepticism and prejudice. "Much like the wily patient," she explains, "the welfare queen is discursively constructed as a marriage of contradictions." Bridges, like Angela Davis in Unit III (reading 10), draws connections between the controlling image of the welfare queen and the twenty-first-century US political economy of race and gender, which continues to proactively disadvantage and disparage Black women without, as she notes, explicitly using racist and sexist terminology. As social construc-tions, the welfare queen and the wily patient are both archetypes that allow for the "easy" categorization of patients while absolving the people doing the categorizing from the racist and sexist ideologies driving these categories. In this sense, Alpha becomes a quintessential site of color-blind racism, which Eduardo Bonilla-Silva, Helen Neville, and many other social scientists have described as the dominant racial paradigm of the contemporary United States. Color-blind racism allows for the enactment of specifically racist behaviors within a social architecture that masks and hides the very racism it facilitates. As Bridges illuminates, the political and economic realities of the patients at Alpha are somewhat irrelevant within the walls of the hospital—intersecting ideologies of race, class, and gender shape their experiences, and the patients find ways to respond to these oppressive structures accordingly.

37. Wily Patients and Welfare Queens[*]

Within Alpha staff folklore exists the wily patient—a health care-seeking subject whose crushing stupidity is matched only by her formidable duplic-ity. Alpha staff tends to perceive as contemporaneous these contradictory characteristics.

At Alpha, pregnant women with appointments to see their prenatal care providers are required to collect and submit urine so its glucose and protein levels can be measured. Subsequent to giving the staff persons working behind the front desk her clinic card (on which is stamped the patient's name, address,

---

* Excerpted from K. M. Bridges, *Reproducing Race: An Ethnography of Pregnancy as a Site of Racialization* (Berkeley: University of California Press, 2011), 202–203, 205–206, 211–213, 226–227.

and insurance provider), appointment slip, and registration receipt, the woman is instructed to take a paper cup and plastic tube and "do your urine." Indeed, one of the first Spanish colloquialisms I learned when I began conducting patient intake was "Haga la orina"—"Make urine." The woman is then allowed entrance behind a secured door that separates the waiting area from the internal labyrinth composed of doctors' and nurses' examination rooms. The pregnant patient is expected to use the internal restrooms to urinate into the cup, pour the urine into the tube, and seal the tube with a rubber stopper. She will usually keep the tube of urine with her until a Patient Care Associate (PCA) calls her to take the urine from her and record her blood pressure and weight.

After being told to "do your urine" at their first two or three prenatal care appointments, most patients realize that they must submit urine at every visit and, as a result, without prompting, take a paper cup and plastic tube for the purpose of collecting urine. However, there are always new patients. These women are often confused when the person conducting their intake points to the stack of cups and piles of tubes on the front desk and simply says, "Do your urine." Consequently, there is the occasional circumstance where a woman so instructed returns to the front desk after using the internal restroom and attempts to hand the person conducting intake an uncovered cup of urine. Instead of understanding such confusion as resulting from a lack of proper instruction, these incidents are largely explained in terms of patient "stupidity."

I witnessed such an attempt one day when I was behind the front desk observing the clinic. Sandra, a PCA who took great pride in her Jamaican heritage and who was sitting beside me, also observed the confused woman's attempt to give Minnie, a Puerto Rican intake worker who had worked in Alpha for over twenty-five years, the cup of urine. She laughed at Minnie, who was contorting her face in disgust, and said:

> These patients do the strangest things. When patients do that to me, I say to them, "What do you want me to do with that? Drink it?" They do the strangest things. You tell them to pee in the cup, they bring back [feces] in the cup. I used to work in the urology clinic and you tell them to pee in the cup, and they come back with semen in the cup. These patients are so stupid. So stupid.

Sandra's comments about the stupidity of Alpha patients are representative of a sentiment shared by many of the ancillary staff, who largely understand the patients seeking care at Alpha to be "stupid" people who frequently manifest their lack of intelligence in "strange" ways. The above example of the confusion generated by a poorly clarified directive to "do your urine," and the willingness of the staff to place it within a larger ideology of patient stupidity, is one of many.

According to the story articulated and accepted by most Alpha ancillary staff, when one finds oneself performing intake work behind the front desk of the Women's Health Clinic (WHC), one must be prepared to defend the clinic against the pilfering of its resources by patients. According to this mythology, although it is deplorable that patients tax the hospital of its resources by their sheer existence as patients—each *one* demanding expensive services the cost of which the hospital can only hope to recover from depleted state and federal coffers—the leeching of the hospital's assets by the patient does not end there. Indeed, patients are not satisfied to merely consume reasonable portions of the public-hospital-as-governmental-largesse. Through their cunning, the patients attempt to steal more time than that allotted to them, more resources than those allocated to them, and more services than those deserved by them. Thus, Alpha intake workers must always be primed to identify patient greed and deception, then act to protect the hospital from exploitation.

The fear of the swindling of clinic resources is manifest in the belief that many obstetrics patients "steal" Medicaid from the hospital. As previously noted, because Alpha, as a public hospital, is obliged to provide medical care to all patients without regard to their ability to pay, all obstetrics patients are encouraged to sign up for Medicaid if they do not already have it. Medicaid coverage means the hospital ultimately will be reimbursed by state and federal governments for the cost of the services it provides pregnant women, as opposed to absorbing the cost of the care itself. Thus, located within the WHC, among the examination rooms, ultrasound scanning rooms, and sites in which to dispose of biological waste, is the finance office, which assists patients in the Medicaid subscription process. The expectation is that once the hospital has successfully aided a woman in her pursuit of Medicaid coverage of her prenatal care expenses, the woman will continue receiving her care at Alpha, allowing the hospital to receive Medicaid money from the government. However, many private hospitals in New York City will accept patients with Medicaid coverage, although (unlike Alpha) they will not assist patients in applying for it. Consequently, there is an articulated worry among Alpha staff that many patients begin prenatal care at Alpha for the sole purpose of enlisting the hospital to help them acquire Medicaid, after which they will take their business (and the government dollars associated with it) to another hospital.

The two characteristics outlined above, stupidity and duplicity, coexist within the mythology of the patient. Although they are contradictory—indeed, if patients are as stupid as staff believe them to be, they would lack the intelligence to decipher the cumbersome and abstruse Alpha bureaucracy well enough to manipulate and abuse it—the Alpha patient nevertheless embodies the paradox. The intersection of these contradictions in the fantasy of the patient produces the "wily patient." Interestingly, the figure of the wily patient bears a striking similarity to another ubiquitous character within political and popular discourse: the figure of the "welfare queen."

Much like the wily patient, the welfare queen is discursively constructed as a marriage of contradictions: She is uneducated, yet informed enough to make lucrative her reproductive capabilities. She is stupid, yet smart enough to shift to the government the costs of maintaining her (luxurious, or at least undeservedly excessive) lifestyle to the tune of billions of dollars a year. Descriptions of the welfare queen abound: "If one takes a serious moment to envisage what the 'typical' welfare recipient looks like, perhaps the image is one of an urban, black teenage mother, who continually has children to increase her benefits and who just lies around all day in public housing waiting for her check to come" (Note 1994, 2019). In other descriptions, the excessiveness of the welfare queen's enjoyment of governmental largesse in the form of cash assistance is underscored: "At worst, the conjured image is one of a gold-clad, cadillac-driving [sic], welfare queen who buys steak and beer with food stamps" (2019).

Former President Ronald Reagan should be credited with introducing the figure of the welfare queen to the nation and ensuring her popularity. Reagan insisted that she was made possible by "extreme" redistributive policies and social programs authored by liberal politicians; moreover, she exemplified everything that was wrong with "big government." The welfare queen was strategically deployed by Reagan. As Smith (2007) writes, the figure of the welfare queen—and the extramarital sex and blatant immorality she implies—enabled Reagan to enlist the support of the religious right in his efforts to reduce the size of social welfare programs. In so doing, he reiterated the perception that "out-of-wedlock births, rather than structural conditions, . . . cause impoverishment among single-mother-headed families" (104). But, what was key in Reagan's construction of the myth of the welfare queen was the sense that the single mother who received public assistance took more than what she needed; moreover, the structure of the programs allowed her to do so. The "typical welfare mother was bent on extracting every last penny from the poverty programs by fraudulently exaggerating the neediness of her household" (106). Hence, we arrive at Reagan's oft-cited, hyperbolic fantasy of the welfare queen: "One of Reagans favorite anecdotes was the story of a Chicago welfare queen with '80 names, 30 addresses, 12 Social Security cards and tax-free income over $150,000'" (Edsall and Edsall 1991, 148).

In the figure of the welfare queen, not only do contradictions intersect, but they appear to exist in an imperfect dialectic. The prospective welfare queen's lack of education and intelligence compel her, in the face of certain death/poverty, to shrewdly capitalize upon her childbearing capabilities, or, rather, she shrewdly produces children, for which the government compensates her. She calculatingly produces more children to increase the size of government payments to her. Her scheme is successful, as she avoids the necessity of selling her labor (i.e., working) while simultaneously enjoying anything from a comfortable to a lavish standard of living. However, her cunning ultimately reveals her stupidity: although she receives a cash subsidy increase for an additional child, the newest child nevertheless effects a reduction in the per capita income of her individual family members. Her stupidity prevents her from realizing the failure of her cunning. And the dialectic continues.

Although the figures of the wily patient and the welfare queen are analogous insofar as both are paradoxical unions of incongruous qualities, an important characteristic distinguishes them: the welfare queen is decidedly raced as Black. "By the 1990s, the image of the welfare queen had fully developed, and visual images in the media routinely displayed her as a black woman" (Onwuachi-Willig 2005, 1971). Meanwhile, the wily patient, capable of being recognized in any patient who presents herself (or himself) to the front desk of the Alpha Women's Health Clinic, appears to be un-raced. That is to say, all patients seeking care or services from Alpha may embody the wily patient without regard to a patient's ascribed race.

But, it is important to keep in mind that the figure of the welfare queen has never been explicitly raced as Black. Rather, the figure allows those who refer to it to gesture toward race—to speak about it—without expressly mentioning race at all. As noted by Marian Wright Edelman, "'[W]elfare' is not a direct signifier for race. Instead, it is but a 'code word' for race" (Note 1994, 2019). In fact, it is possible to conceive of the term "welfare" as a failed euphemism for race. It has failed insofar as euphemisms are generally polite methods of referencing topics perceived to be impolite; yet, there is very little polite in the signifier "welfare" as it is presently understood. I am reminded of my interview with eighteen-year-old Monica, who I initially met when she was pregnant with her first child. At the time of the interview, she was five months pregnant with her second child. After she had apprised me of the breathtakingly massive number of hardships she was experiencing—finishing high school, securing child care and housing, negotiating her own legal troubles, and coercing her intermittently unemployed and incarcerated boyfriend to provide financial assistance for their children—I suggested that her burdens might be reduced somewhat if she applied for and received welfare. She expressed profound disgust at the prospect:

Monica: I really don't want to go there. Welfare is not . . . my mother never had welfare. My sister's on welfare, but she really needs the extra money. But, I don't want to do that. My mother doesn't, so why do I have to?
Khiara: Why don't you like it so much?
Monica: Welfare just sounds so bad. It does.

Khiara: But it helps, though.

Monica: [mouthing the words to herself] Welfare. Welfare. [To me] It don't even
sound right. I don't like it. Old people in the projects maybe. I don't do
that. It would make me go crazy.

For Monica, even the word "welfare" itself did not "sound right." That
is, the things welfare signified were so noxious that they had managed to cor-
rupt the signifier itself. Indeed, there is very little euphemistically polite about
welfare. Irrespective of whether "welfare" was ever intended to be a courte-
ous term of art, very few would disagree that when one speaks of the "welfare
queen," one is speaking of a derided, debased, and *raced* figure.

The implicit racialization of the wily patient reveals that there is a closer
affinity between it and the welfare queen than was previously imagined. As
noted above, the welfare queen is itself a figure that, like the wily patient, is
only implicitly racialized. As noted above, "welfare" is a "code word" for race,
not a synonym. Smugly race-neutral on its face, references to "welfare" autho-
rize debates about whether race is really what is under discussion. Harrison
(1998) makes this point when she notes, "We find ourselves debating whether
current political discourses on . . . welfare reform . . . encode race and reinforce
racial domination . . . " (610). The figure of the welfare queen functions to
disarticulate race, while ironically, simultaneously allowing those who conjure
it to evoke race nonetheless. In this way, the welfare queen appears to be a not-
so-distant relative of the tacitly raced wily patient whose racial Otherness is
mostly unmentioned but constantly suggested. Hence, the wily patient is more
like the welfare queen in racial terms than not, both for its dissimulation of
race and its evocation of it nevertheless.

The similarities shared by the figures of the wily patient and the welfare
queen, in terms of the contradictory characteristics that define them as well
as their common implicit racialization, might not be understood as a mere
fluke. That is, the welfare queen and the wily patient are parallel figures because the latter might be understood as a simple reflection of the former as she
is imagined in the particular social context of a public obstetrics clinic where
the "undeserving" poor are provided with Medicaid to finance their pregnan-
cies. One might even argue that welfare legislation, which generates the welfare apparatus begrudgingly and with a contemporaneous problematization of
those who benefit from it, produces the wily patient insofar as she is, by definition, a potential/possible/likely welfare queen. To take an argument made by
Piccato (2001) in his incisive study of early twentieth-century criminology in
Mexico and adapt it for my own purposes, Temporary Assistance for Needy
Families (TANF) and its coercive, punitive, and reluctantly charitable state
strategies have perpetuated the vilified figure of the welfare queen; moreover,

it has created suspected welfare queens out of poor women. To the extent that the wily patient is marked as poor by her mere presence at a public hospital, she should be considered the embodiment of that suspicion. In other words, the wily patient might be understood as that which is engendered when suspicion of the welfare queen's presence is materialized within the WHC. The point is underscored if one considers that, at Alpha, the wily patient is frequently manifested precisely during her pregnancy. The wily patient's pregnant body is not read as a symbol of infinite possibility, joy, or self-fulfillment—a reading that may only be reserved for the non-poor. Rather, in light of TANF and the condemnation of welfare mothers in political and popular discourse, the (poor) wily patient's pregnancy is realized as the event that makes the welfare queen possible, the condition that makes the entire welfare apparatus necessary.

Nancy J. Hirschmann

Nancy Hirschmann is a professor of political theory at the University of Pennsylvania and a preeminent political scientist who has served as the vice president of the American Political Science Association. Her scholarship has encompassed the areas of the history of political thought, analytic philosophy, and the applications of political theory in public policy, though she is best known for her contributions to the study of women in politics and feminist political theory. Recently, her work has taken a turn to the critical study of another dimension of difference—disability—which is highlighted in the following excerpt from her 2012 essay in the journal *Politics & Gender*.

Though she begins the essay with a crisp declaration, I suggest we take Hirschmann's treatise here quite seriously: Hirschmann is reflecting on decades of feminist scholarship that has ignored the politics of *disability*, "a term that refers exclusively to what society, social conditions, prejudices, biases, and the built environment have produced." Disability studies is not "new," and in many ways that is precisely Hirschmann's point. Scholars at the relative periphery of the social sciences and humanities—even natural and applied sciences!—have been researching and theorizing disability for decades, and yet the feminist mainstream has been painfully slow to incorporate disability into research on social inequalities as anything more than a tokenized gesture or afterthought. Rather than displace gender with disability, Hirschmann makes an impassioned plea here for the substantive, committed incorporation of disability studies into the mainstream of feminist and antiracist work. She reminds us that disability intersects with all dimensions of identity, and that disability is a meaningful axis on which other oppressions are framed and distributed across populations. For example, how might the experiences of a veteran of color with a physical disability who relies on military benefits for health care differ from a deaf child born to affluent parents with private health insurance? And how do the physical and intellectual differences among persons with disabilities affect how we understand racial, ethnic, and gender differences that we might otherwise imagine as manifesting in a disability-free vacuum? In the interest of continuing to innovate intersectional research and politics, we should especially consider Hirschmann's conclusion, in which she argues not for the abandonment or flattening of differences, but for a reckoning with the pervasiveness of difference in human experience. Her provocative move to embrace a focus on "sameness" is politically risky and not easily dismissed; readers may not agree with Hirshmann, but she does compel us to consider the epistemological and political risks of studying inequality exclusively through a logic of difference.

38. Disability Is the New Gender*

Disability is the new gender. I make this claim with trepidation and a sense of irony. Certainly, disability studies today is like women's studies was in the 1970s and 1980s, when feminist scholars had to convince colleagues in "mainstream" political science that gender was something worth attending to, that it was a serious enterprise, and that it should be part of the mainstream. The fields of history and English have been somewhat more welcoming of disability as a valid topic of study, just as these fields preceded political science in realizing that gender was an important category of study. But political science has been slow to catch on.

Feminist and disability theory also share a deep concern about the body and bodily difference. Feminists, of course, have been at the forefront in recognizing the importance of the body. But we tacitly operate from a particular body. We assume certain reproductive capacities, certain body parts, certain capabilities. Philosophers like Nussbaum presuppose a certain kind of "capability" that effectively bars seriously disabled individuals from full membership and participation in relevant communities (Nussbaum 2000; 2006). Lesbian feminism, transgender theory, as well as postmodern theory have challenged feminism on these assumptions to some degree, raising the question of what "woman" means, of who "counts" as a woman, and the potential oppressiveness of the boundaries of identity. But even these feminists have excluded disability from the categories in need of inclusion (Samuels 2002). And feminists have even used disability as a pejorative term to describe what patriarchy has

---

* Excerpted from N. J. Hirschmann, "Disability as a New Frontier in Feminist Intersectionality Research," *Politics & Gender* 8 (2012): 396–405. Reproduced with permission.

done to women, "crippling" our abilities and imaginations (Young 1980). Asch and Fine (1988, 4) maintain that some feminists exclude disabled women from study for fear that they will reinforce stereotypes of women as dependent.

Yet disability theorists maintain that disability is not a disadvantage; it is a difference. We argue that what makes something a disability is not bodily difference itself—not impaired vision, or weak or missing limbs, or cognitive impairments—but rather the social contexts in which they exist. For instance, using a wheelchair does not itself constitute a "disability": rather, the built environment, with its curbs and stairs, disables some bodies from moving freely.

In this view, which disability scholars call the "social model" of disability, disability is a social construction in the most obvious sense: Because of the ways that social relations, the built environment, laws, customs, and practices are structured and organized, certain bodies are disabled, and other bodies are facilitated. Impairment is seen as a natural part of biological life, not "abnormal," and is incorporated into a person's sense of self. *Disability* is thus a term that refers exclusively to what society, social conditions, prejudices, biases, and the built environment have produced. Disability is thus not applicable to the body per se but to the body in a hostile social environment.

The social model of disability has certain shortcomings, of course; some bodily impairments are sources of suffering and frustration, disabling no matter what social context. Furthermore, focusing exclusively on the social ironically obliterates the body from view; we fail to see the suffering caused by physical conditions that cannot be addressed through accommodation. This may be seen to parallel feminist arguments over the relationship between sex and gender; if the body is always already social, then sharp lines between the medical and social models cannot be drawn.

The social model of disability is nevertheless important, and it coheres with insights made by feminists for decades that it is not that women are naturally unable to do things ranging from being professors and chief executive officers to weight lifters and firefighters, but rather that they have been prevented and restrained from doing so by norms, laws, practices, customs, and regulations that "disable" their minds and bodies from achieving whatever they otherwise could, just as stairs "disable" a wheelchair user from entering a building. Feminists have also been at the forefront of understanding the value of difference, arguing that even if women do want to be professors, CEOs, weight lifters and firefighters "just like men," they also, even simultaneously, may want to do those things differently: Being "just like men" is not the goal, any more than the disabled want to be able-bodied.

This is the most difficult idea for most nondisabled people to grasp: "Who would want to be deaf/blind/in a wheelchair/have cerebral palsy?" the thinking goes, "of course such people want to be 'normal.'" But in fact they do not;

multiple studies show that levels of happiness are the same for disabled people as nondisabled people, and the major frustration for the former is the prejudicial attitudes and treatment, the blockages of a hostile built environment, all of which make living in their bodies harder. They are all barriers, constraints, to living their lives as they wish. So they do not want to change their bodies; they want to change these barriers. They want the able-bodied to see these facets of the world *as* barriers and not as inevitable or natural. For instance, the bitter division between the hearing and Deaf communities over the use of cochlear implants, devices which are "hard-wired" into the brain to create sound waves to enable deaf people to "hear," stems from the fact that many Deaf people do not want to hear but wish to preserve Deaf culture and sign language. In fact, they do not consider deafness a disability at all.

This should sound familiar to feminist and queer theorists. For years, being gay was considered a psychological disorder that had to be "cured," and indeed even now hostility toward gays, lesbians, and transgendered individuals operates out of a tacit assumption that such individuals are perverted or abnormal. Feminists, too, are familiar with this line; just two years ago, a well-respected and even adored senior male political theorist asked me, "But don't most women really, fundamentally, want to be men? I mean, women are so subordinated in so many ways, and men have such freedom and power, don't they all really want to be men?" Granted, there was more context to this conversation than I can present here, but this was 2010, not 1940.

Additionally, the ways in which the disabled are shunned and demonized parallels ways in which gays, lesbians, and particularly transgendered people are: Both relate to the anxiety that Butler identified about the "undecidability" of the body, the notion that our bodies are not essentially given to us, nor static and unchanging, but rather in states of flux and uncertainty. Butler upended feminist theory when she challenged the accepted wisdom that "sex" constituted the biological reality of female bodies whereas "gender" constituted human-made social roles, arguing instead, following Foucault, that sex and the sexed body itself are socially constructed and constituted by language and discursive practices (Butler 1990). This way of understanding the sex/gender relationship recast our understanding of the body and introduced the notion that central aspects of identity—gender, sexuality, physical capability—are not fixed but in flux, not in our control.

Understanding the intersections of disability with gender and sexuality can thus yield productive new insights and complicate feminist analysis. But disability is more than simply another "case" to be added to intersectionality, or another intersection with gender and sexuality; considering the intersections of disability with gender and sexuality also raises methodological issues about how intersectionality research is conducted. Often, intersectionality is conceptualized as a crossroads, with single lines of identity crossing at discrete points, a conception that fails to capture the depth of the degree to which various aspects of our identity and situation shape all others. Even the more inclusive conception of a Venn diagram, with overlapping planes, presumes a combination of two separate and distinct identities that happen to overlap.

Disability, however, presents intersectionality within intersectionality. I mean two things by this. On a simple level, if gender and sexuality studies is interdisciplinary because its subjects are themselves already intersectional, and if disability studies is as well, then the intersections between these fields, and between disability and gender and sexuality, are intersections of intersections— perhaps a double-helix imagery rather than a crossroads or Venn diagram.

On a more complicated—and perhaps controversial—level, I would venture to say that disability presents intersectionalities within intersectionality because of the role and meaning of difference. I think feminist approaches to intersectionality have been limited in part because, no matter how much feminists remind ourselves that "women" occupy all racial, ethnic, religious, class, and sexuality positions, one tends not to hold all of that multiplicity in mind when one uses the term—we are sometimes better at calling for intersectionality and proclaiming its importance than we are at actually doing it. It is a feminist truism how "different" women are from one another, and such difference is said to make the category "woman" impossible. And yet we use the term for the most part without confusion, incorporating those differences into our usage. Despite our repeated insistence that women are so different from one another, perhaps we share more than we differ.

Saying this makes me nervous, I admit, threatening a return to the 1980s' essentialism debate and I do not mean to suggest that. Indeed, I find myself surprised at my own position, having argued against the unifying and unitary understanding of categories like "women" or "white" or "lesbian" or "black" (Hirschmann 1992; 2003). And yet such arguments, no matter how politically inspiring they are, increasingly strike me as intellectually empty because of the work being done on disability, an identity category that truly embraces "difference" in a way that feminism could learn from.

For disability is so very variant as to strike at the core of human identity. As Thomson (1997) argues, the disabled are "the ultimate other," far more than women or people of color, because the able-bodied know that they could become disabled at any time, and they fear that possibility. Or as Seibers puts it, "Disability is the other other that helps make otherness imaginable. . . . In no other sphere of existence . . . do people risk waking up one morning having become the persons whom they hated the day before" (2008, 48, 26).

Although we might like to think that awareness of this possibility would make us more sympathetic to persons with disabilities, the evidence runs against it: Why is there still such resistance to the Americans with Disabilities Act (see O'Brien 2004)? Why, as Watson (1998, 161) notes, do "disabled people face a daily barrage of images of themselves as other, as unworthy, as something to be feared"? Why have "ugly laws" existed in our history, forbidding disabled people from appearing in public, even to use the streets (see Schweik 2010)? The disabled body, as Wendell (1996) puts it, is "the rejected body," and it is fear of this body that makes the nondisabled work so hard to cast disabled people as "different" and "other."

Even deeper are the differences of disabled persons from one another; differences so deep as to make it virtually impossible to have a category of "disability." Is the person with cerebral palsy at all like the blind person, the person with a prosthetic leg, the deaf person? In what regard, exactly? The differences among disabilities is so profound as to make the differences between gay and straight women, or black and Latina women, seem small by comparison. Indeed, working in disability theory has made me realize how problematic, perhaps even narcissistically self-indulgent, our feminist debates over difference have been. We are much more similar to one another than are persons with divergent disabilities and impairments; and yet they see themselves as a community. How is this possible?

I believe it is because disability studies enacts intersectionality in a way that feminists have not even begun to: in a deep, profound way that understands that intersections mark not just our differences but our connections, as well. In feminism, we use intersectionality to distinguish ourselves: Intersectionality theory tells me that as a professional, straight, white woman, for instance, I am different from black, working class, lesbian women. Too often there seems no recognition of what we also share.

Disability theory similarly recognizes that the struggles that I encounter in dealing with my body are different from those encountered by a blind person, a person with postpolio syndrome, or a person with only one arm. But it maintains that this difference is precisely what makes me the same as all these others. The disability understanding of intersectionality is not the Venn diagram, or the crossroads, or even perhaps the double helix, but more like Gilligan's conception of the "web," where we are linked to each other sometimes directly, other times indirectly through a complicated path of connections (Gilligan 1982; Hirschmann 1992).

Perhaps that simply demonstrates another way in which disability studies today is like feminism of the 1980s; but I do not mean to imply a naive nostalgia for the "good old days" when second-wave feminism "discovered" the political power of relationship and connection. For that work predated the important contributions of intersectionality theory, particularly by women of color, concerning the exclusion of various kinds of experiences and identities

(Crenshaw 1991). But webs contain multiple kinds of intersections, complex patterns of connections and interrelations, and capture what I think disability theory does much better than current feminist theory: namely, showing and theorizing our connections, and not just our differences. Disability, I believe, can help feminism develop intersectionality's truly radical potential: namely, the ways in which "difference" is just another word for being human.

METHODS

What Do We Do Now?

Patrick R. Grzanka

Black feminist cultural theorist Jennifer C. Nash (2008) has been a vocal critic of intersectionality on the grounds of wanting to push the field forward, particularly in the interest of questioning some of the root assumptions that she sees driving the field. She frames the stakes accordingly:

> The important insights that identity is complex, that subjectivity is messy, and that personhood is inextricably bound up with vectors of power are only an analytic starting point; it is time for intersectionality to begin to sort out the paradoxes upon which its theory rests in the service of strengthening its explanatory power. (13–14)

In social science, "explanatory power" is the traditional litmus test by which social theory is measured. If intersectionality is conceptualized as a social theory or a loose connection of affiliated social theories, then one primary way to evaluate its theoretical fortitude is to assess how good intersectionality is at describing empirical reality, that is, how the world works. In order to conduct these kinds of "tests," we are faced with a paradoxical problem rooted in theory's conceptual cousin: methods.

Methods are the tools by which the empirical universe is explored; in social science, methods are how data (in all its varied forms) are collected, generated, and analyzed. Social theory is based in reality, and social scientists access that reality through empirical methods. By this logic, methods generate theory, and theory is continually evaluated and refined via the continuous application of methods. So while theory and methods are often placed in a binary or dualistic configuration wherein they oppose one another or in which one can be pro-theory and anti-methods (and vice versa), theory and methods are always bound up in one another. Furthermore, much of what gets called "theory" in the social sciences (e.g., poststructuralist deconstruction) goes by the term "method" in the humanities, so the dividing line between the two is blurry and evasive when traveling across disciplines. When thinking about the problem of methods in intersectionality, accordingly, we are never talking about methods alone, but instead about how methods can contribute to the refinement of the theory and how theory can catalyze new thinking about methods.

"Methodology," as defined by sociologist Sharlene Nagy Hesse-Biber (2007), refers to the conceptual frameworks by which particular research methods are deployed. In this sense, methodology is rooted in epistemology, because methodology refers to the assumptions about reality that guide the strategic application of methods. From Hesse-Biber's position, intersectionality can actually be understood as a kind of methodology insomuch as intersectionality may serve as a frame or lens that guides the execution of empirical inquiry, albeit in widely diverse and divergent forms (e.g., from quantitative survey research in demography to qualitative textual analysis in communication studies). In one of the most widely cited articles on intersectionality, sociologist Leslie McCall (2005) addresses the dearth of discourse on methodology in intersectionality by mapping out the range of approaches to social categories (i.e., race, gender, sexuality, class, ability, nation, age, etc.) found in the field. She organizes intersectional methodologies in a tripartite framework:

1. **Anticategorical complexity.** These approaches generally deconstruct or dismantle categories such as race, gender, and sexuality; they focus on their historical contingency and arbitrariness, undermining the validity of categories or their ability to adequately capture the complexity of human experiences; they assert that categories are always about hierarchies and drawing boundaries. Implicit in this approach is the idea that using social categories in research on difference reinstalls and reinscribes the very systems and regimes that social justice work tries to critique.

2. **Intracategorical complexity.** These approaches look within categories, especially those defined by multiple dimensions of difference (e.g., Black women), to expose the underexplored complexities inherent to these categories; while these approaches may undermine categorization or approach them obliquely, they do not necessarily reject the use of categories altogether. Instead, they insist that categories contain more within-group differences than typically assumed, often explicitly demonstrating the inadequacy of standard categories to reflect lived experiences and social realities.

3. **Intercategorical complexity.** These approaches provisionally adopt salient social categories to reveal the configurations of inequalities between groups, or to expose the relationships of domination and subordination between multiply marginalized and privileged social constituencies. Though acknowledging the limitations and dynamic nature of social categories, these approaches highlight the relationships between inequalities and social categories themselves, but insist upon the material reality of social categories insomuch as they predict and explain empirically verifiable differences in access to resources, power, life chances, etc.

By anchoring this taxonomy in intersectional researchers' approach to categories, McCall is able to incorporate both a wide range of research methodologies and an equally wide range of research methods from across the disciplines. She effectively broadens what constitutes intersectionality to include an essentially infinite variety of methodological approaches insomuch as they take into consideration the interactions between multiple social categories. Though she explicitly favors the third approach, intercategorical complexity, the popularity of her work and its extensive uptake may be attributed to how flexibly she envisions intersectionality's insights can be applied in diverse sites of critical social research.

Nearly ten years after the publication of that 2005 essay, McCall (with Kimberlé Crenshaw and Sumi Cho) revisited the issue of methodologies in a special issue of the journal *Signs* on intersectionality. In surveying the "methodological insurgencies" characterizing some strands of intersectionality alongside the more methodologically conservative approaches that apply intersectionality within well-established disciplinary guidelines, they explained that:

Implicit in this broadened field of vision is our view that intersectionality is best framed as an *analytic sensibility*. If intersectionality is an analytic disposition, a way of thinking about and conducting analyses, then what makes an analysis intersectional is not its use of the term "intersectionality," nor its being situated in a familiar genealogy, nor its drawing on lists of standard citations. Rather, what makes an analysis intersectional— whatever terms it deploys, whatever its iteration, whatever its field or discipline—is *its adoption of an intersectional way of thinking about the problem of sameness and difference and its relation to power*. This framing—conceiving of categories not as distinct but as always permeated by other categories, fluid and changing, always in the process of creating and being created by dynamics of power—emphasizes what intersectionality *does* rather than what intersectionality *is*. (Cho, Crenshaw, and McCall 2013, 794) [emphasis added]

In expressing intersectionality as an "analytic sensibility," these leaders of the field position it as more closely aligned with epistemology and methodology than with methods per se. Intersectionality, according to their logic, is a lens and a commitment, rather than a prescribed set of methodological procedures. This means that virtually any method can be considered an intersectional one, so long as the conceptualization of categories is multiplicative and dynamic, and that power is foregrounded.

With "analytic sensibility," Cho, Crenshaw, and McCall (2013) also effectively circumvent criticisms of the field that insist intersectionality develop more specific and robust methods (for an overview of such criticisms see Davis 2008; Carbado 2013; Nash 2008). This criticism is linked to concerns about (inter) disciplinarity, that is, whether or not intersectionality is best pursued within the boundaries of disciplines or through the subversion or transcendence of those boundaries. On this point of contention, the literature is indecisive and offers several tenable philosophies. On the one hand, intersectionality's initial articulations by the Combahee River Collective and Black feminist writers such as Audre Lorde and bell hooks lacked investment in disciplinary norms or procedures. In *Black Feminist Thought* (1990/2000), Patricia Hill Collins writes from the discipline of sociology but in imaginative ways and with an overt commitment to coalition-building across disciplines and institutional spaces. Twenty years after the initial publication of that book, Collins (2009) posited several paradigmatic questions as she looked ahead toward the next iterations of intersectional research:

> Continuing to move the field forward requires that expansive approach to intersectionality engage some thorny questions. For one, can the expansive approach taken to intersectionality that seemingly emerges from and remains central to interdisciplinary endeavors work within disciplines? Is intersectionality inherently oppositional to traditional disciplinary approaches to knowledge production and the social conditions that accompany them? Or can intersectionality be recast solely as a theoretical frame that might reform existing disciplinary paradigms? Under what conditions does this kind of scholarship and praxis flourish, and what conditions foster its demise? (xii)

Concluding with a cautious and even foreboding tone, Collins challenges the field to consider whether or not the initial interdisciplinary innovations that marked the inception of the movement in academia are sustainable without adaptations and negotiations that facilitate intersectionality's application in traditional disciplinary spaces. The question of applying intersectionality within a traditional discipline begs the concomitant question: will intersectionality transform disciplines, or be disciplined by them?

Though this book is interdisciplinary insomuch as it places a wide variety of disciplinary perspectives in conversation and many of the approaches featured here are interdisciplinary, the scholars featured in the volume broadly and this unit specifically do not share a unified perspective on interdisciplinarity. For example, Elizabeth Cole's (2009, reading 41) essay in *American Psychologist* excerpted here plainly states that methodological innovation and interdisciplinary collaboration are *not* requisite elements of intersectional research. To the contrary, Cole addresses her work to psychologists who may be unwilling to learn new methods but simultaneously seek to incorporate intersectionality into their work. The danger in this case, of course, is whether or not such "inclusion" of intersectionality in psychological research occasions substantive engagement with human cultural diversity or superficial multiculturalism. And yet Cole also stresses how "the application of the three intersectional questions I have outlined here does require that researchers rethink the relationship between their conceptualization of social categories and their methodological choices" (178–179). Cole's colleague Lisa Bowleg (2008, reading 40) offers a somewhat dissenting view and spends much of the time in her essay insisting that business-as-usual psychological research methods and methodologies are mostly unfit to tackle the complexities of intersectionality.

Beyond the debates over interdisciplinarity, Jasbir Puar (2007, reading 42) argues that intersectionality is mired in epistemological assumptions that inhibit its ability to do truly transformative work. From the interdisciplinary locus of women's, gender, and queer studies, she closes this unit with an excerpt from *Terrorist Assemblages* that offers a potent, controversial critique of intersectionality's explanatory power and radical potential (or lack thereof):

> As a tool of diversity management and a mantra of liberal multiculturalism, intersectionality colludes with the disciplinary apparatus of the state—census, demography, racial profiling, surveillance—in that "difference" is encased within a structural container that simply wishes the messiness of identity into a formulaic grid, producing analogies in its wake and engendering what Massumi names "gridlock": a "box[ing] into its site on the culture map." (212)

Puar provokes a theoretical mediation on the utility of the intersection metaphor and of the very "analytic sensibility" on which Cho, Crenshaw, and McCall (2013) locate intersectionality's strength. Rather than close a conversation, Puar's work can incite radical imaginings that push social justice scholar-activisms in new directions, even if that means away from the intersections.

As Collins (1990/2000) elaborated early on, intersectionality is a *critical* social theory, which means that it is squarely committed to social justice; as Mendieta elaborates, "Critical social theory always has a practical, transformative, generative telos that is guided by injustice in its time and social locus" (2012, 459). While there may be a strategic benefit in rendering intersectionality into a theory and *not* a method, there may also be some advantages to retaining an investment in methods as we dialogically conceive of new ways to map inequalities, generate theories, and challenge institutionalized oppressions. I borrow the term "theory-methods package" from sociologist Adele Clarke (2005) to suggest that we not prematurely foreclose upon thinking of intersectionality methodologically. If we consider intersectionality to be a collection or even "assemblage" (Puar 2007) of theory-methods packages, then intersectionality does not have to be either inherently disciplinary or interdisciplinary, nor does it have be to be "just" theoretical or strictly methodological. As the selections in this volume demonstrate, there is general agreement that intersectionality is invested in doing something—that is, transforming institutions and structures—and abandoning considerations of methodologies and methods may inadvertently position intersectionality in the realm of abstraction so antithetical to its politics (Collins 2009, excerpted in Unit II as reading 7).

References and Further Reading

Bowleg, L. 2008. "When Black + Woman + Lesbian ≠ Black Lesbian Woman: The Methodological Challenges of Qualitative and Quantitative Intersectionality Research." *Sex Roles* 59: 312–325.

Brah, A., and A. Phoenix. 2004. "Ain't I a Woman? Revisiting Intersectionality." *Journal of International Women's Studies* 5: 75–86.

Carbado, D. W. 2013. "Colorblind Intersectionality." *Signs: The Journal of Women in Culture and Society* 38: 811–845.

Cho, S., K. W. Crenshaw, and L. McCall. 2013. "Intersectionality Studies: Theory, Applications, and Praxis." *Signs: The Journal of Women in Culture and Society* 38: 785–810.

Choo, H. Y., and M. M. Ferree. 2010. "Practicing Intersectionality in Sociological Research: A Critical Analysis of Inclusions, Interactions, and Institutions in the Study of Inequalities." *Sociological Theory* 28: 129–149.

Clarke, A. 2005. *Situational Analysis: Grounded Theory After the Postmodern Turn.* Thousand Oaks, CA: Sage Publications.

Cole, E. R. 2009. "Intersectionality and Research in Psychology." *American Psychologist* 64: 170–180.

Collins, P. H. 2009. "Foreword: Emerging Intersections—Building Knowledge and Transforming Institutions." In *Emerging Intersections: Race, Class, and Gender in Theory, Policy, and Practice,* edited by B. T. Dill and R. E. Zambrana, vii-xiii. New Brunswick, NJ: Rutgers University Press.

Davis, K. 2008. "Intersectionality as Buzzword: A Sociology of Science Perspective on What Makes a Feminist Theory Successful." *Feminist Theory* 9: 67–85.

Dhamoon, R. K. 2011. "Considerations on Mainstreaming Intersectionality." *Political Research Quarterly* 64: 230–243.

Dill, B. T., and M. H. Kohlman. 2011. "Intersectionality: A Transformative Paradigm in Feminist Theory and Social Justice." In *The Handbook of Feminist Research: Theory and Praxis,* second edition, edited by S. N. Hesse-Biber, 154–174. Thousand Oaks, CA: SAGE Publications.

Dill, B. T., S. M. Nettles, and L. Weber. 2001. "Defining the Work of the Consortium: What Do We Mean by Intersections?" *Connections.* Consortium on Race, Gender and Ethnicity. http://www.crge.umd.edu/pdf/RC2001_spring.pdf.

Ferguson, R. A. 2012. "Reading Intersectionality." *Trans-Scripts* 2: 91–99.

Hancock, A.-M. 2007. "When Multiplication Doesn't Equal Quick Addition: Examining Intersectionality as a Research Paradigm." *Perspectives on Politics* 5: 63–79.

Hancock, A.-M. 2008. "Intersectionality as a Normative and Empirical Paradigm." *Politics & Gender* 3: 248–254.

Hesse-Biber, S. N. 2007. "Feminist Research: Exploring the Interconnections of Epistemology, Methodology, and Method." In *Handbook of Feminist Research: Theory and Praxis,* edited by S. N. Hesse-Biber, 1–24. Thousand Oaks, CA: Sage Publications.

Kohlman, M. H. 2006. "Intersection Theory: A More Elucidating Paradigm of Quantitative Analysis." *Race, Gender & Class* 13: 42–59.

Lewis, G. 2009. "Celebrating Intersectionality? Debates on a Multi-faceted Concept in Gender Studies: Themes from a Conference." *European Journal of Women's Studies* 16: 203–210.

MacKinnon, C. 2013. "Intersectionality as Method: A Note." *Signs: The Journal of Women in Culture and Society* 38: 1019–1030.

McCall, L. 2005. "The Complexity of Intersectionality." *Signs: The Journal of Women in Culture and Society* 30: 1711–1800.

Mendieta, E. 2012. "Mapping the Geographies of Social Inequality: Patricia Hill Collins's Intersectional Critical Theory." *Journal of Speculative Philosophy* 26: 458–465.

Nash, J. C. 2008. "Re-thinking Intersectionality." *Feminist Review* 89: 1–15.

Puar, J. K. 2007. *Terrorist Assemblages: Homonationalism in Queer Times.* Durham, NC: Duke University Press.

Puar, J. K. 2012. "'I'd Rather Be a Cyborg than a Goddess': Becoming-Intersectional in Assemblage Theory." *philoSOPHIA* 2: 49–66.

Reed, T. V. 2001. "Heavy Traffic at the Intersections: Ethnic, American, Women's, Queer, and Cultural Studies." In *Color-Line to Borderlands: The Matrix of American Ethnic Studies,* edited by J. E. Butler, 273–292. Seattle, WA: University of Washington Press.

Simien, E. 2007. "Doing Intersectionality Research: From Conceptual Issues to Practical Examples." *Politics & Gender* 3: 264–271.

Warner, L. R. 2008. "A Best Practices Guide to Intersectional Approaches in Psychological Research." *Sex Roles* 59: 454–463.

Weber, L. 2009. *Understanding Race, Class, Gender, and Sexuality: An Intersectional Framework.* Second edition. New York: Oxford.

Avtar Brah and Ann Phoenix

"Methods" do not only apply to data collection and analysis, but to the careful art of crafting and using social theory. Avtar Brah (now retired from her post as professor of sociology at Birkbeck, University of London) and Ann Phoenix (professor on the Faculty of Children and Learning at the Institute of Education, University of London) offer a reminder that intersectionality—as a critical social theory—is susceptible to cooptation and stagnation like any political or intellectual movement. In 2004, they "revisited" intersectionality in the *Journal of International Women's Studies* to do some important contextualizing in light of the war against Iraq. They raise provocative questions about the ability of intersectional critiques to challenge new versions of old scripts about White people saving third world women of color from men of color (and themselves). They also consider the politics of space through the analytic of "diaspora," and consider the relationships between intersectional thought and postcolonial theories. Intersectionality has the potential to be disruptive of modernist paradigms, but not if intersectional critique is uncritically embedded in Western narratives and assumptions that refuse to do more than acknowledge globalization and transnational social dynamics. Thinking beyond the artificial boundaries of nations in order to understand how citizenship and nationality are coproduced with race, gender, class, and other highly variable dimensions of difference is already a part of the intersectional project as defined by US Black feminists. But then why does "nation" sometimes feel like an afterthought in intersectional theorizing? What might it mean for the future of intersectionality if non-US subjects were more than "incorporated" into the framework? To borrow a phrase from Black feminist literary critic Mary Helen Washington, what would happen to intersectionality if we put transnationalism in the center?

39. Occupy Intersectionality*

It is worth bearing in mind that the phrase, "Ain't I a Woman?" was first introduced into North American and British feminist lexicon by an enslaved woman Sojourner Truth (the name she took, instead of her original name Isabella, when she became a travelling preacher). It predates by a century some of our more recent feminist texts on the subject such as Denise Riley's (2003/1988) *Am I That Name?* or Judith Butler's *Gender Trouble* (Butler, 1990). It is as well to remember in this regard, that the first women's antislavery society was formed in 1832 by black women in Salem, Massachusetts in the USA. Yet, black women were conspicuous by their absence at the Seneca Falls Anti-Slavery Convention of 1848 where the mainly middle class white delegates debated the motion for women's suffrage. Several questions arise when we reflect on black women's absence at the Convention. What, for instance, are the implications of an event which occludes the black female subject from the political imaginary of a feminism designed to campaign for the abolition

---

* Excerpted from A. Brah and A. Phoenix, "Ain't I a Woman? Revisiting Intersectionality," *Journal of International Women's Studies* 5 (2004): 75–86.

of slavery? What consequences did such disavowals have for the constitution of gendered forms of "whiteness" as the normative subject of western imagination? How did events like these mark black and white women's relational sense of themselves? Importantly, what happens when the subaltern subject—black woman in this case—repudiate such silencing gestures?

We know from the biographies of black women such as Sojourner Truth that many of them spoke loud and clear. They would not be caged by the violence of slavery even as they were violently marked by it. Sojourner Truth's 1851 speech at the Women's Rights Convention in Akron, Ohio, very well demonstrates the historical power of a political subject who challenges imperatives of subordination and thereby creates new visions. This power (which, according to Foucault, simultaneously disciplines and creates new subjects) and its consequences are much bigger than the gains or losses of an individual life who articulates a particular political subject position. Sojourner Truth was born into enslavement (to a wealthy Dutch slave-owner living in New York). She campaigned for both the abolition of slavery and for equal rights for women. Since she was illiterate throughout her life, no formal record of the speech exists and, indeed, two different versions of it are in existence (Gates and McKay, 1997).

What is clear is that the words of Sojourner Truth had an enormous impact at the Convention and that the challenge they express foreshadowed campaigns by black feminists more than a century later:

> Well, children, where there is so much racket, there must be something out of kilter, I think between the Negroes of the South and the women of the North—all talking about rights—the white men will be in a fix pretty soon. But what's all this talking about? That man over there says that women need to be helped into carriages, and lifted over ditches, and to have the best place everywhere. Nobody helps me any best place. And ain't I a woman? Look at me! Look at my arm. I have plowed (sic), I have planted and I have gathered into barns. And no man could head me. And ain't I a woman? I could work as much, and eat as much as any man—when I could get it—and bear the lash as well! And ain't I a woman? I have borne children and seen most of them sold into slavery, and when I cried out with a mother's grief, none but Jesus heard me. And ain't I a woman? . . .

This cutting edge speech (in all senses of the term) deconstructs every single major truth-claim about gender in a patriarchal slave social formation. Political identity here is never taken as a given but is performed through rhetoric and narration. Sojourner Truth's identity claims are thus relational, constructed in relation to white women and all men and clearly demonstrate that what we call "identities" are not objects but processes constituted in and through power relations.

It is in this sense of critique, practice and inspiration that this discourse holds crucial lessons for us today. Part lament, but defiant, articulating razor sharp politics but with the sensibility of a poet, the discourse performs the analytic moves of a "decolonised mind", to use Wa Thiongo's (1986) critical insight. It refuses all final closures. We are all in dire need of decolonised open minds today. Furthermore, Sojourner Truth powerfully challenges essentialist thinking that a particular category of woman is essentially this or essentially that (e.g. that women are necessarily weaker than men or that enslaved black women were not real women). This point holds critical importance today when the allure of new Orientalisms and their concomitant desire to "unveil" Muslim women has proved to be attractive even to some feminists in a "post September 11" world.

There are millions of women today who remain marginalized, treated as a "problem", or construed as the focal point of a moral panic—women suffering poverty, disease, lack of water, proper sanitation; women who themselves or their households are scattered across the globe as economic migrants, undocumented workers, as refugees and asylum seekers; women whose bodies and sexualities are commodified, fetishised, criminalized, racialised, disciplined and regulated through a myriad of representational regimes and social practices. So many of us, indeed, perhaps, all of us one way or another, continue to be "hailed" as subjects within Sojourner Truth's diasporic imagination with its massive potential for un-doing the hegemonic moves of social orders confronting us today. She enacts dispersal and dissemination both in terms of being members of a historical diaspora but equally, in the sense of disarticulating, rupturing and de-centring the precariously sutured complacency and self-importance of certain feminisms.

Since Sojourner Truth many feminists have consistently argued for the importance of examining "intersectionality". A key feature of feminist analysis of "intersectionality" is that they are concerned with "decentring" of the "normative subject" of feminism.

The concept of "simultaneously interlocking oppressions" that were local at the same time as they were global was one of the earliest and most productive formulations of the subsequent theorisation of a "decentred subject" (see, e.g. hooks, 1981). As Norma Alacom, in her analysis of the book *This Bridge Called My Back*—a North American collection of political writings by women of colour—later suggested, the theoretical subject of *Bridge* is a figure of multiplicity, representing consciousness as a "site of multiple voicings" seen "not as necessarily originating with the subject but as discourses that traverse consciousness and which the subject must struggle with constantly." This figure is the bearer of modes of subjectivity that are deeply marked by "psychic and material violence" and it demands a thorough "reconfiguration of feminist theory" (Alacom in Anzaldúa 1990: 359–365).

In Britain, we were making similar claims when women of African, Caribbean, and South Asian background came to be figured as "black" through political coalitions, challenging the essentialist connotations of racism (Grewal et al., 1988, Brah 1996, Mirza 1997). This particular project of Black British feminism was forged through the work of local women's organisations around issues such as wages and conditions of work, immigration law, fascist violence, reproductive rights, and domestic violence. By 1978, local groups had combined to form a national body called the Organisation of Women of Asian and African Descent (OWAAD). This network held annual conferences, published a newsletter, and served as an active conduit for information, intellectual conversations and political mobilisation. The ensuing dialogue entailed sustained analysis of racism, class, and gender with much debate as to the best means of confronting their outcomes whilst remaining alive to cultural specificities:

> Our group organises on the basis of Afro-Asian unity, and although that principle is maintained, we don't deal with it by avoiding the problems this might present, but by having on-going discussions. . . . Obviously, we have to take into account our cultural differences, and that has affected the way we are able to organise. (OWAAD cited in Mirza 1997:43)

This careful attention to working within, through and across cultural differences is a highly significant heritage of this feminism and it is one that can be used as a resource for working with the question of cultural difference in the present moment when, for example, differences between Muslim and non-Muslim women are constructed as posing insurmountable cultural differences. Internal conflicts within OWAAD, as amongst white women's groups, especially around homophobia, proved salutary so that, even as British "black feminism" assumed a distinctive political identity separate from "white feminism", engaging the latter in critical theoretical and political debate, it was not immune to the contradictions of its own internal heterogeneity. These internal conflicts within and between different feminisms prefigured later theories of "difference".

Recognition of the importance of intersectionality has impelled new ways of thinking about complexity and multiplicity in power relations as well as emotional investments (e.g. Arrighi, 2001; Kenny, 2000; Pattillo-McCoy, 1999). In particular, recognition that "race", social class and sexuality differentiated women's experiences has disrupted notions of a homogeneous category "woman" with its attendant assumptions of universality that served to maintain the status quo in relation to "race", social class and sexuality, while challenging gendered assumptions. As such, intersectionality fits with the disruption of modernist thinking produced by postcolonial and poststructuralist theoretical ideas.

Feminist theories of the 1970s and 1980 were informed by conceptual repertoires drawn largely from "modernist" theoretical and philosophical traditions of European Enlightenment such as liberalism and Marxism. The "postmodernist" critique of these perspectives, including their claims to universal applicability, had precursors, within anticolonial, antiracist, and feminist critical practice. Postmodern theoretical approaches found sporadic expression in Anglophone feminist works from the late 1970s. But, during the 1990s they became a significant influence, in particular their poststructuralist variant. The work of scholars who found poststructuralist insights productive traversed theoretical ground that ranged from discourse theory, deconstruction, psychoanalysis, queer theory, and postcolonial criticism. Contrary to analysis where process may be reified and understood as personified in some essential way in the bodies of individuals, different feminisms could now be viewed as representing historically contingent relationships, contesting fields of discourses, and sites of multiple subject positions. The concept of "agency" was substantially reconfigured, especially through poststructuralist appropriations of psychoanalysis. New theories of subjectivity attempted to take account of psychic and emotional life without recourse to the idea of an inner/outer divide. Whilst all this intellectual flux led to a reassessment of the notion of experiential "authenticity", highlighting the limitations of "identity politics", the debate also demonstrated that experience itself could not become a redundant category. Indeed, it remains crucial in analysis as a "signifying practice" at the heart of the way we make sense of the world symbolically and narratively.

Overall, critical but productive conversations with poststructuralism have resulted in new theories for refashioning the analysis of "difference" (Butler, 1990; Grewal and Kaplan 1994; Weedon 1996; Spivak, 1999). One distinctive strand of this work is concerned with the potential of combining strengths of modern theory with postmodern insights. This approach has taken several forms. Some developments, especially in the field of literary criticism have led to "postcolonial" studies with their particular emphasis upon the insight that both the "metropolis" and the "colony" were deeply altered by the colonial process and that these articulating histories have a mutually constitutive role in the present. Postcolonial feminist studies foreground processes underlying colonial and postcolonial discourses of gender. Frequently, such work uses poststructuralist frameworks, especially Foucauldian discourse analysis or Derridean deconstruction. Some scholars have attempted to combine poststructualist approaches with neo-Marxist or psychoanalytic theories. Others have transformed "border theory" (Anzaldúa 1987; Young, 1994, Lewis 1996; Alexander and Mohanty-Talpade 1997; Gedalof, 1999; Mani, 1999; Lewis, 2000). A related development is associated with valorisation of the term diaspora. The concept of diaspora is increasingly used in analysing the mobility of peoples, commodities, capital and cultures in the context of globalisaton and transnationalism. The concept is designed to analyse configurations of power both productive and coercive in "local" and "global" encounters in specific spaces and historical moments. In her work Brah (1996, 2002) addresses the concept of "diaspora" alongside that of Gloria Anzaldúa's theorisation of "border" and the widely debated feminist concept of "politics of home". The intersection of these three terms is understood through the concept of "diaspora space" which covers the entanglements of genealogies of dispersal with those of "staying put". The term "homing desire" is used to think through the question of home and belonging; and, both power and time are viewed as multidimensional processes. Importantly, the concept of "diaspora space" embraces the intersection of "difference" in its variable forms, placing emphasis upon emotional and psychic dynamics as much as socio-economic, political and cultural differences. Difference is thus conceptualised as social relation; experience; subjectivity; and, identity. Home and belonging is also a theme of emerging literature on "mixed-race" identities which interrogates the concept of "race" as an essentialist discourse with racist effects (Tizard and Phoenix 2002/1993, Zack 1993; Ifekwunige 1999; Dalmage, 2000). Accordingly, the idea that you are mixed-race if you have black and white parents is problematised. Instead the analytical focus is upon varying and variable subjectivities, identities, and the specific meanings attached to "differences".

In 2003, the second war against Iraq has brought into relief many continuing feminist concerns such as the growing militarization of the world, the critical role of the military industrial complex as a technology of imperial governance, the feminisation of global labour markets and migration flows, the reconstitution of differentially racialised forms of sexuality as a constitutive part of developing regimes of "globalisation", and the deepening inequalities of power and wealth across different regions of the world. A historically-rooted and forward looking consideration of intersectionality raises many pressing questions. For example: What are the implications for feminisms of the latest forms of postmodern imperialisms that stalk the globe? What kinds of subjects, subjectivities, and political identities are produced by this juncture when the fantasy of the veiled Muslim woman "in need of rescue," the rhetoric of the "terrorist", and the ubiquitous discourse of democracy becomes an alibi for constructing new global hegemonies? How do we challenge simplistic binaries which posit secularism and fundamentalism as mutually exclusive polar opposites? What is the impact of these new modes of governmentality on the lives of differentially exploited, racialised, ethnicised, sexualised, and religionised humans living in different parts of the world? What do these lived experiences say to us—living as we do in this space called the west—about our own positionalities, responsibilities, politics, and ethics? We have tried to indicate that feminist dialogues and dialogic imaginations provide powerful tools for challenging the power games currently played out on the world stage.

Lisa Bowleg

In the following essay from the 2008 special issue of *Sex Roles* on intersectionality, George Washington University psychologist Lisa Bowleg does something that academics rarely do: expound upon their *mistakes*. In this dazzling research report, Bowleg explores how she embarked upon a major research project without considering how intersectionality shaped the lives of her participants, who were Black lesbians. She details the ways in which every level of the project—from the assumptions undergirding her research questions and study design to the individual interview questions, measurement tools, and data analysis—resulted in a skewed account of these women's lives. Learning from these mistakes, Bowleg then took up an intersectional approach and reconfigured her methods and aims. She is ultimately critical of psychology's reluctance to embrace intersectional approaches, and she suggests that the legacy of "positivism" is at least partially to blame for the anti-intersectional thinking that pervades much of contemporary psychology. Positivism, championed by early social scientists such as founding sociologist Emile Durkheim, assumes a stark division between the researcher (i.e., subject, where biased subjectivity is thought to reside) and his object of study (i.e., object, in which the holy grail of objectivity lives). In the interest of cultivating objectivity (read: Truth with a capital "T"), traditional positivism seeks to remove all prejudice and influence of the researcher on the scientific process. You can imagine what the scholars in this volume might have to say about the idea that researchers are simply neutral, dispassionate observers of reality. . . .

Bowleg does not, however, argue here that quantitative methods are useless or that qualitative methods are perfect. Rather, she insists, "we need new analytical tools and strategies to assist in understanding the complexities of intersectionality." Bowleg demands much from social scientists seeking to do intersectional research, because her argument here is that merely knowing how to execute research methods is insufficient. Researchers must understand the beliefs and assumptions (i.e., epistemology; see Unit II) that produce a particular method, so that those assumptions can be assessed, critiqued, and modified as necessary. As intimidating as it might be, researchers must be prepared to imagine new methods that better assess the dynamic relationships between lived experiences and hierarchical social structures. Bowleg concludes by pointing toward multidisciplinary collaboration as the most readily available and efficacious tool for combating methodological stagnation and for promoting new tools with which to dismantle the master's house of positivism.

40. When Black + Woman + Lesbian ≠ Black Lesbian Woman*

The discipline of psychology has not fared well in terms of promoting the understanding of intersectionality. Despite an abundance of theories on social identity within psychology, the prevailing view of social identities is one of unidimensionality and independence, rather than intersection. A notable exception is Ransford's (1980) multiple jeopardy-advantage (MJA) hypothesis which posits that people occupy various social status positions that intersect to create a "unique social space" (p. 277). This unique space manifests as outcomes that one's social status location (e.g., race) alone cannot explain. Instead, this space can be explained only by the intersection of one of more social status positions (e.g., race, sex, class, sexual orientation) to yield multiple jeopardy (i.e., the intersection of two or more low social status positions) or multiple advantage (i.e., the intersection of two or more high social status positions). Deaux's (1993) work reconstructing social identity to recognize multiple dimensions of social identity is another exception to the rule, as are numerous examples within feminist psychology. Though explicit mention of the term *intersectionality* is rare, feminist psychology has been far more progressive than mainstream psychology in recognizing the intersections between women's experiences of structural inequality based on race, gender, class, and sexual orientation (e.g., Greene 1997; Reid and Comas-Diaz 1990; Weber 1998).

Because the lives of Black lesbians are rooted in structural inequalities based on the intersections of sexual orientation, sex, gender, and race (see Greene 1995), Black lesbians are an ideal population in which to study intersectionality. Intersectionality examines how distinctive social power relations mutually construct each other, not just that social hierarchies exist (Collins 1998). At the micro level, a small empirical literature base has examined the

---

* Excerpted from L. Bowleg, "When Black + Woman + Lesbian ≠ Black Lesbian Woman: The Methodological Challenges of Qualitative and Quantitative Intersectionality Research," *Sex Roles* 59 (2008): 312–325. Reprinted with permission from Springer Science + Business Media. Some in-text citations have been excised for length.

intimate relationships (Hall and Greene 2002; Mays and Cochran 1988; Peplau et al. 1997), health care (Cochran and Mays 1988), mental health (Cochran and Mays 1994), workplace (Bowleg et al. 2008), active coping (Bowleg et al. 2004), and multiple minority stress and resilience (Bowleg et al. 2003) experiences of Black lesbians. Other relevant scholarship, most of it focused on predominantly White middle-class lesbian, gay, and bisexual (LGB) populations has addressed the minority stress experiences of LGBs (Brooks 1981; DiPlacido 1998; Meyer 2003) and the dual identity experiences of lesbians (Fingerhut et al. 2005).

Two studies, the *Black Lesbians Stress and Resilience Study* (BLSR), a mixed methods study with Black lesbians in southern California (Bowleg, manuscript in preparation; Bowleg et al. 2008, 2004, 2003), and a qualitative study with a subsample of Black lesbians in Washington, DC who were part of the *Trials and Tribulations Study* (TT), a larger study of Black lesbian, gay, bisexual and transgender (LGBT) people (Bowleg, manuscript in preparation) provide the foundation for the methodological challenges that I highlight in this article.

The goal of both studies was to explore and examine experiences of multiple minority stress and resilience relevant to the intersections of race, sex/gender and sexual orientation for Black lesbians. Despite the researchers' interest in the intersection of and social inequality based on these identities, much of it prompted by the primary author's own experience as a Black lesbian, the research team knew virtually nothing about intersectionality theory or research. The proof: none of the literature review sections of these articles reference a single intersectionality theorist, or even mention the word *intersectionality.* Instead, the prevailing wisdom of the triple jeopardy approach to Black lesbians' experiences (e.g., Greene 1995) informed much of the empirical exploration of what Bowleg et al. (2003) called at the time "multiple marginalized identities" (p. 89). The researchers' realization that virtually every methodological choice made in these studies reflected an additive approach (Black + Lesbian + Woman), antithetical to the theoretical fidelity of intersectionality would come later, most of it revealed through the research participants' poignant and complex narratives about the intersections of ethnicity, sex/gender, and sexual orientation in their lives. Thus, trial and error, those two marvelous teachers, inform the methodological issues that I discuss relevant to measurement, data analysis, and interpretation.

Obviously, asking good questions is vital to intersectionality research too, but doing so well can be quite challenging. At issue is how to ask questions about experiences that are intersecting, interdependent, and mutually constitutive, without resorting, even inadvertently, to an additive approach. The additive approach posits that social inequality increases with each additional stigmatized identity. Thus, a Black lesbian would be multiply oppressed because of the combination of her ethnicity, sexual orientation, and sex/gender (i.e., triple jeopardy). Critics reject the additive approach because it conceptualizes people's experiences as separate, independent, and summative (Collins 1995; Cuadraz and Uttal 1999; Weber and Parra-Medina 2003). Furthermore, they disavow the additive approach's implication that one's identities and/or discrimination based on these identities can be ranked. Weber and Parra-Medina have asked rhetorically: "How can a poor Latina be expected to identify the sole—or even primary—source of her oppression? How can scholars with no real connection to her life do so?" (p. 204). They contend further that people can be members of dominant and subordinate groups (e.g., a White man with a physical disability) simultaneously thereby rendering the ranking exercise futile. Alas, what holds in theory does not always translate easily to practice. Indeed, I would argue that it is virtually impossible, particularly in quantitative research, to ask questions about intersectionality that are not inherently additive.

The conceptual framework of triple jeopardy (Greene 1995) shaped the design of both the BLSR (Bowleg et al. 2008, 2003) and TT (Bowleg, manuscript in preparation) studies. Applied to Black lesbians, this framework is implicitly additive: Black lesbians are subject to prejudice and discrimination based on their ethnicity, sex, and sexual orientation. Three lessons from these studies are key: (1) ask an additive question, get an additive answer; (2) the problem of attempting to measure intersectionality through addition; and (3) ask precisely what you want to know.

Ask an Additive Question, Get an Additive Answer

Consistent with the additive approach, Bowleg (manuscript in preparation) posed questions in the qualitative phase of the TT study that implied that participants' identities could be isolated and ranked:

> Some of the people we've spoken to have told us that when it comes to their identities, they are Black first, and gay, lesbian or bisexual second. Other people said that they are gay or lesbian first and then Black or female, second. Still others have said that they don't feel as if they can rank these identities. In terms of your life, do you rank these identities, that is by race, sexual orientation, gender or anything else?

Not surprisingly, many interviewees responded in kind. That is, they ranked their identities. For example, Loretta, a 33 year old lesbian noted that she did rank her identities. "I think I do. I'm African American first but for a while I was lesbian first and before that I was just [Loretta] and couldn't understand what all the fuss was about" (Bowleg, manuscript in preparation).

Although Maggie, a 27 year old lesbian initially challenged the request to rank her identities, noting, "[No]. I've thought about that and I don't think I can," she nonetheless proceeded to do just that:

> No, I would say that I'm gay first because being a lesbian has had such an impact in my life that it has put me into a different category than just being an African American. It seems like if I were going to be discriminated against about something that would be the first thing. If someone had a choice to hate me or discriminate against me for something that I was that would probably be the first thing picked. And that is the thing I feel I am discriminated against the most. So then that seems to have the biggest impact so I guess that's why it gets first place. And then second place is being Black. Regardless of where I go being Black in any part of the world being Black is an issue. Even in Black countries it's an issue. Black women and White woman get treated differently in every country.

By contrast, others such as Karen, a 36 year old lesbian, reflected the intersectionality perspective with their rejection of the notion that they could rank their identities. Karen observed, "No, I always resort to 'there is no higher political repression.' So I personally don't ascribe to that I'm Black first, lesbian second, woman third. I'm all those."

Attempting to Measure Intersectionality Through Addition

Another question from the Bowleg TT study asked: " . . . If someone dropped in from another planet and asked you to tell them about your life as a Black lesbian woman. First, what would say about your life as a Black person?; Woman? Lesbian?; and Black lesbian woman?" It is obvious now in retrospect that a truly intersectional question would simply ask the respondent to tell about her experience without separating each identity. This is precisely what Karen implied in her response to the question about her life as a Black or African American woman?: "Well, you probably could combine all those statements." The research suggests that even if the interviewer omitted the question singling out each identity, respondents might still seek to do so. For example, at a later point in the interview when asked, "In terms of your own life, what are some of the things you like most or the advantages about being Black and lesbian?" Karen countered, "Not Black, lesbian, and woman? Just Black and lesbian?" Her questions seeking clarification highlight the importance of articulating intersectionality explicitly in interview questions. Even if a respondent asks an interviewee to disaggregate identities, it seems advisable for the interviewer not to do so, but to instead invite the interviewee to discuss her identities and experiences however they best resonate with her. Karen's counter questions are also a fitting example of the problem of assuming that the experience of being a woman is subsumed within that of being lesbian.

Ask Precisely What You Want to Know

The aforementioned measurement mistakes notwithstanding, an interview question in Bowleg's BLSR study elicited narratives that captured the experience of intersectionality. For example, in response to the question, "What are some of the day-to-day challenges that you face in terms of your race, gender and/or sexual orientation?" Nancy, a 44 year old lesbian with a physical disability stated: "Getting listened to. I think that a lot of time people discredit me because I am a Black lesbian, who walks with a cane most of the time." Ethnicity, sex, sexual orientation and disability intersect in Nancy's narrative; these are not discrete identities.

In the TT study, Johanna, a 36 year old woman who said that she sometimes identified as lesbian and other times as a lesbian-identified bisexual depending on her audience, described the intersection of her identities this way:

> I clearly . . . see myself as Black first. Although . . . I feel that . . . I am not just Black, but I'm also a woman, I'm lesbian identified bisexual, I also come from a working class background. So I see those other parts of myself.

Johanna's presentation of her identities was seamless; the absence of the conjunction *and* in her description underscores her perception of her identities as intersectional rather than additive. Noteworthy in Johanna's mention of socioeconomic class, an identity that the interviewer did not ask about explicitly, is the reality that interviewers are limited in the number of different identities about which they can ask questions. It is simply not practical for an interviewer to ask an exhaustive list of questions about intersecting identities (e.g., class, disability status, etc.). If the researcher asks the question well, however (i.e., by inviting participants to discuss any other dimensions that are important to them), then the interviewee can add, as Johanna did class and other dimensions that the researcher might otherwise have overlooked.

Asked how she typically described herself, Kim, a 33 year old lesbian interviewee from the TT study explained, "I think I usually describe myself as a Black lesbian or African American lesbian cause it feels like I have to carve myself some space for myself there because there isn't already." Thus, for Kim the intersection of these identities formed an interdependent identity that she presented to the world rather than a summation of additive identities.

By contrast, in response to the same question others such as Leslie, a 48 year old lesbian in the BLSR study (Bowleg et al. 2003) separated each identity, illustrating a disconnect between how the researchers intended to have the question answered (i.e., with a focus on all of the intersecting identities rather than single identities) and how Leslie perceived and interpreted the question (i.e., additively):

> Well, the primary challenge would be around race . . . Because it's like every day you get up and you don't know if you will get to work without one of these mad dog police pulling you over and getting into a beef and you get arrested; then you lose your job. You don't know if you'll get home at night. You don't know if when you go shopping they'll put security on you and be following you around the store. The queer part is probably something . . . I personally encounter in up close relationships so it would probably be in a work environment or just out in the street where maybe a guy is hitting on me or something. And the woman part is kind of like the same [as the queer part] where you interact with men on the street and at work with your coworkers or bosses (p. 14).

As for how one might measure intersectionality quantitatively, none of the options are ideal. For example, in the quantitative phase of the BLSR study, Bowleg et al. (2004) gave participants the option of using a five-point Likert-type scale (1 = strongly agree, 5 = strongly disagree) to indicate the extent to which they agreed or disagreed with statements such as: "Racism is a much more serious issue in my life than homophobia" and "Racism is a much more serious issue in my life than sexism" (p. 234). In retrospect, this approach seems farcical for all of the obvious and previously stated reasons. Nonetheless, it has prompted me to think how I would ask the question with another similar study. I remain stumped. The simplest, albeit inadequate approach appears to be the inherently additive *check all that apply* option:

> In the past year, would you say that you have experienced stress as a result of discrimination due to your race, sex, and/or sexual orientation? If so, please indicate by *checking all that apply* below, the response that best describes the basis for the discrimination you experienced. Was it primarily because of your:
>
> ❏ Race   ❏ Sex   ❏ Sexual orientation

The BLSR (Bowleg et al. 2008, 2003) and TT (Bowleg, manuscript in preparation) research experiences of Bowleg et al. have yielded some clear insights about asking questions intersectionality. The most obvious is that no part of the question should even hint at addition. For example, if I were to ask a question about day to day challenges today, I would ask something like this: "Now, I'd like you to tell me about some of the day-to-day challenges that you face as a Black lesbian woman." That is, I would not use a phrase such as "race, gender and/or sexual orientation" in which the presence of the conjunctions *and/or* could imply that I wanted the experience recounted serially (race, then gender, then sexual orientation) or that these identities could or should be separated.

Going forward, there are two key points to which researchers should attend in constructing questions about intersectionality. First, questions about intersectionality should focus on meaningful constructs such as stress, prejudice, discrimination rather than relying on demographic questions alone (Betancourt and Lopez 1993; Helms et al. 2005; Weber and Parra-Medina 2003). Second, questions should be intersectional in design; that is they ought to tap the interdependence and mutuality of identities rather than imply as the BLSR (Bowleg et al. 2008, 2003) and TT (Bowleg, manuscript in preparation) studies of Bowleg et al. did, that identities are independent, separate, and able to be ranked.

My clarity on the aforementioned points notwithstanding, there are other measurement issues with which I continue to grapple, however. For example, I am increasingly agnostic about how much energy ought to be expended on asking the right question to measure intersectionality. Overzealous focus on designing the perfect qualitative or quantitative question harkens back to positivism's ontological tenet that there is some single fixed reality (see Tashakkori and Teddlie 1998) about intersectionality that can be measured if only the researcher had just the right question. Yet, as Nancy and Leslie's different answers to the same question demonstrate, there is no single reality about the experience of one's intersecting identities, only multiple constructed realities about one's own experience of intersectionality. As for asking questions about intersectionality in quantitative research, I question whether the positivistic assumptions implicit in quantification are compatible with intersectionality research.

Interdependence, multi-dimensionality and mutually constitutive relationships form the core of intersectionality, attributes that contradict the positivist assumptions inherent in most quantitative approaches. Since I use both quantitative and qualitative methods in my research, it should be obvious that I have no interest in resurrecting that tired and ultimately futile debate about the superiority of quantitative versus qualitative methods. Rather, my argument here is that the positivist paradigm that undergirds much (but not all) quantitative research appears to be orthogonal to the complexities of intersectionality. A researcher's philosophical or "qualitative stance" (Marecek 2003, p. 49) exemplified by an epistemological commitment to "situating . . . investigations in specific historical, social, and cultural contexts" (Marecek 2003, p. 56) is paramount; not whether the questions they ask to measure intersectionality are qualitative or quantitative.

As for the statistical tools that we use to analyze quantitative intersectionality data, Audre Lorde's (1984) famous quote, the "Master's tools will never dismantle the master's house" (p. 111) seems apt here. That is, the statistical methods, even those that test interactions, were not designed with the study of intersectionality in mind. Rather, statisticians rooted in positivistic paradigms developed statistical assumptions of linearity, unidimensionality of measures, uncorrelated error components and the like (McGrath and Johnson 2003) that do not reflect the real world complexities of intersections of race, sex/gender and sexual orientation. In short, we need new analytical tools and strategies to assist us in understanding the complexities of intersectionality.

Examining intersectionality from multidisciplinary perspectives is a signature strength of scholarship on intersectionality. Scholars from disciplines as varied as women's studies, Black feminist studies, social epidemiology, sociology, critical theory, legal studies, and psychology have all made important contributions to advancing knowledge about the experience of intersectionality. Nonetheless, this disciplinary dispersion also reflects a "balkanization of research on social inequality . . . that has precluded integrated knowledge across systems of oppression" (Reskin 2002 as cited in Weber and Parra-Medina 2003, p. 200). An essential response to this balkanization of research is multidisciplinary teams of researchers composed of qualitative analysts and statisticians to develop and advance methodological knowledge about interdisciplinary research. At issue is not just an expansion of methodological expertise; multidisciplinary teams challenge the predominant post-positivist paradigm in which most traditionally trained researchers are steeped by "incorporating more dimensions, situationally specific interpretations, group dynamics and an explicit emphasis on social change" (Weber and Parra-Medina 2003, p. 222).

Elizabeth R. Cole

The publication of University of Michigan psychology, African American studies, and women's studies professor Elizabeth Cole's essay on intersectionality in the flagship journal of the American Psychological Association (APA) was a watershed moment for intersectionality in quantitative social science. Every member of the APA receives a subscription to *American Psychologist,* and I was thoroughly surprised when I saw the word "Intersectionality" on the cover of that issue in April 2009, because as Shields (2008, Unit III, reading 13) and Bowleg (2008, reading 40) have already explained, psychology has been particularly recalcitrant in embracing intersectional ideas. In this work,

Cole addresses a diverse audience of psychologists from across the discipline, many who are likely quite skeptical of the ideas she is advocating. Her writing suggests that she anticipated questions such as: "What makes this more than a buzzword? How is this relevant to my work? How will this advance the science? Isn't this sociology? I already study race—how can I study gender, too? Shouldn't we leave this to the folks in women's studies?" This essay is, among other things, a carefully executed argument in which Cole does the work of convincing her readers to keep listening to what she has to say.

Cole takes a markedly more moderate approach than Lisa Bowleg does in the previous essay. Though she does suggest interdisciplinary collaboration, Cole explicitly writes that psychologists need not *necessarily* learn new methods to develop intersectional research projects. Instead, Cole offers three guiding questions that psychologists should ask themselves throughout the research process (e.g., design, data collection, analysis and interpretation, reporting, etc.). These questions are broad enough to apply to most kinds of social research and specific enough to catalyze intersectional analyses by rethinking the relationships between research questions and research methods. She follows up each question with examples from the literature that demonstrate the potency and rigor of intersectional research design and methods. Ultimately, I read Cole as encouraging us to consider what additional questions beyond these three we might pose for our own research.

41. Intersectional Psychology: (At Least) Three Questions*

Psychologists are increasingly concerned with the effects of race/ethnicity, gender, social class, and sexuality on outcomes such as health and well-being, personal and social identities, and political views and participation. However, little work has considered how these categories of identity, difference, and disadvantage are jointly associated with outcomes.

Such questions may be understood within the rubric of *intersectionality*, which feminist and critical race theorists developed to describe analytic approaches that consider the meaning and consequences of multiple categories of social group membership. However, psychologists have been slow to incorporate this concept into their work because there are no established guidelines for empirically addressing research questions informed by an intersectional

---

* Excerpted from E. R. Cole, "Intersectionality and Research in Psychology," *American Psychologist* 64 (2009): 170–180. Copyright © 2009 by the American Psychological Association. Reproduced with permission. The use of this information does not imply endorsement by the publisher.

framework (McCall, 2005). Given this gap, some psychologists might imagine that to address intersectional questions, it is necessary to develop complex designs involving prohibitively large samples or to enlist the cooperation of an interdisciplinary team to triangulate the problem. Although this is not the case, an intersectionality framework does ask researchers to examine categories of identity, difference, and disadvantage with a new lens.

I propose three questions psychologists might ask as a strategy for addressing intersectional questions in psychology research: First, who is included within this category? Second, what role does inequality play? Third, where are there similarities? These questions are not mutually exclusive; in fact, each question builds on insights generated by the previous one.

1. Who Is Included Within This Category?

At the simplest level, psychologists can begin to consider the intersectional nature of the social categories they study by reflecting on who is included within a category. This question draws researchers' attention to diversity within categories. Because certain groups have been systematically underrepresented in psychology research (e.g., people of color, S. Sue, 1999; poor women, Reid, 1993), subcategories that only partially represent a larger category have often been taken as representative of the whole category. For example, because of the use of student samples (S. Sue, 1999), much of what is known about women in psychology is based on responses from women who are White and often middle class. An intersectional approach is an antidote to this erasure.

Moreover, the question may also encourage researchers to study groups belonging to multiple subordinated categories, such as women from racial/ethnic minority groups. This attention to those who have traditionally been excluded, perhaps the oldest approach within intersectionality studies, thwarts any tendency to view a category in essentialist terms, both by illuminating what is overlooked when a social category is assumed to include only certain (usually privileged) subgroups of that category and by representing diverse experiences contained within categories defined by multiple identities (e.g., the category of Black women includes women of different social classes and sexualities). Asking who is included within a category can facilitate representation of those who have been overlooked and the repair of misconceptions in the extant literature. The need for representation was well illustrated by early work on intersectionality showing that a single-axis framework that defines disadvantage only in terms of group members who are otherwise privileged systematically excludes members of multiply subordinated groups (Crenshaw, 1989/1993; King, 1988).

However, turning scholarly attention to groups who experience disadvantage based on membership in multiple categories is more than a matter of equity or inclusiveness. Such inclusion transcends representation, offering the possibility to repair misconceptions engendered by the erasure of minority groups and the marginal subgroups within them. First, by focusing on groups that have been neglected, researchers are better able to arrive at a contextualized understanding of the groups' experiences, rather than viewing them in terms of the way they depart from norms based on dominant groups (Weber & Parra-Medina, 2003). Second, analyses that presume to focus on, say, gender, without consideration of other category memberships, implicitly assume a host of other social statuses that usually go unnamed in American culture: middle-class standing, heterosexuality, able-bodiedness, and White race (D. W. Sue, 2004). Scholars who attend to which groups are represented and which tend to be excluded—either by focusing their work on members of subordinate groups (hooks, 1984) or, conversely, by explicitly identifying and investigating the multiple identities that define privilege (see, e.g., Farough, 2006; Kuriloff & Reichert, 2003)—disrupt these assumptions by identifying the ways that race, class, or other identities shape the meaning of gender (Higginbotham, 1992).

Considering who is included within a category accomplishes more than mere inclusion; it improves psychologists' ability to theorize and empirically investigate the ways social categories structure individual and social life across the board. Thus, intersectionality is not only a tool to understand the experiences of minority group members. Nevertheless, increasing attention to diversity within social groups is not sufficient to address the psychological meaning of race, gender, and other social categories. Sociologists remind researchers that the social practices that construct race and gender involve hierarchy and inequality (Bonilla-Silva, 1997; Risman, 2004). Yet, when researchers attend to who is included within the social categories they study, with particular attention to groups that have been traditionally overlooked, social and material inequality between groups may be treated only implicitly (why, after all, have some groups been studied to the exclusion of others?). These concerns are addressed by the second question.

2. What Role Does Inequality Play?

Categories such as race, gender, social class, and sexuality do not simply describe groups that may be different or similar; they encapsulate historical and continuing relations of political, material, and social inequality and stigma. Mahalingam (2007) characterized intersectionality in terms of the "interplay between person and social location, with particular emphasis on power relations among various social locations" (p. 45). Asking what role inequality plays draws attention to the ways that multiple category memberships position individuals and groups in asymmetrical relation to one another, affecting their perceptions, experiences, and outcomes. This question helps psychologists to view constructs such as race and gender as structural categories and social processes rather than primarily as characteristics of individuals, a move consistent with recent methodological critiques (Helms, Jernigan, & Mascher, 2005) and social constructionist approaches within psychology (e.g., Jost & Kruglanski, 2002). Moreover, sociologists argue that constructs like race (Bonilla-Silva, 1997) and gender (Risman, 2004) affect beliefs about what is possible or desirable and define the contours of individuals' opportunities and life chances through social and institutional practices. Considering the role of inequality helps psychologists see individuals as embedded in cultural and historical contexts, a tradition that has deep roots within the discipline but one that has languished recently.

Femininity, long conceptualized within psychology in terms of traits and/ or behavior, provides a rich test case for such an analysis. Girls and women are pressured to conform to feminine norms, including beauty, cultivation of feminine traits, performance of normative heterosexuality including motherhood, development of domestic skills, and sexual restraint. For much of U.S. history, however, economic exploitation, stereotyping, and lack of legal protection (Collins, 1990) served to deny Black women (and other women of color; see, e.g., Espiritu, 2001) the protections femininity is purported to afford. This history led Collins (2004) to argue that these benchmarks of femininity "become a normative yardstick for all femininities in which Black women [and other women of color] are relegated to the bottom of the gender hierarchy" (p. 193; Higginbotham, 1992). In response, Black women activists have long asserted their femininity, and accordingly their respectability, as a means to claim entitlement to legal protection and civil rights (Giddings, 1985).

Cole and Zucker (2007) explored Black and White women's perceptions of femininity in light of this history. Confirmatory factor analysis of national survey data showed both groups used the same dimensions to conceptualize femininity: feminine traits, appearance, and traditional gender beliefs. However, for White women, traditional gender ideology was negatively related to feminist identification. Among Black women, those who placed a high value on wearing feminine clothing were more likely to identify as feminist, and Black women rated appearance items as more important to them. Black women were also more likely than White women to identify as feminists, arguably because the experience of racial oppression sensitizes Black women to issues of sexism. Craig's (2002) historical research can help explain why these aspects of femininity have different political meaning for Black and White women: Black women have traditionally used a strategy of scrupulous attention to appearance to challenge stereotypes of Blacks as uncivilized and sexually immoral. Thus, Black and White women's social locations, defined by structural relations of inequality rooted in history and culture, explained patterns of similarity and difference in the findings: Black and White women had similar views about the components of normative femininity; Black women reported higher levels of feminist identification because of double discrimination; and structural relations between White and Black women explain why feminine appearance bears a different association with feminism for each group. These findings address all three permutations of intersectionality as theorized by Crenshaw (1989/1993).

Weber and Parra-Medina (2003) have made a useful distinction between looking "downstream" for causes (i.e., in individual behavior that might be associated with social category membership) and "upstream" at "the group processes that define systems of social inequality" (p. 190), such as laws, institutional practices, and public policies. Consideration of the role of inequality can help psychologists look upstream by drawing attention to how groups stand in relation to each other and to public and private institutions, including families, schools, workplaces, and the law, and, correspondingly, how political, material, and social inequality lead to class, race, and gender differences in outcomes (see, e.g., Eagly & Wood, 1999; Glick et al., 2004; Lott, 2002; Reid, 1993). Asking this second question helps avoid the risk of treating socially constructed categories as though they refer to static and ahistorical constructs. However, to deeply engage this question, psychologists would be well served to supplement their training with interdisciplinary study in history, sociology, or other social sciences and/or to pursue collaborative relationships with scholars in other disciplines.

3. Where Are There Similarities?

The third way to reconceptualize social categories to address intersectional research questions entails seeking sites of commonality across difference. Asking where there are similarities encourages researchers to reassess any presumption that categories of identity, difference, and disadvantage define homogeneous groups as they look for similarities that cut across categories. Looking for commonality across difference entails viewing social categories as reflecting what individuals, institutions, and cultures do, rather than simply as characteristics of individuals. This shift opens up the possibility to recognize common ground between groups, even those deemed fundamentally different by conventional categories.

This way of approaching intersectional research questions is grounded in the work of authors who have used the concept as a tool for political organizing. Urging intersectional analysis to address important differences within groups, Crenshaw (1994) criticized agencies serving women who had experienced intimate partner violence for overlooking how statuses such as poverty and immigration status fundamentally shape certain women's specific needs; if these needs were not addressed, the agencies were not meeting the needs of some women. Unfortunately, this key insight of intersectionality—the heterogeneity of groups—is easily misconstrued to suggest that identity groups can effectively organize around only the most specific, and thus the most limited, constituencies. Cohen (1997) exploded this misreading, advocating that social change organizations should not mobilize on the basis of shared identities (which inevitably exclude some people). Instead, she noted that oppression operates through a series of interlocking systems that cut across conventional identity categories. Specifically, she suggested that lesbian and gay political activists have a limited constituency if their organizing is based only on identity. However, many of the political issues that concern activists offer opportunities to build coalitions among diverse groups who are disadvantaged by public policies that attempt to regulate sexuality or that confer resources and privileges on the basis of sexual behavior. When seen through this lens, women on welfare targeted by marriage incentive policies have important shared interests with gay men and lesbians whose sexuality and intimate partnerships are also stigmatized and proscribed (Cohen, 1997).

Cohen's (1997) argument is groundbreaking because psychologists tend to see certain identities as totalizing and determinative, as trumping all others. For example, Higginbotham (1992) argued,

> Race not only tends to subsume other sets of social relations, namely, gender and class, but it blurs and disguises, suppresses and negates its own complex interplay with the very social relations it envelops. *It precludes unity with the same gender group, but often appears to solidify people of opposing economic classes* [italics added]. (p. 255)

Such insights can be powerful in research related to social issues and public policy, as these examples show. Although grounded in insights from political organizing, looking for commonality across difference suggests how an intersectional analysis can generate innovative research questions. The activists who developed coalition-building strategies recognized that the diversity within a group (e.g., the racial diversity among women or the class diversity among Blacks) provides opportunities to reach across perceived boundaries to identify common ground with other communities. Dworkin's (2005) work makes clear how failing to see these commonalities raises the likelihood that researchers may misunderstand how multiple social structures—gender, race, sexuality—shape sexual behavior with potentially tragic consequences. In this, she implicitly made an argument about gender that is analogous to Helms, Jemigan, and Mascher's (2005) rethinking of psychologists' methodologies for studying race; they recommended that psychologists move away from viewing race as an independent variable and instead operationalize specific mechanisms through conceptual variables. The examples I have described suggest that some research related to social issues, public policy, and practice engages these principles of coalition in an untheorized way. The concept of intersectionality offers a way to bring this insight to bear in future research.

Implications for Research

To translate the theoretical insights of intersectionality into psychological research does not require the adoption of a new set of methods; rather, it requires a reconceptualization of the meaning and consequences of social categories.

These conceptual questions have implications for each stage of the research process. When researchers ask who is included within a category, it encourages them to understand all their participants in terms of the multiple social categories of identity, difference, and disadvantage they represent and to attend to groups that are often overlooked in psychology. This question does not imply that any given study ought to include individuals representing every permutation of race, gender, class, or other social identity; not only is this practically impossible, it is properly the cooperative work of a field. Rather, attention to who is included within any category of interest, with particular attention to groups that have often been excluded, is meant to encourage psychologists to view all samples in terms of their particularity and to attend to diversity within samples. Psychologists who ask this question may also be more likely to consider studying groups that have been overlooked by researchers. Reading the literature in psychology with this question in mind can make systematic omissions in sampling obvious.

The question of what role inequality plays makes the greatest demands at the level of hypothesis generation and interpretation of findings. This question helps researchers view the participants and phenomena they study as grounded in social and historical contexts: Race, gender, sexuality, and class, as well as other social categories, structure groups' access to social, economic, and political resources and privileges. Jackson and Williams's (2006) work on public health crises among the Black middle class illustrates the insights resulting from this question. They noted that although higher social class is related to decreased rates of suicide for Whites, the association is positive for Black American men. To understand this finding, they pointed to three sources of psychological stress related to this group's structural position in terms of race, class, and gender: stressors of racist experiences, the recency and fragility of middle-class status for many Blacks, and disappointment that occupational advancement has not been commensurate with educational achievement for many Black men. By conceptualizing race, gender, sexuality, and class as simultaneously shaping this group's experience, Jackson and Williams looked for explanations in terms of structural inequality upstream, rather than primarily at the level of individual differences.

Asking what role inequality plays may lead researchers to look for both similarities and differences across groups. This leads to the third question, Where are the similarities? This question represents the greatest departure from viewing social categories as defining fundamentally different types of people. Often researchers use social categories of identity, difference, and disadvantage primarily to define groups whose difference is a testable hypothesis, which, if not supported, defaults to similarity. Testing these differences rarely provides insight into the psychological experience implicit in the categories or the practices that create and maintain them. If psychologists conceptualize social categories as defining structural relations with implications for individual, social, and institutional practices, they must attend to both differences and similarities, even among groups that appear to be disparate. Because these similarities may not be obvious, addressing the question of commonalities across difference may entail conducting exploratory analyses or using interpretive qualitative methods. At the level of sampling, this question encourages researchers to include diverse groups within their studies, groups chosen not only in terms of group membership, but also in terms of shared relations to power.

What I am suggesting here is distinct from Hyde's (2005) gender similarities hypothesis. Hyde argued that meta-analytic review of the gender difference literature finds many more similarities between women and men than differences; much of what might appear to be gender differences can be shown to be a function of the different contexts that men and women typically find themselves in by virtue of their social roles. In contrast, looking for commonality across differences does not suggest researchers should reexamine the magnitude or extent to which there are differences between groups defined on one social category (e.g., gender). It is critically important from an intersectional standpoint that in recognizing similarities, researchers remain sensitive to nuanced differences across groups, even when similarities are found. For example, although middle-class Black men and working-class White men might experience some of the stressors they face in similar ways, their experiences are not equivalent or identical.

What then are the implications of an intersectional analysis for research methods? Certainly the first tool that many research psychologists would reach for to address questions of how outcomes are related to multiple group memberships is a research design in which social categories are treated as independent variables with main effects and interactions. Despite the power of this method to address certain intersectional research questions, it would be a mistake to reduce the nuanced theoretical concept of intersectionality to include only the type of associations that can be modeled through the use of interaction effects. One limitation to this approach arises from the fact that social categories, such as race and gender, are confounded in individuals; this means that any survey question that asks participants to report whether their experiences were a function of one category membership rather than another may be eliciting flawed data.

Testing intersectional research questions by looking at interactions between categories can undertheorize the processes that create the categories represented as independent variables. Put another way, treating race and gender as independent variables suggests that these social categories are primarily properties of individuals rather than reflections of macrolevel social practices linked to inequality (Weber & Parra-Medina, 2003). These observations suggest that the inclusion of statistical interactions among race, gender, and other social categories in multivariate analyses is not, in and of itself, sufficient to develop what Smith and Stewart (1983) called a "truly interactive model of racism and sexism" (p. 6) without reconceptualizing the ways researchers use race, gender, and other social categories.

The skeptical reader may ask what the critical lens of intersectionality can add to his or her research program, particularly if the work is not focused on members of subordinated groups. Although grounded in the lived experience and critique of those at the convergence of multiple stigmatized identities, the implications of the concept of intersectionality are more expansive. As Hancock (2007b) has argued, intersectionality does not simply describe a content specialization addressing issues germane to specific populations. Rather, it also is a paradigm for theory and research offering new ways of understanding the complex causality that characterizes social phenomena.

Jasbir K. Puar

Over the past several years, Jasbir Puar's work has become synonymous with criticisms of intersectionality. Her trailblazing book *Terrorist Assemblages* (2007) has experienced tremendous uptake in scholarship on inequalities, and a close read of that text reveals a protracted thesis on the limitations of intersectionality as a lens or method. In the excerpt below, Puar suggests the weaknesses of intersectionality (as a research paradigm) to do the radical work she thinks necessary for transformational social theory and politics. Puar is an associate professor of women's studies at Rutgers University, and her work engages the fields of critical ethnic studies, cultural studies, feminist globalization studies, queer theory, and sexuality studies; her major contribution to social theory so far has been the concept of "homonationalism," which denotes the nexus of sexual politics and American discourses on terrorism in the twenty-first century. As she explains, "At this historical juncture, the invocation of the terrorist as a queer, nonnational, perversely racialized other has become part of the normative script of the U.S. war on terror" (37). Accordingly, to Puar, contemporary LGBT social politics cannot be understood outside the context of global counterterrorism measures and vice versa.

Puar begins below by revisiting Michel Foucault's important concept of "biopower," which refers to the various tools of discipline and surveillance deployed by modern institutions to manage and control populations. Though this section may be difficult to comprehend for readers unfamiliar with Foucault's work, Puar's explanation of Butler and Mbembe's re-readings of Foucault is essential to understanding what she means by "assemblage" and how she arrives at her critique of intersectionality. By investigating the various ways that biopower and biopolitics have been taken up by scholars in different disciplines, namely queer studies and critical race studies, Puar shows how the theory has been transformed to meet the political investments of its practitioners. She is telling a story—a version of a story—and she uses this narrative to arrive at questions about the power of life and the power of death, and how these powers are used by, for, and on queer subjects in our contemporary moment of "counterterrorism," perpetual war, and rampant forms of nationalism and xenophobia. We then pivot to her discussion of identity politics, which is where intersectionality comes front and center. For Puar, intersectionality remains invested in identity in ways that undermine the entire point of the intersectional project: "that identities cannot so easily be cleaved," as she puts it. A focus on identity disempowers theorists from being able to address the complicated terrain of contemporary biopolitics. Rather than simply critique, she offers "assemblage" as an alternative way of theorizing intersectional identities. Instead of identity, which Puar reads as the privileged unit of intersectionality, assemblage is the privileged unit of her "affective politics." I include this explicit criticism of intersectionality not in the interest of fostering consensus or dissent, but to encourage us all to think about how being self-reflexive and proactively critical of social theory can generate exciting new possibilities for identifying inequalities, explaining complex systems of power, resisting oppression, and promoting justice.

42. **From Intersections to Assemblages***

In 1992, Judith Butler, faulting Foucault's *The History of Sexuality* for his "wishful construction: death is effectively expelled from Western modernity, cast *behind* it as a historical possibility, surpassed or cast *outside* it as a

---

* Excerpted from J. K. Puar, *Terrorist Assemblages: Homonationalism in Queer Times* (Durham, NC: Duke University Press, 2007).

non-Western phenomenon," asks us to revaluate biopolitical investment in fostering life from the vantage point of homosexual bodies that have been historically cathected to death, specifically queer bodies afflicted with or threatened by the HIV pandemic, For Foucault, modern biopower, emerging at the end of the eighteenth century, is the management of life—the distribution of risk, possibility, mortality, life chances, health, environment, quality of living—the differential investment of and in the imperative to live. In biopower, propagating death is no longer the central concern of the state; staving off death is. Cultivating life is coextensive with the sovereign right to kill, and death becomes merely reflective, a byproduct, a secondary effect of the primary aim and efforts of those cultivating or being cultivated for life. Death is never a primary focus; it is a negative translation of the imperative to live, occurring only through the transit of fostering life. Death becomes a form of collateral damage in the pursuit of life.

This distancing from death is a fallacy of modernity, a hallucination that allows for the unimpeded workings of biopolitics. In *Society Must Be Defended,* Foucault avers, "Death was no longer something that suddenly swooped down on life, as in an epidemic. Death was now something permanent, something that slips into life, perpetually gnaws at it, diminishes it and weakens it." Butler, transposing the historical frame of Foucault's elaboration of biopower onto the context of contemporary politics of life and death, notes the irony of Foucault's untimely death in 1984 due to causes related to AIDS, at that time an epidemic on the cusp of its exponential detonation. Thus, Butler's 1992 analysis returns bodies to death, specifically queer bodies afflicted with or threatened by the HIV virus.

With a similar complaint, albeit grounded in the seemingly incongruous plight of colonial and neocolonial occupations, Achille Mbembe redirects our attention from biopolitics to what he terms "necropolitics." Mbembe's analysis foregrounds death decoupled from the project of living—a direct relation to killing that renders impossible any subterfuge in a hallucinating disavowal of death in modernity—by asking, "Is the notion of biopower sufficient to account for the contemporary ways in which the political, under the guise of war, of resistance, or of the fight against terror, makes the murder of its enemy its primary and absolute objective?" For Foucault, massacres are literally vital events; for Mbembe, they are the evidence of the brutality of biopower's incitement to life.

For a millisecond, we have an odd conflation and complicity, rendering necropolitical death doubly displaced: first by biopolitical antennae of power, and second by the theorist who describes them. Laboring in the service of rational politics of liberal democracy, biopolitical scopes of power deny death within itself and for itself; indeed, death is denied through its very sanction. In *The*

History of Sexuality, Foucault, himself ensnared in the very workings of biopolitics, a disciplinary subject of biopolitics, denies death within biopolitics too. However, in *Society Must be Defended,* he contends that the "gradual disqualification of death" in biopolitical regimes of living stigmatizes death as "something to be hidden away. It has become the most private and shameful thing of all (and ultimately, it is now not so much sex as death that is the object of a taboo)." This privatization of death, Foucault indicates, signals that in the quest to optimize life, "power no longer recognizes death. Power literally ignores death."

Mbembe's "death-worlds" of the "living dead," on the other hand, may cohere through a totalizing narrative about the suffocation of life through the omnipotent forces of killing. In the face of daily necropolitical violence, suffering, and death, the biopolitical will to live plows on, distributed and redistributed in the minutiae of quotidian affairs not only of the capacity of individual subjects but of the capacity of populations: health, hygiene, environment, medicine, reproduction and birthrates (and thus fertility, child care, education), mortality (stalling death, the elongation of life), illness ("form, nature, extension, duration, and intensity of the illnesses prevalent in a population" in order to regulate labor production and productivity), insurance, security. These "technologies of security" function to promote a reassuring society, "an overall equilibrium that protects the security of the whole from internal dangers," and are thus implicated in the improvement of the race through purification, and the reignition and regeneration of one's race.

While questions of reproduction and regeneration are central to the study of biopolitics, queer scholars have been oddly averse to the Foucauldian frame of biopolitics, centralizing instead *The History of Sexuality* through a focus on the critique of psychoanalysis and the repressive hypothesis, implicitly and often explicitly delegating the study of race to the background. Rey Chow notes the general failure of scholars to read sexuality through biopower as symptomatic of modernist inclinations toward a narrow homosexual/heterosexual identitarian binary frame that favors "sexual intercourse, sex acts, and erotics" over "the entire problematic of the reproduction of human life that is, in modern times, always racially and ethnically inflected." I would add to this observation that the rise of the centrality of *The History of Sexuality* in queer studies has been predominantly due to interest in Foucault's disentanglement of the workings of the "repressive hypothesis" and his implicit challenge to Freudian psychoanalytic narratives that foreground sexual repression as the foundation of subjectivity. (In other words, we can trace the genealogic engagements of *The History of Sexuality* as a splitting: scholars of race and postcoloniality taking up biopolitics, while queer scholars work with dismantling the repressive hypothesis. These are tendencies, not absolutes.) It is also the case, however, that scholars of race and postcoloniality, despite studying the intersections of race and sexuality, have only recently taken up questions of sexuality beyond the reproductive function of heterosexuality. While Chow's assessment of western proclivities toward myopic renditions of sexuality is persuasive, the relegation of the sexual purely to the realm of (heterosexual) reproduction seems ultimately unsatisfactory. In the case of Chow's project, it allows her to omit any consideration of the heteronorms that insistently sculpt the parameters of acceptable ethnics. Moreover, nonnormative sexualities are rarely centered in efforts elaborating the workings of biopolitics, elided or deemed irrelevant despite the demarcation of perversion and deviance that is a key component of the very establishment of norms that drive biopolitical interests.

Many accounts of contemporary biopolitics thus foreground either race and state racism or, as Judith Butler does, the ramification of the emergence of the category of "sex," but rarely the two together. In this endeavor I examine the process of disaggregating exceptional queer subjects from queer racialized populations in contemporary U.S. politics rather than proffer an overarching paradigm of biopolitical sexuality that resolves these dilemmas. By centering race and sexuality simultaneously in the reproduction of relations of living and dying, I want to keep taut the tension between biopolitics and necropolitics. The latter makes its presence known at the limits and through the excess of the former; the former masks the multiplicity of its relationships to death and killing in order to enable the proliferation of the latter. The distinction and its attendant tensions matter for two reasons. First, holding the two concepts together suggests a need to also attend to the multiple spaces of the deflection of death, whether it be in the service of the optimization of life or the mechanism by which sheer death is minimized. This bio-necro collaboration conceptually acknowledges biopower's direct activity in death, while remaining bound to the optimization of life, and necropolitics' nonchalance toward death even as it seeks out killing as a primary aim. Following Mbembe, who argues that necropolitics entails the increasingly anatomic, sensorial, and tactile subjugation of bodies—whether those of the detainees at Guantanamo Bay or the human waste of refugees, evacuees, the living dead, the dead living, the decaying living, those living slow deaths—it moves beyond identitarian and visibility frames of queerness to address questions of ontology and affect.

Second, it is precisely within the interstices of life and death that we find the differences between queer subjects who are being folded (back) into life and the racialized queernesses that emerge through the naming of populations, thus fueling the oscillation between the disciplining of subjects and the control of populations. Accountable to an array of deflected and deferred deaths, to detritus and decay, this deconstruction of the poles of bio- and necropolitics also foregrounds regeneration in relation to reproduction. We can complicate, for instance, the centrality of biopolitical reproductive biologism by expanding the terrain of who reproduces and what is reproduced, dislodging the always already implicit heterosexual frame, interrogating how the production of identity categories such as gay, lesbian, and even queer work in the service of the management, reproduction, and regeneration of life rather than being predominantly understood as implicitly or explicitly targeted for death. Pressing Butler on her focus on how queers have been left to die, it is time to ask: How do queers reproduce life, and Which queers are folded into life? How do they give life? To what do they give life? How is life weighted, disciplined into subjecthood, narrated into population, and fostered for living? Does this securitization of queers entail deferred death or dying for others, and if so, for whom?

There is no entity, no identity, no queer subject or subject to queer, rather queerness coming forth at us from all directions, screaming its defiance, suggesting a move from intersectionality to assemblage, an affective conglomeration that recognizes other contingencies of belonging (melding, fusing, viscosity, bouncing) that might not fall so easily into what is sometimes denoted as reactive community formations—identity politics—by control theorists. The assemblage, as a series of dispersed but mutually implicated and messy networks, draws together enunciation and dissolution, causality and effect, organic and nonorganic forces. For Deleuze and Guattari, assemblages are collections of multiplicities:

> There is no unity to serve as a pivot in the object, or to divide in the subject. There is not even the unity to abort in the object, or "return" in the subject. A multiplicity has neither subject nor object, only determinations, magnitudes, and dimensions that cannot increase in number without the multiplicity changing in nature (the laws of combination therefore increase as the multiplicity grows). . . . An assemblage is precisely this increase in the dimensions of a multiplicity that necessarily changes in nature as it expands its connections. There are no points or positions. . . . There are only lines.

As opposed to an intersectional model of identity, which presumes that components—race, class, gender, sexuality, nation, age, religion—are separable analytics and can thus be disassembled, an assemblage is more attuned to interwoven forces that merge and dissipate time, space, and body against linearity, coherency, and permanency. Intersectionality demands the knowing, naming, and thus stabilizing of identity across space and time, relying on the logic of equivalence and analogy between various axes of identity and generating narratives of progress that deny the fictive and performative aspects of identification: you become an identity, yes, but also timelessness works to consolidate the fiction of a seamless stable identity in every space. Furthermore, the study of intersectional identities often involves taking imbricated identities apart one by one to see how they influence each other, a process that betrays the founding impulse of intersectionality, that identities cannot so easily be cleaved. We can think of intersectionality as a hermeneutic of *positionality* that seeks to account for locality, specificity, placement, junctions. As a tool of diversity management and a mantra of liberal multiculturalism, intersectionality colludes with the disciplinary apparatus of the state—census, demography, racial profiling, surveillance—in that "difference" is encased within a structural container that simply wishes the messiness of identity into a formulaic grid, producing analogies in its wake and engendering what Massumi names "gridlock": a "box[ing] into its site on the culture map." He elaborates:

> The idea of positionality begins by subtracting movement from the picture. This catches the body in cultural freeze-frame. The point of explanatory departure is a pin-pointing, a zero point of stasis. When positioning of any kind comes a determining first, movement comes a problematic second. . . . Of course, a body occupying one position on the grid might succeed in making a move to occupy another position. . . . But this doesn't change the fact that what defines the body is not the movement itself, only its beginnings and endpoints. . . . There is "displacement," but no transformation; it is as if the body simply leaps from one definition to the next. . . . "The space of the crossing, the gaps between positions on the grid, falls into a theoretical no-man's land."

Many feminists, new social movement theorists, critical race theorists, and queer studies scholars have argued that social change can occur only through the precise accountability to and for position/ing. But identity is unearthed by Massumi as the complexity of process sacrificed for the "surety" of product. In the stillness of position, bodies actually lose their capacity for movement, for flow, for (social) change. Highlighting the "paradoxes of passage and position," Massumi makes the case for identity appearing as such only in retrospect: a "retrospective ordering" that can only be "working backwards from the movement's end." Again from Massumi: "Gender, race and sexual orientation also emerge and back-form their reality. . . . Grids happen. So social and cultural determinations feed back into the process from which they arose. Indeterminacy and determination, change and freeze-framing, go together."

For example, intervening in the circuitous debates in "lesbian studies" regarding the preoccupation of the invisibility of lesbian sexuality in representational formats, Annamarie Jagose discourages attempts to restore integrity to a lesbian figure by countering its derivative status through the representational tactics of excavation, restoration, and visibility. For Jagose, the "prioritizing

[of] sequence over visibility" is not a substitution of tropes. Rather, sequence informs the very logic that drives desires for visibility, both chronological (lesbian as second order to the first orders of heterosexuality, vis-à-vis sexuality, and male homosexuality, vis-à-vis gender) and retrospective (lesbian as anachronistic and belated, linked to the "reparative project of constructing lesbian history"). Instead, she argues, it is the regulatory and "self-licensing logic of sexual sequence" itself that produces hierarchies of intelligibility for *all* sexualities and thus must be interrogated, rather than restoring the lesbian to proper representational visibility, a tactic which merely reiterates the centrality of sexual sequencing rather than deconstructing its frame, reifying the politics of recognition, retribution, and rehabilitation rather than transforming their utility. An embracing of derivative status reveals, Jagose claims, that "categories of sexual registration themselves, not lesbianism particularly, are always secondary, always back formations, always belated." The "certified specification of lesbian difference" is thus a tautological endeavor whereby "problem and solution, cause and effect repeatedly assume each other's form."

"Grids happen." As such, intersectional identities and assemblages must remain as interlocutors in tension, for if we follow Massumi's line of thinking, intersectional identities are the byproducts of attempts to still and quell the perpetual motion of assemblages, to capture and reduce them, to harness their threatening mobility. Endless becomings surface on our radar screens when, drawing on philosopher Henri Bergson, Massumi tells us, "Position no longer comes first, with movement a problematic second. It is secondary to movement and derived from it. It is retro movement, movement residue. The problem is no longer to explain how there can be change given positioning. The problem is to explain the wonder that there can be stasis given the primacy of process."

Identity is one effect of affect, a capture that proposes what one is by masking its retrospective ordering and thus its ontogenetic dimension—what one was—through the guise of an illusory futurity: what one is and will continue to be. However, this is anything but a relay between stasis and flux; position is but one derivative of systems in constant motion, lined with erratic trajectories and unruly projectiles. If the ontogenetic dimensions of affect render affect as prior to representation—prior to race, class, gender, sex, nation, even as these categories might be the most pertinent mapping of or reference back to affect itself—how might identity-as-retrospective-ordering amplify rather than inhibit praxes of political organizing? If we transfer our energy, our turbulence, our momentum from the defense of the integrity of identity and submit instead to this affective ideation of identity, what kinds of political strategies, of "politics of the open end," might we unabashedly stumble upon? Rather than rehashing the pros and cons of identity politics, can we think instead of affective politics?

Displacing queerness as an identity or modality that is visibly, audibly, legibly, or tangibly evident—the seemingly queer body in a "cultural freeze-frame" of sorts—assemblages allow us to attune to movements, intensities, emotions, energies, affectivities, and textures as they inhabit events, spatiality, and corporealities. Intersectionality privileges naming, visuality, epistemology, representation, and meaning, while assemblage underscores feeling, tactility, ontology, affect, and information.

EPILOGUE

Frontiers
Bonnie Thornton Dill

As a young sociologist, working with other women of color in my discipline to better understand and explain the relationship between the distinctive experiences of women like ourselves and the social structures that frame our lives, I never imagined that the description we provided of our work—"exploring the intersections of race, class, and gender"—would resonate so well with the explorations of others, morph into the single term "intersectionality," and become part of a theoretical and analytical construct that would energize debate and discourse for three decades. Neither did I imagine that the impact of that set of ideas would find broad global or multidisciplinary application.

It is exciting, therefore, to see how Grzanka's reader charts this scholarly trajectory; to wander through its presentation of different origin stories; and to engage in interesting and illuminating debates about such things as the concept's applicability to non-US settings, its place as theory or method or both or neither, its gains and losses as it crossed borders and expanded its lens beyond its earliest frames of reference, and its newest challenges.

As someone who has tried to codify this concept, to provide definitions and applications, and to establish its importance as an analytic tool in the social sciences and humanities, I find it both troubling and exhilarating to read these essays in collection and in the context that Grzanka provides for them in his introduction to the volume.

And here we are. Almost fifty years after the Voting Rights Act was passed, it has been gutted by the Supreme Court. Forty years after *Roe v. Wade* made abortion legal, access to this service is being erased in many states across the country. Forty-six years after *Loving v. Virginia,* the right to marry is slowly and fitfully being extended to more US citizens, while our national angst about the growing presence of some immigrant groups threatens to undermine the goal of cultural diversity buried in the Hart-Cellar Immigration Act of 1965. This changing political and social landscape makes it clear that struggles for social justice are unending. Victories of the past have to be sustained in the present, and new forms of discrimination and exclusion must continuously be addressed.

The significance and utility of intersectionality lies in acknowledging these realities. Intersectionality grew out of particular historical moments and sets of social and geographic locations. Its multiple origin stories suggest that the ideas that characterize it arose in a number of different locations at different times and in response to different sets of specific circumstances. From my perspective, this variety indicates both the depth of the need that the concept addresses and its scope as an analytical and social tool. Inability to capture the breadth and diversity of approaches within a single definition or category is an apt metaphor for the work intersectionality does in insisting on multiple axes rather than a single-axis analysis. Finally, efforts to apply these ideas globally—shifting, remodeling, and even contorting them in the process—is additional testament to the fundamental importance of the questions that lie at the heart of this scholarship. From my perspective, the purpose of intersectional ideas is to illuminate the complexities of exclusion; to reveal the interconnectedness of power embedded in different social structures; and to provide a tool that could be used to pry loose notions of separation and discreteness to reveal the interconnections that were always already operating beneath the surface.

The scholarship of intersectionality is part of a social justice project: an effort to address questions about the nature of inequality and the sources and systems that maintain injustice and exclusion. The goal is to unveil structures of power so that we may design policies, programs, and actions that will reduce their grip or eliminate them entirely. These are, of course, timeless issues, and because all of these dimensions are always in flux, we face great challenges in claiming to know what we think it is we know. Because intersectional approaches grew out of the experiences of the most oppressed groups—Black and Brown women in the United States—they have the potential for broad impact among and on behalf of oppressed and excluded minorities in other locations. For the same reasons, however, intersectionality has also faced barriers to adoption and diffusion in academia and in social policy.

So, the new frontiers are new, not because there are many new inequalities (though there certainly are some) but because old inequalities of race, class, gender, sexuality, and disability, among others, are manifested in new ways and require new tools to examine, expose, and dismantle them. Racial, class, and gender oppression and exclusion are manifest in the school-to-prison pipeline and in child-welfare policies that remove children from so-called "negligent" mothers who are disproportionately poor women of color. They are apparent in the efforts to eliminate access to free and low-cost family planning, birth control, and abortion services across many states and to deny higher education to undocumented adults brought here as children. Under the pressure to secure individual rights and freedom, such as the right to bear arms or "stand your ground," it has been too easy to deny the exclusion of group rights to people whose opportunities have been historically and contemporarily constrained through structural inequalities. The challenge for intersectional scholars today is not to trap ourselves in a tower of ideas but to make sure that our scholarly debates about terminology, approaches, and assumptions are meaningful and productive, so that we can apply both our old and new insights to generate strategies to address experiences of injustice on the ground. Ultimately, the value in identifying new scholarly frontiers in the scholarship and writing about intersectionality is to reveal new understandings and approaches that help us do the work of reducing inequalities and expanding social justice.

INDEX